The Land Before Her

Annette Kolodny

The Land Before Her

Fantasy and Experience

of the American Frontiers,

1630–1860

The University of North Carolina Press

Chapel Hill and London

Library of Congress
Cataloging in Publication Data

Kolodny, Annette, 1941–
The land before her.

Bibliography: p.
Includes index.
1. Women pioneers—United States.
2. Frontier and pioneer life—United
States.
3. Women in popular culture—United
States.
4. Women in literature.
5. Frontier and pioneer life in literature.
6. United States—Territorial expansion.
I. Title.
E179.5.K64   1984   973'.088042
83-10629

ISBN 0-8078-1571-3
ISBN 0-8078-4111-0 (pbk.)

Set in Galliard by G&S Typesetters
Designed by Naomi P. Slifkin

95 94 93   7 6 5 4

The author is grateful for permission to re-
produce passages from the following:

Margaret Atwood, *The Journals of Susanna
Moodie,* copyright © 1970 by Oxford
University Press Canada.
Louise Bogan, "Women," from *The Blue
Estuaries* by Louise Bogan (The Ecco
Press, 1968). Copyright © 1968 by
Louise Bogan. Used by permission.
Marie Harris, *Interstate* (Slow Loris Press,
1980), copyright © 1980 by Marie
Harris.
Judith McCombs, *Against Nature: Wilder-
ness Poems* (Dustbooks, 1979), copyright
© 1979 by Judith McCombs.
Adrienne Rich, "From an Old House in
America," in *Poems: Selected and New,
1950–1974,* by Adrienne Rich, used by
permission of the author and the publisher, W. W. Norton and Company, Inc.,
copyright © 1975, 1973, 1971, 1969,
1955 by W. W. Norton and Company, Inc.

Dorothy Scarborough, *The Wind,* copyright © 1929 by Dorothy Scarborough;
copyright © renewed 1953 by Mary
Daniel Parker; reprinted, Austin: University of Texas Press, 1979. Used by permission of the University of Texas Press.
Ruth Whitman, *Tamsen Donner: A Woman's
Journey* (Alice James Books, 1977), copyright © 1977 by Ruth Whitman. By permission of the author.
Portions of Chapter 2 appeared in somewhat different form in *Women's Language
and Style,* edited by Douglas Butturff and
Edmund L. Epstein (L and S Books,
1978), copyright © 1978 by E. L. Epstein, and in *Women and Language in Literature and Society,* edited by Sally
McConnell-Ginet, Ruth Borker, and
Nelly Furman, copyright © 1980 by
Praeger Publishers. Reprinted with the
permission of Praeger Publishers. A substantial portion of Chapter 3 first appeared in *Critical Inquiry* 8, no. 2
(Winter 1981): 329–45.

For
Daniel Peters
husbandloverbrotherfriend

Contents

We may accept it as an omen for ourselves, that it was Isabella who furnished Columbus with the means of coming hither. This land must pay back its debt to woman.

—Margaret Fuller, "The Great Lawsuit. Man *versus* Men. Woman *versus* Women," in *The Dial* (1843)

Men have given us all their experience, from Moses down to the last village newspaper; and how much that is palatable have they said of woman?

—Elizabeth Cady Stanton, in *The Una* (1843)

Not only a firm purpose, a clear insight, a brave soul, and a true moderation are needed to effect the desired change in the social and political position of woman, but a positive knowledge of all that relates to her past condition.

—Caroline Healey Dall,
in *The Una* (1855)

Preface

The purpose of this study is to chart women's private responses to the successive American frontiers and to trace a tradition of women's public statements about the west. The attention accorded letters and diaries should not suggest that this is a study of the daily lives of pioneer women, however. Nor should the analysis of three centuries of published materials suggest that I have attempted any definitive literary history.

Although I have made extensive use of letters and diaries composed between 1630 and 1860, I have not attempted a revisionist history of the westward movement as seen through the eyes of women. Such a history is nonetheless long overdue, and I sincerely hope my chapters may encourage further work toward that end. In that event, my contribution may be the reminder that white women began as pioneers to this continent in the seventeenth century. Only by acknowledging the fullness of that history will we be able to grasp the continuities linking later generations with what had gone before.

The formal literary materials treated here were chosen not for their literary character or putative excellence (questionable criteria, at best), but for the light they cast on women's developing literary response to the fact of the west. Even familiar writers and genres are examined apart from the critical categories that currently define them. Thus, transcendentalism does not govern my reading of Margaret Fuller, nor does Puritan piety account for the appeal of the first Indian captivity narratives. I focus, instead, on the imagery through which the landscape is rendered and assimilated into meaning.

My subject, then, is neither social history nor literary history, but the sequence of fantasies through which generations of women came to know and act upon the westward-moving frontier. In the process of projecting resonant symbolic contents onto otherwise unknown terrains—a process I designate here as fantasy—women made those terrains their own. Fantasy, these chapters argue, allowed women to enact relational paradigms on strange and sometimes forbidding landscapes. And fantasy, shaped as much by personal psychology as by social context and changing geography, gave rise to a progression of popular texts in which women expressed their unique sense of the frontier's significance.

Because the boundaries of what Americans denominated "the west," "the middle west," and "the far west" were continually changing between 1630 and 1860, these terms cannot always correspond to "the West" or "Middle West" of modern usage. For consistency, therefore, such generalized geographical designations are lowercased in this book, with the context of the usage providing information as to the specific region intended.

My abiding concern for landscape as a symbolic (as opposed to a geographic) realm derives from the conviction that, in addition to stringent antipollution measures and the development of wind, water, and solar energy sources, we need also to understand the unacknowledged fantasies that drive us either to desecrate or to preserve the world's last discovered Earthly Paradise. For, as the materials examined in these pages should remind us, the landscape is the most immediate medium through which we attempt to convert culturally shared dreams into palpable realities. Our actions in the world, in short, are shaped by the paradigms in our head. But not until those paradigms are brought to conscious awareness can we begin to pick and choose among them, letting go of those by which we would relentlessly destroy our surroundings and holding onto those by which we might protect and preserve the continent as a home for all its creatures.

Noting that male fantasies had taken hold from the beginnings of exploration, governing subsequent Euro-American relations with the landscape, I turned to these first in *The Lay of the Land*. Frightened and dismayed by the implications of the male images, I then turned to women's materials, hoping to discover some alternative metaphorical design—one that would lead us away from our destructive capacities. What I found both sustained and disappointed my initial optimism. Like their husbands and fathers, women too shared in the economic motives behind emigration; and like the men, women also dreamed of transforming the wilderness. But the emphases were different.

After initial reluctance at finding themselves on the wooded frontiers of the northeast and the Ohio valley, women quite literally set about planting gardens in these wilderness places. Later, they eagerly embraced the open and rolling prairies of places like Illinois and Texas as a garden ready-made. Avoiding for a time male assertions of a rediscovered Eden, women claimed the frontiers as a potential sanctuary for an idealized domesticity. Massive exploitation and alteration of the continent do not seem to have been part of women's fantasies. They dreamed, more modestly, of locating a home and a familial human community within a cultivated garden.

The image of the garden as domestic space, however, will disturb some readers. For, simply put, that is not a fantasy we traditionally associate with the conquering heroes of a new frontier. Indeed, in that sense, there are no legendary heroes here and no recovered myth of a female Daniel Boone. What I offer, instead, is some suggestion as to why the women who were at home in the wilderness—like Mary Jemison and Rebecca Bryan Boone—never achieved mythic status. I offer, as well, the courage of a young bride, three months pregnant, who rode horseback over the Alleghenies to a fledgling frontier settlement at the confluence of the Ohio and Muskingum rivers. And I argue for the imaginative daring of the domestic fictionists who challenged outright the nation's infatuation with a wilderness Adam.

If we judge these women and their writings by the ideological predispositions of late twentieth-century feminism, their aspirations seem tame, their fantasies paltry and constricted. But when analyzed as part of the worlds in which the women actually lived, those same fantasies emerge as saving and even liberating. I ask the reader, therefore, to consider the social and historical contexts in which these women dreamed their dreams of a frontier garden and, with that, to appreciate the psychological fortitude required to evade the power and cultural pervasiveness of male fantasy structures.

For myself, I have long ceased to lament the absence of adventurous conquest in women's fantasies before 1860 and have come now to regret men's incapacity to fantasize tending the garden. For, given the choice, I would have had women's fantasies take the nation west rather than the psychosexual dramas of men intent on possessing a virgin continent. In the women's fantasies, at least, the garden implied home and community, not privatized erotic mastery.

Because the analyses here depend on a written record, the fantasies in question are largely those of relatively privileged, if not always wealthy, middle-class women. From the illiterate, the unschooled, as from those who could never afford time away from their labors for diaries and correspondence, we hear nothing direct in these pages. At best, we catch whispers of their silenced voices in the observations of their more privileged sisters. The literary materials, too, were composed by women with solid middle-class backgrounds (except perhaps for Alice Cary); and their works were directed almost universally at middle- and upper-class sensibilities—that is, women with the means to purchase books and the leisure to read them. The domestic fictionists' frontier Eve is thus a distinctively middle-class invention: a vehicle for projecting the Victorian values of a genteel east onto an imagined bourgeois west.

My decision to treat only materials written in English derived from the impossibility of making adequate cross-language and cross-cultural comparisons were I to attempt to deal with the variety of ethnic groups in the changing west. Moreover, since I sought to place women's responses to the new landscapes within a developing *popular* culture about the west, I necessarily restricted myself to the dominant language and its speakers. As a result, this study must ignore the unique multinational mosaic that was increasingly the pattern along the agricultural frontier after 1830.

The deplorable omission in this regard is the black woman (who, after all, also spoke English). But here I am faced with a recalcitrant historical record: I have been unable to locate adequate or relevant materials composed by African-American women on the frontier during the period covered in this study (1630–1860). Which is not to say that I have located no black women on the frontier. To the contrary: Mary Jemison credits "two negroes, who had run away from their masters," with helping her and her children survive the bitter winter of 1779. While one of her rescuers is clearly male, the other is never identified by gender and may well have been a woman. Additionally, while traveling the Mississippi River on a flatboat in 1784, Elizabeth House Trist records meeting "a Mullato Woman nam'd Nelly," who offers "water mellons, green corn, apples—in short, everything that she had was at our service." Although Nelly apparently gave Trist and the flatboat crew "the history of her life," Trist did not think to record that history. And we cannot be certain that Nelly herself could either read or write.

My discussion of the narratives of white women captured by Indians must also point to the sorry unavailability of black women's writings from the early frontier. For, in the language of white women taken against their will into the world of the Indian, we hear echoes of the slave narratives later composed by black women, recounting the years these women experienced themselves as captive among alien and predatory whites. Unfortunately, the structural and stylistic affinities between the captivity narratives and the slave narratives—both essentially accounts of captivity amid powerful Others—are beyond the purview of a study focused on the frontier before 1860. In a subsequent volume, however, I will use the writings of frontier black women—writings that only become available in any quantity after 1870—and there I will attempt to make precisely such connections. In the meantime, I simply point to the obvious correspondences between these genres in the hope that I may interest others in rethinking and reassessing their historical interconnections.

In the work at hand, I examine the captivity narratives for the light they cast on pioneer women's developing responses to the raw frontier, and I do not pursue any extensive examination of their writers' attitudes toward the Indian. In the aggregate, however, my treatment of all the works in this study should suggest the sheer variety of white women's perceptions of the Indian population. And in noting women novelists' willingness to contemplate intermarriage between the Indian and the white woman in their fictions, I tried to emphasize these women's radical departure from the often racist reticences of their male contemporaries. Even so, having strictly limited my focus to fantasies of the landscape (with which, to be sure, the Indian was often inextricably linked in the imagination), I cannot pretend to any comprehensive treatment of white women's responses to the Indian here. But I hope I have at least managed to point to a rich area for future inquiry.

Finally, let me caution the reader against assuming that the fantasies that sustained women to the edge of the Missouri went unchanged as the frontier jumped two thousand miles to the Pacific. Nor should the reader underestimate women's capacity to enter into new and different fantasies as they left the rolling middle western prairies to take up homes in the Rockies, the wooded Pacific coastal ranges, and the high plains of the Dakotas. But that is another story—and one that must wait for a second volume.

Acknowledgments

Time and support for research and writing were provided by fellowships from the National Endowment for the Humanities, the Ford Foundation, the Rockefeller Foundation, and the John Simon Guggenheim Memorial Foundation. Without their generosity, and the encouragement it represented, this book could not have been completed.

Since 1975, when I first began researching this project, I have had the good fortune to come under the friendly guidance of a number of excellent librarians and knowledgeable staff people. These include Anna B. Allan, Ellen Neal, Julius Ruff, Richard A. Shrader, and their Director, Carolyn A. Wallace, of the Southern Historical Collection, Wilson Library, at the University of North Carolina Library, Chapel Hill; Director James D. Hart and the staff of the Bancroft Library, University of California, Berkeley; Sheryl K. Williams, Assistant Curator and Head of the Kansas Collection, University of Kansas Library; Judith A. Schiff, Chief Research Archivist at Sterling Memorial Library, Yale University; and all those behind the desks who so patiently retrieved manuscripts or rare books at the Beinecke Rare Book and Manuscript Library of Yale University, the Massachusetts Historical Society, and at the Library of Congress. My especial debt, however, is to Reina Hart, Hugh Pritchard, Melinda Regnell, Jane Russell, and Mylinda Woodward of the Dimond Library, University of New Hampshire, all of whom were indefatigable in helping me to locate rare primary source materials and ingenious in their use of interlibrary loan facilities.

When I could not visit their collections in person, David Kinnett, Manuscript Librarian of the Iowa State Historical Department, and Eve Lebo of the Archives and Manuscripts Division, Suzzallo Library, University of Washington, both extended their time and expertise through correspondence.

Robbins Paxson Gilman, President of the Historical Society of Exeter, New Hampshire, offered a special boon when he opened his home to share family papers, heirlooms, and memorabilia.

In ways too numerous to catalogue here, this project has benefited from the help, advice, and support of Harriette Andreadis, Bill Andrews, Everett Emerson, Bob Giffin, Elizabeth Hampsten, Verna and C. Hugh Holman, Aldona Hoppe, Helen Deiss Irvin, Nancy Irving, Mary Kelley, David Levin, Lillian Schlissel, Ellen Messer-Davidow, Joel Myerson, Mary Beth Norton, Marjorie Pryse, Tricia Rooney, Anne B. Shteir, Henry Nash Smith, Margaret Solomon, Laurel Thatcher Ulrich, Dick Vitzthum, and Larry Ziff. My sincere gratitude to each.

The intelligence, enthusiasm, and dogged determination of two extraordinary research assistants, Sheryl Snaper Perey and Pat Riley, must, however, be credited with keeping me going when my own energies were flagging. With unfailing patience, Sheryl Snaper Perey helped me to locate primary source materials and then organized, catalogued, and annotated stacks of manuscript items. Pat Riley researched manuscript holdings at the Earl Gregg Swem Library of the College of William and Mary in Virginia; and she tracked the trail of family letters from one archive to another, from New England to the Pacific Northwest. Together, both devoted countless hours to transcribing thousands of pages of often faded or mutilated handwritten documents. As a result, I hope they feel that this book is also, in some way, *theirs*.

A deeply personal debt is owed to my friend and former colleague, the late Dawn Lander Gherman. For it was she who first urged upon me the importance of the Indian captivity narratives that finally figured so prominently in this study. Although Dawn and I came to different conclusions about the significance of that genre, no investigation of women's responses to wilderness can begin without reference to her groundbreaking Ph.D. dissertation, "From Parlour to Tepee: The White Squaw on the American Frontier" (University of Massachusetts, 1975). For the adventuresomeness of her intellect, for her deeply held political commitments, for her caring and kindness—in short, for all that makes a friend—she is sorely missed.

The years in which this book was researched and written coincided with a prolonged and difficult period in my professional life. Indeed, what was at stake was whether or not I was to have a professional life. In addition to the strength and support derived from those I have already named, I also drew special sustenance over the years from all those who contributed to my legal fund; from my students at the University of New Hampshire; from Judy, Gary, and Peter Lindberg, who surrounded me with their love and courage; from Norman S. Grabo, who never let me think that I might fail; from Iris Tillman Hill and Sandy Eisdorfer of the University of North Carolina Press, who waited patiently and eagerly and caringly; and from Nancy Gertner, Ann Lambert Greenblatt, and Byrna Aronson, who guided me through a legal nightmare to eventual victory, all the while urging me to continue writing and offering unstinting friendship.

Finally, my most profound gratitude must go to my husband, Daniel Peters, to whom this book is dedicated. He was and is always there for me. With him, all these years—and even during the difficult times—I have known myself embraced by joy.

Abbreviations

AAR	*Autobiography and Reminiscences*
ANH	*A New Home—Who'll Follow?*
ATH	*A True History of the Captivity and Restoration of Mrs. Mary Rowlandson*
CL	*Clovernook* (1852)
CL, 2d ser.	*Clovernook* (1853)
DB	*Biographical Memoir of Daniel Boone*
DL	*Decennium Luctuosum*
FL	*Forest Life*
HFD	*Humiliations follow'd with Deliverances*
I	*India: The Pearl of Pearl River*
MJ	*The Narrative of the Life of Mrs. Mary Jemison*
MK	*The History of Maria Kittle*
MV	*Mabel Vaughan*
Pinckney	*Letterbook of Eliza Lucas Pinckney*
PL	*Life in Prairie Land*
PS	*The Pet of the Settlement*
SL	*Summer on the Lakes, in 1843*
T	*Texas: Observations, Historical, Geographical and Descriptive*
Trist	Diary of Elizabeth House Trist
Trumbull	*The Adventures of Colonel Daniel Boone* (1786)
WC	*Western Clearings*
WH	*The Western Home*

I am an American woman:
I turn that over

.   .   .   .

I am not the wheatfield
nor the virgin forest

—Adrienne Rich,
  "From an Old House in America"

Prologue
Dispossessed of Paradise

Leaving the Old Homestead, by James F. Wilkins (1854).
Courtesy Missouri Historical Society

By the time European women began to arrive on the Atlantic shores of what is now the United States, the New World had long been given over to the fantasies of men. At the end of the fifteenth century, Christopher Columbus remained convinced that the biblical Garden of Eden lay farther up the Orinoco River than he had been able to explore. At the end of the next century, according to the London investor, Richard Hakluyt, Sir Walter Raleigh swore that he could not be torn "from the sweet embraces of . . . Virginia."[1] From the beginning of exploration, then, sailors' reports of a "delicate garden abounding with all kinds of odoriferous flowers" became inextricably associated with investors' visions of "a country that hath yet her maydenhead."[2] Encouraging Raleigh to make good on his promise to establish a permanent colony in Virginia, Hakluyt prophesied in 1587, "If you preserve only a little longer in your constancy, your bride will shortly bring forth new and most abundant offspring, such as will delight you and yours."[3] By the beginning of the eighteenth century, it was relatively commonplace for colonial promoters to promise prospective immigrants a "*Paradise* with all her Virgin beauties."[4]

The psychosexual dynamic of a virginal paradise meant, however, that real flesh-and-blood women—at least metaphorically—were dispossessed of paradise. From the early decades of the seventeenth century onward, therefore, the English-speaking women who are the subject of this study struggled to find some alternate set of images through which to make their own unique accommodation to the strange and sometimes forbidding New World landscape.

To appreciate the difficulty of that struggle, we need only remind ourselves of the persistent pervasiveness of the male configurations. Specific geography, apparently, had little effect on the power of the projection. In 1609, one promoter of English immigration to Virginia promised there "Valleyes and plaines streaming with sweete Springs, like veynes in a naturall bodie," while just seven years later, Captain John Smith praised New England as yet another untouched garden, "her treasures hauing yet neuer beene opened, nor her originalls wasted, consumed, nor abused."[5] The fantasy even constituted a cognitive component in the writing of history. Translating the excitement that attended the first discovery of the Connecticut River into the rhythms of sexual conquest, in his 1725 verse history of Connecticut, Roger Wolcott depicted an ardent mariner "press[ing] / upon the virgin stream who had as yet, / Never been violated with a ship."[6] In a 1903 essay for the *Atlantic*, the eminent frontier theorist, Frederick Jackson Turner, described how "this great American West" made over

"European men, institutions, and ideas . . . and . . . took them to her bosom." If less overtly erotic in his imagery than Wolcott, Turner nonetheless echoed two centuries of promotional documents when he defined an American wilderness that had once "opened new provinces, and dowered new democracies in her most distant domains with her material treasures."[7]

To the initial fantasy of erotic discovery and possession, settlement added the further appeal of filial receptiveness. The American husbandman was cast as both son and lover in a primal paradise where the maternal and the erotic were to be harmoniously intermingled. As Hector St. John de Crèvecoeur put it in the eighteenth century, the European becomes the American "new man" "by being received in the broad lap of our great *Alma Mater*."[8] Invoking an idealized nation of small yeoman farmers, all working in "the spirit of brotherly harmony" and prospering as a result of the generous fertility of the American landscape, Crèvecoeur put forth what he believed was a design "uncontaminated either by spoils or rapine."[9]

But of course the fantasy was never "uncontaminated." Not even the "American Belisarius," Crèvecoeur's emblem of the son "prepared to begin the world anew in the bosom of this huge wilderness," could avoid arousing the jealousy of his land-hungry brothers-in-law.[10] For, the suppressed infantile desires unleashed in the promise of a primal garden were inevitably frustrated and thwarted by the equally pressing need to turn nature into wealth. In a capital-accumulating economy, this demanded, on the one hand, competition—even between brothers—and, on the other, a willingness to violate the very generosity that had once promised an end to such patterns. Ultimately, "the success of settlement depended on the ability to master the land, transforming the virgin territories into something else—a farm, a village, a road, a canal, a railway, a mine, a factory, a city, and finally, an urban nation."[11] In that process, those (like Crèvecoeur) who sought fraternal community at the maternal board witnessed, instead, every husbandman's fierce rivalry to possess America's favors for himself. The result, almost immediately, was a reflexive recoil before the incestuous consequences of incompatible filial and erotic impulses. Indeed, as early as 1656, John Hammond of Maryland cried out against the specter of a giving and fertile landscape "deflowred by her own Inhabitants, stript, shorne and made deformed."[12]

Until there were no more regions upon which to project the fantasy, the characteristic gesture in the face of its frustration was simply to displace the garden westward. With frightening regularity, the promise and its disappointment were succeeded by guilt and anger as, again and again, Americans found themselves bearing witness to the mutilation and despoliation of their several newfound Earthly Paradises. Returning to California ten years after his first enthusiastic visit there in 1849, Bayard Taylor reluctantly acknowledged that "Nature here reminds one of a princess fallen into the hands of robbers, who cut off her fingers for the sake of the jewels she wears."[13] Such cautionary images notwithstanding, until the outbreak of Civil War in 1861, nineteenth-century Americans were repeatedly admonished to believe that "we are still in Eden."[14]

Out of the tensions inherent in the recurrent pursuit of the fantasy, white male America forged for itself the saving myth of "the solitary, Indian-like hunter of the deep woods."[15] Adapted to life in the wilderness, but not in the settlements, his figure suggests at least the possibility of harmonious intimacy between the human and the natural, free of the threat of violation. In his earliest incarnation, he is Daniel Boone, seduced by the "second paradise" of Kentucky.[16] In subsequent incarnations he is Davy Crockett, Kit Carson, and a host of "mountain men" who first trapped and traded in the Rockies. In literature, he is James Fenimore Cooper's Leatherstocking, unquestionably the culture's most enduring portrait of the isolate woodland son, enjoying a presexual—but nonetheless eroticized—intimacy within the embraces of the American forest.[17]

Adhering to the underlying fantasy components, the myth of the woodland hero necessarily involves a man (as Natty Bumppo calls himself) "'form'd for the wilderness'"[18] and a quintessentially feminine terrain apparently designed to gratify his desires. The myth, thereby—like the fantasy—excludes women. In the idealized wilderness garden of what R. W. B. Lewis calls "the noble but illusory myth of the American as Adam,"[19] an Eve could only be redundant.

Rebecca Bryan Boone was therefore early edited out of her husband's story. Cooper's Leatherstocking twice rejected the temptations of the human female. And Frederick Jackson Turner, writing what he conceived to be history rather than myth, revealed that, for him, the wilderness would ever be the preserve of the white male hunter. Taking his images from Boone and Leatherstocking, Turner described how "the wilderness masters the colonist" by "strip[ping] off the garments of civilization and array-[ing] him in the hunting shirt and the moccasin."[20]

Thus denied a place beside the abiding myth of an American Adam, American women were understandably reluctant to proclaim themselves the rightful New World Eve. When they at last began to embrace that identity, in the nineteenth century, they were already redefining the meaning of the garden and, with that, radically reshaping the wilderness Adam as well. Having for so long been barred from the fantasy garden, American women were also, at first, wary of paradisal projections onto the vast new landscape around them. Their imaginative play, instead, focused on the spaces that were truly and unequivocally theirs: the home and the small cultivated gardens of their own making. Then, with the movement of the frontier beyond the forested Ohio valley and out onto the open, parklike prairies of the middle- and southwest, women's public and private documents alike began to claim the new terrain as their own. Even as husbands and fathers looked with suspicious eye upon the treeless prairies and clung, when they could, to the edges of the woods. The prairie, however, spoke to women's fantasies. And there, with an assurance she had not previously commanded, the newly self-conscious American Eve proclaimed a paradise in which the garden and the home were one.

Still, it must be recalled that during her earliest years on this continent, the Euro-American woman seems to have been the unwilling inhabitant of a metaphorical landscape she had had no part in creating—captive, as it were, in the garden of someone else's imagination.

Though few European men possessed more than scant knowledge of the new continent, none journeyed to it without some sense of "the good land whether we are goeing."[21] Before setting sail, John Winthrop was prepared to compare Massachusetts to "the lande of Canaan," and, upon arrival on that rocky coast, he wrote his wife in England, "my deare wife, we are heer in a Paradice."[22] To be sure, the Puritan identification with an Old Testament exodus invited such imagery. But even *with* that religious sanction, the women in Winthrop's colony generally avoided these usages. Also a passenger aboard the *Arbella* in 1630, Anne Bradstreet remembered only that her "heart rose" against what she saw when she first "came into this Covntry."[23] And in 1645, after some years living near Salem, Joan White complained of being "shut up for a long space of time living far in the woods."[24]

It may be more than coincidence, then, that the single narrative form indigenous to the New World is the victim's recounting of unwilling captivity and that, in English, the history of this genre begins with a Puritan woman. Governor Winthrop may have declared Massachusetts "a Paradice." But Mary White Rowlandson, dragged by Indians from her Lancaster home into the woods beyond, in 1675, found herself threatened by a "vast and desolate Wilderness."[25] The pious Puritan women who read and reread her phenomenally successful narrative of that captivity, we may speculate, identified with more than its anti-Indian sentiments and read beyond the overlay of religious interpretation. For what the captivity story provided was a mode of symbolic action crucial to defining the otherwise dangerous or unacknowledged meaning of women's experience of the dark and enclosing forests around them.

To escape the psychology of captivity, women set about making their own mark on the landscape, reserving to themselves the language of gardening. "An innocent and delightful amusement," Eliza Lucas Pinckney called it in the eighteenth century.[26] Neither paradisal nor gendered, the vocabulary of garden and gardener evaded the disappointments inherent in the male fantasies. What it offered was a socially sanctioned means of altering the landscape while delimiting the imaginable scope of that alteration. Even as she reclaimed a substantial plantation from the wilderness, for example, Eliza Lucas Pinckney would accept no title beyond "head gardener."[27]

Women seem not to have reacted against the land with violence not simply because they never dreamed of it as an object of sexual conquest, nor simply because they had evaded the frustrations of irreconcilable desires. They had, in addition, taken on a set of images that limited the very contexts of imaginative possibility. Thus, women avoided male anguish at lost Edens and male guilt in the face of the raping of the continent by confining themselves, instead, to the "innocent . . . amusement" of a garden's narrow space.

Moreover, having come to these shores with no fantasied attachment to the primal wild in the first place, women could—with perhaps greater equanimity than men—accept its disappearance. What women were apparently less willing to accept was the single-minded transformation of nature into wealth without any regard for the inherent beauty of the place. Although, from the Atlantic seaboard to the Ohio valley, women eagerly looked toward the clearings for signs of farm and settlement, they nonetheless cried out against "the total extirpation of the forest." On the Michigan frontier of 1836, Caroline Kirkland castigated "the Western settler" for regarding the trees "as 'heavy timber,'—nothing more. He sees in them only obstacles which must be removed," and so intent is he on the clearing process, Kirkland complained, that "not one tree, not so much as a bush, of natural growth, [can] be suffered to cumber the ground, or he fancies his work incomplete."[28] Kirkland's was not a lone voice here.

The uncomfortable sense of bearing witness to a vanishing Eden runs like a leitmotiv through nineteenth-century writing as, increasingly, Americans recognized the waste and unnecessary destruction that had accompanied the westward movement.[29] Belatedly, but wholly in keeping with the tenor of her day, Lydia Sigourney warned at mid-century, "'Twere well / Not as a spoiler or a thief to prey / On Nature's bosom."[30] Like Bayard Taylor after his second visit to California, Sigourney's language hints at an unarticulated suspicion that something is seriously amiss in male responses to the frontier. But, without any available psychological paradigm through which to probe those suspicions, both writers had to settle, at best, for a catalogue of consequences. What distinguished women's vision of those consequences from men's was women's suggestion that two rather different fantasies were on a collision course.

"Man's warfare on the trees is terrible," Sigourney intoned, because the masculine transformation of the wilderness into profit threatened women's transformation of the wilderness into home. Where clearing knows no check, she emphasized, the human habitation "stands / Unblessed by trees" and therefore vulnerable "to the burning noon."[31] The American Adam whom Sigourney's contemporaries were then reinventing for their westernized domestic fictions was thus, appropriately, a rejection of such designs. In Maria Susanna Cummins's *Mabel Vaughan* (1857), Eve's consort, on his own, creates a home with a view.

The beauty of the view did not become a recurrent theme for women, however, until the early decades of the nineteenth century brought them out of the forests and onto the open and flowering prairies of Illinois, Wisconsin, and Texas. At this point, beginning with Mary Austin Holley's *Texas* (1833), women too joined in as promotionalists for a New World Eden. In eastern Texas in 1831, Holley claimed to have found a "land . . . literally flowing with milk and honey."[32] Some ten years later, on a summer tour of the middle west, Margaret Fuller declared the Rock River country of Illinois "the very Eden which earth might still afford."[33] The American Eve had at last found her proper garden. With their parklike and flowered expanses alternating with stands of trees, the prairies seemed to offer nothing of the claustrophobic oppression of a wooded frontier. If anything, they resembled in large the treed lawns and flower beds with which women had always dreamed of surrounding home.

More than that, the prairies invited metaphors of intimacy—as had the forests for men. Eliza Farnham saw the "great and generous land" of central Illinois "in the light of a strong and generous parent,"[34] while on the prairies outside of Chicago, Margaret Fuller regained a realm where "nature still wore her motherly smile" (*SL*, p. 60). No less powerful in their psychic content than the male metaphors, the women's do not appear to have invited either erotic mastery or infantile regression. Instead, the women reveal themselves healed, renewed, revitalized—and even psychically reborn—in a country, as Margaret Fuller put it, "such . . . as I had never seen, even in my dreams, although those dreams had been haunted by wishes for just such an one" (*SL*, p. 36). In "a garden interspersed with cottages, groves, and flowery lawns" (*SL*, p. 67), women like Fuller recovered what the dark, embracing forests of the male imagination had always denied them: a garden that reflected back images of their own deepest dreams and aspirations.

For roughly thirty years, then—from about 1830 through 1860—women's public writings about the west purposefully and self-consciously rejected (or refined) male fantasies, replacing them with figures from the female imagination. In place of intimate woodland embraces, women hailed open rolling expanses broken, here and there, by a clump of trees. In place of pristine forests, women described a cozy log cabin where "eglantines and wood-vine, or wild-cucumber, [had been] sought and transplanted to shade the windows."[35] And, in their promotional writings, as in their domestic novels set in the west, women writers stripped the American Adam of his hunting shirt and moccasins, fetching him out of the forest and into the town.

Private writings, the historical record, and even some firsthand observers, however, point to large discrepancies between the fantasy and the daily experience. If the domestic fictions of the 1850s habitually sent their heroines out to fledgling townships or prospering settlements at the edge of the agricultural frontier, few early pioneer women, in fact, enjoyed such community. In central Illinois, for example—a favorite setting of the domestic fictionists—there were only about eight people to the square mile during the antebellum decades, and homesteads were generally separated rather than clustered.

Even more important: few women were actually able to enjoy the new landscape in the way the promotionalists had promised. As on every previous frontier, it was men who reaped the pleasure of the garden. As one Wisconsin farmer recalled in 1869, when he had first come to it some thirty years before, "the country was all open and free to roam over." But it was the men who had done the roaming, he made clear. "We could roam and fish, or hunt as we pleased, amid the freshness and beauties of nature." "With our wives," though, he continues, it was different: "From all these bright, and to us fascinating scenes and pastimes, they were excluded. They were shut up with the children in log cabins."[36] Margaret Fuller had noted the same thing during her summer in Illinois and Wisconsin in 1843. Unwittingly reviving the captivity design where she herself had undergone a kind of psychic liberation, Fuller complained that "while their husbands and brothers enjoyed the country in hunting or fishing," the pioneer women she met, by contrast, "found themselves confined to a comfortless and laborious indoor life" (*SL*, p. 117). The dream of a domestic Eden had become a nightmare of domestic captivity.

For all that, the fantasy remained intact. Promulgated by promotionalists intent on making the frontier attractive to women and popularized by domestic fictionists eager to use an idealized west to point up the shortcomings of a corrupt and corrupting east, there remained, until the outbreak of Civil War, the enticing image of a flowered prairie paradise, generously supporting an extended human family, at the center of which stood a reunited Adam and Eve.

That the prairie Eden, more often than not, proved *only a fantasy* does not diminish its importance. For the history of the metaphoric structures through which Euro-American women gradually went from feeling themselves "shut up . . . in the woods" to celebrating "a garden interspersed with cottages, groves, and flowery lawns" is more than a history of stylistic change or private psychological predilections. It is a history of personal attitudes, fears, and desires shared by generations of women and cast— sometimes fitfully, sometimes artfully—into public form, so as to forge the ongoing collective fantasies through which the American Eve encountered and accommodated herself to the changing American frontiers. What we trace here, in short, are the successive psychic strategies for survival that were, for pioneer women, no less crucial than the imaginative structures through which generations of men followed in the footsteps of Daniel Boone and believed themselves "invited to possess this *promised Land . . .* laid out *as an Earthly Paradise*." [37]

The danger in examining the projections of fantasy is the temptation to construe them as unmediated models of behavior. In fact, what we are examining here are not blueprints for conduct, but contexts of imaginative possibility. Fantasy, in other words, does not necessarily coincide with how we act or wish to act in the world. It does, however, represent symbolic forms (often repressed or unconscious) that clarify, codify, organize, explain, or even lead us to anticipate the raw data of experience. In that sense, fantasy may be mediating or integrative, forging imaginative (and imaginable) links between our deepest psychic needs and the world in which we find ourselves.

Consider, for example, seventeenth- and eighteenth-century women's fearful fantasy of captivity in a hostile wilderness. The recurrence of these narratives surely suggests an imaginative elaboration of Elizabeth House Trist's sense of being "oppress'd with so much wood towering above me in every direction and such a continuance of it." [38] What the captivity fantasy does not predict is Trist's capacity to pursue what, in 1784, was a most unusual journey for a woman. Soon after penning these lines, and with only Alexander Fowler, an old family friend, and Polly, a female acquaintance from Philadelphia, for company, Trist took leave of the frontier settlement of Pittsburgh to travel the Ohio and Mississippi rivers as far as Natchez. It would thereby be shortsighted to conclude from the popularity of the captivity genre or from women's repeated wariness of "tak[ing] up my abode in a howling wilderness" [39] that, were it up to women only, the frontier would never have been pushed very far west.

What we can say, instead, is that while women's apparently deep-seated hostility to the dark and enclosing forests of the northeast and the Ohio valley was palpable, it was not paralyzing. Indeed, it is even possible that the conventions of the captivity narrative helped women to locate and mediate their fears through a fantasy of displacement, thus obviating the paralysis that can accompany unattended psychic distress. The young bride who saw herself going off to "a howling wilderness," after all, also professed herself "willing to leave."[40]

By the same token, the fact that a fantasy is frustrated by intractable realities does not mean that it loses either force or vitality. In the face of a disappointing daily reality, fantasy may still continue to link us to the possibilities of our world. Thus, even after ten rather unsettled years in Iowa, one native New Englander still clung to images from the pages of the domestic fictionists, explaining to her husband in 1856, "Sometimes a vision of a pleasant home with a garden and flowers and creeping vines, and children and husband dear all at home, no more to roam, comes over me, and I confess I look forward to its reality with anticipated pleasure."[41]

Having offered that caveat against any *necessary* correspondence between fantasy and behavior, it would nonetheless be disingenuous of me to ignore the tantalizing speculation, suggested everywhere in these materials, that, had women's fantasies been in control (rather than men's), westward migration might have taken a different course. Too many possible differences immediately suggest themselves. To begin with, relations between whites and the native inhabitants might never have become so brutal, and white anxiety about intermarriage between the two populations might not have grown so fierce. Additionally, because they harbored a dream of the west as an idealized community, women probably would not have mythologized Daniel Boone or the lone cabin in the wilderness. And removals to the frontier would have involved not isolated farmsteads but what one Kansas pioneer woman contentedly remembered as an "ambitious little county seat . . . laid out in true generous Western fashion over a square mile or so of charming hill and dale, its modest frame houses . . . separated by wide stretches of greenest verdure."[42]

Looking toward the frontier not simply as a place to begin anew but, as well, as a realm in which to continue and even hallow the past, women would have transferred many more of the tokens of prior homes and earlier gardens than male migration patterns allowed. Once arrived on a new frontier, women would have settled in permanently, unimpressed by appeals to an El Dorado further west and generally uncomfortable with the nomadic existence of successive removes. And when settled in, women would have set about transforming the wilderness not into portable wealth but into what one Nebraska newcomer called a "sanctuary of domestic happiness."[43] Indeed, if Caroline Kirkland's comments may be taken as representative (rather than simply as the preferences of women of her class), it appears that female pioneers would have monitored the clearing process to preserve attractive views, preserve shade trees for houses and town squares and, just generally, preserve some reminder of the original beauty of the place. For pioneer women, in other words, the proverbial Garden of the West pointed not simply to a fertile landscape, but to a complex integration of home and community made possible by that fertility.

To be sure, these are not large claims. But then it would be naive to expect that the first development of women's frontier fantasies could have given rise to radically unprecedented shapes or patterns. The forms a fantasy may take, after all, are constrained by what the culture makes available to imagination. During the formative years traced here, women's fantasies about the west took shape within a culture in which men's fantasies had already attained the status of cultural myth and at a time when woman's sphere was being progressively delimited to home and family. What women eventually projected onto the prairie garden, therefore, were idealizing and corrective configurations drawn from the spheres in which their culture had allowed them imaginative play.

To put it another way: wherever fantasies come from—subconscious mental processes or biologically based urges—they always wear cultural clothing. Thus, men sought sexual and filial gratifications from the land, while women sought there the gratifications of home and family relations. Each in their own way, however, enacted sanctioned cultural scripts.

In emphasizing the cultural contexts of fantasy, I wish also to temper the implication that, by tracing the domesticating components of women's frontier fantasies, I am perpetuating the time-worn cliché that women are the civilizing force on any new frontier. Admittedly, it is a view put forth by many of the women quoted here. But the statement holds true only if herb gardens, flower beds, or attractively planted town squares alone are taken as signifiers of civilization. Clearly, that will not hold. The tilled field and the blacksmith shop, too, signify. What must be understood, therefore, is that a shaded town square or eglantine around a cabin window represent not civilization per se but the signs of white *women* in a particular historical and cultural context. In their homes, their flower beds, their town squares, women preserved to themselves some part of the landscape otherwise physically appropriated by men for the marketplace and metaphorically appropriated by men for erotic conquest. In other words, beyond the published texts and private letters and diaries in which they gave verbal expression to their fantasies, eighteenth- and nineteenth-century women utilized what they could of their surroundings—as men had always done—to announce their presence and imprint their dreams.

A rider emerging from the Michigan woods onto the prairies in 1840 would have known that white men were in the vicinity from the sudden appearance of girdled trees, tilled fields, and waving wheat. Catching sight of a honeysuckle vine trained round a cabin door, or an herb garden adjacent, the rider would also have been reminded that women, too, had been a'westering.

I never chose this place
yet I am of it now

—Adrienne Rich,
   "From an Old House in America"

Book One
From Captivity to Accommodation,
1630–1833

Fort Harmar as drawn by Joseph Gilman. Reproduced from S. P. Hildreth's *The Pioneer History of the Ohio Valley* (1848), courtesy the University of North Carolina Library

Women have no wilderness in them,
They are provident instead

—Louise Bogan, "Women"

1 Captives in Paradise

In contrast to a wealth of descriptive documents composed by explorers, promoters, and the founders of early settlements, little remains to tell us how women regarded their new environment, once they, too, began to cross the Atlantic for these shores. Some years after the event, Anne Bradstreet confided to her children that when she first "came into this Country" in 1630, she had "found a new world and new manners" against which her "heart rose"; and, in 1645, Joan White told her minister that when she first arrived in New England, she had felt "shut up for a long space of time . . . in the woods."[1] But such brief and scattered hints of at least initial antipathy toward the translation from civilized England to the rocky and wooded coast of Massachusetts record only the confidences of private moments. They were never intended to become part of that growing body of literature in and through which New World immigrants recorded for future generations the story of their conquest of and accommodation to the new continent. Even so, the tenor of those confidences suggests that it may have been no accident that when Mary White Rowlandson broke traditional Puritan sanctions against women making public statements, the story she told was one of unwilling captivity and forced removal to a "vast and desolate Wilderness."[2] With the 1682 publication of *A True History of the Captivity and Restoration of Mrs. Mary Rowlandson*, therefore, begins the public record of American women's encounter with the wilderness places of the New World landscape.

The first printed account of a New Englander captured by Indians (though Rowlandson was not the first from the Bay Colony to be captured), Rowlandson's narrative opens with the Indians' early morning raid on Lancaster, Massachusetts, in February 1675, and then goes on to detail her subsequent "eleven weeks and five days" among the Narragansetts (*ATH*, p. 29). No doubt composed with her minister husband looking over her shoulder (and later published with an accompanying sermon by him),[3] Rowlandson's *A True History* converts private experience into a story with symbolic significations for a Puritan community that already tended to view itself as a suffering and embattled Old Testament Israel surrounded by enemies. Noting Rowlandson's repeated efforts to illuminate "the works of the Lord" (*ATH*, p. 11) in all that befell her, combined with her frequent "recourse to jeremiad texts," most scholars have concentrated on the complex layers of religious symbolism embedded in the work.[4] What has attracted less comment is the fact that Rowlandson's narrative also comprises the first published account of a white woman's journey through what she perceived as a "vast and desolate Wilderness" (*ATH*, p. 4).

At the outset at least, the physical and the religious journeys are almost indistinguishable. Indeed, as Richard Slotkin points out, "for Rowlandson . . . time is marked not in temporal days but in 'Removes'"—or relocations from one Indian encampment to another—which constitute both "spatial and spiritual movement away from civilized light into Indian darkness."[5] Each successive remove away from the Massachusetts settlements thus pits Rowlandson against not only the physical wilderness of the Connecticut River valley but against an all-embracing "Wilderness condition" (*ATH*, p. 6). Nonetheless, as the narrative continues, the spiritual and the physical journeys get progressively sorted out (though they never wholly lose their symbolic interconnections). The Indians, who had earlier been characterized as a "company of hell-hounds" (*ATH*, p. 3), gradually take on individual personalities; and within their society, Rowlandson manages to carve out an economic niche for herself with her knitting skills. If the extra food or special favor she receives in exchange for her stockings and caps thus enable her to negotiate the often treacherous political terrain of her captivity, so too, a Bible given to her by one of the Indians helps her to negotiate the spiritual desolation of her "Wilderness condition," serving as a "guide by day, and my Pillow by night" (*ATH*, p. 18). The only terrain she can never negotiate on her own is the landscape itself.

Repeatedly, Rowlandson records her admiration for the "*Squaws* [who] travelled with all they had, bag and baggage, and yet . . . got over this River" with an ease she cannot imitate (*ATH*, p. 9). For her, the several crossings and recrossings of the Connecticut River and its tributaries leave her "so weak and feeble, that I reeled as I went along, and thought there I must end my days at last" (*ATH*, p. 20). Weakened by cold and hunger, burdened by her pack, and further weighed down by fears for her two children who have also been captured but are separated from her, Rowlandson finds the winter journey unremittingly difficult. At times, the landscape reflects back images of her fears, as when a "Swamp by which we lay, was as it were, a deep Dungeon" (*ATH*, p. 10). At other times, her description of the geography mirrors her physical state, as when she recalls passing "over tiresome and wearisome Hills" on the eleventh remove. "One Hill was so steep," she explains, "that I was fain to creep up, upon my knees: and to hold by the twigs and bushes to keep my self from falling backward. My head also was so light, that I usually reeled as I went" (*ATH*, p. 14).

Never does she suggest that she perceives any beauty in the landscape, and only once does she record that the landscape provided her sustenance *directly*—that is, without the Indians' intercession. This occurs on the twelfth remove when, "so hungry I could not sit," she ventures away from the encampment "to see what I could find. Walking among the Trees," she writes, "I found six Acorns and two Chestnuts, which were some refreshment to me" (*ATH*, p. 15). This one instance notwithstanding, and despite the fact that complaints of hunger echo like a refrain throughout these pages, Rowlandson never acquires more than rudimentary knowledge of the wilderness fare that allows the Indians to survive (especially after the English have destroyed their corn). "Their chief and commonest food was Ground-nuts," she recalls, continuing: "they eat also Nuts, and Acorns, Hartychoakes, Lilly-roots, Ground-beans, and several other weeds and roots that I know not" (*ATH*, p. 28).[6]

On her own, Rowlandson's narrative strongly hints, she could not survive. The landscape into which she has been taken is one she believes cannot sustain her and whose physical hardships might well destroy her. Thus, threatened both by her Indian captors (and what appear to her as the vagaries of their intentions toward her) and by "the vast and howling Wilderness" (*ATH*, p. 10) through which they take her, Rowlandson meekly submits before what she accepts as God's rightful chastening and consoles herself by recalling the settlements upon which she has been so rudely forced to "turn my back" (*ATH*, p. 4). By the sixth remove, still "mourning and lamenting, leaving farther my own Countrey," she says she "understood something of Lots Wife's Temptation, when she looked back" (*ATH*, pp. 9–10).

Notwithstanding the apparent aptness of the comparison, the destroyed habitation for which Rowlandson yearns is no Sodom or Gomorrah but, quite the opposite, one of the many fledgling Bay Colony townships that represented Puritan hopes of raising Jerusalem anew in America. The analogue appropriate to *that* dream—and, as her minister husband may have pointed out, of greater significance to the entire Puritan enterprise—was the Old Testament type of *Judea capta*, the image of Israel suffering in Babylonian captivity. It is an image that, like an undercurrent, governs much of the narrative, becoming explicit in Rowlandson's depiction of her eighth remove, when she is taken by canoe across the Connecticut River to a large convocation of Indians at the camp of their leader, "King Philip." Here she is "amazed at the numerous Crew of Pagans," many of whom soon "gathered all about me, I sitting alone in the midst." In this situation, she writes, "I fell a weeping," noting that this "was the first time to my remembrance, that I wept before them. Although I had met with so much Affliction," she repeats, "and my heart was many times ready to break, yet could I not shed one tear in their sight" (*ATH*, p. 11). By dwelling at length on the scene, emphasizing her unusual crying there, Rowlandson lays both the emotional and the pictorial groundwork for the biblical type she is about to invoke. For, whatever meaning her weeping in the midst of her captors on the banks of the Connecticut River may have held for her at the time, once reunited with her family (with both her children also rescued) and resettled in Boston, Rowlandson attaches to it an interpretation that is at once intimately personal and communally resonant. "Now I may say," she writes, "as in *Psal.* 137. 1. *By the Rivers of Babylon, there we sate down, yea, we wept when we remembered Zion* (*ATH*, p. 11).

Ever attentive to local possibilities for exemplum and exhortation, New England divines were quick to seize upon the emblematic, *typick* features inherent in the increasing incidence of captivity. For general theological purposes, Rowlandson's insistence that she had been preserved by "the Lord by his Almighty power" (*ATH*, p. 3) proved invaluable for teaching congregations that, during times of trial, "we must rely on God himself, and our whole dependence must be upon him" (*ATH*, p. 36). For more immediate theocratic (and essentially political) purposes, the pattern of capture and suffering followed by redemption might signify a promise that New England's current problems—Indian wars, crop failures, epidemic disease, or even bad weather—were similarly a divinely mandated "scourging," at once justified by the community's momentary backsliding but essentially temporary in nature.

The dramatic wilderness journeyings of the captives, moreover, allowed—indeed, demanded—a renewed appreciation of the conflicting images guiding the physical removal of the Puritans from the spiritual Babylon of England to the uncharted forests of New England. On the one hand, entry into the New World wilderness called forth the types of Moses and John the Baptist, who dared the wilderness to test and ultimately to revitalize their religion. On the other hand, what appeared to many as the untamed savagery of the New England landscape—an image comprising both the terrain and its native inhabitants—suggested that perhaps one Babylon had simply been abandoned for another. The dark forest recesses, controlled by those who were thought to be the very "bond-slaves of Sathan,"[7] thus easily suggested themselves as yet another type through which to signify the notion of spiritual wilderness. As a result, Babylon, a favored Puritan signifier for human corruption and spiritual wasteland, was symbolically transposed from a desert cityscape to a forested landscape.

In the Puritan sermon's rhetorical emphasis upon this Americanized Babylon, the captivity story—*especially when its protagonist was a woman*—proved repeatedly useful. For nowhere in American experience would the authors of these jeremiads find a more affecting image of New England as *Judea capta* than in the languishing figure of a Puritan woman held captive in the rugged wilderness retreats of the Indian. Cotton Mather, in particular, sought to exploit these possibilities—even where, as in the case of Hannah Dustin, the applicability of the story to his intended purpose was, at best, imperfect.

In the spring of 1697, a week "before a General FAST," Mather delivered a "humiliation" sermon in Boston that rested, for its dramatic impact, on "a Notable Deliverance lately Received by some English Captives, From the Hands of Cruel Indians."[8] Composed near the end of a decade of almost uninterrupted warfare between New England and the newly allied Indian and French troops (called "King William's War"), Mather's text emphasizes the French and Indian threat as one among several justifiable "*Scourges* of Heaven" sent to punish and to humble the chosen "for our Delinquencies" (*HFD*, pp. 4–5). The persuasiveness of his closing admonition that the congregation confess its sins and, in so doing, humble itself before God, therefore, rests on Mather's ability to induce in his listeners a felt perception of the implied cause-and-effect relationship between the "*Spiritual Plagues* whereto we are abandoned" and the fact of the community "*Humbled* by a Barbarous Adversary once and again let loose to *Wolve* it upon us" (*HFD*, pp. 34, 33). The emotional, if not the logical, link between the two lay in Mather's earlier paragraph-long rumination on the image of *Judea capta*, which, imaginatively at least, prepared the audience for the captivity story to follow. His listeners, in effect, were being invited to experience their community's spiritual vulnerability through the biblical type, and then, more dramatically, their own individual vulnerability through identification with an actual captive woman who exemplifies the type.

In exploring the implications of his chosen image, Mather suggests that New England's problems bear out the prophecy in Isaiah concerning the Daughter of Zion: "*She being Desolate, shall sit upon the Ground.*" "When *Zion* was *Desolate*, by the Roman Conquest," he reminds his audience, "there were Coins made in Commemoration of that Conquest, and on those Coins there was a Remarkable Exposition of this Prophecy. On the Reverse of those Medals, which are to be seen unto this Day, there is, *A Silent Woman sitting upon the Ground, and leaning against a Palm-tree, with this Inscription* JUDAEA CAPTA." Mather first repeats his description of the figure on the Roman coin and then redesigns it so as to make it explicitly applicable to New England: "Alas, if poor *New-England*, were to be shown upon her old Coin, we might show her *Leaning* against her Thunderstruck *Pine tree, Desolate, sitting upon the Ground*" (*HFD*, p. 31). The full impact of the image, however, is meant to take hold retrospectively, as listeners recognize its resonances in the captivity story that Mather introduces as an "*Example* . . . Subservient unto the main Intention" of his "Discourse" (*HFD*, p. 40). The problem is that Hannah Dustin's story cannot, in fact, consistently correspond to his design.

Supposedly based on the woman's own recounting of the events, Mather's version opens, as had Rowlandson's, with a detailed description of the Indians' intrusion into the Dustins' Haverhill, Massachusetts, household. A week-old infant is slain, and the house set on fire. Hannah Dustin, still recuperating from childbirth, and her nurse, Mary Neff, are taken captive.[9] Within a few days of their captivity, Dustin and Neff are forced to travel, on foot, over 150 miles and are then given over to the charge of an Indian family that had earlier been converted to Catholicism by the French. Thereafter, they travel with this family who have in their charge, as well, "an English Youth, taken fom *Worcester*" some months before (*HFD*, p. 45).

Approaching "a Rendezveuze of Salvages, which they call a *Town*" (probably somewhere north of what is now Concord, New Hampshire), the women are informed by their captors "that when they came to this Town, they must be Strip't, & Scourged, and Run the *Gantlet*, through the whole Army of Indians" (*HFD*, p. 45).

Modern anthropology suggests that, among many tribes in the northeast, the running of the gauntlet may have been less an act of vengeance than a prelude to the ritual adoption of captives. But Dustin obviously did not know this—nor would it have comforted her if she had. For her the gauntlet could only represent an unacceptable physical threat. As a result, as Mather informs his listeners, one night while still about a week's journey from the rendezvous, Hannah Dustin "took up a Resolution, to Imitate the Action of *Jael* upon *Sisera*." Rousing from sleep "the *Nurse*, and the *Youth*, to assist her" and "furnishing themselves with *Hatchets* for the purpose, they struck such Home Blowes, upon the Heads of their *Sleeping Oppressors*, that e're they could any of them struggle into any effectual Resistance, at the Feet of those poor Prisoners, . . . *there they fell down Dead*. Onely one *Squaw* Escaped sorely wounded," we are informed, "and one *Boy*." The brief narrative then ends with an acknowledgment of the former captives' presence in the audience: "But cutting off the Scalps of the *Ten Wretches*, who had Enslav'd 'em, they are come off; and I perceive, that newly arriving among us, they are in the Assembly at this Time, to give Thanks unto, *God their Saviour*" (*HFD*, pp. 46–47).

At one point, just before the description of the slaughter of the sleeping Indian family, Mather interrupted the flow of the narrative to ask his audience, parenthetically, "Syrs, can we hear of these things befalling our Neighbours, & not *Humble* our selves before our God!" (*HFD*, p. 46). The parenthesis was meant to remind the "assembly" that they were to interpret the story in a specific way: as an example of God's chastening followed by His merciful deliverance, and not as an instance of Amazonian determination and effectiveness. The danger, of course, as Mather too well understood, was that stories of "captives who escaped from the Indians by [their individual] strength or cunning might suggest that man could rely on his own strength for salvation."[10] To curtail *that* response—a response that the narrative certainly invited—Mather did what he could to emphasize some features of Dustin's adventure while suppressing others.

To heighten the story's correspondence with the *Judea capta* type, Mather underscores Dustin's feminine vulnerability by stressing her convalescence from the recent childbirth. Playing upon the Puritan identification of the Babylonian captivity with Roman (or, in Mather's view, Papist) conquest, he somewhat embarrassedly acknowledges that the Indian family is faithful in its daily prayers, but then insists that "these *Idolaters*, were, like the rest of their whiter Brethren *Persecutors*, and would not Endure that these poor *Women* should Retire to their *English Prayers*" (*HFD*, p. 44). Mather then attempts to justify the dramatic center of the narrative—the captives' slaughter of the sleeping Indian family—by comparing it to Jael's slaying of Sisera in Judg. 4:21. That biblical precedent has the effect, also, of suggesting images of Israelite captivity because Sisera was the commander of the army of a king of Canaan into whose hands the Israelites had fallen. Finally, though, Mather has to mediate the sheer brutality of the act—an act almost unseemly for a Puritan woman. This he does by claiming that "she thought she was not forbidden by any *Law*, to take away the *Life*, of the *Murderers*, by whom her *Child* had been butchered" (*HFD*, p. 46).

Clearly, Mather was attempting, however awkwardly, to exploit material inherently intractable "unto [his] main Intention" (*HFD*, p. 10). He might edit or refine Dustin's story, but substantially recast it he could not. Dustin's spectacular escape, followed by her appearance before Boston's General Court, scalps in hand, to collect her bounty, were simply too well known. And not a few in his audience, Mather may have suspected, were attending the lecture that day in order to hear the story again and to view, firsthand, the celebrated former captives. Having thus run the risk of losing some control over his material, and all too aware that precisely those aspects of the story that had so riveted public attention tended to subvert his rhetorical purposes, Mather closed his sermon with "An Improve-

ment," a clearly articulated interpretive comment that enjoined congregation and returned captives alike to perceive in these events not the assertion of human capacities but "a Surpassing *Providence*" (*HFD*, p. 48).

Still, Mather apparently did not rest secure that his message was clear
enough. When, a few months later, he prepared the sermon for publication, he appended to it "A Narrative of *Hannah Swarton*, containing a
great many wonderful passages, relating to her Captivity and Deliverance."
Indeed, had Dustin's sensational escape not obsessed the public imagination, or had Dustin not planned to attend the Boston "lecture," Mather
might well have preferred to use the Hannah Swarton story in the original
sermon. For with none of the subversive implications that marked Dustin's
captivity, Hannah Swarton's first-person narrative returns readers to the
pattern begun by Rowlandson: it exhibits the traditionally feminine—and,
for Mather's purposes, the typologically useful—response that John Seelye
has termed "passive forbearance in the face of adversity."[11] As such, it more
perfectly advances the *Judea capta* type that Mather had been at such great
pains to impose on Hannah Dustin.

Additionally, perhaps because it was a first-person account that largely
escaped Mather's editorial meddlings, Hannah Swarton's narrative restores
what Mather had repressed in the Dustin account—the captive's detailed
recollection of what it was like to be "hurried up and down in the Wilderness" (*HFD*, p. 52). Mather may have seen no reason to cut such material
from the Swarton narrative because he realized that it dramatically underscored his rhetorical intentions, even as it also emphasized the dangers of
removing from established towns. Because Swarton saw her captivity as a
just punishment for her family's decision to leave "the Publick Worship
. . . to Remove to the North part of *Casco-Bay*, where there was no
Church, or Minister" (*HFD*, p. 55), her story thus tended to discourage
the growing atomism of the Puritan settlements, an atomism against
which Mather himself so often inveighed.

The Indian raid on the Maine coastal fort at Casco Bay, in May of 1690,
resulted in the death of Hannah Swarton's husband. She and her children
were taken captive, but, as had been Mary Rowlandson's experience,
Hannah Swarton, too, was quickly separated from her children and
granted little "Liberty to Discourse with them" (*HFD*, p. 51). Again like
Rowlandson, Swarton appears not to have cried before her captors, reporting that "they would threten to kill us, if we cryed each to other"
(*HFD*, p. 51). The physical hardships of her sojourn with the Indians
similarly repeat Rowlandson's. Her feet "Pinched with Snow, Cold, and
Ice" (*HFD*, p. 53),[12] Swarton labors over "steep and hideous *Mountains*
one while, and another while . . . *Swamps* and Thickets of Fallen Trees"
(*HFD*, p. 59).

Although Swarton follows Rowlandson in establishing the spiritual bar-
renness of this landscape, bewailing the fact that she has no "*Bible* or *Good
Book* to look into" (as had Rowlandson), her narrative, for the most part,
stresses its physical discomforts. She even seems to have felt compelled to
explain at one point, "being continually in danger of being killed by the
Indians, or pined to Death with Famine, or tired to Death with hard Travelling, or pinched with Cold, . . . I was so amazed with many Troubles,
. . . that I had not time or leisure so composedly to consider of the great
Concernments of my Soul" (*HFD*, p. 56). It was an apologia, no doubt,
directed at an audience she knew to be familiar with Mary Rowlandson's
best-selling and often-reprinted narrative. For, if Swarton had not read
that text before her own captivity, we may be certain she read it upon her
return, recognizing it as a model by which to organize the meaning of her
experience and a model, as well, by which her readers' expectations would
have been molded.

In fact, like Rowlandson's, Swarton's captivity narrative *is* about "the
great Concernments of [her] Soul." And what comes to concern her most
in this regard is not surviving the physical hardships of the woods—
though that is certainly difficult enough—but surviving incarceration
among the French in Canada, "for fear lest I should be overcome by them,
to yield to their Religion" (*HFD*, p. 59). Thus, upon her arrival in
Quebec, "after many weary Journeys, through Frost and Snow" (*HFD*,
p. 59), Swarton's narrative swerves from one kind of spiritual testing to
another. If her time in the woods has brought Swarton to a renewed appreciation of God's justice and mercy in punishing and then sustaining her
through physical trials, her more comfortable captivity among the Catholic French tests her capacity to hold on to that newly won faith.

Whether consciously intended or not, the passage that enunciates that
transition symbolically summarizes what has already been suffered while,
at the same time, it prepares readers for what is about to begin. Walking
away, alone, from her Indian master, to approach the outskirts of French
settlement at Quebec, Hannah Swarton leaves behind her, as she goes, a
trail of blood on the otherwise pristine winter landscape: "The Snow
being knee deep, and my Legs and Hams very sore, I found it very tedious
to Travel; and my sores bled, so that as I Travelled, I might be Tracked by
my Blood, that I left behind me on the Snow" (*HFD*, p. 60). Suggestively
an *imitatio* of Christ, and thereby a foreshadowing of things to come, the
image also serves to remind readers of Swarton's physical frailty in an inhospitable landscape. More ominously still, the fact that she may "be
Tracked by my Blood" associates her with a vulnerable and hunted prey. In
either interpretation, however, the landscape is quite literally marked by
the sign of her suffering; and at a deeper, perhaps unconscious level, that

marking betokens how inappropriate is her presence here: it stains the whiteness.

The second half of Swarton's narrative details her three and a half years among the French at Quebec. There she successfully resists the priests' overtures and comes to the "Ravishing Comfort" that "God was my God, and my Sins were pardoned in Christ." The only sin to which she specifically refers, "that Sin which had been especially a Burden to me, [is] namely, *That I left the Publick Worship and Ordinances of God, to go and Live in a Remote Place*" (*HFD*, pp. 67–68). This act stands in her mind as the figurative abandonment of the faith to which she has now returned. All that remains, then, to complete the multileveled pattern of redemption is her return "to the Country *from whence I had been Scattered*" (*HFD*, p. 70). It is Boston, the center of New England's Puritan way, where she arrives "in Safety . . . in November, 1695" (*HFD*, p. 72), to which she refers here—and not to the Maine outpost. The physical return to Boston, "our Desired Haven" (*HFD*, p. 72), in other words, underscores and reinforces the earlier spiritual return.[13]

As Mather no doubt perceived when he published the narrative, the point was at once religious and political: for, if the scattering of God's chosen "*far off among the Heathen*" follows upon their decision "*to go to live in a Remote Place, without the Publick Ministry*" (*HFD*, pp. 69, 68), then, at least by implication, Swarton's story suggested that without that ministry—and the orderly planting of towns that it represented—the frontier was no more than an extension of the wilderness, at once spiritually desolate and militarily vulnerable. Mather would have had no quarrel with such a reading. Its admonitory effect would help to preserve the theocratic structure of the Puritan community, even as—or perhaps because—it repudiated the outermost edge of the frontier as a landscape upon which readers might, with comfort, imagine themselves.

Mather's interest in these captivity narratives, it must be understood, had little to do with the meaning of captivity as a catalyzing event in an individual's life, and even less with responses to the wilderness. His interest, almost always, was in the captivity story's adaptability to the *Judea capta* type and, with that, its utility as a dramatic exemplum through which to call the larger community to a renewed sense of its original covenantal obligations. Understanding these motives, we also understand why, with numbers of popular and pious male captivity narratives available, Mather and his brethren utilized, whenever possible, the stories of female captives. "*The Fearful Sex*,"[14] as Mather phrased it, more perfectly accommodated the interpretive biblical type because female captives (with the possible exception of Dustin) could be so easily identified with the shrinking, passive vulnerability that was at its heart. Thus, when Mather composed the *De-cennium Luctuosum*, his "History of . . . the Long War, Which New-England hath had with the Indian Salvages, From the Year, 1688. To the Year, 1698," he included, in addition to detailed descriptions of border warfare, a number of captivity stories, all of it once again designed to persuade "*a Sinful People*" to amend their backsliding ways (*DL*, p. 29). What is noteworthy here is that the captivity stories involve male and female captives in almost equal numbers (including an expanded version of Dustin's experiences). And yet, when summarizing "the Condition of the Captives"—and presumably here he meant all of them—Mather reverts to the gender of the biblical type, insisting that the meaning of these events may only "truly . . . be Express'd in the Terms of the ancient *Lamentations . . . The Daughter of my People, is in the Hands of the Cruel* (*DL*, p. 50).

The legacy of these interpretive strategies, repeated over and over again in the sermons and published writings of several generations of New England divines, is one that is still with us. For, however unintended, the appeal to the religious significance of *Judea capta* initiated the familiar image of a meek and frightened white woman, suffering in the wilderness—an image linked in the popular imagination not with a symbolic Babylon but with the forested landscapes of the New World. At the end of the seventeenth century, Cotton Mather transferred the symbolism of the Roman coin's "*Silent Woman sitting upon the Ground, and leaning against a Palm-tree*" to a New England *Judea capta*, "Leaning against her *Pine tree, Desolate, sitting upon the Ground*" (*HFD*, p. 31). By the end of the next century, so familiar had these usages become that it was a relatively easy task for Ann Eliza Bleecker to tap her readers' sympathies by exploiting that same image on behalf of her 1790 fictional captivity, *The History of Maria Kittle*.[15] Captured during one of the many periods of hostility that made up the French and Indian Wars, Bleecker's heroine is forced "through almost impenetrable swamps" and across a "rapid river" until, "overcome by sorrow and fatigue," she "sunk helpless at the foot of a tree" (*MK*, p. 25). The seventeenth century's *Judea capta* had simply been recast as the eighteenth century's sentimental heroine, wandering "sad and benighted" in the wilderness (*MK*, p. 25).

Like Rowlandson and Hannah Dustin, the fictional Maria Kittle sees her children slain in the Indian raid. As in Hannah Swarton's narrative, Bleecker also emphasizes "Maria's inability to travel, her feet being greatly swoln and lacerated by the flinty path" (*MK*, p. 43). But beyond these resemblances, twice in the narrative, Bleecker recapitulates the symbolic emblem through which Cotton Mather had once interpreted more authentic stories, picturing Maria "seating herself silently under a spreading tree," where, unseen by her captors, she "indulged herself in the luxury of sorrow" (*MK*, p. 39). Thus had the sermons and sermonizing of the Puritans succeeded in codifying imaginative contents that have ever after made their way into our popular literature.

Whether by men or by women, the narratives composed by Puritans rescued or ransomed from Indians display little understanding of or sympathy for the Indian and no liking whatever for the wilderness through which the captive was forced to travel. In fact, the depictions of the Indians in these narratives were sometimes exploited as justifications for the genocidal tendencies of the Puritans, while the wilderness came conveniently to symbolize the antithesis of that Paradise that the Puritans believed could be regained only in the towns and congregations. Thus, in the earliest captivity narratives, Indian and forest alike functioned as symbolic props in a preconceived cultural script, the central focus of which was always the spiritual drama of affliction and redemption.

By the second half of the eighteenth century, however, with Puritan influence severely diminished and Boston's grip on colonial printing presses forever loosened, the popularity of the form continued unabated, but the narratives themselves began to shed much of their original controlling religious structure. Now, whether authentic, a sensationalized version of some earlier text, or wholly invented, and wherever they might be published, the captivity narratives responded to the changing needs of a different generation of readers. This was the generation that made its way to the Saluda–Cumberland Gap and across the Alleghenies. And this was the generation that declared its independence from the crown, in part because of what it perceived to be inept British administration of the western lands. Readers such as these required different imaginative constructs for the New World wilderness than ever the town- and church-centered Puritans dreamed of.

The avatar of that transition and the figure who most enduringly embodies the myth of America's westward expansion is Daniel Boone, passed down to us in later incarnations as Cooper's Leatherstocking, Faulkner's Boon Hogganbeck, and A. B. Guthrie's Boon in *The Big Sky*. As a literary artifact, Boone's legend begins in 1784, when John Filson appended to *The Discovery, Settlement And Present State of Kentucke* a first-person narrative entitled *The Adventures of Col. Daniel Boon, one of the first Settlers*. Supposedly taken down by Filson from Boone's dictation (though probably largely an invention of Filson's pen), *The Adventures* comprises autobiography and reminiscence, a history of the Indian Wars, a promotional tract, and incidents of captivity. The character of captivity, however, has changed radically: no longer the event that structures the narrative, Boone's two captivity experiences are subordinate to the larger design, which is essentially about the conquest of the wilderness. Additionally, the experience itself has changed from one of unwilling captivity to almost compliant adoption. The Indians' "affection for me was . . . great," Boone boasts. "[I] was adopted, accordin to their custom, into a family where I became a son, and had a great share in the affection of my new parents, brother, sisters, and friends."[16]

Immediately and enormously popular, Boone's *Adventures* was quickly reprinted as a separate text, sometimes whole, but more often in edited versions. Among the most famous (and often reprinted) of these editings was one produced in 1786 by the Norwich, Connecticut, printer, John Trumbull. Trumbull trimmed Filson's complex and multilayered representation so that what emerged was a portrait of Boone as a man of the wilderness rather than the settlements and, as he has ever after been known, as a man of action rather than contemplation. The result, however, was a text too short to be profitably published by itself, and so, with it, Trumbull also bound "A Narrative of the Captivity and Escape of Mrs. Francis Scott, an Inhabitant of Washington County, Virginia," taken from recent newspaper accounts.[17] Trumbull's conscious motive, no doubt, as Slotkin suggests, was simply "to satisfy his audience's demands by . . . combin[ing] two major forms . . . the Indian war narrative," which, in Trumbull's version, had come to dominate the Boone text, "and the captivity narrative."[18] But, in so doing, he also succeeded in placing side by side those patterns through which Americans were coming to image male and female experience at the edge of the frontier.[19] For, by being juxtaposed to the newly emergent narrative of male westward conquest, the now familiar female captivity narrative helped readers locate those changing features that were to become constitutive of the developing male myth. By the same token, the radically revised male narrative helped readers recognize the enduring features of the corresponding female text at a period when the female captivity narrative was also shedding the cultural scriptings of the Puritans and, like Scott's, attending less to the trials of captivity and more to the hardships of the wilderness.

The Scotts settled on the edge of the frontier that Boone himself had earlier helped to open.[20] But where Boone, in 1769, eagerly chose to "resign my domestic happiness . . . to wander through the wilderness of America" (Trumbull, p. 3), Scott, in 1785, is forced into that wilderness against her will. Boone, when captured, is easily adopted and acculturated to Indian ways, "often . . . hunting with them, and frequently gain[ing] their applause for my activity at our shooting matches" (Trumbull, p. 9). Scott, when taken, never even contemplates adoption but is always "anxiously looking for an opportunity to make her escape" (Trumbull, p. 18). Boone effects his escape and returns expeditiously to the settlements. Scott escapes only to find herself "without any provisions, having no kind of weapon or tool to assist her in getting any, and . . . also knowing that a vast tract of rugged high mountains intervened, between where she was and the inhabitants eastwardly, . . . and she almost as ignorant as a child of the method of steering through the woods" (Trumbull, pp. 19–20). Exhausted and close to starvation, she is quickly "reduced to a mere skeleton" (Trumbull, p. 22). The abundant wildlife that sustained Boone appears to her also, but it cannot provide her with food. Instead, "from the tenth of July to the eleventh of August, she had no other subsistence but chewing and swallowing the juice of young cane stalks, Sassafras leaves, and some other plants she did not know the name of" (Trumbull, p. 23). Finally, where everything in the Boone text emphasizes Boone's woodcraft as responsible for his ability to negotiate "a journey of 160 miles" in only four days after his escape from the Indians (Trumbull, p. 10), everything in the Scott narrative makes clear that, without such skills, she is dependent on chance and circumstance. When confronted with a valley that "parted into two, each leading [to] a different course," Scott miraculously chooses correctly, but the basis of her choice is hardly one upon which she might repeatedly rely: the flight of two "beautiful bird[s] . . . . determined her choice of the way" (Trumbull, pp. 22–23).

If Daniel Boone was seduced by "the ample and beauteous tracts" of the wilderness (Trumbull, p. 5), Francis Scott experiences herself abandoned to it, at once its victim and prey. In contrast to the solitary Adamic Boone who "esteemed" Kentucky "a second paradise" (Trumbull, p. 6), Scott is rather a hapless Eve, bitten on the ankle by "a venomous snake" and characterized by the third-person narrative as "a forlorn creature" (Trumbull, pp. 22, 23). At the end of his narrative, Boone looks back upon his years in Kentucky to exult over the "Peace" that now "crowns the sylvan shade." Identifying himself with the patriarchs to whom the Puritans earlier paid homage, he announces himself "an instrument ordained to settle the wilderness" (Trumbull, p. 15). At the end of her narrative, Scott is grateful to be quit of the wilderness, continuing even so "in a low state of health." And she looks back upon her experience on the Virginia-Kentucky border only to "remain inconsolable for the loss of her family" (Trumbull, p. 24), all of whom were killed when Indians attacked their frontier cabin on the Clinch River and dragged Scott herself in the woods.

Having been offered to the public as companion pieces, the Boone and Scott narratives offered readers a striking contrast. Through Boone, who found Kentucky a landscape of "astonishing delight" (Trumbull, p. 5), the white male imagination continued to project, ever westward, its endless dream of rediscovering Paradise. As represented by the captivity narrative of Francis Scott, the white female continued to encounter only the implacable and hostile American wilderness of "inexpressible affliction" (Trumbull, p. 21).

Despite instances of white women who, when given the choice, preferred to remain with their adoptive Indian families, and despite the shift in male narratives from captivity and suffering to adoption and acculturation, from the seventeenth century through the beginning of the nineteenth century, certain features of the women's captivity narratives remained stubbornly resistant to change. While a narrative like Scott's, for example, dispensed with the religious typology that had informed the earlier Puritan texts, thus causing one Boston printer to preface the whole with his own choice of scriptural passages,[21] it nonetheless repeated Rowlandson's distress at traveling through "a vast and desolate Wilderness, I know not whither" (*ATH*, p. 4). To explain such continuities, we have to go beyond the observation that the Puritan *Judea capta* was easily adapted to the popular literary conventions of the eighteenth century and reappeared in sentimental fictions like Bleecker's *The History of Maria Kittle*. We have to understand, as well, the particular historical and experiential contexts in which these narratives were being composed and read.

The second half of the eighteenth century was a period of steady and persistent movement westward, interrupted only briefly by the Revolutionary War, and later renewed on the very roads that had been built to transport contending armies. Once peace was declared, Americans eagerly made their way across the Alleghenies, even as President Washington invited "the sons and daughters of the world [to] . . . *Increase and Multiply*"—especially on "the fertile plains of the Ohio," which, he boasted in a letter to Lafayette, "we have opened." It was, he assured his correspondent, a "Land of promise, with milk and honey."[22] And so it proved for many of the men who made or recouped their fortunes there. But for their wives, often enough, removal to the frontier meant only, as one woman observed, "enduring the hardships incident to the emigrant life."[23]

A case in point is the Gilman family of Exeter, New Hampshire. Joseph Gilman had been a partner in a dry-goods business from which, out of his own pocket, he helped supply New Hampshire's Revolutionary forces with ammunition, blankets, and clothing. The promissory notes and paper currency issued him by a provisional congress as partial payment proved worthless once hostilities were over; and, much to his chagrin, the once-prosperous Gilman found himself suddenly, at age fifty-one, impoverished and in debt. Having "speculated in Ohio land" at the close of the war, he decided, in the autumn of 1788, to remove there permanently with his wife and son. It was obviously a precipitous move, and one for which his neighbors (and, presumably, his creditors) were unprepared. Describing that sudden departure, many years after the event, an Exeter friend of Rebecca Ives Gilman recalled that "one night, unknown to everybody, . . . she and her husband with all their moveables left the town on their way to Ohio. AND THE MORNING SHOWED ONLY A DESERTED HOME. Had an earthquake happened it could not have occasioned more consternation." A little neighbor boy reported "that his mother [had] cried all the day after they left Exeter," his mother being "very fond of Mrs. G. who was idolized in Exeter." Clearly, it was a close and affectionate circle that the Gilmans left behind them when they departed for the Ohio, and a circle that, had it known of their financial difficulties, would have acted to keep the family in New Hampshire. "Friends said, if they had known their intention they should not have gone," remembered the woman friend from Exeter. "Thirty or 40 years afterwards," when the two met again in Philadelphia, the Exeter woman "reported this to" Rebecca Ives Gilman. "Would to heaven they had known it, she replied."[24]

Joseph Gilman appears to have found the land of milk and honey promised by Washington. Despite continuing depredations by the Indians and some initial financial uncertainty, he was nonetheless soon writing relatives in the east that he was "fully satisfied" with the "goodness" of the land.[25] Of his wife we read little in his letters beyond an occasional greeting that she sends to relatives in New England and scattered comments on the state of her health. Only once, in a letter of 1790, does Gilman share anything of his wife's response to their Marietta home: "M^{rs} G admires the country," he writes, "the temperance of the Climate and Singing of birds in Winter charm her."[26] That fond reassurance notwithstanding, the forty-two-year-old woman who had been so unceremoniously ushered out of her beloved Exeter home to begin the long trek over the mountains had not happily or easily adapted to life in the fledgling Marietta settlement at Fort Harmar. Years later, Rebecca Ives Gilman, now "an old lady bowed by affliction more than by years," confided a description of quite different experience to her old friend from Exeter. As the friend reported it, "She told me that she had learned to milk the cow and used to sit with the pail and looking up to heaven, say 'are these the stars and the moon I used to see at Exeter?' And sob and cry as loud as a child, and then wipe her tears and appear before her husband as cheerful as if she had nothing to give her pain."[27] The stars and the moon, of course, were the same. But nothing else on that frontier held their familiarity. Still, like every captive from Rowlandson on, Rebecca Ives Gilman, too, went meekly westward and held back her tears before those who had brought her, against her will, into the wilderness.

It was a pattern of experience that would be repeated daily, on frontier after frontier, well into the nineteenth century. Then, "tired of his Michigan farm," a man might go "out to the 'diggings' in Illinois, Wiskonsan, or Iowa." Asked "how she likes the change," his wife "will try perhaps to put the best face on the matter," but, as Caroline Kirkland observed in 1842, "if she be of the more timid and gentle nature, . . . she will answer with silent tears, which however will be carefully concealed from her husband."[28] For these women, the popularly reprinted narratives of female captivity—retaining many features from Rowlandson and including many reprintings of Rowlandson's seventeenth-century original—mirrored back crucial aspects of their frontier experience. To Rebecca Ives Gilman, the journey with her husband and son from the established and cultured town of Exeter to the edge of the frontier at the wooded confluence of the Ohio and Muskingum rivers, surrounded by hostile Indian tribes, must have seemed like removal to a desolate wilderness, indeed. In her situation, there would have been a poignant familiarity in Rowlandson's description of "turn[ing] my back upon the Town, and travel[ling] with them into the vast and desolate Wilderness, I know not whither. It is not my tongue, or pen can express the sorrows of my heart, and bitterness of my spirit, that I had at this departure" (*ATH*, p. 4). The anger such women felt (but dared not express) toward the husband who had staked the family's future on the availability of rich lands on the frontier might thus, through the captivity narrative, vicariously be displaced onto the dark and dusky figure of the Indian, a projection of the husband's darker side. And the anguish they dared not demonstrate may have seemed less a burden when they read of other women, similarly "afraid of dropping a Tear" before those who had forced them into so inhospitable an environment (*DL*, p. 50).

In some of the later narratives, where captivity and its delineation were comparatively brief, or where, as in Scott, the woman quickly escapes, the captivity structure functioned to elaborate possibilities first hinted at by Rowlandson. It functioned, in short, almost as a pretext for establishing what had now become the central drama of the story: the woman's suffering in the wilderness. Those women who came from the towns and small cities, especially, would have recognized echoes of their own bewilderments in the captivity heroine's lack of wilderness skills, empathizing with Francis Scott in being "almost as ignorant as a child of the method of steering through the woods" (Turnbull, pp. 19–20). Rebecca Ives Gilman, we recall, had to *learn* to milk the cow in Ohio; it was something she had never been required to do in her town home in Exeter, New Hampshire.

At the very least, however, these narratives offered models of the kind of passive forbearance that some readers were themselves practicing—and on a recognizable terrain. For those women who did not themselves choose relocation to the frontier, in other words, the female captivity narrative may have offered the only available literary vehicle through which, whether as readers or as writers, they might safely confront the often unhappy experiences of their westward migration.

2 Gardens in the Wilderness

Through the early decades of the nineteenth century, echoes from the language of the captivity narratives continued in the letters and diaries of women trying to grasp the meaning of their experience on the New World landscape. As late as 1823, Hannah Robbins Gilman repeated Mary Rowlandson's phrasing when she described her earlier removal to frontier Ohio in 1790 as "tak[ing] up my abode in a howling wilderness—a land inhabited by savages and beasts of prey."[1] In 1801, returning to her father's North Carolina plantation after fourteen years in England (where she had been raised by relatives of her deceased mother), seventeen-year-old Eliza Carolina Burgwin called up images from some of the more lurid reprintings of Francis Scott's captivity, to which unscrupulous printers had added prefaces promising that the narrative depicted the "hideous, shocking and frightful Beasts who inhabit the Wilderness of America."[2] As the carriage in which she rode approached her father's grounds, Eliza became apprehensive at the "narrow" lane "thro' a pine forrest . . . & expressed to the driver a dread of 'Wild Beasts'—emerging from the woods."[3]

Reared in Plymouth, Massachusetts, as the daughter of a Congregational minister, and thus heir to the typological frameworks of Rowlandson's thought, Hannah Gilman discovered within the "howling wilderness" the figurative garden that had eluded the Puritans but which had always been promised by the Old Testament precedents. "We were blest with children," Hannah recalled in 1823, "our substance increased—to whatever we turned our hand, we were prospered," and, "in a few years, we were able to set under our own vine and fig tree—and have none to make us afraid."[4]

Gilman's capacity to shun the captivity pattern and to embrace "a howling wilderness" as "my beloved home"[5] resulted from several factors. To begin with, as a young bride eager to begin a new life, she had "felt willing to leave Parents—doating parents—Brothers—sister—and the most affectionate of friends and acquaintances."[6] Following her wedding, and before setting out across the mountains, moreover, she had enjoyed several months of visits to friends and relatives in New England, in company with her husband, saying good-bye.[7] Unlike the captivity heroine, and unlike her mother-in-law—who had made the same journey two years earlier— Hannah Gilman had not been abruptly or unceremoniously uprooted.

No less important, the twenty-two-year-old newlywed, now three months pregnant, was greeted at Fort Harmar by Rebecca Ives Gilman, a loving and affectionate surrogate mother, and by a community of former New Englanders all busily engaged in erecting on the banks of the Ohio "a new England village," as later travelers would describe Marietta.[8] Soon enough, the wilderness took on more familiar markings. By 1797, with local Indian tribes signed to treaties of peace, the Gilman families were among the first to move out of the small log cabins surrounding the protective grounds of Fort Harmar,[9] building for themselves adjacent two-story, white-clapboard, double-chimney "colonials" with shuttered windows, as might be seen anywhere in New England. Two years earlier, having visited with her parents in Plymouth, Hannah brought back with her, at her husband's request, "a Box of [s]cions," thus helping to establish in Ohio the orchards she had earlier known in Massachusetts.[10]

By contrast, Eliza Burgwin saw herself as, in fact, inhabiting the wilderness of the captivity narratives—even though, unlike Gilman, she returned to a region that had been settled and cultivated for over sixty years. Still, to eyes accustomed to the streets of Bristol, England, and to the nearby suburb of Alveston (where she had attended school), the town of Wilmington, North Carolina, in 1801, "had a singular, wild, appearance" and, as Eliza added in her diary, "a most unciviliz'd one." Her fears of "'Wild Beasts'—emerging from the woods" were therefore real enough—even though, as she also noted in her diary, the driver had expressed himself "perfectly astonish'd" at her question, asking, "'What sort 'o Wild Beastess Missus?'"[11] That Eliza Burgwin had returned to nothing like a raw wilderness is not the point. The "Isolation" she experienced was no less distressing for that, prompting her to ask of her diary, "Could I have been a greater exile even in India"? For, however extensive were the grounds of "The Hermitage," nonetheless they could not alleviate Eliza's disappointment at discovering "there were no neighbors within visitting walking distance"; nor could the plantation's formal English gardens lessen the sense of entrapment for a girl who remained "afraid to ride thro' the woods alone." Her "heart . . . crushed" by these unexpected and unfamiliar circumstances, Eliza echoed the sentiments of the typical captivity heroine, complaining to her diary, "I had left all who lov'd me, all I lov'd."[12]

The contrasting responses of these two women to their new homes may be due, at least in part, to their different opportunities to create a personal garden in what seemed to them alien territory. Because Benjamin Ives Gilman's letters to his wife are full of details about planting and the seasonal progress of fruits and vegetables, we may surmise that Hannah Gilman evinced an avid interest in these subjects (even though her letters from her early years in Ohio no longer exist); and we know that she helped him to obtain seeds and scions in New England for cultivation in Ohio.[13] Arriving on grounds long ago laid out according to her elderly father's tastes, and now maintained by slaves, Eliza Burgwin had no means of making any similar imprint on an unfamiliar soil. And so, to her, the "wild" and "unciviliz'd" environs of Wilmington, North Carolina, felt like a wilderness entrapping her in "thraldom" on the aptly named Hermitage estate.[14]

Indeed, the letters and diaries composed by other women during the eighteenth and early nineteenth centuries strongly support the speculation that the gardens to which women personally attended were crucial in helping them to domesticate the strangeness of America. That most women did not become so traumatized by the dislocations of pioneering as to feel themselves "lost in the green west" (as one nineteenth-century novelist phrased it)[15] often appears directly related to their capacity either to create such a garden or at least to project its possibility onto the forested wilderness. Nowhere is this more clear, perhaps, than in the earliest surviving travel diary of a white woman who crossed the Alleghenies, wintered in Pittsburgh, and then proceeded on, in the spring of 1784, down the Ohio and into the Mississippi River as far as Natchez. Seriously considering the prospect of "end[ing] my days in the Western country," Elizabeth House Trist everywhere sought out on her journey the open clearings of recognizable settlement or, where these were lacking, the signs that such settlement might soon be possible. The raw, uncultivated wilderness she could never embrace, except on that rare occasion when she discovered what to her "look[ed] like a garden."[16]

During the Revolutionary War years, following the lead of men like Daniel Boone, small parties of emigrants from Virginia and the Carolinas moved into Kentucky, settling along the Cumberland and Kentucky rivers. With General Cornwallis's surrender at Yorktown in October 1781 and the ensuing rumor of imminent peace, Americans from both the north and the south renewed their push across the Alleghenies. New Englanders generally headed for Ohio and the Northwest Territory, while those from the middle and southern states either continued into Kentucky and then into the Illinois Territory beyond, or else began to navigate the Mississippi River southward toward Natchez. The Louisiana Purchase was still some years off. Even so, the bravado that followed upon the defeat of Great Britain awakened dreams of continental destinies and this, combined with Spain's relatively negligent administration of the area, encouraged many Virginia planters to invest in speculative purchases on both sides of the lower Mississippi. Having seen their soil progressively depleted by the single-minded cultivation of tobacco, the Virginians were now looking with interest toward the promised fertility of the Mississippi River basin. Soon after the cessation of hostilities, they began to locate settlements in and around Natchez, forming the nucleus for what was later to become the state of Mississippi.

Among those attracted to the area was Nicholas Trist, formerly a British officer but now, having resigned his commission, a naturalized citizen of the new nation who had purchased land along Bayou Manchac, below Baton Rouge. In 1783 he sent his wife "Marching orders" to leave her home in Philadelphia and meet him at Natchez (Trist, Dec. 27, 1783). Elizabeth House Trist kept a diary of her journey. What remains of it begins in late December 1783, when she set out from Carlisle, Pennsylvania, to cross the mountains, arriving in Pittsburgh on January 9, 1784. There she remained until May, when spring thaws made the rivers navigable again, enabling her to board a flat boat down the Ohio and then into the Mississippi, bound for Natchez. The choice of route was no doubt determined both by the fact that the mountain barriers were more easily circumvented in Pennsylvania than elsewhere and by the happy coincidence that a business associate of her husband's, Alexander Fowler, was available to guide her across the mountains and then house her with his family in Pittsburgh. Elizabeth Trist and a female traveling companion, Polly, were thus comfortably settled for the winter with "Mr. and Mrs. Fowler," who, as she later wrote, "treated us with every possible attention" (Trist, May 20, 1784).

Less than thirty years later, in the autumn of 1810, a young New Englander named Margaret Van Horn Dwight would follow the same route across the mountains, sighting "Waggons without number" on what had by then come to be called "the old Pennsylvania road." For her the road would prove "better than we expected."[17] But in the harsh winter of 1783–84, following military roads—some of which dated back to the Seven Years War—Trist found only treacherous footing for her horse, especially in places where on one side "was a thicket and on the other a precipice" (Trist, Dec. 31, 1783). And once "the snow began to fall," she encountered the mountains in their most inhospitable mood (Trist, Dec. 30, 1783). Twice she recorded "Snow up to the Horses bellies" and complained of her own "great difficulty . . . stick[ing] upon the Horse." When her saddle came loose while the little group essayed an "allmost perpendicular" ascent up Tuscarora Mountain, Trist was able to proceed only because Fowler managed to dismount and adjust her straps. "Had I dismounted," she wrote, "I believe I must have Perished for I cou'd not have mounted again and I am certain I cou'd not have walk'd 2 or 3 miles through the snow it was so deep" (Trist, Dec. 31, 1783).

Relieving the "cold and fatigue" (Trist, Jan. 8, 1784) of the daylight travel were the several forts, inns, or private homes where, nightly, the threesome stopped for food, rest, and shelter. To leave the warmth of even the rudest cabin took some courage, however, as when Trist rose from her bed to discover that "the whole Earth appeared like Glass and so cold that we hardly had resolution to set out." But set out they did, riding into what Trist later characterized as "cold so intense that I was allmost dead" (Trist, Jan. 7, 1784).

Enduring "excessive cold" and maneuvering treacherous inclines where the horses were "scarse able to keep their feet" (Trist, Jan. 8, 1784), Trist nonetheless seems to have been eyeing the surrounding countryside with avid curiosity. Her diary records not only sights of historical interest (generally military forts) and vignettes of evening hospitality and entertainment but detailed commentary on the landscape through which she traveled. Coming upon the Juniata River on New Year's Day, 1784, she noted that its "situation is very pretty" and then continued: "I was very much pleased with the prospect of the country which is Mountainous and the river Juniatta running through these Mountains for a 100 miles a clear beautiful stream. . . . it affords fine fish and from its being shaded with evergreens its beauty was much heighten'd at this season" (Trist, Jan. 1, 1784). The next day, having passed through "a Valley partly surrounded by a pretty Stream a Branch of the Juniatta call'd Rhea Stone," she again noted that "the country looks beautiful even in this dreary Season" (Trist, Jan. 2, 1784).

In entries such as these, where observations of natural beauty include also some hint of the potential for human settlement ("it affords fine fish"), Trist's voice anticipates that of John Filson's Daniel Boone narrative, which would see its first printing later that same year in Delaware. Touring Fort Ligonier, the site of engagements between British and French troops during the 1760s, Trist added to her impressions of the fort ("the best stockade in the Western country") her impressions of its surroundings: "the land in this Neighbourhood is very fertile and the country seems pleasant" (Trist, Jan. 6, 1784). Even where, as when ascending "the Allegany Mountain," she passed "over some very poor barren land," Trist still anticipated Filson's Boone by noting that "there was plenty of game" (Trist, Jan. 4, 1784).

In fact, only two things distinguish Trist's voice from that of Boone: her studied avoidance of paradisal projections and her apparent inability to praise the Pennsylvania frontier simply for the beauty of its untouched wilderness state. Boone, of course, had also entered Kentucky with an eye toward prospective settlement. But what had kept him there alone for an entire winter (1770–71), "explor[ing] a considerable part of the country, each day equally pleased as the first," were "the diversity and beauties" of undisturbed primal nature.[18] Trist, by contrast, could be pleased only by the palpable signs of advancing (or at least potential) settlement. Even her appreciation of "something enlivening and delightful" in the valley enclosed by "a Branch of the Juniatta call'd Rhea Stone" emanated from her happy discovery that the valley sheltered the village of Bedford, which "consists of about 100 Houses, some of them very good" (Trist, Jan. 2, 1784). And although she found the beauty of the Juniata "much heighten'd . . . from its being shaded with evergreens," nevertheless Trist would not join Boone in "esteem[ing]" the scene "a second paradise."[19] Instead, as she rather curtly noted in her diary, "I cou'd not but figure to my self that this must be the Lethe tho the fields were not Elysium" (Trist, Jan. 1, 1784).

Elysium, for Trist, implied not the wilderness but the assurance that the wilderness would soon be turned into something else. In an entry that approvingly rehearsed just how much had changed in the intervening years, Trist observed of the area west of Carlisle, "this country in the last war was the frontier." What she encountered there during the last days of December 1783, however, was the settled hospitality of an elderly couple, once early pioneers in the area. Her imagination was caught by the contrast between the old people's "former sufferings" and, having "lived to see an end to them," their contented present. Now enjoying a peaceful and healthy old age in a house shared with their son and his wife and children, the pioneer couple represented for Trist "a true picture of rural felicity." There, amid the rugged mountain passes of the Alleghenies, Trist recorded, "it gave me pleasure to see so much harmony subsist among them" (Trist, Dec. 29, 1783). It was an emblem of America for which Crèvecoeur strove in everything he wrote and the emblem upon which Jefferson was to stake his political career. For Trist, it meant the promise of the human garden that would one day displace the wild. And this is what she everywhere sought—not only in the mountains but in and around Pittsburgh, where she arrived, at last, on January 9, 1784.

Fort Pitt, at the forks of the Ohio, had originally been built by the French as Fort Dusquesne; but soon after its capture and renaming by the British, in 1758, it became a mecca for British colonists from the northeast who wanted to move out onto the Allegheny plateau. By 1764, settlement near the fort had increased so substantially that Pittsburgh was formally laid out as a grid of streets forming a municipality. Coming upon it twenty years later, Elizabeth House Trist described a "town" of "about a hundred buildings all (except, one, stone and one or two frame) . . . built of logs and they in a very ruinous state" (Trist, Jan. 9, 1784). By the time she left Pittsburgh the following May, she had accommodated herself sufficiently to its architectural infelicities to conclude that on "the whole I like the situation of Pittsburg mightily and was there good Society I shou'd be contented to end my days in the Western country" (Trist, undated [May 1784] entry).[20]

Whether the possibility that her husband's land speculations might require her to end her "days in the Western country" had made of Trist an especially curious visitor, or whether the simple need to escape the winter's confinements had made an adventurer of her, Trist took every opportunity the following spring to explore what she perceived to be a "land . . . exceeding rich." She particularly reveled in the early blossoming of "a fine orchard belonging to the Garrison" and then went on to describe "an abundance of Maple trees" on the other side of the Monongahela River that were yielding "quantitys of sugar. I pd a visit to their camps in the time of their sugar harvest . . . and was much pleased with the excursion," she explained, because "the vegetation being much quicker on that side of the river[, it] presented to our view a beautiful verder a sight that we had been a stranger to for some time" (Trist, undated [May 1784] entry).

Nothing outside of town impressed her as much, however, as "the low land lying between the river and the high lands or hills, . . . called bottoms. Nothing can exceed the quallity of those grounds," she averred, because "in the month of May they look like a garden such a number of beautiful flowers and shrubs." It was not the cultivated garden of settlement, but only "*like* a garden." Still, it was as close to the human imprint as raw nature could anticipate, and Trist enthusiastically catalogued the familiars she found there: "several wild vegetables that I would give the preference to [over] those that are cultivated[;] Wild Asparagus[,] Indian hemp, shepherd sproats, lambs [quarters], &cc—beside great abundance of Ginsang, Gentian and many other aromatic." The accuracy of her catalogue notwithstanding, it was still largely an *imagined* garden that Trist contemplated on the outskirts of Pittsburgh. For, even after twenty years of settlement, Pittsburgh remained comparatively rude, its mostly log dwellings surrounded by dense woods and forested hills. "If the country which is mountainous was cleared it wou'd be beyond description beautiful," Trist wrote. But in 1784, as even she had to admit, "the timber is very large" and, being so, it tended to obstruct her desired vision (Trist, undated [May 1784] entry).

It was an obstruction she was psychologically unprepared to tolerate. Contemporary aesthetic predilections for artfully arranged long views and "beautiful prospects," moreover, are inadequate to explain the quality of her intolerance, an intolerance that became acute during "an excursion over the Monongahala to the Cherties settlement" about ten miles from Pittsburgh, where "Mr. Fowler has a fine tract of land laid out in farms." Her expectations of the place were belied by what she actually encountered: "Here and there a farm wou'd present it self to our view with a few acres around it cleared but the country is yet in a very rude state." Were it cleared, she was certain, "it wou'd afford many beautifull prospects it being Hilly and the land of a superior quallity" (Trist, undated [May 1784] entry).

Up to this point, her statements seem simply to repeat a general eighteenth-century blindness to the beauty of any densely wooded and uncultivated landscape. Indeed, such statements had been literary commonplaces in America since the middle of the century—as when, in 1758, Thomas Godfrey complained of the woods surrounding Fort Henry:

> Here no enchanting prospects yield delight,
> But darksome forests intercept the sight.[21]

In the popular literature of the period, male responses to such forested enclosures involved either happy capitulation (as in Daniel Boone) or, as in David Humphreys's *A Poem on Industry*, aggressive alteration:

> Let the keen adze the stubborn live-oak wound—
> And anvills shrill, with stronger strokes resound.[22]

But neither of these responses seem to have been available to Trist.

Unable to discover the "beautifull prospects" she sought, and apparently incapable of calling forth anything resembling Humphreys's imagined transformation of the scene, Trist repeatedly complained of feeling "confin'd" within thick woodlands that offered only "a little opening now and then." Increasingly anxious at the "very confined Prospect," her agitation heightened until she felt "oppress'd with so much wood towering above me in every direction and such a continuance of it." And here intolerance turned to terror, as Trist described the physical symptoms of the anxiety that held her in its grip: "I began at last to conceit myself Attlass with the whole World upon my shoulders. My spirits were condenc'd to nothing" (Trist, undated [May 1784] entry). Like the Puritan woman who told her minister in 1645 how she had suffered from being "shut up for a long space of time living far in the woods,"[23] Trist too sought escape. "My head began to ach[e]," she recorded, "and I returned to town quite sick" (Trist, undated [May 1784] entry).

The next line of the diary begins the final Pittsburgh entry, dated May 20, 1784. As though in direct response to what she had just written, Trist there reversed earlier, more sanguine comments about the place, now declaring that she "left Pittsburg with as little regret as I ever did any place that I had lived so long in" (Trist, May 20, 1784). What she could not know then, of course, was that the river voyage would bring her into realms where her spirits would again be "condenc'd to nothing."

The trip down the Ohio, though, gave no hint of what lay ahead. As this portion of the water voyage began, Trist noted only that "things wear a smiling aspect," and she continued to observe the fertility of the landscape, describing the first island encountered in the river as "about a mile in length and very fertile as is most of the land in this country" (Trist, May 20, 1784). The next day when the boat docked at Wheeling to take on fresh supplies, she expressed her pleasure in the booming settlement she found there and in the garden-like appearance of the place. Declaring herself "allmost in extacy at the magnificence of the display of nature" in Wheeling, Trist described "the trees . . . decked in all their gay attire and the earth in its richest verdure." What she could not comprehend were the emigrants who arrived in Wheeling in "blooming May," only to push on down the river. "Yet the people seem to have caught the infection of the country," she explained to herself, "a desire for the Kentucki" (Trist, May 21, 1784).

What Trist was observing, of course, was the fact that, upon the close of the Revolution, the Ohio quickly became a well-traveled road to the expanding western frontiers, with settlement locating itself on either bank and along its tributaries. Passing "salt river which runs up in the Kentucke settlements," Trist characteristically noted, "I am informed there are a number of good Plantations up on this river" (Trist, June 4, 1784). By 1784, as a result, game along the banks of the Ohio was already disappearing. "We have not seen any wild beasts till today a bear presented himself to our view," Trist wrote on the fourth day out of Pittsburgh (Trist, May 23, 1784). And, three days later, she recorded "disappointment" that "our hunters return'd without any game . . . as we expected to have had some fresh meat for dinner"—a disappointment that led her to conclude that "there are such numbers of boats continually going down the river that all the game have left the shore" (Trist, May 26, 1784). Two weeks later, when some of the crew again went on shore "to hunt," they "killed a tame cow which they mistook for a Buffaloe" (Trist, June 6, 1784). Those who fancied they were Daniel Boone, we may surmise, were less eager to perceive the changes that Trist so easily accepted. Not until they had passed the falls at Louisville did crewmen go "on shore to hunt" with success. This time, "being gone several hours," they "returned with a deer the first wild meat we have had" (Trist, June 5, 1784).

During a nine-day stopover in Louisville, occasioned by the boat's running aground on the rapids, Trist and Polly were "met by several Gentlemen that I had the pleasure of being acquainted with" (Trist, May 27, 1784). These included former Virginians who, with their families, were removing to Louisville. The physical discomforts of her stay at Fort Nelson were thus mitigated by her pleasure at discovering more refined society relocating itself westward. In her diary she recorded that she joined "in several little dances that were made on . . . our accounts," and she decided that, all in all, she had "experienced the greatest attention and politeness from several Gentlemen and particular marks of friendship" (Trist, May 28, 1784). Despite some inclement weather and the boat's running aground, therefore, Trist's journey down the Ohio had proven a comparatively easy passage through a landscape marked by the familiarities of settlement, old acquaintances, and "wild ginger which grows in great abundance along the banks" (Trist, May 24, 1784). Not unsurprisingly, then, the general tone of her Ohio entries approved "the country [for being] very healthy and the land very fertile" (Trist, June 10, 1784).

This changed as she entered "the back waters of the Mississippi." Here, we "proceed on our voyage but very slow," she noted, because "the current [is] very dead." Her closing entry for June 12, 1784, tells us that the boat "made fast to the shore for the night as it is thought unsafe to enter the Mississippi in the dark" (Trist, June 12, 1784). But the next morning "the Grand Riviere" turned out to be no more hospitable than its backwaters. To her dismay, Trist found "the water of the Mississippi uncommonly low so as to discover a large sand bar." Her boat passed this hazard safely, but still, Trist insisted, "the navagation of this river is rendered dangerous." That night, at anchor on the river, "about 7 miles below the Ohio," she protested that the cool evening air provided "no comfort" because of "the musquitos" (Trist, June 13, 1784). After this, her diary entries habitually recorded complaints about weather, illness, fevers, mosquitoes, and the many difficulties of navigating the river's treacherous channels.

The land along the banks offered no compensating welcome. When the boat anchored briefly "about 3 miles below the mouth of the Ohio," near Fort Jefferson, Trist was dissuaded from going ashore "as it was not certain what Indians might be there." From the crew who did disembark she received only "a very unfavorable account of the place": "the worst situation of any upon the river the land very low" (Trist, June 13, 1784). The unremitting wildness of the shore line, moreover, prohibited her usual imaginative play. On June 14, she eagerly looked toward "a fine high situation," reporting that "I am told there is to be a town laid out here very soon" (Trist, June 14, 1784). But more characteristic of her impressions along the Mississippi was her June 16 entry: "we pass'd two Glades the only clear land I have seen" (Trist, June 16, 1784).

No longer does she seem able to contemplate ending "my days in the Western country." The Mississippi—with its "passionate sort of a climate," its wilderness shoreline, and its fever-laden mosquitoes—persuades her only that "all the wealth of the Indies wou'd not induce me to live in a Musquitoe country" (Trist, June 17, 1784). Not even the rare clearing or a grove of wild fruit could induce her to imagine any gardens here; instead, she harked back to what had been left behind. Coming upon "a very pretty glade full of fine ripe plumbs," she commented, "there are great quantitys of them growing in this country but I dont think they are as large as those that grow in Pennsylvania" (Trist, June 22, 1784).

As the shoreline failed to reflect back what she would see there, Trist's diary increasingly recorded human wretchedness—her own and Polly's (both sick with intermittent fevers)—and that of "a poor family encamp'd at this place . . . call'd Lonce la Greece . . . 80 miles from the Ohio" (Trist, June 16, 1784):

> a man and his wife their father and mother and five children, left the
> Natchez seven months ago on their way to cumberland river and
> had not a morsel of bread for the last three months. they had buried
> one the oldest of their sons a little while before, the poor little chil-
> dren when they saw us cry'd for some bread. our Gent. gave them
> some flour and I had the pleasure to contribute to the hapiness of
> the women by giving them some tea and sugar—which was more
> acceptable to them than diamonds or pearls. (Trist, June 15, 1784)

The encounter afforded the diarist a sobering reminder of the hardships endured by most who traveled west—hardships resulting, in part, from the poverty that had driven them to the frontier in the first place. At the same time, the encounter also reminded her of just how privileged her own situation really was: "every one thinks their troubles the greatest, but I have seen so many poor creatures since I left home who's situation has been so wretched that I shall begin to consider my self as a favored child of fortune" (Trist, June 15, 1784). It was a philosophy she would soon enough need to call upon for solace.

Reputed to be "the best hunting ground anywhere on the river," the stopover at Lonce la Greece was intended to replace "provisions" that were "allmost exhausted." But the "hopes of killing some deer" proved fruitless, and "the men returned without even having fired a gun." While she was not unmindful of the need to replace diminishing food stores, Trist nonetheless "lament[ed] the loss of this day" because, by stopping, they had lost a favorable wind. By this time Trist was desperate to be done with her passage down the Mississippi, confiding to her diary, "my patience is allmost exausted . . . what with the Musquitos and head winds I am allmost sick." An earlier spring departure might have made the passage more tolerable, even "pleasant," she admitted, but a boat builder's delay in Pittsburgh left them at the mercy of the June heat and the shallow channels of the summer season. "At present there is nothing but trouble," she concluded (Trist, June 18, 1784).

The statement coincides with her coming in sight of "the first of the Chickasaw Bluffs . . . which is 201 miles from the Ohio." As the bluffs overwhelmed and dwarfed her, she experienced an anxiety not unlike that which overcame her in the woods outside of Pittsburgh, near the Cherties settlement. Only here she ascribed to the Mississippi, her agent of passage into the frightening realms, her own sense of entering where she does not belong:

> I have various ideas about this river. some times conceit I am got to the far end of the world or rather that it is the last of Gods creation and the seventh day came before it was quite finish'd. at other times I fancy there has been some great revolution in nature and this great body of water has found a passage where it was not intended and tore up all before it. the banks are now about 50 feet high very ragged and every here and there great pieces of the earth tumbling in to the water often great trees go with it. . . . All together its appearance is awfull and Melancholy and sometimes terrific. (Trist, June 18, 1784)

From the river, however, there was no escape to town. At best, she could compute progress toward her destination. Two days later, having passed the bluffs, she impatiently recorded, "a week this day since we entered the Mississippi and have not got 300 mile" (Trist, June 20, 1784).

Not until June 30, more than two weeks after her entry into the Mississippi, did Trist report "the first settlement we saw on the river." When her boat anchored at the settlement, Trist went ashore to avail herself of the refreshment of "water mellons green corn apples" and conversation with "a Mullato woman named Nelly." But "after spending a couple of hours," Trist related that "we took our departure" (Trist, June 30, 1784). The stopover thus constituted only a brief interlude in what was otherwise a steady emotional decline. "I can hardly keep my self alive. . . . I am every day more anxious to be at the end of my journey or voyage" (Trist, June 26 and June 28, 1784). The mood of the June 28th entry may perhaps be explained by the boat's having earlier that day been driven "against a large tree . . . by the violence of the current." "For my part," Trist wrote, "I gave my self up. I did not even see a probability of saving my life" (Trist, June 28, 1784). Even so, she did survive—as did the boat. But her "poor little Dog" was taken by alligators the next day (Trist, June 29, 1784).

Though no further dramatic incidents ensued, and despite what was now her proximity to her destination, Trist's diary entries continued to betray a growing anxiety. On July 1, "within a few miles of the Natchez," her "journey . . . most completed," she wrote, "my heart sinks within me and I feel so weak that I can hardly keep my self a live." Not even the knowledge that "three days more I shall be happy in sight of the Natchez" alleviated her distress. "What can cause these sensations?" she queried. The information that reached her that afternoon may have answered her question. The boat having docked "to unload some flour" before going on to Natchez (Trist, July 1, 1784), it is probable that there the news caught up with Trist that her husband had died five months earlier—while she, all unknowing, passed the winter in Pittsburgh. With the July first entry, the diary abruptly breaks off, mid-sentence and mid-page.

After surveying the writings of men like Daniel Boone and Alexander Henry, Richard Slotkin concludes that "the characteristic American gesture in the face of adversity is . . . immersion in the native element, the wilderness, as the solution to all problems, the balm to all wounds of the soul, the restorative for failing fortunes."[24] But for Elizabeth House Trist, the wilderness itself had been the problem, wounding her soul with its oppressive forests and towering rock formations, "condenc[ing]" her "spirits . . . to nothing," and taking her husband—first in exploration and now in death. For her, "immersion in the native element" had never been possible. Her husband's pioneering footsteps into the Mississippi Territory would be followed by those of their son.[25] But Trist herself returned a widow to her mother's boardinghouse in Philadelphia.

If, through the beginning of the nineteenth century, American women shied away from paradisal projections, they nonetheless seemed eager to tend the garden. "Those that would be satisfied to see every thing here perfect," mused Cornelia Greene in 1800, "have ill health." But then, as she continued in a letter to cousins on Jamaica, "even in Paradise the Wicked would be miserable." For her own part, Greene made clear that she had "never expected to find any thing extraordinary & never saw any thing very pleasing" about Cumberland Island, off the coast of Georgia, to which her family had so optimistically removed during the turbulent years of revolution. And so, to her mind, she was "the most blessed."[26] As perhaps she was. Instead of suffering any disappointing encounter between exaggerated paradisal expectations and Georgia realities, Cornelia Greene was creating a surer garden, one of her own making. "Do not forget my ripe fruit which I intreated you to send me," she reminded her cousins, adding, "any flower or fruit which you can share & send to me would be a great acquisition to our country as well as a gift of highest prize."[27] It is a refrain that dominates the extant letters and diaries of generations of American women, whether they write from settled landscapes or from the frontier. For, in the exchange of cuttings, scions, seeds, and overripe fruit (for its seeds) and in the exchange of information about their garden activities, women shared with one another both their right and their capacity to put their personal stamp on landscapes otherwise owned and appropriated by men.

For Frances Ann Tasker Carter, "to live in the Country, and take no pleasure at all in Groves, Fields, or Meadows," would have been "a manner of life too tedious to endure." Wife to Robert Carter III and mistress of his extensive Nomini Hall plantation in tidewater Virginia, she did much more than merely "take pleasure" in the plantation's grounds. She insisted also that they be planned to suit *her* tastes. As her children's tutor recorded in his 1773–74 diary, "Mrs. Carter told the Colonel [her husband] that he must not think her setled . . . til he made her a park and stock'd it."[28] At the same time, while her husband permitted "large Quantities of Land" to be planted in a manner that quickly depleted fertility,[29] Frances Carter superintended the smaller garden plots from which, year after year, the family gathered its fruits and vegetables. In February, she ordered "the Gardener to sew Lettice, & plant Peas . . . in the Garden" and, with some pride, according to the young tutor from Princeton, she showed him her "Apricot-Grafts; Asparagus Beds &c." A New Englander with regional suspicions of southerners, and a Princetonian with decidedly limited opinions of female intelligence, young Philip Vickers Fithian seemed clearly impressed that his mistress knew what she was about in her garden. In December, after walking together in one of the many plots surrounding the main house, the tutor recorded that he had "ask[ed] her some questions upon a Row of small slips—To all of which she made polite and full answers; As we walked along she would move the Ground at the Root of some plant; or prop up with small stickes the bended *scions*."[30]

In the early decades of the eighteenth century, the Swedish botanist, Carl Linnaeus, taught his classification system to his eldest daughter and thereby helped to legitimize "botanizing" as an acceptable activity for women.[31] But for women in America, the recognition of "several wild vegetables" (Trist, undated [May 1784] entry) or the domestication of local flora in home gardens denoted something far more crucial than pleasant outdoor recreation. For women on the frontiers, especially, these implied a form of survival on unfamiliar terrains. Many times widowed on the treacherous frontier, Ann Kennedy Wilson Poague Lindsay McGinty came to what is now Mercer County, Kentucky, in December 1775, "& in the Cource [of] that winter & spring following," as she later recalled, she worked with her then husband, William Poague, to clear "about ten acres of ground & planted it in Corn the same spring that being the first clearing that appeared to have been made at that place."[32] She then took stock of the wilderness around her and devised a means of using the fibers of "nettles and other weeds" that grew so abundantly there as a substitute for flax, thereby supplying her family with a usable cloth for the warm winter garments they so urgently required.[33]

Complementing (perhaps even accelerating) this process of adaptive familiarization—and due largely to the exigencies of colonial existence—was the fact that American women were also gradually securing a modicum of legal control over some of the land they were being asked to call home. Though it was not the case in earlier decades, by the end of the seventeenth century, generally, women who were single or widowed could hold property anywhere in the colonies. And even married women could, in a technical sense, claim ownership—though, legally, their husbands still held complete control of all property and could dispose of it at any time without their wives' consent. By the end of the eighteenth century, however, it was not unusual for fathers to bequeath land to their daughters as well as to their sons (though this hardly became the rule and, for the most part, land still remained predominantly under male title).[34]

Still, the same contingencies of colonial existence that were thus slowly altering centuries of English custom in land ownership did make available to American women opportunities for land management that would have been unimaginable to their counterparts in Europe. Take, for example, the young Eliza Lucas. Born in the West Indies and educated in England, she found herself, at age sixteen, managing three plantations in South Carolina. The oldest of the four children of George Lucas, a lieutenant colonel in the British army, Eliza was brought to America in 1738 when her father, seeking a more congenial climate for his ailing wife, removed his family to a plantation on Wappoo Creek that he had inherited from his father. The next year, a maritime conflict between England and Spain forced him to return to his military post in Antigua. From then until his death in 1747, Lucas remained abroad on military assignments and never saw South Carolina again. In his absence, his oldest child attended to the plantation's business, experimenting with diversified crops at Wappoo and, among these, developing a strain of indigo that was eventually to provide a staple crop for the colony.

From Eliza's letterbook, it is clear that, at first, she perceived herself as no more than her father's agent, carrying out "*his* plantation affairs" and relying on him for direction. In July 1740, her letterbook records that she wrote her father a "very long letter on his plantation affairs and . . . on the pains I had taken to bring the Indigo, Ginger, Cotton and Lucerne and Casada to perfection, and had greater hopes from the Indigo (if I could have the seed earlier next year from the West India's) than any of the rest of the things I had tryd."[35] At this point, Eliza was only seventeen and still rather tentatively assuming her new role. Two years later, confident in the success of her management, she asserted a clear independence of her father's guidance, confiding in a letter to her friend, Mary Bartlett, "I am now making a large plantation of Oaks which I look upon as my own property, whether my father gives me the land or not" (*Pinckney*, p. 38).

More and more pursuing her own inclinations in the management of her father's properties, Eliza Lucas not only asserted her determination to plant what she wanted but she pursued her own taste in the aesthetic design of the grounds. Not for her were "the mounts, Wilderness, etc." with which other southerners sought artfully to define "a fine prospect" on their estates. Which is not to say that Eliza was wholly unimpressed by elaborate contrivances such as a "charming spott where is a large fish pond with a mount rising out of the middle . . . and upon it is a roman temple." Clearly, as revealed in a 1743 letter to Mary Bartlett, the intended effect was not lost on her. Even so, she insisted, "what immediately struck my rural taste," were not the artful manipulations of sense and sensibility but, instead, "a thicket of young tall live oaks where a variety of Airry Choristers pour forth their melody." Thus, while her wealthier neighbors might indulge the period's taste for artfully contrived landscapes, Eliza Lucas seems to have been immune to the Arcadian fantasies shaping these "very handsome Gentlemens Seats" (*Pinckney*, pp. 60–61). Her characteristically eighteenth-century impulse to make of her landscape a living emblem was, by contrast, far more modest. In the spring of 1742, she contemplated a cedar grove (usually associated with gloom or contemplation) in which "to connect . . . the solemnity (not the solidity) of summer or autumn with the cheerfulness and pleasure of spring, for it shall be filled with all kind of flowers, as well wild as Garden flowers, with seats of Camomoil and here and there a fruit tree—oranges, nectrons, Plumbs, &c." (*Pinckney*, p. 36).

Happily for her, Eliza Lucas had quickly decided that she liked "this part of the world," assuring Mrs. Bodicott, her good friend and former teacher in England, "I really do" (*Pinckney*, p. 6). What seems to have enabled this speedy accommodation was the fact that Eliza found herself "in the Country" but not isolated from town or neighbors. Only "17 mile by land and 6 by water from Charles Town," Wappoo was also immediately surrounded by "6 agreeable families" on nearby plantations. Perhaps even more important was the unique opportunity to design a landscape according to her own choosing and, in that process, indulge unstintingly in what she termed the "innocent and useful amusement" of gardening (*Pinckney*, p. 35). For, despite the fact that, as she herself admitted, "I have the business of 3 plantations to transact, which requires much writing and more business and fatigue of other sorts," Eliza Lucas habitually asked her correspondents to picture her as a woman in "the Garden, which I am very fond of" (*Pinckney*, p. 7).

She invoked the image whether describing the planting of a grove, the seeding of a cash crop, or the domestication of wild flowers. It is an apparently disingenuous emphasis for a woman burdened with the management of three plantations. But, as her later letters make abundantly clear, the seeming oddity of her usage derives from the fantasy she was all along projecting. The fact is, Eliza Lucas wanted to see herself not as the agrarian entrepreneur she was but as a humble gardener at work amid the receding wilderness places of America.

When she married Charles Pinckney, a childless widower twenty years her senior, Eliza removed first to his Belmont plantation on the Cooper River and then, in 1753, her husband having been named a colonial commissioner to the crown, she found herself again in England. That country's war with France precipitated the couple's return to South Carolina where, a few months later, in July of 1758, Charles Pinckney died of malaria. His able widow took on the management of plantation business. Just as she had so many years earlier, when describing her activities at Wappoo, Eliza Lucas Pinckney once more reported herself "tak[ing] pleasure in" her garden. "I think it an Innocent and delightful amusement," she repeated (*Pinckney*, p. 185). This time, however, the essential fantasy underlying that "amusement" was explicitly imaged.

In a letter of 1762, written from her Belmont plantation on the Cooper River to friends outside of London, Eliza described herself as inhabiting "a little hovel . . . quite in a forrest." However ill-managed the estate had been during the Pinckneys' absence abroad, and without discounting Eliza's possibly playful inclination to cater to a Londoner's faulty notions of life in the colonies, the gracious mansion at Belmont was hardly a "hovel," nor were its grounds any kind of "forrest." The exaggeration makes sense only if we recognize the writer's eagerness to convey a quality of experience that depended not so much on the physical geography as on an imagined one. "We found it in [such] ruins when we arrived from England," she wrote of the Belmont grounds, "that I have had a wood to clear" (p. 185). In actuality, of course, the widow Pinckney and her servants were cutting back the overgrowth of several years of neglect. Even so, the image she preferred was of a woman clearing a primary garden for herself in the wilderness area just beyond the line of urban settlement: "I have a little hovel about 5 mile from town, quite in a forrest where I find much amusement 4 or 5 months in the year, and where I have room enough to exercise my Genius that way. . . . I am my self head gardener, and I believe work much harder than most principal ones do" (*Pinckney*, p. 185). Except for the limited time allotted (she need be there only "4 or 5 months in the year"), the impression evoked by these lines is of a woman situated, under rather humble circumstances, upon a landscape neither settled nor wholly wild, but certainly within the pale of civilization. The area to which the writer attends, moreover, is sufficiently circumscribed to be called a garden and to permit a lone woman to exercise her "Genius" upon it. Only with that image firmly established does she allow reality to intrude, finally admitting to her London correspondent that she has, in fact, been modernizing the grounds of an estate "laid out in the old taste."

Were such phrasings not everywhere to be found in the letters and diaries of eighteenth-century American women, they would perforce be labeled the peculiar idiosyncrasy of this disingenuous South Carolinian. But when measured against similar ploys in the writings of her contemporaries, Eliza Lucas Pinckney's repeated reliance on a highly stylized vocabulary of gardening and modest dwellings begins to suggest the imaginative resources through which women of her time and class sought a more secure cognitive hold on the American landscape. Even on her attractive Birdwood plantation, for example, Elizabeth House Trist claimed to inhabit only a humble "Cabbin."

In 1801, writing from Virginia to her former neighbor and then-president, Thomas Jefferson, in Washington, Trist reported a recent "dreadfull hail storm" from which "the Sky lights at Monticello I hear has not escaped." Her own dwelling, happily, "experienced no damage except the blowing down of a few pannel of fence." What saved it, she emphasized, was neither its grandeur nor its size, but instead its very humility: "I expected that our Cabbin wou'd have been carried off by the Wind, but its humility not its strength preserved it."[36] The facts of her social situation belie the rhetoric of her description. Having grown to manhood and successfully petitioned for a small inheritance from his father's family in England, her son had purchased Birdwood, adjacent to Monticello. Born into a solidly middle-class Quaker merchant family in Philadelphia and now welcomed into comfortable business and planting families in Virginia, Elizabeth House Trist may not have enjoyed the most luxurious dwelling in Virginia, but her home was far from what even then would have been labeled merely a "Cabbin."[37]

As in the letters of Eliza Lucas Pinckney, the imagery is at once pointed and consistent. But in Trist it bridges years and disparate landscapes alike. The comfortable, if limited, circumstances that attached to the ancient Pennsylvania pioneer couple as "a true picture of rural felicity" also defined what she would see at Birdwood. "Had we a more convenient establishment," she boasted in her letter to Jefferson, "as it is, I don't know that I wou'd exchange with any of you in the Grand City." After all, she explained, her "grain is flourishing," she and her family "have few temptations to extravagance," and, all in all, "we . . . enjoy good health and of course appetites to relish our homely fair."[38]

It would appear therefore that Trist's accommodation to any American landscape—be it wild or well settled—depended on her capacity to experience it as what Leo Marx and others have labeled "the middle landscape": that is, that band of log cabins and small but prospering farms and grazing lands newly wrested from the wilderness.[39] In Virginia, she painted herself inhabiting a cabin and "relish[ing] . . . homely fare." In frontier Pennsylvania, she sought out the clearings of early settlement and delighted in finding hints of the cultivated kitchen herb gardens that might one day replace the forests. Thus could she negotiate the passage from urban Philadelphia to forested frontier and even contemplate ending her days in the "Western country." For what Trist transported with her wherever she went was a fantasy of "rural felicity," a fantasy not unlike Eliza Lucas Pinckney's self-portrait as a gardener in a retreating "forrest." The only difference was that, in addition to the images honed by fantasy, the young Eliza Lucas, like so many other immigrant women, brought with her to South Carolina seeds and cuttings from the landscapes she had known earlier (in this case, in England and the West Indies). To make a home of the place, both needed to be implanted on the alien soil. Physically *and* imaginatively, in short, the pioneer women of America *carried their roots with them.*

That the garden they invoked was to be neither a rediscovered Eden (only "*like* a garden," Trist emphasized) nor any fortuitously found paradise also should not surprise. Young women educated in eighteenth-century England and America had never been trained to identify "paradise" with a geographical terrain; for them, the word resonated with other meanings entirely. Schooled in the attitudes of pious domesticity then deemed appropriate for genteel young women, Eliza Carolina Burgwin brought with her to North Carolina in 1801 a strict notion of the "various duties in their various stations . . . appointed to each Sex. To man's more vigorous frame & intellect, Manual labor, and scientific pursuits were appropriated; whilst the office of gentle Woman, was to render Home a Paradise, by the strict enactment of her several domestic duties."[40] From the late eighteenth century through the opening decades of the nineteenth, phrasings like this were commonplace on both sides of the Atlantic. In Philadelphia, even the comparatively progressive Susanna Rowson taught her female charges that it was their particular duty to create a "paradise at home."[41]

As a result, "paradise" implied radically different places when used by men and by women. For men the term (with all its concomitant psycho-sexual associations) echoed an invitation for mastery and possession of the vast new continent. For women, by contrast, it denoted domesticity. Thus, while men sought new Edens and created new Arcadias for themselves, working "the keen adze" and altering the landscape to make it comply with their dreams of receptive and bountiful realms, women patched Pine Tree quilts, appliqued counterpanes with brightly colored Rose of Sharon designs, and cultivated small gardens in order "to render Home a Paradise."

3 The Lady in the Cave

In a 1773 reprinting of Mary Rowlandson's captivity narrative, the original pious title and the accompanying sermon by her minister husband were removed, and the title page now carried a woodcut of a woman shooting at four men (presumably Indians). "An image hardly justified by the contents of the book," as John Seelye has pointed out,[1] it was nonetheless an image pertinent to the imaginative requirements of a generation determined to transplant itself westward, a generation in which young women like Hannah Robbins Gilman would declare themselves "willing to leave Parents . . . and take up my abode in a howling wilderness."[2] For what a later generation sought to divine in narratives like Rowlandson's was not the story of patient suffering but a gesture of defiant survival. In the years just before and after the Revolution, as a steady stream of emigrants crossed the mountains in small family groups, this was no idle theme.

The anxiety attendant upon such relocations rested not only on an appreciation of the physical dangers and hardships but on a far deeper fear of the loss of civilization itself. The savagery of the woods and of their native inhabitants, many eighteenth-century observers believed, would inevitably make savages of the whites who tried to remove there.[3] Despairing at what he had himself seen of the northeastern "back settlers," Hector St. John de Crèvecoeur made his fictional Farmer James insist that "there is something in the proximity of the woods, which is very singular." "By living in or near the woods," James averred, settlers' "actions are regulated by the wildness of the neighborhood."[4] The Anglican minister, Charles Woodmason, traveling in the Carolina backcountry in the years just before the Revolution, confided similar concerns to his journal when he noted that he found the Flat Creek settlers "as rude in their Manners as the Common Savages, and hardly a degree removed from them."[5]

When applied to women, such fears became even more virulent in their expression, suggesting a culture that felt itself more profoundly threatened by the specter of the white woman—as opposed to the white man—gone savage. Charles Woodmason, for example, deplored his encounters with the "barefooted and Bare legged" women of the Carolina backcountry, all of them, in his view, "Quite in a State of Nature." Particularly distressing to the good preacher was the women's habit of "Rubbing themselves and their Hair with Bears Oil and tying it up behind in a Bunch like the Indians."[6] Somewhat more restrained in his *Letters from an American Farmer*, Crèvecoeur also noted the pernicious influence of the woods on the families of those who chose to settle there. "Their wives and children live in sloth and inactivity," he wrote, the parents raising "a mongrel breed, half civilized, half savage."[7]

Indeed, throughout the eighteenth century, much though they wanted to, Americans seemed incapable of sustaining the image of a woman adapted to life along the frontier and yet untainted by "ruggedness or Immodesty." That such women existed, we have ample evidence in the journals and diaries of the men who encountered them. Nonetheless, what consistently marks these entries is the tone of surprise. When Philip Ludwell helped survey the westernmost boundary between Virginia and the Carolinas in 1710, for example, he and his party came upon the frontier cabin of a Mrs. Jones. Subsequently, Ludwell recorded in his journal that, "It is said of this Mrs. Jones . . . that she is a very civil woman and shews nothing of ruggedness or Immodesty in her carriage, yett she will carry a gunn in the woods and kill deer, turkeys, &c., shoot down wild cattle, catch and tye hoggs, knock down beeves with an ax and perform the most manfull Exercises as well as most men in those parts."[8] The muted disbelief betrayed by Ludwell's transitional "yett" springs from contemporary notions that a woman simply could not master the skills requisite for survival at the edge of the frontier without becoming either masculinized or Indianized.

At least in part, the phenomenal popularity of John Filson's original Daniel Boone narrative may have been due to the fact that it effectively quieted fears of white male degeneracy in the woods by substituting for those fears the heroic myth of white male conquest of the wilderness. By demonstrating all the woodcraft and hunting skills of the Indian while, at the same time, firmly associating himself with white agricultural settlement, Filson's Boone responded to those like Crèvecoeur who panicked at the notion that, near the woods, men might abandon the plow and "degenerate altogether into the hunting state."[9] Boone the isolate hunter, after all, was also the protector of the fledgling Kentucky settlements, declaring himself, in Filson's 1784 text, "an instrument ordained to settle the wilderness."[10]

Fears for the fate of white women in the wilderness could be quieted by no correspondingly mythic figure. Rebecca Bryan Boone and her daughters as yet remained only shadowy characters in Filson and, in printer John Trumbull's 1786 editing, their presence was even further diminished.[11] In 1787, however, there appeared from the pen of some still unidentified author a strange and haunting narrative that, perhaps without quite understanding its own motivations, offered at least the fantasied possibility of a civilized white woman's lone survival in the wilderness places of America. This was "A Surprising account of the Discovery of a Lady who was taken by the Indians in the year 1777, and after making her escape, She retired to a lonely Cave, where She lived nine years," first printed in *Bickerstaff's almanack, for the year* . . . *1788*, and then widely and repeatedly reprinted (at least twenty-five different times) through 1814.[12] It was composed as a letter from a pseudonymous Abraham Panther to an unnamed correspondent and has thus popularly come to be known as the "Panther Captivity" (a title under which it has sometimes been reprinted).

As the letter opens, the writer is apparently responding to his correspondent's request for some account of a recent journey into "the Western wilderness." No doubt intentionally echoing Filson's narrative of *The Adventures of Col. Daniel Boon*, the writer here explains that he and a companion, "Mr. Isaac Camber," were "determin[ed] to penetrate the Western wilderness as far as prudence and safety would permit," and, in the course of that journey, "travelled for thirteen days in a westerly direction." Again echoing Boone's enthusiasm for the fertility and beauty of the Kentucky landscape, combined with his hunter's pleasure at the abundance of game to be found there, Abraham Panther similarly notes that he and Camber found the land "exceeding rich and fertile," emphasizing "the very great variety of birds and wild beasts, which would frequently start before us."[13] "As we had our muskets," he adds, these "contributed not a little to our amusement and support."

On the fourteenth day of their travels, the two men are enjoying a particularly "agreeable picturesque prospect" when they are surprised at the sound of a voice nearby. "Uncertain whether the voice was a human one, or that of some bird," they decide to proceed up the hill, from which the sound seemed to come. Daniel Boone, too, had described "gain[ing] the summit of a commanding ridge." What he encountered there, to his "astonishing delight," were "the ample plains, [and] the beauteous tracts" that later drew him to resettle in Kentucky.[14] By contrast, what Panther and Camber discover as they mount their "high hill" is the palpable symbolization of what remains just below the surface in Boone, even as that mythic hero recounts his virtual seduction by "the beauties of nature I found here."[15] Following a small foot path to the top of the hill, the letter writer and his companion "passed around a large rock, and through a thicket of bushes at the end of which was a large opening." And there, "to our inexpressible amazement," Panther writes, "we beheld a most beautiful young LADY sitting near the mouth of a cave."

As they approach the woman, who is not yet aware of their presence, they are halted by the barking of "a dog which we had not before observed." Alarmed by the dog's barking, the woman "started up and seeing us, gave a scream and swooned away." Upon her recovery, the two men quiet her apprehensions, and "having convinced her of our peaceable dispositions," they are invited into the cave where "she refreshed us with some ground nuts, a kind of apples, some Indian cake and excellent water. We found her to be an agreeable, sensible lady," the letter continues, "and after some conversation we requested to know who she was and how she came to this place." At this point, the text swerves from a Boone-like narrative of masculine adventure in the wilderness to a surprising version of the by now familiar female captivity narrative.

What is surprising about the woman's story is not that she has spent relatively little time in captivity or that she has subdued at least her second captor; there were already precedents for these in earlier narratives.[16] What is surprising here is that her sojourn in the woods, following upon her escape, has reduced her neither to "a mere skeleton" nor to the "forlorn creature" that characterized Francis Scott and so many other escaped female captives.[17] And, more surprising still, she has managed to sustain herself in the wilderness and survive there, on her own, for nine years. As such, her first-person narrative, embedded within the Panther letter and thereby interrupting the masculine hunting story that it would otherwise recount, suggests a subtle readjustment in Americans' imaginative vision of the place and person of the white woman in the wilderness.

"I was born near Albany in the year 1760," the lady begins, the only child of "a man of some consequence and of considerable estate." At age fifteen she fell in love with a young clerk whom the father had recently introduced into the household. The growing attachment between the two had to be concealed, however, because, as she explains, her father being "excessively eager in pursuit of riches," he could not be expected to "countenance our loves or consent to my marriage with a man destitute of fortune." Nonetheless, the father one day discovers the couple together and, "with an angry countenance upbraided my lover . . . and after calling him many hard names, dismissed him with peremptory order never again to enter his house." By means of a secret correspondence, the young lovers manage to remain in contact, finally devising a plan to "retire into the country, to a little hut." Her father, "enraged at my elopement," subsequently hires several men to pursue the couple and thereby drives them "further back in the country . . . there to wait till time should calm my father's rage, or effectually cool his resentments."

By traveling deeper into the wilderness, the couple evades the father's hired men, only to fall captive to Indians. The young man is "barbarously murdered," at the sight of which the girl "fainted away and lay some time motionless on the ground." When she regains consciousness, she discovers that her Indian guard has joined his fellows in singing and dancing, and so she takes the opportunity to withdraw "by degrees into the bushes." Now safely escaped from her Indian captors, she still feels herself "surrounded, as I supposed, on all sides by danger . . . without a guide to direct, or friend to protect me." At this juncture, most previous narratives had emphasized the woman's lack of woodcraft, detailing her sense of being lost in a trackless wilderness and her inability to find sufficient food to stave off starvation. In the Panther Captivity, however, while the lady acknowledges that she "wandered about for 14 days without knowing whether I went," the text also insists that raw nature provided at least a modicum of adequate food and shelter: "By day the spontaneous produce of the earth supplied me with food, by night the ground was my couch, and the canopy of heaven my only covering."

"In the afternoon of the fifteenth day," her story continues, she is "surprized" by "a man of gigantic figure walking towards me." Concluding escape to be impossible, she allows the man to overtake and then lead her to the cave she now inhabits. Here, her captor first feeds her, "after which he stretched himself out upon a long stone covered with skins which he used as a bed, and several times motioned to me to lay myself beside him." When the girl declines "his offer," the giant fetches his "sword and hatchet . . . motion[ing] to me that I must either accept of his bed or expect death for my obstinacy." Still she declines, insisting that "I . . . was resolved to die rather than comply with his desire." At that, the giant binds her, "insinuating that he left me till next morning to consider his proposal." While he sleeps, the girl chews away at her bark bindings, frees herself, and despairing of eluding "him by flight," she determines instead to kill her captor:

> I did not long deliberate, but took up the hatchet he had brought, and summoning resolution I with three blows effectually put an end to his existence. I then cut off his head, and next day having cut him into quarters drew him out of the cave about half a mile distance, when after covering him with leaves and bushes I returned to this

place. I now found myself alone in possession of this cave in which are several apartments. I found here a kind of Indian corn which I planted, and have yearly raised a small quantity, here I contented myself as well as I my wretched situation would permit—here have I existed for nine long years, in all which time this faithful dog which I found in the cave has been my only companion, and you are the only human beings who ever heard me tell my tale.

With that, the young woman's "narration" is completed, accompanied by "a plentiful shower of tears."

The voice of the letter writer then resumes the narrative, detailing the next day's tour of the cave's four compartments (which contain "a spring of excellent water"; a cache of "four skulls," presumed to be those of "persons murdered by the [former] owner of the cave"; a supply of weapons, including "three hatchets, four bows and several arrows, one large tinder box, one sword, one old gun"; and a number of animal skins "and a few cloathes"). "After continuing in the cave five days" more, Panther writes his correspondent, he and his companion "proposed returning home and requested the lady to accompany us." "At first she refused to quit her cave," he continues, "but after some persuasion she consented." He then briefly summarizes the homeward journey, expanding only on accompanying "the lady, agreeable to her desire, to her father's house." By this time the old man is quite ill and "did not at first recognize his daughter. But being told who she was," he revives briefly "and then tenderly embraced her crying O! my child, my long lost child." He faints and is again revived—this time sufficiently long enough to hear his daughter's story, to acknowledge that "he had been unjustly cruel to her," and, at the last, to ask her forgiveness. Once more, then, the old man loses consciousness, but now all efforts to revive him fail. His death brings his daughter "a handsome fortune," and she, in her turn, "notwithstanding his cruelty," is "deeply affected at his sudden death." So ends both the letter and its writer's recounting of "this adventure the most singular and extraordinary of my life."

Clearly, disparate generic sources contribute to the Panther Captivity. These include the male narrative of wilderness adventure, the captivity narrative, the sentimental romance, and Indian fertility myths. In the course of the letter, however, the original meaning or intent of each of these is either quietly subverted or altogether superseded. The male adventure is displaced by a narrative of female adventure. The now standard narrative of enforced female captivity in the wilderness approaches instead— and for the first time in popular literature—accommodation to the wild. The passive languishing heroine of sentimental romance demonstrates her capacity to survive on her own in the woods. And the slaying of the corn god here makes possible not a tribe's but a white woman's continued existence. Separately and together, these generic alterations all move toward an image of a white *lady's* (and I use that term purposefully) capacity to survive and sustain herself in realms previously penetrated only by Indians or by the likes of Daniel Boone. What have survived with her, moreover, are the identifying markers of civilized femininity.

Despite her nine-year sojourn in the woods, as the text is careful to emphasize, the "beautiful young LADY" of the Panther Captivity still displays the unmistakable features of a stereotypic middle-class heroine from the sentimental romance tradition. She swoons and cries copiously and, overcoming the limitations of her circumstances, shows herself a gracious hostess to her unexpected guests. Like many well-bred young ladies of the period, she has a small dog for her pet. And her singing, while it harmonizes so perfectly with her surroundings that the hunters cannot distinguish it from birdsong, also functions to suggest the more civilized musical adornments to which middle-class women, both in novels and in life, were trained. In other words, the lady of the Panther Captivity is decidedly "feminine" in all the ways that contemporary readers would have understood the term.

What dramatizes that identification, ironically, is the very act that seems so singularly out of keeping with her sentimental origins: her murder and dismemberment of her giant captor. But when we recall that what is being protected in that act is the lady's chastity, we appreciate the ingenuity with which the author of the Panther Captivity managed to bend the outlines of an Indian fertility myth to the requirements of sentimental fiction. For the act not only assures the white *woman's* survival—since she now possesses the corn that will sustain her—but it also marks the white *lady's* survival—since what has been overcome is not merely the threat of sexual violation but the threat of being given over to the inherent brutality of the wilderness itself.

Apparently because the man inhabits a cave and speaks a language the lady cannot understand, most commentators have simply assumed that this second captor, too, is Indian. In fact, the text never identifies him one way or another, and his cave is said to contain the implements of both the red man and the white. Insofar as he is left so carefully *un*identified, therefore, the "man of a gigantic figure" easily takes on the period's fearful conceptions of the very wilderness he seems to master: overpowering, potentially brutal and brutalizing, essentially promiscuous, and wholly uncivilized. And it is to this—the symbolization of the uncivilized brutality of the wilderness—as much as it is to his physical body that the heroine of the Panther Captivity successfully refuses to surrender.

A century earlier, although everything he wrote about the wilderness (and the Indians who were to him its emblem) hinted at it, Cotton Mather found himself incapable of offering a similar interpretation of Hannah Dustin's slaying of her captors. For, in 1697 Massachusetts, Mather remained committed to a religious typology that yoked him to the image of a Puritan *Judea capta*.[18] In the intervening decades, however, the culture's shared images of itself had changed dramatically, with a new secular typology now placing a gun in Mary Rowlandson's hands. Simply enough, those who witnessed the frenzied selling off of public lands that had followed the Revolution[19] needed heroines different from a cringing Maria Kittle or a "forlorn" Francis Scott,[20] no less than—like the earlier Puritans—they needed reassurances that for women to enter the woods did not mean that they would inevitably be "regulated by the wildness of the neighborhood."

By utilizing the trappings of familiar genres and fitting these to elements taken from Indian legend, the Panther Captivity was the first American text to fulfill the new fantasy requirement, mirroring back, with symbolic exemplariness, the hopes and anxieties attendant upon American women's increasing removal to the frontier. At the same time, the way in which the Panther Captivity attempted to project that experience was not, after all, so far off the mark. If its heroine's nine-year isolation is extreme and improbable, it nonetheless honors the very real loneliness of the cabin-bound pioneer woman, often separated from her nearest frontier neighbor by many miles. That the lady survives by yearly planting a crop of Indian corn echoes the fact that the first crop planted for survival in those days *was* corn— planted by the women and children between the stumps of the trees felled by their husbands and fathers. And, further, like most women who entered the wilderness at the end of the eighteenth century, this lady does not go there on her own; she first follows a man's lead into the forest.

At the end of the eighteenth century, with Americans self-consciously (albeit naively) declaring their independence of European antecedents and eagerly hastening to populate the lands newly opened in the west, two images competed for precedence in the public imagination, each claiming to carry within itself the fulfillment of the promise of a New World Eden. The one, given imaginative expression by Crèvecoeur and then codified as political doctrine by Jefferson, embraced an expanding agricultural republic of small, family-sized farms, their yeoman owners the backbone of democracy and proof against the corruptions of greedy commerce.[21] The other, anarchic in its implications, elevated to the status of heroic myth the figure of Daniel Boone as the solitary white hunter amid seductive and untouched wilderness spaces. At stake in these competing images was more than the new nation's choice of a defining fantasy for itself. At stake, as well, were competing and contradictory strategies for being in and relating to the vast uncharted wilderness lying just beyond the outermost edge of settlement. Structured as a series of radical displacements involving both these image possibilities, the Panther Captivity cleverly exploited the gender of its characters in such a way as to play out and comment upon precisely this crisis of identity facing the new nation.

In concentrating on the generic roots of the narrative, Richard Slotkin detects within the Panther Captivity a "tension between the traditional captivity pattern, which emphasizes filial reconciliation, and the fertility-myth pattern, which emphasizes the preparation of the new generation to destroy and replace the old." This "tension," he avers, "expresses the dilemma of all men coming of age, inheriting their parents' world, and replacing their sires as the shapers of that world."[22] Interesting and intelligent as this reading is, it nevertheless ignores one crucial fact: the inheritor here is a woman. Were either "filial reconciliation" or the replacement of the "sires" the issue, a male protagonist would better have served the narrative's symbolic purposes. The fact that a female displaces both the giant in the wilderness and her own "blood father in the civilized world"[23] clearly marks those chains of inheritance as radically altered. For what the lady of the Panther Captivity represents, both by virtue of her gender and her experience within the tale, is an order of existence altogether different from those she displaces.

In terms of its symbolic displacements, then, the story held up a mirror to contemporary reality. The wilderness was, after all, being claimed by those who pushed the agricultural frontier westward; and, both symbolically and historically, this implied the presence of women. At the same time, the mercantile commercial interests of the recent colonial past, it was hoped, were to be replaced by the more benign economic organization of a nation of cultivators. And insofar as men function as hunters in the narrative, only the lady, as the sole white cultivator, thus stands as the appropriate heir to her father's "considerable estate."

Indeed, the narrative's careful concern to date and place itself suggests that such eco-political implications were not wholly unintentional. The lady tells the hunters that she "was born near Albany in the year 1760" and describes her father as "a man of some consequence and of considerable estate in the place where he lived." At the time of her birth, Albany was the central base for British fur-trading interests, competing with the French at Montreal for control over that trade. The counting houses at Albany made fortunes for the merchants who traded with the Iroquois, even as they harnessed English dreams of empire in the Northwest Territory to an economy based on hunting and allied to mercantile interests. No contemporary reader would have been ignorant of these facts; and, for such a reader, the conclusion that the girl's father had amassed his wealth through the fur trade would have been probable, if not inescapable.

By the time the girl falls in love "with a man destitute of fortune," she is fifteen; the year is 1775. Colonial relations with the kinds of mercantile interests that dominated Albany were now strained to the limit. By the time she is forced into the woods because of her greedy father's disapproval of the match, it is 1776; the next year, pursued by her father's hired men, she is first captured by Indians. In these same years a newly independent nation challenged the authority of what it perceived to be the unconscionable greed of George III. Eschewing commercial interests, at least in their public rhetoric, more radical and avowedly idealistic elements within the Revolution broke from the protections of a parent nation and sought to project the image of an independent republic of yeoman farmers. In gross outline (if not in detail), the lady's adventures coincide with these historical events. In rejecting her imperious and greedy father, she is forced into a new relationship with the American wilderness, depending upon its cultivation for her survival. As a result, it is with her nine-year sojourn as a cultivator behind her that she eventually displaces her father, just as it is as a civilized white that she had earlier displaced her wilderness captor. Through its avatar, the *lady*, in other words, white civilization displaces the wilderness with agriculture while, simultaneously, in a series of events roughly coincident with revolutionary history, the independent cultivator displaces the man of international commerce.

I do not mean to suggest that the lady's story was consciously composed as an allegory on the birth of a nation. But I do mean to suggest the ways in which the narrative's purposeful assignment of gender at once pitted civilization against the wilderness and then inevitably suggested to contemporary readers that cluster of ideological associations surrounding the symbol of a resplendent Lady Columbia. At the close of the Revolution, Columbia was most often depicted sheathing her sword and turning from deeds of war to the peaceful pursuit of agriculture. Generally pictured with a laden cornucopia or with sheaves of native corn, that female symbol of the new nation was thus repeatedly used to call forth the virtues of agriculture over the exploitive interests of commerce.

Because the lady's story adheres to the requirements of both the captivity narrative and the sentimental romance by allowing for a final reuniting of and reconciliation between father and daughter, it invites the illusion that the narrative's competing elements—the wilderness versus civilization; agriculture as opposed to hunting and commerce—have been similarly reconciled. But such is not the case. For, once the lady's story is reinserted back into the frame of the Panther letter (with its own store of telling information), the drama reemerges a second time—this time in the shape of a confrontation that denies even the possibility of reconciliation. At stake here are competing patterns of intrusion: the white woman's intrusion into a wilderness that Panther and Camber had "imagined totally unfrequented" and her consequent conversion of that wilderness into a cultivated garden; and, against this, the two hunters' intrusion into—and, finally, termination of—the lady's wilderness idyll. In these oppositions resides the symbolization for the ideological conflict that is at the heart of the narrative's fascination.

Although the style of his letter establishes Abraham Panther as a gentleman, within the text he and his companion function essentially as hunter-adventurers, much in the tradition of Daniel Boone. "Determining to penetrate the Western wilderness" for their amusement and curiosity (as Boone had first ventured into Kentucky), they boast that "our muskets contributed not a little to our amusement and support." Again like their prototype, they encounter a "beautiful," "rich and fertile" landscape that affords them a "very comfortable living." Part of what comprises the beauty and contributes to their comfort is perhaps suggested by the decidedly sexual contours of the topography through which they move when approaching the lady's cave. To begin with, they "were observing a high hill, at the foot of which ran a beautiful stream, which passing through a small plain, after a few windings lost itself in a thicket." Following the mysterious voice, they "proceed up the hill" (first "crossing the brook"), "and arriving at the top of the hill, passed round a large rock, then through a thicket of bushes at the end of which was a large opening."

The quality of penetration implied here, however, leads not to further intimacy with the landscape (as it had for Boone) but, instead, to the discovery of a human female who has already appropriated that landscape for herself. And precisely at this point—with the lady's presence making all too palpable the unacknowledged male fantasy and, at the same time, annihilating its possibility—the male adventure narrative gives way to the female's. Little wonder that the two hunters later urge the lady to return with them to civilization. For what she has introduced into the wilderness is not only the fleshly fact of the male fantasy projection but, as well, a way of relating to the wilderness that is altogether different from the men's—and, potentially, a threat to it.

For her part, the lady's responses suggest that she, too, perceives something vaguely threatening in her visitors. Their first appearance causes her to scream and faint away, and, as Panther himself admits, it was only with some effort that he and his companion "convinced her of our peaceable dispositions." When the two men "proposed returning home," the lady is at first reluctant to accompany them. "At first she refused to quit her cave," Panther reports, "but after some persuasion she consented." The lady's history, of course, supplies ample justification for her reactions. The suddenness of the men's appearance evokes her father's earlier intrusion into "a little garden adjoining our house," the trysting place for her and her lover. The two men's very presence suggests the "several men" hired by her father "to search the country in pursuit of us." And her giant captor, whose cave contained a store of weapons, may perhaps also be divined in their musket-wielding shadow. That Abraham Panther is, in fact, appropriately to be associated with such figures is strongly implied by his decision to return to civilization with a selection of the cave's contents, "which," he informs his correspondent, "are now in my possession." These include "the bows, some arrows, the sword and one hatchet." Since the information serves in no obvious way to forward the action of the story, we must assume that the author of the Panther Captivity included it as a clue to his larger thematic concerns. At the very least, Panther's decision to take possession of the weaponry reinforces his identification as a hunter, even as it marks him as another in the chain of males in the story who either commands or wields the instruments of bloodshed.[24] (The lady, by contrast, makes no further mention of using the cave's implements once she has dispatched its owner.)

When, however reluctantly, the lady allows herself to be persuaded to quit her cave and return to civilization, the Panther Captivity endeavors to maintain both of its fantasy possibilities at once. The cultivator takes her place within the settlements, while the wilderness is once more available to the sole possession of the hunters. With only a slightly different twist, it is the identical status quo with which the more familiar narratives of female captivity also ended. This similarity suggests that the captivity narratives portraying frail and helpless white women suffering in the wilderness served certain male imaginative purposes as well as female. For, while identification with such images may have allowed for the symbolic projection of real women's fears of and resistances to the wilderness frontier, the images themselves enjoyed the further admonitory effect of dissuading women from picturing themselves as at home in the deep woods. Thus, for all of its otherwise unique features, the Panther Captivity finally followed its prototypes in imaginatively helping to maintain the wilderness as the exclusive preserve of the white male hunter (accompanied, if at all, by others of his kind or by an Indian companion).

What makes the Panther Captivity so unusual is that it adhered to the essential male fantasy of woodland intimacy while, at the same time, it offered a positive image of the white woman's capacity to survive and plant gardens in that same wilderness. In so doing, it catered, in symbolic terms, to opposing and contradictory dreams. I emphasize *symbolic* here because I do not mean to suggest that the Panther Captivity defines agriculture as a female activity. Clearly, most Americans recognized that both hunting and farming were essentially masculine pursuits, the wooden plow of the eighteenth-century farmer having been thought too heavy for most women to guide (though we know some did). The gender markings are important not for the real-life behaviors they imply but for the different symbolic contents they held for contemporary audiences. And, at the heart of those symbolic contents, as I have been suggesting all along, was the fact of the significance of women's increasing advance onto the frontier. For, coincident with their arrival, agriculture began to displace hunting (both for sustenance and for peltry) as the means of survival.

In the end, of course, the nation took to its heart the heroic mythology of the wilderness hunter, eschewing the hybridized romance of the wilderness cultivator suggested by the Panther Captivity. To be sure, Americans could not have held onto both. For, in fantasy as in life, if the wilderness was to be possessed by the cultivators, then it could be no place for the hunters; and if the hunters triumphed, then however appealing their gardens, the cultivators would have to be barred (or removed). And so, while historically the wilderness *was* given over, frontier by frontier, to the cultivators, in fantasy it forever remained the domain of the male hunter-adventurer (albeit stripped of his commercial and settlement associations). Daniel Boone emerged from his original incarnation as a brooding, meditative protector of the settlements to become Boone the isolate white, male hunter, companion to the Indian and, in Slotkin's words, "the version of the American myth that attained the widest currency."[25]

Even so, it seems that women, at least, held to the dream of creating gardens in the wilderness. And this, perhaps, explains the appeal of the Panther Captivity for that generation of readers who grew to maturity between its first appearance in 1787 and its last known printing in 1814. For them, as they watched the selling off of public lands in the west, its odd pastiche of generic sources delineated what all the Boone narratives evaded: that is, the symbolic terms of the then competing fantasy possibilities—in one of which women's fantasies found their first palpable expression.

> *"Some folks is born afraid of the
> woods and all wild places, but I must
> say they've always been like home
> to me."*
>
> —Sarah Orne Jewett,
> "The Queen's Twin"

4 Mary Jemison and Rebecca Bryan Boone: At Home in the Woods

Always disturbing to a white society determined to replace the forests and their native inhabitants with "a civilized Manner of Living" was the specter of white children, once having experienced Indian ways, forever attached to them. At a prisoner exchange between the Iroquois and the French in upper New York in 1699, Cadwallader Colden observed that "notwithstanding the French Commissioners took all Pains possible to carry Home the French, . . . few of them could be persuaded to return." "The English had as much Difficulty. No Arguments, no Intreaties, nor Tears of their Friends and Relations, could persuade many of them to leave their new Indian Friends and Acquaintance." Even among those who were so persuaded, Colden continued, "several . . . in a little Time grew tired of our Manner of living, and run away again to the Indians, and ended their Days with them."[1] In the next century, Benjamin Franklin echoed Colden's observations, noting that

> when white persons of either sex have been taken prisoners young
> by the Indians, and have lived a while among them, tho' ransomed
> by their Friends, and treated with all imaginable tenderness to pre-
> vail with them to stay among the English, yet in a Short time they
> become disgusted with our manner of life, and the care and pains
> that are necessary to support it, and take the first good Opportunity
> of escaping again into the Woods, from whence there is no reclaim-
> ing them.[2]

It was a situation that called into deepest question the Europeans' claim to a superior cultural organization, especially because, as Colden also noted (with no little chagrin), the reverse was never the case. "Indian Children have been carefully educated among the English, cloathed and taught, yet," he conceded, "I think, there is not one Instance, that any of these, after they had Liberty to go among their own People, and were come to Age, would remain with the English, but returned to their own Nations, and became as fond of the Indian Manner of Life as those that knew nothing of a civilized Manner of Living."[3]

As I have suggested earlier, the eagerness with which Americans purchased books like John Filson's *Adventures of Col. Daniel Boon* (along with its many reprintings), Alexander Henry's *Travels and Adventures in Canada and the Indian Territories, Between the Years 1760 and 1776* (first published in 1809), and, beginning in 1823 with *The Pioneers*, James Fenimore Cooper's Leatherstocking novels, was no doubt due—at least in part—to these texts' reassuring response to the gnawing Euro-American fear of Indianization and the accompanying distrust of "escaping . . . into the Woods." For all their temporary adoption into Indian families, and their knowledge of Indian woodcraft, both the real-life Boone and Henry clearly retained their white manners and their allegiance to the settlements; and Cooper's Natty Bumppo always insisted on his "white gifts."[4] All three, moreover, refrained from sexual contact with the Indian. Boone asserted an adoptive family of parents and siblings; Henry lived and hunted with several tribes, but accepted only the brotherhood (and surrogate fatherhood) of Wawatam; and, in *The Last of the Mohicans* (1826), the single novel in which he approached the notion of miscegenation, Cooper had Natty repeatedly insist on his identity as "a man without a cross."[5]

If such were the heroes that white society would publicly take to its bosom, in private that same society wondered and gossiped about the others, those who had escaped "into the Woods" and embraced Indian life to its fullest. For over half a century, for example, Eunice Williams inspired both rumor and curiosity in her native New England. The daughter of the Reverend John Williams, Eunice was taken captive as a small child in the winter of 1704, during the famous French and Indian raid on the town of Deerfield, Massachusetts.[6] She was then adopted by her Indian captors, and, despite many entreaties from various family members, it was more than thirty years before she returned to New England. When she did, first in the autumn of 1740 and then again the next summer, she came accompanied by her Indian husband and their two daughters. She would not, however, make any other concessions to the world of her birth. In consequence, for over fifty years following her visits, local legend attested that she had preferred the Indian blanket to the white woman's dress and had insisted on a tepee pitched on her brother's lawn rather than sleep within his house.[7]

But if stories like these—and there were many others—caught local fancies, they were never the stuff of legend or myth. There were no doubt several reasons for this. In the case of Eunice Williams, the story of her life with the Indians would have been difficult (albeit not impossible) to record since she no longer spoke English and had to communicate with her white family through an interpreter. More important, perhaps, though her marriage to an Indian may have fascinated the residents of Deerfield, few English colonials were as yet prepared to accept the fact of apparently willing miscegenation, especially where the white partner was a woman. (That male hunters and traders often took Indian "squaw wives," as they were scornfully termed, was common knowledge; but most whites preferred to see these as temporary unions of convenience, or else wrote off the white hunter as hopelessly "Indianized.") At the heart of such denials, however, may have been something more than the habitual white terror of interracial mixings. For, to accept a white woman's intimacy with the Indian was, as well, to accept her intimacy with the forest spaces he inhabited. And from the eighteenth century through the first quarter of the nineteenth, as we have seen, those spaces were imaginatively being wrested from the Indian in order to be given over exclusively to the white male hunter. In 1823, exploiting precisely this aspect of the burgeoning Boone mythology, Cooper's Natty Bumppo declared himself "form'd for the wilderness."[8]

Into Americans' studied literary silence on the subject of white-red intermarriage, and into the wilderness preserve of the white male hunter, there intruded in 1824 two landmark texts: Lydia Maria Child's historical romance, *Hobomok: A Tale of Early Times*, and James Everett Seaver's *Narrative of the Life of Mrs. Mary Jemison*. Completed in six weeks and signed only "by an American," *Hobomok* enjoyed immediate success and quickly established its twenty-two-year-old author as the toast of the Cambridge and Boston literati.[9] Daring as was its assertion of a white woman's willing marriage to an Indian, the novel nonetheless escaped censure by portraying its heroine as lonely and despondent—ill-treated by a narrowly Puritanical father, grieving over the recent death of her mother, and convinced that her true love (an Englishman) has been lost at sea. Her marriage to the Indian, whose name served as the novel's title, is thus an act of desperation rather than an assertion of love or desire. At the same time, since Hobomok leaves his native village in order to marry Mary Conant, now pitching his wigwam on the shore outside of Plymouth plantation, he and his bride inhabit neither the Indian wilderness nor the European settlement. Thus, Child was not called upon to imagine a white woman's accommodation to life in the forest.

In the end—despite the fact that the union results in a son, called "little

Hobomok" (but named "'according to the Indian custom, . . . Charles Hobomok Conant'")—the heroine's white lover returns. Aware of his wife's unshakable attachment to her former fiancé, the noble Indian divorces her (Indian-style, by burning "'the witche hazel sticks, which were givene to the witnesses of my marriage'"), and disappears into the forest, never to be seen again. Mary Conant then returns to the Plymouth settlement, reconciles with her father, marries her white suitor and, at the last, sees her mixed-blood son "a distinguished graduate" from Harvard. Her marriage to the Indian is, in a sense, obliterated. The son's real father, we read, "was seldom spoken of; and by degrees his Indian appellation was silently omitted."[10]

Much though he might have preferred it, James Everett Seaver could succeed in no analogous obliteration because, as his subject insisted of her first husband, "strange as it may seem, I loved him!"[11] Indeed, at the heart of *The Narrative of the Life of Mrs. Mary Jemison* was the experiential texture of the world that Child, for all her daring, simply could not imagine—the world of a white woman contentedly adopted into Indian society and happily adapted to life in the wilderness.

In 1823, a small printer and bookseller in upstate New York arranged a meeting between a schoolteacher named James Everett Seaver and an Indianized white woman known locally as "the White Woman of the Genesee." Her name was Mary Jemison. On the Pennsylvania frontier in 1758, at the age of thirteen or fourteen, she had been captured by a raiding party of French and Indians and thereafter adopted into the tribal life of the Seneca. At the time of the interview, Jemison had been residing for over forty years on what had once been tribal land, near modern Geneseo, New York, attracting to herself, among her white neighbors, a reputation for being "the protectoress of the homeless fugitive" and locally "celebrated as the friend of the distressed" (*MJ*, p. viii). Since Jemison was believed to have "arrived at least to the advanced age of eighty years," the purpose of the interview was to elicit from her an accurate account of her life "while she was [still] capable of recollecting and reciting the scenes through which she had passed" (*MJ*, pp. v, ix). In this, Seaver served as amanuensis, for three days diligently recording "her narrative as she recited it" (*MJ*, p. x). For, though she spoke "English plainly and distinctly," Jemison could neither read nor write (*MJ*, p. xi).

In his preface to the narrative that appeared the next year, Seaver claimed a "strict fidelity," assuring readers that "no circumstance has been intentionally exaggerated by the paintings of fancy, nor by fine flashes of rhetoric; neither has the picture been rendered more dull than the original" (*MJ*, p. v). But, in fact, the very circumstances of its composition militated against the narrative's fidelity. The "many gentlemen of respectability" responsible for initiating the project, Seaver revealed in his introduction, did so, among other reasons, "with a view . . . to perpetuat[ing] the remembrance of the atrocities of the savages in former times" (*MJ*, p. ix). A glance at the title page suggests that the printer, J. D. Bemis, thought he had arranged for a conventional captivity narrative. "An Account of the Murder of her Father and his Family; her sufferings; her marriage to two Indians," it promises, and then—with a sensational flourish—the title page added, the "barbarities of the Indians in the French and Revolutionary Wars."

In agreeing to the interview, Jemison may have had her own, quite different purposes, to which Seaver only dimly alludes. "The vices of the Indians, she appeared disposed not to aggravate," he noted in his introduction, while she "seemed to take pride in extoling their virtues" (*MJ*, p. xiii).

Seaver, clearly, had his own agenda. Defining "biographical writings" as "a telescope of life, through which we can see the extremes and excesses of the varied properties of the human heart" (*MJ*, p. iii), Seaver claimed both a didactic and a moral import for the work. Jemison's story, he asserted, "shows what changes may be affected in the animal and mental constitution of man; what trials may be surmounted; what cruelties perpetrated, and what pain endured, when stern necessity holds the reins, and drives the car of fate" (*MJ*, pp. iv–v). "The lessons of distress" to be derived from Jemison's biography, he hoped, would have "a direct tendency to increase our love of liberty; to enlarge our views of the blessings that are derived from our liberal institutions; and to excite in our breasts sentiments of devotion and gratitude to the great Author and finisher of our happiness" (*MJ*, p. vi). That such lessons might not be lost on the children whom he counted in his audience, Seaver "render[ed] the style easy" and gave "due attention" to the "chastity of expression and sentiment." Above all, he promised, "the line of distinction between virtue and vice has been rendered distinctly visible" (*MJ*, p. v).

To insure these *improving* effects, Seaver exploited all the racial assumptions of his era, thus making certain that the subject from whose life the lessons were to be drawn would be clearly identifiable as white. Only then, he seems to have felt, could she attract a sympathetic reading, the image of the "squaw" or the Indianized white woman having as yet gained neither currency nor approbation. If he could not wholly camouflage the fact that both her dress and "her habits are those of the Indians"—since this was well known to the many whites living in the area—he could, even so, clothe her in sturdy virtue and a "naturally pleasant contenance, enlivened with a smile." He repeated the testimony of white neighbors who "give her the name of never having done a censurable act," and, for his own part, he called her demeanor during the three-day interview "very sociable" (*MJ*, p. xiv). He even attributed to her the stock responses of the sentimental heroine—as opposed to the stereotypic notion of the impassive Indian—by noting that "her passions" were "easily excited. At a number of periods in her narration," Seaver wrote, "tears trickled down her grief-worn cheek, and at the same time a rising sigh would stop her utterance" (*MJ*, p. xi).

That Seaver resorted to such devices suggests that he was trying to prepare his audience for what he knew to be a most unusual text; but it suggests also that he himself may not have been fully prepared for the narrative he received. Certainly, nothing in his previous reading experience could have so prepared him. And the fact is, for all its wealth of detail derived from Jemison's experiences among the Seneca and for all its fascinating store of historical information, *The Life of Mrs. Mary Jemison* is an inconsistent, often perplexing document. At times, it simply echoes the conventions of the earlier female captivity narratives or introduces moralizing elements from the sentimental romances with which Seaver was obviously familiar. At other times, it seems almost gratuitously to focus on "the barbarities which were perpetrated upon" white prisoners by their Indian captors (*MJ*, p. 149), as though it were a standard Indian War narrative. But every now and then what seems authentically to have been Jemison's story breaks out of the molds to which Seaver and his backers would consign it, evading the narrative conventions of captivity and sentimental romance alike and becoming, instead, the story of a woman who, in the forested wilderness of upstate New York, knew how to "take my children and look out for myself" (*MJ*, p. 74).

Unusual in a captivity narrative, the opening chapter offers information about Jemison's parents and their immigration from Ireland to a prosperous farm amid "the then frontier settlements of Pennsylvania" (*MJ*, p. 19). In the second chapter, this "little paradise" (*MJ*, p. 20), is rudely disrupted by a "party . . . of six Indians and four Frenchmen" (*MJ*, p. 25), at which point the conventional captivity design takes over. The Jemison family (with the exception of two older brothers) and some neighbors are taken prisoner and, with their Indian captors, "soon entered the woods" (*MJ*, p. 25). The cruelty of their captors and the hardships of their journey are carefully detailed, the language of these passages echoing, like a refrain, features that could be traced back to the earliest Puritan captivities. As they advance deeper into the forest and away from English settlements, for example, the landscape becomes increasingly threatening; on the second night, reminiscent of Rowlandson, they camp "at the border of a dark and dismal swamp" (*MJ*, p. 26).

At this second encampment, the Indians offer the first clue to their intentions. Mary's shoes and stockings are removed and, in their place, she is given "a pair of mocassins." The only other member of the party accorded this treatment is a young boy, son of a neighbor woman who has also been taken. Jemison's mother apparently correctly interpreted these gestures to mean that the Indians intended to "spare" the lives of the two children, "even if they should destroy the other captives." Accordingly, she took the first opportunity to bid her daughter a kind of admonitory farewell. Among other things, she adjured the girl "not [to] forget your English tongue" and to remember "your own name, and the name of your father and mother" (*MJ*, p. 27). The mother's premonitions proved correct. In short order the two children were separated from the rest of the captives, and within two days Mary's fears for the fate of her family are corroborated: the Indians clean and dry her parents' scalps ("yet wet and bloody") in her view (*MJ*, p. 30).

Fearful though she is, escape seems impossible. To leave the Indians would place her "alone and defenceless in the forest, surrounded by wild beasts that were ready to devour us" (*MJ*, p. 34). It was a situation that called forth all the pathos of the sentimental heroines into which the Puritan *Judea capta* had finally degenerated. However Jemison may have actually phrased her dilemma, Seaver had done his homework in other texts. In answer to her question, "But what could I do?," he put into his subject's mouth an assemblage of phrasings repeated from Hannah Swarton through Francis Scott: "A poor little defenceless girl; without the power or means of escaping; without a home to go to, even if I could be liberated; without a knowledge of the direction or distance to my former place of residence; and without a living friend to whom to fly for protection, I felt a kind of horror, anxiety, and dread" (*MJ*, p. 29). Like Rowlandson, Swarton, and the fictional Maria Kittle who followed them, Jemison tells us, "I durst not cry—I durst not complain. . . . My only relief was in silent stifled sobs" (*MJ*, p. 29).

Possibly because there were no available literary models for what followed, beginning with the third chapter Jemison's *Life* swerved radically from conventional formulae and freed itself from most of the rhetorical flourishes that had dominated the second chapter. For in Chapter 3, Mary Jemison is given new clothes, a new name, and is ritually adopted by two sisters of the Seneca tribe, by whom "I was ever considered and treated . . . as a real sister, the same as though I had been born of their mother" (*MJ*, p. 39). Slowly and patiently, her adoptive sisters teach her the Seneca language and train her to the tasks appropriate to Indian women. The Indians' earlier cruelties are now set aside, even effaced, as Jemison describes her new life with these "kind good natured women; peaceable and mild in their dispositions; temperate and decent in their habits, and very tender and gentle towards me" (*MJ*, p. 40).

Although her adoptive "sisters would not allow me to speak English in their hearing," Jemison remained faithful to her mother's entreaties, taking the opportunity, "whenever I chanced to be alone . . . of repeating my prayer, catechism, or something I had learned in order that I might not forget my own language." This, along with opportunities to talk with whites who came among the Indians either as prisoners or as traders, permitted her to retain her spoken English. At the same time, with her "sisters . . . diligent in teaching me their language," Jemison soon found that she "could understand it readily, and speak it fluently" (*MJ*, p. 40). In short, despite efforts to hold onto the English tongue, she was fast becoming acculturated to her new life. Having been "with the Indians something over a year," she recalled, she became "considerably habituated to their mode of living, and attached to my sisters" (*MJ*, p. 43).

Only once during her first year among the Seneca does she seem to have regretted that habituation. When the tribe paid its annual trading visit to Fort Pitt, Jemison confided, "the sight of white people who could speak English inspired me with an unspeakable anxiety to go home with them, and share in the blessings of civilization." But when her adoptive family begins to suspect that the whites may have designs on the girl, they spirit her away and hide her. It "seemed like a second captivity," Jemison told Seaver, but, with "time, the destroyer of every affection," her "unpleasant feelings" faded, "and I became as contented as before" (*MJ*, p. 43). The contentment seems to have been genuine. For, contradicting then current notions of the arduousness of the Indian woman's life, Jemison described a world that—at least until the horrific disruptions of the Revolutionary War—appeared almost idyllic in its repeated seasonal routines.

Her new home, she says, was "pleasantly situated on the Ohio. . . . The land produced good corn; the woods furnished a plenty of game, and the waters abounded with fish." On the upper banks of the Ohio, "we spent the summer . . . where we planted, hoed, and harvested a large crop of corn, of excellent quality" (*MJ*, p. 40). In the autumn, the Seneca moved "down the Ohio . . . till we arrived at the mouth of the Sciota river; where they established their winter quarters" (thus making Jemison the first white woman known to have traveled the Ohio). Hunting—both for food and for "peltry" for trade—sustained the tribe through the winter. "The forests on the Sciota were well stocked with elk, deer, and other large animals; and the marshes contained large numbers of beaver, musk-rat, &c. which made excellent hunting for the Indians." When the hunting season was over, the Seneca "returned in the spring . . . to the houses and fields we had left in the fall before. There we again planted our corn, squashes, and beans, on the fields that we occupied the preceding summer" (*MJ*, p. 41). To these cyclical repetitions, in which "one year was exactly similar, in almost every respect, to that of the others," Jemison seems easily to have adapted, commenting approvingly that they were "without the endless variety that is to be observed in the common labor of the white people" (*MJ*, pp. 46–47).

During her first two years with the Seneca, Jemison was regarded as still a child, and so the only work she records is joining "with the other children to assist the hunters to bring in their game" during the winter months (*MJ*, p. 41). When she achieved the status of an adult, in her view, again her labor "was not severe." "Notwithstanding the Indian women have all the fuel and bread to procure, and the cooking to perform, their task is probably not harder than that of white women, who have those articles provided for them," she told Seaver, "and their cares certainly are not half as numerous, nor as great. In the summer season, we planted, tended and harvested our corn, and generally had all our children with us; but had no master to oversee or drive us, so that we could work as leisurely as we pleased" (*MJ*, pp. 46, 47). The same theme is repeated in a later chapter. While males of the tribe attended to ritual functions and hunting, "their women," she noted, "attended to agriculture, their families, and a few domestic concerns of small consequence, and attended with but little labour." As far as Jemison was concerned, then, "no people can live more happy than the Indians did in times of peace" (*MJ*, p. 64).

What irretrievably tied her to life among the Indians was her marriage, after two years with the Seneca, to a Delaware named Sheninjee: "a noble man; large in stature; elegant in his appearance; generous in his conduct; courageous in war; a friend to peace, and a great lover of justice." Whether what follows indicates the interpolations of her uneasy scribe, or whether Jemison herself inserted the qualifications as a way of softening the implications of her subsequent declaration, we shall never know. "Yet," she hesitates in the narrative we now have, for all these fine traits, "Sheninjee was an Indian. The idea of spending my days with him, at first seemed perfectly irreconcilable to my feelings." Nonetheless, marry him she does, "according to Indian custom," and soon enough she finds herself won over by "his good nature, generosity, tenderness, and friendship towards me," so much so that he "soon gained my affection." "Strange as it may seem," she concludes, "I loved him!—To me he was ever kind in sickness, and always treated me with gentleness; in fact, he was an agreeable husband, and a comfortable companion" (*MJ*, p. 44).

Though the union with Sheninjee was happy, it was not long-lived. After three years of marriage (and the birth of a son), Jemison was persuaded by her Seneca brothers to join them on a trek from the Ohio to the tribal homeland on the Genesee, to winter there with her two sisters (who "had been gone almost two years"). To this, Sheninjee consented, determining in the meanwhile "to go down the river [and] . . . spend the winter in hunting with his friends, and come to me in the spring following" (*MJ*, p. 51). For Jemison, the trip to western New York proved long and difficult. Her clothing was inadequate to the rain and cold weather she encountered and, as a result, she recalled being "daily completely wet, and at night with nothing but my wet blanket to cover me, I had to sleep on the naked ground, and generally without a shelter, save such as nature had provided." "In addition to all that," she emphasized, "I had to carry my child, then about nine months old, every step of the journey on my back, or in my arms." "Those only who have travelled on foot the distance of five or six hundred miles, through an almost pathless wilderness," she concluded, "can form an idea of the fatigue and sufferings that I endured on that journey" (*MJ*, p. 53). Happily, her "brothers were attentive," helping her where they could, and, in due course, the little party "reached our place of destination, in good health, and without having experienced a day's sickness" (*MJ*, p. 54).

Having spent the winter "as agreeably as I could have expected to, in the absence of my kind husband," Jemison then suffered "a heavy and unexpected blow." "In the course of the summer" she received "intelligence that soon after he left me . . . [Sheninjee] was taken sick and died." The "consolation" of her Seneca family helps her through this period so that "in a few months my grief wore off and I became contented" (*MJ*, p. 58). Sufficiently contented that, when a year or two later, the king's bounty offered her the opportunity to be returned to the whites, she remained "fully determined not to be redeemed at that time" (*MJ*, p. 58). Sticking to her resolution, she successfully eludes both the white man and the Indian chief who have decided to return her. Chapter 5 then ends with the information that when her son "was three or four years old, I was married to an Indian, whose name was Hiokatoo, . . . by whom I had four daughters and two sons" (*MJ*, p. 62).

With Chapter 6, the cyclical idyll of Indian life is forever disrupted by warfare between the would-be independent colonies and the English, a contest in which the Seneca sided with the crown. And, at the same time, this chapter reveals that Jemison's second marriage enjoyed little of the mutuality of affection that had marked the first. "During the term of nearly fifty years that I lived with [Hiokatoo]," Jemison insisted, "I received, according to Indian customs, all the kindness and attention that was due me as his wife." But this hardly bespeaks the quality of attentiveness she had received from Sheninjee. Even so, Jemison was apparently reluctant to speak negatively of her second husband (certain, perhaps, that her biographer, on his own, intended to cast the man in no favorable light), and so she simply insisted that Hiokatoo "uniformly treated me with tenderness and never offered an insult" (*MJ*, p. 104). Intent, however, on exploiting the Revolution as the basis for a traditional Indian War narrative, Seaver sought other sources of information about Hiokatoo and, from neighbors and former military men, pieced together the portrait of a formidable "warrior, [whose] cruelties to his enemies perhaps were unparalleled" (*MJ*, p. 104). Large sections of Chapters 7 and 11, in fact, are given over to sometimes lurid details of Hiokatoo's exploits against the Americans.

The same Revolutionary War that gave ample scope to Hiokatoo's prowess as a warrior also forced Mary Jemison to make good use of every survival skill she had learned among the Indians. For her, the test came during General Sullivan's campaign against the tribes of western New York State in 1779. "A part of our corn they burnt, and threw the remainder into the river. They burnt our houses, killed what few cattle and horses they could find, destroyed our fruit trees, and left nothing but the bare soil and timber" (*MJ*, pp. 73–74). The Indians themselves, however, had earlier escaped across the river. After ascertaining that Sullivan's troops were gone from the area, the Seneca returned, only to discover "not a mouthful of any kind of sustenance left, not even enough to keep a child one day from perishing with hunger" (*MJ*, p. 74).

From the war narrative that Seaver now seems eager to pursue, Jemison's own story insistently emerges. With the weather "cold and stormy" and the remnant of her tribe "destitute of houses and food too," Jemison resolves "to take my children and look out for myself, without delay. With this intention," she continues, "I took two of my little ones on my back, bade the other three follow, and the same night arrived on the Gardow [or Gardau] flats, where I have ever since resided" (*MJ*, p. 74). Her independent removal from the rest of the tribe advances the narrative to yet another recounting of adaptive survival—only this time, it is not a white woman's adaptation to life among the Indians but, in its place, an Indianized white woman's successful adaptation to fending for herself on the cleared and open "flats" along the banks of the Genesee River. (Hiokatoo, for most of the war, was away, leading raiding parties against the American frontier settlements.)

Upon her arrival at the Gardau flats, Jemison encounters "two negroes, who had run away from their masters. . . . They lived in a small cabin and had planted and raised a large field of corn, which they had not yet harvested." In exchange for food and shelter for herself and her children, Jemison husks their corn "till the whole was harvested." Residing with the blacks through the "succeeding winter, which was the most severe that I have witnessed since my remembrance," Jemison and her family survive, while other Indians, for want of food, do not. "The snow fell about five feet deep, and remained so for a long time, and the weather was extremely cold; so much so indeed, that almost all the game upon which the Indians depended for subsistence, perished, and reduced them almost to a state of starvation. . . . Many of our people barely escaped with their lives, and some actually died of hunger and freezing" (*MJ*, p. 75).

The following spring she builds her own dwelling on the flats and here, on "extremely fertile" land (*MJ*, p. 96), she has continued to reside until the time of the interview with Seaver. The blacks had remained only two more years and then taken off (probably for Canada). (Hiokatoo had died in 1811.) Though relatively few whites had even seen the area when Jemison first removed there, by the time of the narrative it is well populated, and Jemison now leases part of her considerable holdings (deeded to her by the Indians) "to white people to till on shares" (*MJ*, p. 96).

What is striking about her description of the intervening years—aside, of course, from the drama of their warfare—is the relative absence of Hiokatoo as a presence in the household and the sense that, with Jemison's arrival, the Gardau flats ceased to be part of the wilderness. "My flats were cleared before I saw them," Jemison explains, proffering the Indian legend that they had once been inhabited by "a race of men who a great many moons before [the Indian], cleared that land and lived on the flats" (*MJ*, p. 76). Whether or not a reader accepts such speculation, the impact is immediate and undeniable: the uninhabited flats become a part of the human world, and the reader thereafter ceases to think of Jemison as living in an unremitting wilderness.

No less striking is her emphasis upon her ability to manage for herself. "For provisions I have never suffered since I came upon the flats; nor have I ever been in debt to any other hands than my own for the plenty that I have shared," she boasts (*MJ*, p. 143). With the aid of her children only, she insists, she carried the boards that were to become her permanent home; with her children, she built that home; and even into the present year, she continues the yearly planting of corn:

> I learned to carry loads on my back, in a strap placed across my
> forehead, soon after my captivity; and continue to carry in the same
> way. Upwards of thirty years ago, with the help of my young chil-
> dren, I backed all the boards that were used about my house from
> Allen's mill at the outlet of Silver Lake, a distance of five miles. I
> have planted, hoed, and harvested corn every season but one since I
> was taken prisoner. Even this present fall (1823) I have husked my
> corn and backed it into the house. (*MJ*, p. 142)

Of the eight children to whom she has given birth, three now survive—all daughters. The youngest, with her husband and their three children, also live on the Gardau Tract, while the rest of her family, including "thirty-nine grand children, and fourteen great-grand children," live nearby, "in the neighborhood of Genesee River, and at Buffalo" (*MJ*, p. 143). "Thus situated in the midst of my children," Mary Jemison concluded the narrative of her uncommon life (*MJ*, p. 144).

Richard Slotkin has observed that, "wittingly or unwittingly," Seaver designed this closing to imitate contemporary popular images of a patriarchal Daniel Boone, "seated," at the end of his life, "in the midst of his happy brood of unspoiled 'children of the woods.'"[12] It is an astute observation—except that, once again, Slotkin ignores the crucial fact of gender. A comfortable and secure life "in my own house, and on my own land" (*MJ*, p. 143) bespoke the reward for surmounting wilderness hardships that had previously been accorded to men—but never to a woman—in American literary history. As such, Jemison's *Life* was "revolutionary" not for the generic alterations Slotkin cites,[13] but because it represented the first text in American literature to move a real-world white woman beyond the traditional captivity pattern to something approaching the *willing* wilderness accommodations of a Daniel Boone.[14]

With that switch in gender, moreover, the nature of the accommodation also changed. For, with Jemison, the baggage of familial and communal domesticity began to enter the wilderness preserve of the male hunter-adventurers. To be sure, following the Boone original, many narratives of western exploration had expressed their protagonist's eagerness to locate sites for future settlement, and, in this sense, they too made claims to familial and communal interests. But in point of fact, most of these narratives concentrated on the private pleasures of and solitary intimacy between the white male protagonist and his wilderness surroundings, thus emphasizing the romance of high adventure rather than the prosaic realities of cabin-building and hoeing corn.[15] In sharp contrast to the Adamic paradisal longings of the men, and unlike her fictional prototype in the Panther Captivity, Mary Jemison brought home and family into the cleared spaces of the wild—an act of survival, if not of romance.

It was a transformation for which the American public was ready and eager. Originally conceived of by its first printer, James D. Bemis of Canandaigua, New York, as a volume that would attract readers in the northern and western sections of his home state, *A Narrative of the Life of Mrs. Mary Jemison* did not for long remain "distinctively a New York state book." Publishers across the country recognized its wider appeal, and pirated editions by English printers were soon being sold on both sides of the Atlantic. According to Frank Luther Mott, Seaver had succeeded in producing the unrivaled best seller of 1824, and throughout the rest of the decade his rendering of Jemison's life continued to sell as well as the novels of Scott and Cooper.[16] In 1842 a revised and extended version was published, which also enjoyed several subsequent reprintings. And in 1856 there appeared yet another enlarged edition, also with supplementary and corroboratory materials, called forth, as its publishers noted, by "frequent inquiries . . . for the work."[17]

The public acceptance—indeed, acclaim—with which Child's *Hobomok* and Seaver's *A Narrative of the Life of Mrs. Mary Jemison* had been received in 1824 may well have prompted James Fenimore Cooper's willingness to approach similar themes in *The Last of the Mohicans*, which appeared in 1826. But Cooper's was, at best, only a hesitant approach. Following Child rather than Jemison, he permitted his white heroine no taint of Indianization, let alone any real accommodation to the wild. And, drawing back from the consummation of Indian-white sexuality that had marked both Child and Jemison, Cooper preferred to have his protagonists die and reunite, if at all, in the "'blessed hunting-grounds of the Lenape'"—rather than grapple with the worldly implications of the suggested attraction between Uncas and Cora. So reticent was he on the subject, in fact, that even the unconsummated attraction had to be justified by the hint that the dark-eyed Cora herself carried the blood of darker races (her West Indian mother having been "descended, remotely," from slaves).[18]

Women writers did not share these reticences. Taking full advantage of what Child and Jemison had made imaginatively possible, Catharine Maria Sedgwick offered a white heroine whose romantic attachment to an Indian included a happy accommodation to life in the woods. To be sure, Sedgwick's *Hope Leslie: Or, Early Times in the Massachusetts* depicts almost nothing of the details of Faith Leslie's life among the Indians and thereby, as Dawn Lander Gherman has pointed out, it emphasizes little of "her attachment to the Indian culture in general."[19] But it does at least assert, even if only sentimentally, the appeal of her woodland transformation. As the Indian maiden Magawisca explains to Faith's sister, "When she flies from you, as she will, mourn not over her . . . ; the wild flower would perish in your gardens; the forest is like a native home to her, and she will sing as gayly again as the bird that hath found its mate."[20] Sedgwick had apparently judged popular reading tastes correctly: upon its first appearance in 1827, *Hope Leslie* rivaled the sales of Cooper and Scott. Such was the legacy of Child and Jemison.

Because of its unique emphasis on a white woman's domestic accommodation to the wilderness, the Jemison narrative, by itself, may have also pointed the way to a renewed interest in the history of Rebecca Bryan Boone. For where Rebecca Boone shared with Jemison the stature of a white woman successfully adapted to life in the wilderness, as the wife of America's mythic frontiersman, she attained that stature without assuming any of Jemison's Indian associations. In preparing his *Biographical Memoir of Daniel Boone*, then, Timothy Flint—a man whose eye was always on the main chance—undoubtedly took his cue from the continuing popularity of the Jemison narrative and attributed to his hero's wife "the same heroic and generous nature" he gave her husband.[21] That he did not thereby succeed in delineating a radically new heroine for the frontier west, nor even achieve a portrait with the strengths of Seaver's Jemison, should not surprise. Flint's subject, after all, was Daniel, not Rebecca Boone; and Flint's purpose was to promote settlement of the agricultural frontier. As a result, Rebecca inevitably shrank to a symbolic appurtenance in the face of her husband's overpowering mythic resonances, just as she also shrank to an exemplary elder in the face of Flint's primary concern to attract readers westward. That said, Flint must nonetheless be credited with resurrecting Rebecca Bryan Boone in 1833 from what had then been a half century of almost nameless obscurity.

Although John Filson's 1784 narrative had recognized Boone's "wife and daughter [as] being the first white women that ever stood on the banks of the Kentucke river,"[22] it never named either woman or otherwise gave them prominence. Throughout that spurious first-person narrative, in fact, Rebecca Bryan Boone is denominated simply as "my wife," and her participation in the initial difficulties and dangers of first settlement is nowhere detailed. Only once is she credited with independent action. "During my captivity with the Indians," Boone reports, "my wife, who despaired of ever seeing me again, expecting the Indians had put a period to my life, oppressed with the distress of the country, and bereaved of me, her only happiness, had, before I returned, transported my family and goods, on horses, through the wilderness, amidst a multitude of dangers, to her father's house, in North Carolina."[23] Boone then returns to his recounting of the Indian Wars along the Kentucky frontier and makes no further mention of the wife and family he had brought back from North Carolina and resettled again in Boonsborough in 1780. Filson's *The Adventures of Col. Daniel Boon*, of course, set precedents that subsequent

Boone accounts would follow. Printer John Trumbull's shortened version of Filson, which appeared two years later, even further reduced Rebecca Bryan Boone's (still nameless) role in her husband's story. And in 1813, the year of her death, one Daniel Bryan, claiming kinship, published a verse epic celebrating Daniel's adventures, but Rebecca hardly figures in *The Mountain Muse: Comprising the Adventures of Daniel Boone; and the Power of Virtuous and Refined Beauty.*[24]

Thus, until Daniel Boone's death in 1821, the only published information regarding his wife had to be gleaned from the various reprintings of the Filson or Trumbull narratives and the occasional newspaper interview granted by Boone or by one of his sons. Following Boone's death, the Providence, Rhode Island, printer, Henry Trumbull, brought out yet another version of the Filson text to which he added "a continuation of the life of Col. Boon, from the conclusion of the American and Indian Wars" to the time of his death, attributed "to a near relation of the Colonel . . . who received it from his own mouth." This 1825 expanded version of Boone's life and adventures underscored anew the image of Boone as a gifted hunter and "a great friend to the Indians," but it offered barely a word about Rebecca—beyond, that is, noting her acquiescence to her husband's preference for the "perfect Wilderness." Seeking the society of "the wild animals of the forest . . . in preference to that of his fellow countrymen," this "continuation" narrative explained, Boone removed "with his family," at age 65, "to the Tennessee Country, then almost a perfect Wilderness." Of the family's reaction to the move we learn only that "it is a remarkable fact that the family of Colonel Boon, which was comprised of his wife, two sons and a daughter, were not less pleased with a secluded life than himself."[25] Following Boone to the year of his death in 1821, the Henry Trumbull text did not even mention Rebecca's passing in 1813.

Despite these printed omissions, as a rich fund of oral lore grew up around the great hunter, so too—if to a lesser degree—Rebecca Bryan Boone attracted popular interest. It was said by some that she was a fair shot, by others that she rivaled her husband in marksmanship; and the rumor persisted that she, not her husband (who was often away from home), had taught their sons the use of the gun. As Boone grew older and increasingly enfeebled by rheumatism, moreover, it became common knowledge that Rebecca accompanied him into the woods, helping her husband to bring down the game, aiming and firing when his knotted fingers could not, and generally proving as valuable a companion as any son or Indian might be.[26] But, beyond the occasional newspaper article, little of this made its way into print. Nor did Timothy Flint, when he essayed a comprehensive *Biographical Memoir of Daniel Boone,* make much use of this material—with one prominent exception: out of the oral tradition he plucked the fire-hunt story and thereby forever assured Rebecca a place in the mythic matrix surrounding her husband.

In addition to his literary pretensions, Timothy Flint saw himself as a beneficent promoter of western settlement. In this sense, the 1833 *Biographical Memoir of Daniel Boone* was simply a more dramatic continuation of his earlier, two-volume *Condensed History and Geography of the Western States, or the Mississippi Valley* (1828).[27] Both works, after all, celebrated the struggling early history of a frontier area and then made clear its current appeal to prospective settlers. Where Flint differed from other promotional writers of his day was in his understanding of the need to address women as well as men on the subject of emigration. He did not address them in the same way, however, since, in his view, "men change their place of abode from ambition or interest; women from affection" (*DB*, p. 30). For male readers, therefore, he elaborated the economic gains of emigration and played to their fantasies through the figure of Daniel Boone. For women, he offered Rebecca Bryan Boone, the exemplary model of a woman who, from affection, willingly "follow[ed] her husband to a region where she was an entire stranger" (*DB*, p. 30). Indeed, wherever Flint introduced women in the *Biographical Memoir* he introduced, as well, an embedded exemplum.

His account of the attack on Bryant's Station is a case in point. One of several fortifications along the Kentucky border (near present-day Lexington), Bryant's Station was attacked by Indians in August of 1782. Unable to penetrate the outer fencing, the Indians settled in for a prolonged siege, surrounding the little fort and cutting off its inhabitants from their single source of water, a spring located just outside the perimeter. When the station ran low on water, as Flint tells it, the women, "these noble mothers, wives, and daughters, assuring the men that there was no probability that the Indians would fire upon them, offered to go out and draw water for the supply of the garrison; and that even if they did shoot down a few of them, it would not reduce the resources of the garrison as would the killing of the men" (*DB*, p. 115). Following the historical facts, Flint then pictured the women marching "out to the spring, espying here and there a painted face, or an Indian body crouched under the covert of the weeds. Whether their courage or their beauty fascinated the Indians to suspend their fire," he does not pretend to guess (thus feigning ignorance of Indian fighting habits that—as the Kentuckians had rightly guessed—insured the women's safety). If, historically, the women probably made only a single trip to the spring, each filling her bucket once, Flint would have it "that these generous women came and went until the reservoir was amply supplied with water" (*DB*, p. 115). He was, of course, trying to heighten the drama of the scene.

But he was also, if illogically, designing his exaggeration so as to draw a moral for those "modern wives, who refuse to follow their husbands abroad." If the women of early Kentucky were willing to risk the dangers of Indian attack, he challenges, then how dare "modern wives" object to western migration only on the grounds "of the danger of the voyage or journey, or the unhealthiness of the proposed residence, or because the removal will separate them from the pleasures of fashion and society." These are but selfish and self-indulgent objections, he suggests, and, in their place, he admonishes his female readers, "contemplate the example of the wives of the defenders of this station" (*DB*, p. 115). Or, throughout the *Memoir*, he implies, contemplate the model of Rebecca Bryan Boone: "she" who "followed [her husband] from North Carolina into the far wilderness, without a road or even a trace to guide their way—surrounded at every step by wild beasts and savages" (*DB*, p. 247).

Flint's stories of the "noble" women of Bryant's Station, the women "running balls" in defense of McAfee's Station the following year (*DB*, p. 196), and his assertion that Rebecca Bryan Boone shared with her husband "the same heroic and generous nature" (*DB*, p. 247) should have generated images of strong, independent womanhood on the frontier. But such was not the case. Like his contemporaries, wary of what might be seen as the hardening, or masculinizing, effect of the frontier on women, Flint backed away from these implications of the historical record. And again, Rebecca Bryan Boone proved the vehicle for his intentions. Acknowledging that she had shared with her husband "in all his hardships, perils, and trials," Flint suppressed what might otherwise be concluded from that remark and asked readers to see Rebecca first as "a meek" and then, only secondarily, as a "yet courageous and affectionate friend" to her mate (*DB*, pp. 247–48).

He even discounted what was supposedly Boone's first-person testimony and denied Rebecca her role as the adult responsible for safely returning her little family to North Carolina after her husband's captivity (and presumed death) among the Shawnee. Flint wrote:

> At the close of the summer of 1778, the settlement on the Yadkin [River in North Carolina] saw a company on pack horses approaching in the direction from the western wilderness. . . . At the head of that company was a blooming youth, scarcely yet arrived at the age of manhood. It was the eldest surviving son of Daniel Boone. Next behind him was a matronly woman, in weeds, and with a countenance of deep dejection. It was Mrs. Boone. (*DB*, p. 165)

Contradicting all the earlier Boone narratives derived from Filson, in which Boone clearly credited "my wife" with "transport[ing] my family and goods on horses through the wilderness, amidst many dangers,"[28] Flint here attributes leadership to a "youth" whom he must concede had "scarcely yet arrived at the age of manhood." The resourceful Rebecca, meanwhile, who in 1778 would have been forty-one, is reduced to "a matronly woman" in widow's weeds, passively following her son as she had once meekly followed his father. But so important was it for Flint to project an acceptable femininity, especially in the wilderness, that he thus rewrote what was already familiar and ignored any oral lore that might challenge his (he supposed) comforting stereotype.

Finally, however, it was the myth of Daniel Boone that, in Flint's pages, overwhelmed and buried the reality of Rebecca Bryan. For Timothy Flint, a New Englander lately transplanted to the Ohio, as for others before him, the figure of Daniel Boone took shape around the image of a loner from his earliest days "formed to be a woodsman" (*DB*, p. vi). In the "solitary and trackless wilderness" of Kentucky, according to Flint, Boone experienced "a kind of wild pleasure" (*DB*, p. 44) that is nothing short of erotic. In the woods, "the paradise of hunters" (*DB*, p. 227), Boone grasps at a "fresh and luxuriant beauty" (*DB*, p. 36), enjoying there a solitary winter later recalled as "the happiest in his life' (*DB*, p. 64). Little wonder, then, that the legend that Flint preserved from the oral tradition, concerning Boone's courtship of Rebecca Bryan, projected yet another instance of the hero's "darling pursuit of hunting, . . . which in him amounted almost to a passion" (*DB*, p. 227).

Purporting to record Rebecca's and Daniel's first meeting, the "fire hunt" legend hints at much older literary sources even as it describes a method of stalking deer adopted by the whites from Indian practice. As it begins, a youthful Daniel Boone is engaged "in a fire hunt" one night with a young friend, and Flint carefully explains what this entails:

> The horseman that precedes, bears on his shoulder what is called a *fire pan*, full of blazing pine knots, which casts a bright and flickering glare far through the forest. The second follows at some distance, with his rifle prepared for action. . . . The deer, reposing quietly in his thicket, is awakened by the approaching cavalcade, and instead of flying from the portentous brilliance, remains stupidly gazing upon it, as if charmed to the spot. The animal is betrayed to its doom by the gleaming of its fixed and innocent eyes. This cruel mode of securing a fatal shot, is called in hunter's phrase, *shining the eyes*. (*DB*, p. 26)

When two eyes had thus been shined, Boone—who was the second horse-man, with his rifle at the ready—dismounted and approached his quarry. "Whether warned by a presentiment, or arrested by a palpitation, and strange feelings within, at noting a new expression in the blue and dewy light that gleamed to his heart," Flint declines to guess. "But," he con-tinues, whatever the reason, "the unerring rifle fell," its bullet still in the chamber, "and a rustling told [Boone] that the game had fled. Something whispered him it was not a *deer*; and yet the fleet step, as the game bounded away, might easily be mistaken for that of the light-footed animal" (*DB*, p. 27).

Presuming "that he had mistaken the species of the game," the resolute hunter doggedly pursues his quarry—all the way to the house of his neighbor, "a thriving farmer, by the name of Bryan" (*DB*, pp. 27, 25). Here he discovers Bryan's daughter, "a girl of sixteen, . . . panting for breath and seeming in affright," because she believes she has just been chased out of the woods by a panther. The two are introduced and, as Flint describes it, "the ruddy, flaxen-haired girl stood full in view of her terrible pursuer, leaning upon his rifle, and surveying her with the most eager ad-miration." The moment takes on the colors of a Scott romance: "Both were young, beautiful, and at the period when the affections exercise their most energetic influence" (*DB*, p. 28). With the close of the chapter, the romantic expectations are fulfilled and the informing metaphor completed. As Boone "was remarkable for the backwoods attribute of *never being beaten out of his track*, he ceased not to woo, until he gained the heart of Rebecca Bryan. In a word," Flint concludes, "he courted her successfully, and they were married" (*DB*, p. 29).

If the fire-hunt legend calls to mind medieval allegories in which the hunting of the hart plays out a lover's pursuit of his *dear*, it does so with a difference. In medieval allegories, the hunt begins with the wounding of the hart and terminates with its capture, the symbolic uniting of the lovers thus displacing the prior pursuit. In Flint's *Biographical Memoir of Daniel Boone*, however, the hunting never ceases. The imputed consummation that closes the story does not, in fact, bind Daniel to Rebecca's side. For Boone's "darling pursuit of hunting" is not metaphorical: it *is* his control-ling "passion" (*DB*, p. 227). The "unexplored paradise of the hunter's imagination" (*DB*, p. 48) is the forest here, not the marriage bed. As a result, the Rebecca Bryan of the fire-hunt legend emerges not as a person beloved in her own right but, instead, as a human cipher who has man-aged, if only briefly, to take on the erotic appeal of the wilderness that de-fined her husband's meaning.

Although family members have insisted that the Boones themselves often repeated the story, it is also said that their children refused to believe it. The Boone children were no doubt aware that their father had first seen his future bride when his older sister, Mary Boone, married into the neighboring Bryan family. Fifteen-year-old Rebecca Bryan, of course, had attended that wedding.[29] The modern reader must discount the story on other grounds. For its mythic and medieval sources notwithstanding, the "fire hunt" finally represents not a symbolic courtship but a travesty of courtship, reducing Rebecca to a fleeing incarnation of Daniel Boone's true and overriding love: the hunt.

But Timothy Flint seems to have been both unaware of the story's darker implications and unmindful of the Boone children's well-known skepticism. Therefore, when he included the fire hunt in what was to become what Henry Nash Smith has termed "perhaps the most widely read book about a Western character published during the first half of the nineteenth century,"[30] Flint forever attached the legend's symbolic significations to the woman, thus stylizing what others, after him, would make of her. To be fair to Flint, even if the modern reader cannot rest satisfied with the portrait, it must be said that he did, after all, grant Rebecca Bryan Boone her name and an attentiveness accorded in no previous text. In so doing, he at least made her available to history (even if not to literature).

In *The Pioneer Women of the West* (1852), for example, Elizabeth Fries Ellet repeatedly acknowledged Flint as the source for her chapter on Rebecca Boone.[31] But even without that acknowledgment, Flint's influence would be obvious. Several passages from the *Biographical Memoir* are quoted whole in Ellet (including the fire-hunt legend), while elsewhere Ellet expands on hints taken directly from Flint. Where Flint had maintained the imaginative codes that defined the forests as "the paradise of hunters" (*DB*, p. 85) and relegated to women "a garden spot" (*DB*, p. 85), Ellet personalized Flint's generalization, assigning the "garden spot" specifically to the charge of "Mrs. Boone and her daughters": "They had brought out a stock of seeds from the old settlements and went out every bright day to plant them."[32]

Where Flint and Ellet differed was where the feminine models of their respective decades differed. If, in 1833, Flint had harked back to the passively "meek" sentimental heroines of earlier decades, in 1852 Elizabeth Fries Ellet dropped the word from her description and, instead, cut Rebecca's figure to match the fashion of her own decade's reigning cult of domesticity: "A most faithful and efficient helpmeet had she proved to the pioneer, possessing the same energy, heroism, and firmness which he had shown in all the vicissitudes of his eventful career, with the gentler qualities by which woman, as the centre of the domestic system, diffuses happiness and trains her children to become useful and honored in after life."[33]

The publication of Flint's *Biographical Memoir of Daniel Boone* meant that, as of 1833, Americans enjoyed—for the first time—published access to two real-life white women who had learned to survive in the wilderness and convert it into a home for themselves and their families. It did not mean that Rebecca Boone would henceforth inspire the kind of mythologizing that her husband had, or that either she or Mary Jemison would independently become figures of legend in the nation's shared cultural imagination. All her wilderness survival skills notwithstanding, Jemison had willingly married—indeed, *loved!*—where white society would see only savagery and brutality. Enormously and continuously popular though it was, therefore, Seaver's portrait of Mary Jemison fell short of myth, its white heroine forever tainted by her Indianization. In Flint's pages, an exemplary Rebecca Boone appeared all too infrequently and all too indistinctly to stand proof against the many and changing stereotypes in which others, in the future, would cast her. And by portraying her first and most dramatically as reflected in the flickering and distorting torchlight of her husband's predominating myth, Flint effectively annihilated any possibility that she might achieve mythic status on her own.

Of course we had looked at the land itself—eagerly. . . . It appeared to be well forested about the edges, but in the interior there were wide plains, and everywhere parklike meadows and open places.

—Charlotte Perkins Gilman,
Herland

Book Two
From Promotion to Literature,
1833–1850

Rolling Prairie of Illinois, by Sarah Freeman Clarke. Reproduced from S. M. Fuller's *Summer on the Lakes, in 1843* (1844), courtesy Duke University Library

To go into a country you didn't know about was hard, and to leave the home you had loved all your life was cruel.

—Dorothy Scarborough,
The Wind

5 Mary Austin Holley and Eliza Farnham: Promoting the Prairies

In chastising "modern wives, who refuse to follow their husbands abroad, alleging the danger of the voyage or journey, or the unhealthiness of the proposed residence, or because the removal will separate them from the pleasures of fashion and society," Timothy Flint was being purposefully disingenuous.[1] To be sure, by 1833, the National Road to Wheeling (soon to be extended to Vandalia, Illinois), steam-powered boats ploughing the Ohio and Mississippi rivers, and completion of the Erie Canal, not to mention various state improvements in the way of roads and canals, had all combined to facilitate westward expansion. And the malarial fevers that seasonally attacked newcomers to the Ohio with "agues" were, according to more seasoned settlers, becoming less virulent. Even so, the rigors of the journey were not to be underestimated. Many a woman heading out to Indiana or Illinois in 1833 concluded, much as had Margaret Van Horn Dwight on her way to Ohio thirteen years earlier, "the reason so few are willing to return from the Western country, is not that the country is so good, but because the journey is so bad."[2] The same year that Flint encouraged readers to ignore health considerations, moreover, Hannah Gilman lost her husband to one of the several fevers then raging up and down the Ohio River settlements; and the next year, 1834, she lost a son the same way.

But it had never been to the rigors of the journey or to the unhealthiness of the region that women had mainly objected. Nor had they opposed emigration because it separated them from "fashion and society." What most pioneer women objected to in the removal westward was what Flint did not name (possibly because he appreciated its justice): the irrevocable separation from friends and family. "Mother I want to see you and Father so much the more I think about you the more I want to see you," a young bride, newly moved westward with her husband, wrote back to Virginia in 1837. That the separation might prove uninterrupted and permanent particularly distressed her. "Mother," she continued, "I can scarsly wright fore the tears thinking perhaps we may never see each other in this world again."[3]

Some women mediated the pain of separation by looking to an afterworld in which its "poignant distress" could not recur. Leaving her beloved Virginia for Kentucky in 1819, Rebecca Wilkinson Street invoked precisely such religious comforts in a poem composed to memorialize the occasion:

> Tho' bidding dear friends and connections adieus,
> I trust we shall meet in a world bright and new;
> In regions of holy unchangeable bliss
> We never shall witness a parting like this.[4]

Others, like Hannah Gilman of Marietta, Ohio, sought to bring her parents closer by asking that they have "miniatures" of themselves made up in Boston. Eagerly complying, her mother promised to send out "good likenesses."[5] Hannah also tried to minimize the distance between Ohio and Massachusetts by asking her mother to write more often. "You say that my writing once a month will not supply the place of a long epistle," her mother responded sympathetically, "because you live at too great a distance & want to hear me talk."[6]

For those left behind, the separation was no less wrenching, a fact they were often (if unintentionally) quick to communicate to those setting out. To a young woman on the road from Pennsylvania to Tennessee in 1803, a friend wrote from Philadelphia, informing her that her friends "mourn your departure, as if you were dead; for truely you are dead to some of them, for they never expect to see you again in this world."[7] When the newly married Christiana Holmes Tillson was about to leave Massachusetts for a home in Illinois in 1822, she overheard her grandmother in a verbal slip that communicated similar apprehensions. Watching "the carriage pass her house, and in telling how she felt at parting with her eldest granddaughter, and the sadness it had given her to see the carriage that was to take me away," her grandmother, Tillson recalled, "was not aware that she said 'hearse' instead of carriage."[8]

The letters that followed Hannah Robbins Gilman westward as she left Plymouth, Massachusetts, to cross the mountains with her husband in June of 1790, contained an added note of concern. Jane, her older sister, reminded Hannah of "that *Horrid never to be forgotten Morning*—of our Seperation," adding—as though the underlining had not been sufficiently emphatic—"Such Pangs I am sure I never experienced before."[9] Hannah's mother posted a letter to Rebecca Gilman in Marietta, begging "leave to address her, upon a painful subject . . . that of parting with my dear Child." That Hannah would be happy with her "amiable" life's companion her mother did not doubt. "But when I think of the distance," she confessed, "all the fortitude I am possess'd of is too little to suppress the starting tear." Then, putting aside her own grief in the matter, she entrusted her daughter to a mother-in-law's care, urging that Rebecca Gilman "be a mother to her."[10] Her concern derived from the fact that she knew her daughter to be pregnant. Hannah's sister, Jane, had implored, "Do be Careful of yourself." In Jane's view, "in your Critical Situation," Hannah's journey across the Alleghenics only brought her closer to "an Hour of distress—& *Peril*."[11] It "was a great relefe to my anxious mind," therefore, wrote her grandmother in November, that Hannah had sent news of her "safe arriavel." Still, the grandmother did not rest easy. "My dear child," she continued, "I feel peculiarly distresst on your account as I think you never wanted a mother so much as you do now;" and she reminded Hannah that "we longe to hear good news from a fare country."[12] That news, in fact, had already been sent: on December 9, 1790, Hannah delivered her first daughter, Jane Robbins Gilman, named for the grandmother, mother, and sister she had left behind.

The uncertain mails and the occasional traveler who carried such "good news from a fare country" back across the mountains were never enough to allay the continuing pain of parting, however. Thus, for those who remained at home as for those who ventured west, the intervening landscape loomed as a kind of insurmountable barrier, separating women who had once been close. "I . . . feel as if I must fly to see you," Jane Robbins wrote to her daughter in Ohio in 1797. "But my wings are soon clip't by the great distance of 700 miles."[13] Crossing the Alleghenies in 1810, on her way to relatives in Warren, Ohio, Margaret Van Horn Dwight confided to the diary she was keeping for her cousin in New England, "I do not feel to night, my dear Elizabeth, as if I should ever see you again—3 mountains & more hundreds of miles part us."[14] And in 1823, writing from St. Clairsville, Ohio, to her mother in Wheeling, Eliza Paull complained, "Mother thear appears to be mountains & rivers between us. I dont know how you are."[15]

What Timothy Flint also neglected to mention in his inept attempt to shame women westward were women's legitimate fears of finding themselves alone and isolated on an unfamiliar terrain, and burdened there with the task of maintaining a household in the face of inadequate supplies or improper tools. To be sure, few women in 1833 anticipated, as had Hannah Gilman in 1790, "tak[ing] up my abode in a howling wilderness—a land inhabited by savages and beasts of prey."[16] A steady policy of removing Indians from lands coveted by whites and the sometimes overly zealous activities of the hunters and trappers who preceded the settlers had done much to diminish the imagined menace of both "savages and beasts." In the 1830s, women newly relocated to the Ohio valley complained, instead, of "living in a *wilderness surrounded by strangers*."[17] Increasingly, however, as more women moved into the area, these uprooted easterners found themselves in a town "pleasanter than I expected—the house better," anticipating that "I shall be very happy & contented."[18]

What gave cause for alarm was that, with the 1820s and 1830s, the familiarly forested landscapes of the Ohio were no longer an economically attractive raw frontier. In consequence, the waves of emigration in the later 1820s, peaking in the 1830s, rolled into the Mississippi valley, tentatively approaching the Illinois prairies, while, in the southwest, a few enterprising souls dreamed of planting an American colony in Mexican-owned Texas. Before the anomaly of open grass lands and treeless stretches, the earliest settlers at first clung to the edges of the forest, suspicious of a soil that supported so few trees. "Americans were used to judging the fertility of new land by the kind of trees growing on it," Henry Nash Smith has commented, thus explaining male settlers' long reluctance "to move out upon the fertile and well-watered prairies of Illinois."[19] Men and women alike, it appears, shared that reluctance—even if for different reasons. For where women had earlier expressed fears of the enclosing forests, now they recoiled before "the vastness which oppresses the mind."[20]

Having just crossed over into Illinois at Shawneetown, in 1822, Christiana Holmes Tillson continued across the "bottom prairie" toward her new home near Alton, all the while bravely trying "to make the dismal-looking bottom prairie through which we were passing look cheerful and homelike, merely because it was Illinois." But her will proved inadequate to her desire. Instead of the flowered expanses her husband had promised, she found only "a black and dismal prairie," charred by recent fires. Her disappointment in the terrain, combined with the difficulties of traveling "a horrible corduroy" road and negotiating a muddy swamp, soon led her to admit "that my enthusiasm for western prairies was vanishing."[21]

Her enthusiasm for the frontier cabin knew no longer duration. But because her husband enjoyed substantial economic resources, Christiana Holmes Tillson was rather quickly able to improve and enlarge their crude log cabin into a relatively comfortable home. Not for her were the "cabins without windows and [the habit of] keeping both doors open for the admittance of light," a practice embraced by so many of her neighbors. Nonetheless, established though she was with dishes, cooking utensils, and locally made furniture, Tillson too confronted the challege of "secur[ing] a comfortable living" in the Illinois of 1822. "The indescribable care devolving upon a housekeeper in that new and rough country and the ways and means to which one must resort in order to keep up a comfortable establishment," she later wrote, "absorbed not only the physical strength of a Yankee housewife, but all the faculties of the mind."[22]

Still, despite the pain of separation from friends and family, the discomforts suffered during the journey, the unfamiliar openness of the prairie terrain, and the inevitable burdens of frontier housekeeping, Christiana Holmes Tillson quickly enough found herself happy and contented and began sending home letters in praise of her surroundings. Other women, similarly enchanted with these new open and rolling prospects, made their statements publicly, thus initiating the beginnings of promotional writing by women. Up until the 1830s, most promotional documents ignored women altogether or else, as in Timothy Flint's *Biographical Memoir of Daniel Boone*, they showed their authors' insensitivity to women's particular needs. Popular songs, of course, had always invited "all you girls from New England that are unmarried yet" to take themselves westward where "young husbands you shall get."[23] But subsequent verses never prepared listeners for what they might actually encounter if they followed the song's advice. It was only when women began popularizing the appeals of a prairie frontier to members of their own sex, therefore, that the promotion of the prairie became both effective and persuasive.

To the crudities and roughness of frontier housekeeping, women writers opposed the simplicities it offered, including in their pages helpful hints for baking where there were no ovens and naming local fruits and vegetables suitable for cooking and preserving. To the discomforts of the journey, they opposed the continuing improvements in transportation and, above all, promised a ready-made park at the end of the trail. For, in the writings of women like Mary Austin Holley and Eliza Farnham, what awaited women who ventured onto the prairies was a species of natural garden, the very openness of the prairies giving "the appearance of vast parks, with ornamental trees artificially arranged to beautify the prospect."[24]

The most imaginative stroke of such writers, however, was their psychological responsiveness—something no male writer had yet managed—to the painful separations and ensuing loneliness women had always resisted. On behalf of Texas, Holley bound "emigrant mothers" in love and responsibility to "the infant colony" (*T*, p. 15). In Illinois, the landscape itself, Farnham averred, beckoned as might "a strong and generous parent," ample surrogate for those left behind; while the very "tree[s] and shrub[s] which we planted" served as "companion[s]" during the early years of first settlement (*PL*, pp. iii–iv, 243). Images of artfully arranged parks overcame women's initial distrust of the "dismal prairie." But even more important, the fantasy of a landscape that might figuratively reconstitute some prior domestic community soothed the sense of irrevocable loss. And together, the image and the fantasy effectively abetted that process by which "man creeps outward from the groves and builds his cabin" on the open prairie (*PL*, p. 77).

Addressing herself "to emigrant mothers" and speaking as "one of themselves," Mary Austin Holley tried to supply prospective female emigrants with more useful information "than could be gathered from the more abstract and general views of gentlemen travellers" (*T*, p. 15). Her *Texas: Observations, Historical, Geographical and Descriptive, In a Series of Letters, Written during a Visit to Austin's Colony . . . in the Autumn of 1831* (1833) thus told future Texas "house-keepers" what they should bring with them and cautioned them "that in a new country, they cannot get things made at any moment, as in an old one" (*T*, pp. 123–24). Writing about Illinois a decade later, Eliza Farnham acknowledged that "a large class of minds have no adaptation to the conditions of life in the West," lamenting that "this is more especially true of my own sex" (*PL*, pp. iv–v). Disturbed that too many "ladies . . . cannot endure the sudden and complete transition which is forced upon them by emigration to the West" (*PL*, p. v), Farnham offered in her *Life in Prairie Land* (1846) models of happy accommodation to what was to her the land of the "stirring future" (*PL*, p. 408). "I loved the country" (*PL*, p. v), she declared at the outset, and then proceeded to offer detailed glimpses of frontier domestic arts, social habits, and medicinal lore, as well as useful information on climate, geography, and Illinois flora and fauna.

If, on some subjects, Holley and Farnham repeated material that was also to be found in men's writings, they did so with a difference. Men writing about the prairies often commented on the lack of available "material for finishing houses" and the relative scarcity of labor for their construction. What men did not make clear was what this meant for the woman trying to maintain a home. Only another woman, apparently, could appreciate the importance of preparing a sister for the realities of the wished-for transition from log cabin to framed house:

> One of the most trying conditions of western life is the first winter, which finds the settler moved out of his warm cabin into the new house which he has erected for himself, but not finished. The former tenement has afforded good security against the greatest

cold. Its thick walls, chinked between the logs with triangular bits of wood, plastered neatly in with clay, have been impervious to the biting frost. The wide fireplace has afforded abundant facilities for imparting warmth; and the heavy floor, if well put together, has protected the feet without a carpet. But since the last winter passed away, the new framed house has been erected. Boards split by his own hands form its thin outside walls, and these are generally for the first year the only thing interposed between the bitter elements and the shivering tenants. No wonder, then, that the cups freeze to the saucers while they are at table, or that the chicken or grouse from which they had just breakfasted, is thoroughly frosted over while the housewife is setting away the remains of the meal. (*PL*, p. 199)

The improvements that attend permanent settlement do not come without their prices and inconveniences, Farnham wanted her readers to understand. But no less she wanted them also to understand that the early years of settlement need not be without their comforts. And so, in a passage largely devoted to the cheerless aspects of an unfinished framed house, Farnham embedded the portrait of a well-constructed log cabin, securely protecting its occupants even "against the greatest cold."

It was a purposeful ploy. Each woman, after all, wanted to interest her reader in becoming more than just a reader: she wanted to encourage others to follow her own journey and to become, themselves, settlers in the new prairie west.[25] To effect that goal, Holley and Farnham had to offer women something more than the catalogues of crops or soil types to which the land had been reduced in men's promotional tracts. And that something more, as Farnham phrased it, was "the beauty of order and purity in domestic life" that obtained in the west (*PL*, p. ix). In many of the first prairie cabins, she insisted, "the neatness and order are perfect. Of necessity they have fewer artificial luxuries than the inhabitants of the older regions," but, in her view, this enhanced rather than diminished "the inherent virtues of cleanliness, order, and self-respect." As far as she was concerned, in fact, "a simple [rather] than a complicated style of living" was to be preferred (*PL*, pp. 68–69).

Composed with the encouragement of her cousin, Stephen F. Austin, and with the express purpose of attracting large numbers of emigrants to his Texas colony, Holley's *Texas* made clear both its origins and its intents in a subtitle: *Written during a Visit to Austin's Colony, with a view to a permanent settlement in that country*. That exaggerated forebodings of a difficult frontier existence not put off those who might otherwise contemplate resettlement, Holley—like Farnham—offered her readers an attractive domestic picture, even where "the family had not been here long, and their *cabin* was not yet built." "Mrs. _____, who was, I found, from my native state (Connecticut)," and her family are said to occupy

> a temporary shed among the trees, . . . not impervious to the light, though there was no window. A white curtain supplied the place of a door. The single apartment contained three or four beds, as white as snow. Books, glass, china, and other furniture in polite usage, were arranged in perfect neatness about the room, as best suited the present exigence. It was Sunday evening. Mrs. _____ was seated in a white cambric wrapper and tasteful cap. The children around the door, and the servants, were at their several occupations, or sitting at leisure about the temporary fire-place without. (*T*, pp. 39–40)

The alarm any housekeeper might feel at the prospect of a windowless "shed" so poorly constructed as to be, euphemistically, "not impervious to the light," is dissipated here by Holley's subsequent insistence on the class markers of genteel comfort: books, glass, china, snowy white linens, and, to top it off, the mistress's equally improbable "white cambric wrapper and tasteful cap." The family hearth has been moved out of doors, to be sure, but its symbolic function has not changed: it serves as the center of a relaxed and comfortable domestic scene. That snowy white bedclothes might prove impossible to maintain in such circumstances; or that the scene rested for its comforts on a coterie of servants more numerous than Holley suggests were bits of information purposefully suppressed. In urging other women to follow her own example and remove to Texas, she knew, she had to quiet realistic apprehensions by offering, in their place, tableaux that could be interpreted, like this one, as an authentic "exhibition of peace and happiness" (*T*, p. 40).

What made their versions of emigration so compelling, however, was that Holley and Farnham offered more than just tableaux vivants or recountings of personal history. They made of Texas and Illinois fantasy realms in which the dreams of the culture might come true, as in a "fairy land" (*T*, p. 6). To male yearnings for receptive natural realms, they held out "fertile fields already cleared by the hand of nature, and waiting, as it were, to receive the plough" (*T*, p. 65). To women they held out idealized elaborations of home and family. Which is not to suggest that Holley or Farnham neglected mid-nineteenth-century America's requisite attachment to a quasi-religious romantic nature. "Here, as in Eden," Holley exclaimed of Texas, "man feels alone with the God of nature, and seems, in a peculiar manner, to enjoy the rich bounties of heaven, in common with all created things. The animals, which do not fly from him; the profound stillness; the genial sun and soft air"—all these, she declared, "are impressive, and are calculated, both to delight the imagination, and to fill the heart, with religious emotion" (*T*, p. 127). In Illinois, just a few years later, Farnham proclaimed analogous religious (or, in her view, *spiritual*) upliftings amid "the free untrodden empire of nature!" "My cathedral should be the overhanging cliff, my temple the eloquent shades," she declared, concluding: "Living much with nature, makes me wiser, better, purer, and therefore, happier!" (*PL*, p. 209). The evocative power of such declarations notwithstanding, the fantasy to which each woman attuned her most consistent imagery was not religious but domestic. And the Eden each envisioned partook less of the temple than of the home and family.

The "emigrant mothers" to whom Holley addressed herself, she made clear, were mothers not only to their own families but to the "infant establishment." On their good offices, she emphasized, "the comfort of every family, and the general well-being of the infant colony . . . depends" (*T*, p. 15). As symbolic consort and as co-parent to the "infant state" (*T*, p. 115), she preferred as "their patriarch" her cousin, Stephen F. Austin, whose name the "children will be taught to hold . . . in reverence" (*T*, p. 109). To give a kind of mythic prominence to her rather shy, self-effacing bachelor cousin, she cloaked him in the mantle of that other legendary patriarch "ordained to settle the wilderness," Daniel Boone.[26] In Holley's pages (like Boone in Flint's), Stephen F. Austin emerges as a "hardy and bold pioneer, braving all the dangers of a wilderness infested with hostile Indians, . . . enduring . . . all the exposure and privation of the camp, living for months upon wild horse-flesh, without bread or salt" (*T*, pp. 108–9).

Having established her readers as the mothers and her cousin as the bigger-than-life founding father of "the infant colony," Holley then incorporated a version of Cooper's Natty Bumppo into her family constellation, embracing the fictional loner within "a distinct class" of spoiled sons (*T*, p. 44). These are the Leather Stockings, "privileged character[s]" who engage almost exclusively "in the business of hunting." Employed by the planters and farmers, the Leather Stockings are generally "Indians and Mexicans" and, occasionally, "a white man from the *States*, who has become somewhat de-civilized." Their characteristically rough manners and "rudeness of speech" are tolerated because they supply the planter's table with game. But Holley's description of that tolerance suggests ties familial rather than economic. "These hunters are very profitable to their employers," she acknowledges, but they are also "much cherished in the family, and often become spoiled by familiarity and indulgence" (*T*, p. 43). Cooper used his Leatherstocking as the vehicle for imaginatively preserving the dream of the wilderness for the isolate white male. Unable to tolerate either wilderness or isolates in her domestic vision, Holley adopted the hunter as a son who helps to maintain the extended frontier family.

Holley's adherence to a family configuration for the Texas colony should not obscure, however, her equivalent attentiveness to the imagery of a newfound Eden. A land "literally flowing with milk and honey" (*T*, p. 14), Texas, in Holleys' view, came close to promising "exemption . . . from the primeval curse" (*T*, p. 56):

> The newcomer has but to plant his seeds in the ground, and collect a first supply of live stock to begin with. They need but little or no care afterwards, and the increase is astonishing. . . . A field once planted in pumpkins, seldom needs planting again. The scattered seed sow themselves, and the plants are cultivated with the corn. . . . Corn is obtained in the prairie cane-brakes, the first year, when there is no time to prepare the land, with the plough, by merely making a hole for the seed, with a hoe. Cows and horses get their own living. (*T*, pp. 117–18)

"Domestic animals," she had earlier remarked, "may be reared . . . without trouble or expense" because, "even in the winter season, the pasturage is sufficiently good to dispense with feeding live stock" (*T*, p. 62). And, finally clinching the imputation of a southwestern prairie Eden, Holley described the mandatory "clusters of grapes" growing wild, even "at this moment, (17th December,) . . . of a delicious flavour" (*T*, p. 118).

It was, of course, the identical imagery through which, since the fifteenth century, most promotional documents had attempted to introduce "a terra incognita" (*T*, p. 5) to prospective colonists and investors. The difference was that Holley—unlike her predecessors—could not rest comfortable with all the implications of such language. At the outset, she tried to limit its force, insisting that "in a new community, *labour* is the most valuable commodity." "A soil, that yields the fruits of nearly every latitude, almost spontaneously, with a climate of perpetual summer," may mollify, but it can never eradicate "the primeval curse . . . even here." "Though the land be, literally flowing with milk and honey," she explained, "yet, the cows must be milked, and the honey must be gathered. Houses must be built and enclosures made. The deer must be hunted, and the fish must be caught" (*T*, p. 14).

Clearly somewhat suspicious of any newfound geographical Eden, in the end Holley returned to the theme with which she had begun, now calling forth an Edenic social terrain in which "people are universally kind and hospitable." What excited Holley about Texas, we come to understand, was less its promise of a toilless garden than its simulation of an extended family: "every body's house is open, and table spread, to accommodate the traveller." The true Eden for Holley, in short, was a social Eden, at once egalitarian and harmonious. "There are no poor people here," she wanted to believe, "and none rich" (*T*, pp. 127–28). "Here, as in Eden," she insisted, "man . . . seems, in a peculiar manner, to enjoy the rich bounties of heaven, in common with all created things" (*T*, p. 127). And then, laying bare the essential meaning of her recovered Eden, Holley closed by depicting the Texas settlers as a kind of family united, "bound together, by a common interest, by sameness of purpose, and hopes" (*T*, p. 128).

Eliza Farnham also invoked a fantasy of family, but her fantasy located itself in the physical facts of the Illinois prairies, and it cast her and her prospective reader-settlers not as mothers to an infant colony but as "the sons and daughters of this land" (*PL*, p. 74). The "great and generous land" (*PL*, p. vii), she explained at the outset, "presents itself to my mind in the light of a strong and generous parent, whose arms are spread to extend protection, happiness, and life" (*PL*, pp. iii–iv). At the same time, the woodlands dotting the prairies presented themselves both as family members and as emblems of home. The "heart turns fondly to these tall tenants of the plain as to elder brothers" (*PL*, p. 76), Farnham wrote of the trees, even as she also acknowledged their comforting familiarity, "convey[ing] an idea of home, such as you have borne from the forest-clad states of the east" (*PL*, p. 75).

Indeed, so attached was Farnham to the emblems of familial relations in nature that, at odd moments, she came close to condemning human advances onto the frontier as a threat to the primordial configuration she would see there. A steamboat on the Mississippi in the early spring thus becomes a "monster," because it intrudes upon the

> myriads of wild fowl . . . now engaged in preparing for their young. Here they have built their temporary homes and reared their young from time immemorial. And here, long years ago, they were unmolested in these cares and pleasures. . . . Now, how changed! Monsters plough the bosom of the river, whose hoarse voices ring through the silent valley for miles; whose eyes are fire, whose breath is destruction. Long before they approach, their measured marchings terrify these feathered dwellers in the wilderness, and long after they are past the sound returns, and the disturbed waters roll ashore with an angry splash, as if they would signify their displeasure at such intrusion. (*PL*, pp. 206–7)

Signifying her displeasure at the horrific irony she had uncovered, Farnham here revealed her suspicion that the very means by which the human family gained access to "prairie land" might also prove the means by which the component patterns of her cherished fantasy would be destroyed.

Within the pages of her book, however, the fantasy remained essentially intact. And to it, as had Holley before her, Farnham attached elements from the oldest of American dreams: paradise regained. Standing at the emotional center of *Life in Prairie Land* is a narrative supposedly spoken by the author's sister, Mary, in which she describes her journey to Illinois as a young bride (accompanied by her husband and his father) in the spring of 1829. It is the model journey that the text invites readers to replicate in their own lives and it is, as well, a journey into "'a new creation'" (*PL*, p. 236).

To begin with, Mary declares that she "'rejoiced'" in her springtime trek to Illinois. "'We journeyed several weeks through the blooming orchards and fields of the cultivated country,'" she recalls, "'and at last plunged into the heavy forests of Ohio and Indiana. Here we sometimes slept in our waggon or on the ground and took our meals in the woods'" (*PL*, pp. 235–36). From the point at which she leaves "'the heavy forests'" and gazes for the first time "'upon the great prairie'" (*PL*, p. 236), however, her narrative ceases to be a straightforward travel narrative and begins to embrace symbolic patterns familiar to contemporary readers from Timothy Flint's phenomenally popular *Biographical Memoir of Daniel Boone*. But as always in women's texts, it did so with a difference. Flint's Adamic "new man" had entered upon "the new country" of Kentucky to discover there "the paradise of the first pair."[27] Like Boone, Mary also exults at "'the magnificence of the country to which we were bound.'" But, unlike Boone—who first visited Kentucky in company with male companions and then wintered over there alone—Mary and her husband *are* a pair, suggestively recovering what "the first pair" had lost. Mary remembers:

> "As we journeyed day after day across [the prairies'] heaving, verdant bosom, I seemed to be living in a new world. . . . A new creation was around me. The great, silent plain, with its still streams, its tender verdure, its lovely flowers, its timid birds and quadrupeds, shrinking away from our sight; its soft winds, its majestic storms— was a sublime spectacle! Occasionally a herd of deer bounded across our path, or a solitary pair of grouse, startled from their parental cares, rose and cleft the air like arrows of their old pursuers; but save these we were alone, in silence broken only by our own voices."
> (*PL*, p. 236)

For this moment, at least, the burden of the Fall seems not to be in force.

What follows continues in the same key, even if it does not carry the impact of the initial image of reentry into the garden. In Mary's "'new world,'" neither the silence nor the isolation is disturbing. "'The charms of the country, which never tired with us, the delights of building a new home and beautifying it ourselves, of having everything grow from nature, under our own hands,'" she explains to her sister, "'were ample sources of happiness.'" And for society—until the arrival of other settlers and the birth of their son three years later, that is—Mary claimed the couples' living handiwork: "'Every tree and shrub which we planted in our grounds was a companion, whose growth it was delightful to watch'" (*PL*, p. 243).

Although Farnham claimed never to have been even "once menaced by a venomous or dangerous serpent" in her prairie Eden (*PL*, pp. 134–35); and although Holley claimed a healthy "salubrity" even in "the cold northern winds" (*T*, pp. 119, 121), thereby maintaining her assertion of "a climate of perpetual summer" (*T*, p. 14), neither was disposed to follow what Holley called "the extravagant . . . representations" (*T*, p. 6) of earlier (male) promotionalists. Holley accurately catalogued less fertile soil types in her Texas landscapes and, above all, emphasized the need for labor, "even here" (*T*, p. 14). Farnham's more complex text went one step further, admitting death into the garden. In the course of her chapters, a mother dies as a result of a prairie fire; Mary dies of consumption at age 25; Farnham's infant son dies in the yellow fever epidemic that spread across the plains in 1837; and nature herself, during a period of extended drought, appears "about to light her own funeral pire" (*PL*, p. 259).

Still, the major threat to the paradisal images of each text wears a human face. Amid the Texans' bold defiance of Mexican laws (especially the anti-slavery laws) and talk of open rebellion, Holley regarded with no little apprehension the "civil and political condition," fearing that the hopeful colony might yet prove another "instance of an Eden converted into an abode of sorrow and wretchedness by the folly of man" (*T*, p. 84).[28] Appalled at the greed that seduced men from the plow to "the alluring uncertainties of speculation," Farnham condemned the financial dealings that led to the Panic of 1837 because, having "plunged deeper and deeper into the mazes of [land] speculation" along the frontier, men had ceased "erecting . . . homes" (*PL*, p. 210). And, together, Holley and Farnham both betrayed a decided discomfort with at least some of the alterations going on around them.

Holley decried the bad taste and the bad management that defined "the common practice with settlers here, to cut away every tree of a clearing," because she preferred to see "the noble giants of the forest . . . serve as true parasols to the dwelling they ornament" (*T*, pp. 48–49). Farnham revealed genuine ambivalence toward the "files of earnest men, with hard hands and severe, calculating faces, pass[ing] toward [Illinois] from the east" (*PL*, p. 405), because under their hands, she understood, "nature would be herself no longer. All her former aspect would fade away beneath the despoiling hand that labor would lay upon her charms" (*PL*, p. 404). Having eagerly looked toward the clearings on an earlier Ohio valley frontier, amid the open spaces of the prairies, by contrast, women were no longer desperate for the signs of human habitation that once proved so comforting to them. More easily and immediately at home on the prairies, here they instead voiced doubts as to what settlement might do to the welcoming land.

Having expressed their hesitations, however, both Holley and Farnham went on to encourage the emigration of "industrious mechanics, farmers, and tradesmen," confident "that there was plenty of territory there whereof to manufacture farms, cities, et cet" (*PL*, p. 155). In short, these were not women who abandoned their fantasies. Holley produced an enlarged—and, if possible, even more enthusiastic—edition of *Texas* in 1836. And Farnham closed *Life in Prairie Land* by reasserting familial and Edenic associations.

"Surpassing the gardens of the old world in fertility," wrote Farnham, Illinois promised "a free brotherhood" to a human family that—as in Holley—stands "united as to the great purposes of life" (*PL*, p. 408). Despite her losses and sufferings there, the country "enchain[ed] our affections," she insisted (*PL*, p. 396). In her preface, Farnham had declared that when "compelled to return to the crowded and dusty marts of the East, I did so with many and deep regrets" (*PL*, p. v); the book she wrote bears ample witness to the honesty of that opening. Indeed, at times it feels like a personal journal written to evoke some happier prior landscape. Only here the writer is in the urban east, her love for the frontier west, "the land of my heart," having become the "attachment" she now cannot bear to "sever" (*PL*, p. vi).

Despite the rout at the Alamo, the Battle of San Jacinto, and the subsequent declaration of independence in 1836, followed by several years of unsuccessful petitions to become part of the United States, Texas enjoyed a steady increase in population throughout the 1830s and 1840s. Despite the Panic of 1837 and the economic depression that followed, both of which closed banks and wiped out thousands of small farmers along the agricultural frontier, the western prairies continued to attract settlers, enjoying a marked increase in migration during the second half of the 1840s. To the imperial designs of a land-hungry populace, Mary Austin Holley's 1833 and 1836 editions of *Texas*, along with Eliza Farnham's 1846 publication of *Life in Prairie Land*, added an element of imaginative play. That is, they introduced (to their women readers especially) welcome images of a congenial landscape upon which *familiar* fantasies might be played out.

To women afraid of finding themselves either "shut up . . . in the woods"[29] or exposed on some "naked expanse" (*PL*, p. 76), Holley and Farnham offered comforting counter-images. On a landscape "fancifully diversified with prairie and woodland" (*T*, p. 65), Holley seems to have intuited, both these fearful responses would be obviated. Repeatedly emphasizing the unique mixture of closed and open spaces, Holley declared that it was "the alternate woodland and prairie, which make the peculiar beauty of a Texas landscape."[30] Moreover, the "elevated prairie . . . with occasional *points* and *islands* of timber," in Holley's view, gave "the plains the appearance of vast parks, with ornamental trees artificially arranged to beautify the prospect" (*T*, p. 62). Farnham, too, seems to have appreciated that alternation because, over and over again, she praised the frequent stands of woodland dotting the Illinois prairies as a "familiar alternative to which the mind recurs when it is weary of the majesty which lies beyond" (*PL*, pp. 75–76). Everywhere on the prairies, then, both authors agreed, one encountered only "delightful scenery" (*T*, p. 78) and the open prospects for which Elizabeth House Trist had once felt so desperate in the woods outside of Pittsburgh. As far as Holley was concerned, echoing Trist in the previous century, "nothing was wanting, but neat white dwellings, to complete the picture" (*T*, p. 31).

What the prairies seemed to offer, in fact—as the Pennsylvania woods in 1784 had not—was a receptive screen for precisely such projections. And so, as we have seen, each writer, in her own way, painted "with the pencil of fancy" (*T*, p. 66) familial and domestic designs, even as she tried to map for her readers the geographical details of the world around her. That both Holley and Farnham pitched their promotionalism in a domestic key was perhaps as much a personal choice as it was a nod in the direction of their anticipated (female) readership. For the family configurations dominating the two works catered not only in a general way to the domestic pieties of mid-nineteenth-century America but, in particular, they articulated the psychological needs and emotional yearnings of their individual authors.

When Mary Austin Holley first visited Texas, during the fall and winter of 1831, she was a forty-seven-year-old widow, well educated, genteel, but impoverished, caring for an unruly (and probably mentally incapacitated) teenage son and fond of sending occasional bolts of expensive cloth to a married daughter in Kentucky.[31] Since her husband's death in 1827, she had supported herself as the live-in tutor to the children of a wealthy French-speaking Creole family in Louisiana. An older brother who had already established himself in Texas first interested her in the colony by showing her maps on which were penciled those portions of land to be allotted to members of the Austin family who settled there. "Like the in-gathering of the Jews!," she had quipped, eagerly contemplating the pros-pect of renewed family ties and the possibility of providing for her son's future.[32] Her cousin Stephen's promise to reserve land for her on Gal-veston Bay clinched her determination to go and see for herself. As she would later put it in her book, casting herself in the third person, "allured . . . by the flattering representations of the country, . . . and tempted by the very liberal terms of settlement . . . [and] above all, impelled by a de-sire, which every widowed mother will know how to appreciate, of making some provision for an only son . . . , favoured, also, by a previous personal acquaintance with Col. Austin himself, and encouraged by a brother al-ready established in the country, she resolved to go" (*T*, p. 11). The result, she wrote, was a determination "to choose this spot for her home" (*T*, p. 12).

. The truth is, during this first trip to Texas, Holley never set foot on the land that had been promised her. Her firsthand knowledge of the colony was confined to observations made from the deck of a schooner as she sailed up the Brazos River and then to day excursions in and around her brother's home at Bolivar, where she resided the entire time. (The regional climatic and geographical comparisons in her book were gathered from conversations with others, mostly from her brother and cousin.)[33] Her limited experience of the Texas countryside notwithstanding, Holley found what she was looking for: the promise of an intact family and a do-mestic security she had not known since the death of her husband.[34] Such ties may have been especially important to her because, as a child, she had lost her father to a yellow fever epidemic. When her father's estate was set-tled, it was found that he had left his family practically destitute. At age ten, therefore, the little girl was taken into the home of an uncle, a success-ful businessman in New Haven, while her five brothers and one sister were farmed out to other relatives.

Texas now seemed to be promising to gather in the Austin clan. One brother and several cousins were already there and, as if to elaborate the design, the whole of its social structure struck Holley as one happy ex-tended family. No less important, the "infant colony" itself promised to restore her role as a mother to a thriving offspring and to supply her with an appropriate patriarch consort in the person of her cousin, nine years her junior, Stephen F. Austin. The attachment was more than symbolic— though its symbolic aspects clearly appealed to her.[35] A later diary of Hol-ley's and extant letters between the two cousins indicate a growing roman-tic attachment that, had not political difficulties in Texas and Austin's un-timely death in 1836 intervened, might well have ended in marriage.[36] At the very least, however, those letters, plus her various newspaper articles about Texas, suggest that Holley never chose to distinguish between her attachment to her cousin and her commitment to the "infant establishment" to which he had dedicated his adult life. As a result, it was her own idiosyncratic fusion of protective parental concern and familial commitment that she projected as the experience of all women who would come as "emigrant mothers" to the fledgling Austin colony.

Eliza Farnham, by contrast, preferred to see herself as a daughter welcomed by "a strong and generous parent" (*PL*, pp. iii–iv) and as a sibling able to turn to the trees "as to elder brothers" (*PL*, p. 76). Precisely, in short, the relationships of which she had been deprived in childhood. Born Eliza Wood Burhans in Rensselaerville, New York, in 1815, she had lost her mother in 1820. Her father—whom the growing girl always suspected to have been involved with another woman—decided then to break up the family and distribute his five children to various friends and relatives. Little Eliza was taken to western New York state, where she found herself under the domination of a harsh and parsimonious foster mother who discouraged the child's intellectual curiosities and considerably restricted her physical freedom as well. Finally, in 1830, an uncle brought the unhappy fifteen-year-old to eastern New York where, with the help of one of her brothers, she managed a little more than a year of study at a Quaker boarding school. For a time she supported herself by teaching, and then, again with her brother's aid, she enrolled in the Albany Female Academy. She was so eager to succeed there that, soon after the first-year examinations, she collapsed from exhaustion. When she recovered (and probably also at family urging), she decided to join a married sister in the new prairie west, arriving in Tazewell County, Illinois, in 1835.

In what we crudely denominate "real life," Farnham in Illinois—like Holley in Texas—found a family for herself. Her sister Mary's family immediately welcomed her. Then, in July 1836, after little more than a year in Tazewell County, Eliza Wood Burhans married Thomas Jefferson Farnham (a young lawyer who was later to distinguish himself as an explorer and promoter of the Far West). Their first son was born in 1837. But, as the metaphors in *Life in Prairie Land* make clear, Farnham also found in Illinois a natural world that, imaginatively at least, seemed to compensate for the family she had lost in childhood.

As an ungendered "parent," the "magnitude, . . . fertility, . . . [and] kindliness" (*PL*, pp. iii–iv) of the landscape compensated at once for both father and mother. And the trees represented "elder brothers" and "an idea of home" (*PL*, p. 76)—from both of which she had been too early separated. Indeed, some psychologists would suggest that the imagined recovery of the childhood configuration enabled the performance of her adult roles as wife and mother. Be that as it may, the prairies of Illinois certainly conferred emotional fulfillments that ten years in western New York never had.

If Farnham's foster mother had ridiculed the growing girl's interest in books, nature in Illinois appeared a benign teacher, addressing the newcomer with lessons that "are purifying, ennobling, and elevating" (*PL*, p. iv). If Farnham's foster mother had held the girl to repressive standards of decorous behavior, the Illinois prairies offered "'social and physical freedom . . . in their most enlarged forms'" (*PL*, p. 89). The "delightful recreations" of autumn "wood-parties," for example, saw Farnham and her female companions "mounted, . . . without our riding dresses, that we may not be cumbered with them when we reach the wood." "Away we go," she exulted, "free as the winds. North, south, east, or west, the way is equally open." Only step outside your cabin door, Farnham seemed to be promising women like herself, and you too will once again become a happy daughter, with "a larger liberty" than you have elsewhere known (*PL*, pp. 172–73).

When Mary Austin Holley acknowledged that her responses to Texas were "very like a dream or youthful vision realized" (*T*, p. 127) and Eliza Farnham disclosed that the composition of her Illinois sketches had allowed her to "live again in the land of my heart" (*PL*, p. vi), both tacitly owned up to the fact that, at least in part, they were engaged in fantasy. To paint, as Holley put it, "with the pencil of fancy . . . rural cottages, with the flocks of the herdsman, and all the various indications of human activity and domestic happiness" (*T*, pp. 66–67) was not, however, to project only the personal or the idiosyncratic onto the Texas plains. No one's fantasies, after all, exist in a vacuum. And in the case of the familial and domestic fantasies of the two most successful female promotional writers of mid-nineteenth-century America, especially, the genteel domestic ideology of a rising middle class was powerfully at work.

As one popular novelist declared on behalf of the American woman in 1838, "Home was her true sphere."[37] This meant that she was to begin life as the dutiful daughter of loving but guiding parents and then assume a central role in a household of her own, serving there as the keeper of the symbolic hearth, spiritual guide to a loving husband and teacher and moral arbiter to their obedient offspring. If life rarely comported with these patterns, they were nonetheless the only patterns the culture offered as desirable. Not even the growing ranks of feminists attacked the validity of these roles, preferring instead to call for changes in the educational, legal, and economic constraints traditionally attached to these roles. As a result, popular magazines, sermons, and the sentimental domestic fictions of the day all combined to make of this home-centered life pattern *the* model for female life experience or, where that failed, the model for fantasy reveries of what might or ought to be. What Holley and Farnham projected onto the Texas and Illinois prairies, therefore, represented more than their unique personal psyches. Their projections encompassed the very imagery through which most women of their day either experienced or wished to experience their lives.

What constituted the especial appeal of *Texas* and *Life in Prairie Land*, however, was their further suggestion that the familial configuration might reach beyond the cabin door. The frontier was itself an extended family, both books seemed to imply, and "the beauty of order and purity in domestic life" (*PL*, p. ix) pervaded all relationships. This, too, came out of the much-vaunted domestic ideology. For while the popular women's fictions of the 1830s and 1840s assumed that a woman would find her "greatest happiness and fulfillment in domestic relations," they included in those relations, as Nina Baym has pointed out, "not simply [her duties] as spouse and parent, but the whole network of human attachments based on love, support, and mutual responsibility."[38] Historian Mary Kelley has noted that the woman was to be more than simply the "central figure in the home." Indeed, that centrality was to make of her, as well, "a reformer of and servant to an American society judged to be in dire need of regeneration."[39] In other words, as Baym concludes, "domesticity [was] set forth as a value scheme for ordering all of life" in the hope that, eventually, "home and the world would become one."[40]

Nowhere in mid-nineteenth-century America did such a fusion seem imminent. Except, perhaps, in the idealized prairie west mapped by Holley and Farnham. If, as Mary Kelley urges, the "domestic dream" of the sentimental domestic fictionists was "the home—christened Eden,"[41] then in Holley and Farnham, a societal Eden and the individual home at last became one on a landscape that had always been christened Paradise. As promotional tracts, to be sure, *Texas* and *Life in Prairie Land* were consequential in attracting settlement to the prairies. But a no less enduring legacy may have been the spate of women's fictions set on western landscapes that became so popular in the 1850s. For what the promotional writers had made available to the novelists of their day was a new backdrop for domestic fantasies that were now wearing thin in the town houses and tenements of an industrializing northeast and on the plantations of a slavery-ridden south.

6 Margaret Fuller: Recovering Our Mother's Garden

When Mary Austin Holley first visited Texas in the autumn of 1831, she brought rose slips from her daughter's garden in Kentucky to plant around her brother's home at Bolivar; some years later, she set out "the first strawberries in Texas."[1] If the women who first contemplated making a home for themselves on the vast expanse of the American prairies thus felt the need to bring their gardens with them, a later generation claimed to discover on those same prairies a ready-made "garden interspersed with cottages, groves, and flowery lawns."[2] The promotional appeals to a prairie Eden had had their effect—even on a self-willed New Englander who anticipated only antipathy at "'the encircling vastness,'" a woman who came "to the west prepared for the distaste I must experience at its mushroom growth" (*SL*, pp. 35, 28).

To be sure, Margaret Fuller was not contemplating settlement nor was she even an early visitor to a raw frontier. In 1840, the year Eliza Farnham left Illinois for upstate New York, bidding farewell to the "land of the . . . stirring future,"[3] more than a third of the nation's population lived west of the Appalachians. Indeed, in May of 1843, as Margaret Fuller took the train to Buffalo and from there a steamer across the Great Lakes to Chicago, a thousand emigrants in ox-drawn covered wagons were beginning the "Great Emigration" overland to Oregon. For those less intrepid, however, the comparative speed and relative comfort of the rail and steamboat systems offered Illinois and the Wisconsin Territory as easily accessible destinations, even as these same conveyances also carried summer tourists anxious to throw off "the routine that so easily incrusts us" (*SL*, p. 170). It was thus a middle west undergoing rapid expansion and even more rapid change that Margaret Fuller visited in the summer of 1843.

All of this she duly noted. But what make her observations of particular interest is that they betray the frustration of the very fantasy that the women promotionalists were then promising as daily reality to their sisters who would come as settlers to the prairies. For, like Holley and Farnham before her, Margaret Fuller too believed that she had discovered on these open and rolling grasslands "the very Eden which earth might still afford" (*SL*, p. 122). Unlike Holley and Farnham, she came to understand and—more important—to express, as they could not, how that Eden might at once exist and yet be unavailable to women.

Scarcely a year after she gave up her editorial duties on the *Dial*—a year filled with writing, translating, and conducting her famous "conversations" for women in order to eke out a precarious living—Margaret Fuller reluctantly accepted a gift of fifty dollars from her friend, the liberal Universalist minister, James Freeman Clarke, so that she might join him and his sister on a tour of what was then still denominated the American Northwest. It was her first trip beyond the confines of New England and upstate New York. With her, as she took the train from Boston to Buffalo, were three close friends: Caroline Sturgis, who left the party at Buffalo, and James Freeman Clarke and his sister, the artist and illustrator, Sarah Freeman Clarke. The little party stopped first at Niagara Falls and then, taking the steamer out of Buffalo, traveled five and a half days to Chicago. From there, James Freeman Clarke returned to the east, entrusting the two women to the care of his brother, William Hull Clarke, who owned a business in Chicago. After two weeks in that city, William Hull Clarke seated his two visitors in a horse-drawn covered wagon, loaded it with provisions, and struck out across the south end of De Kalb County, through Lee County, to the Rock River country, proving himself, as Fuller would later write, "a guide, equally admirable as marshal and companion, who knew by heart the country and its history" (*SL*, p. 36).

After a fortnight's ramble, the three returned to Chicago, and from there Margaret and Sarah journeyed on by boat to Milwaukee. In Milwaukee, the women hired a driver and a carriage to take them on a similar exploration across the Wisconsin Territory. On both occasions, while Sarah Freeman Clarke filled a sketch pad, Margaret Fuller kept a journal. In it, she noted down all that she encountered and experienced, hoping thereby "to woo the mighty meaning of the scene, perhaps to foresee the law by which a new order, a new poetry, is to be evoked from this chaos" (*SL*, p. 28). The fruit of that wooing was *Summer on the Lakes, in 1843*, published the next year in Boston and illustrated by Sarah's sketches. It was Margaret Fuller's first original book (her previous books having been translations from the works of German authors).

Despite having "come to the west prepared for the distaste I must experience at its mushroom growth" (*SL*, p. 28), and despite some initial apprehension at the unaccustomed openness of the terrain, Fuller, like Holley and Farnham, was captivated by the landscape. If "at first, the prairie seemed to speak of the very desolation of dulness," once she had taken her first ride out and "seen the flowers, and observed the sun set with that calmness seen only in the prairies, and the cattle winding slowly to their homes in the 'island groves,'" she admitted that she "began to love, because I began to know the scene, and shrank no longer from 'the encircling vastness'" (*SL*, pp. 34–35). That vastness, in fact, quickly took on the association it had held for Holley: the open and rolling prairies dotted with "island groves" struck Fuller as parklike and cultivated. "Illinois," she observed, "bears the character of country which has been inhabited by a nation skilled like the English in all the ornamental arts of life, especially in landscape gardening." "The villas and castles seem to have been burnt," she acknowledges, "but the velvet lawns, the flower gardens, the stately parks, . . . the frequent deer, and the peaceful herd of cattle," all these remain (*SL*, pp. 43–44).

If her first view of the prairie flowers, then in full bloom, evoked "a sort of fairy-land exultation never felt before" (*SL*, p. 34), so too the "excursion of two or three weeks" (*SL*, p. 35) across Illinois represented a kind of paradise regained. Setting forth "in a strong wagon, . . . loaded with every thing we might want . . . for buying and selling were no longer to be counted on" (*SL*, pp. 35–36), Fuller and her companions wandered at their leisure, following neither road nor guidebook, and depending on the kindness of the climate or the hospitality of the local farmhouses for the night's lodging. Having thus radically dispensed with "the routine that so easily incrusts us" (*SL*, p. 170), Fuller could compare her liberation to nothing less than the original earthly ideal. "There was neither wall nor road in Eden," she noted, and "those who walked there lost and found their way just as we did" (*SL*, p. 65).

Precisely this idealized, Edenic quality impelled Fuller to caution her readers to expect neither guidebook nor conventional travel diary as its result. She eschews references to mileage or direction because "I . . . do not know how many miles we travelled each day, nor how many in all." And she will not note landmarks or waystations of "the geography . . . inasmuch as it seemed to me no route, nor series of stations, but a garden interspersed with cottages, groves, and flowery lawns, through which a stately river ran." Instead of the conventional catalogue of places and facts, in other words, Fuller explains that "what I got from the journey was the poetic impression of the country at large"; and that, she insists, "is all I have aimed to communicate" (*SL*, p. 67). To put it another way: what she got from the journey—whether in Illinois or Wisconsin—was less an impression of physical topography than an immersion in the fantasies that

that topography seemed to invite. And what she communicated—even if unwittingly—was her own idiosyncratic version of the domestic dreams awakened for Holley and Farnham on similar landscapes.

The "poetic impression" that Fuller repeatedly sought in Illinois and the Wisconsin Territory was the "habitation of man" settled unobtrusively "like a nest in the grass, . . . thoroughly . . . harmonized with what was natural" (*SL*, p. 38). So taken was she with the parklike beauty of the prairie that she did not wish to see it displaced by settlement. At the same time, however, she recognized in the fertile and well-watered grasslands a potential economic refuge from the hard scrabble farms of her native New England, where sons fled to the cities or the frontier to seek a livelihood and daughters left home for fourteen-hour days and slave wages in the proliferating textile mills and shoe factories. Obviating "those painful separations, which already desecrate and desolate the Atlantic coast," Fuller believed, were the prairies, where "whole families might live together," generation upon generation. Here, she mused, "the sons might return from their pilgrimages to settle near the parent hearth," and "the daughters might find room near their mother" (*SL*, p. 60).

To protect both features of her vision—the beauty of the landscape and the unbroken, prospering family—Fuller insisted that, on the expansive prairies, "a man . . . may have water and wood and land enough" and yet still "afford to leave some of it wild, and to carry out his own plans without obliterating those of nature" (*SL*, p. 60). With all the zeal of a promotionalist—or, in her case, the fervor of a fantasist—she pointed to the home of "an Irish gentleman," praising "the unobtrusive good taste of all the arrangements, [which] showed such intelligent appreciation of the spirit of the scene." Since Illinois is already a natural park, she explains, "his park, his deer-chase, he found already prepared; he had only to make an avenue through it" (*SL*, p. 45). Elsewhere, at "a double log cabin" near the town of Oregon, Illinois, she describes what is to her eye, "the model of a Western villa. Nature had laid out before it grounds which could not be improved" (*SL*, p. 58). Nor have its owners made any attempt to do so, she implies.

The few improvements she did applaud enhanced rather than disfigured the landscape, in her view, because they stood as emblems of the idealized domesticity she would see in the west. Around the door of one cabin "grew a Provence rose, then in blossom. Other families," she adds, "brought with them and planted the locust. It was pleasant to see their old home loves, brought into connection with their new splendors" (*SL*, p. 39). Within the cabins thus adorned she looked for a scene in which "female taste had veiled every rudeness—availed itself of every sylvan grace" (*SL*, p. 58). Where such expectations were fulfilled—the sylvan home harmonizing with an unspoiled terrain—Fuller enjoyed days of "unalloyed, spotless happiness," declaring herself, as Elizabeth House Trist never dared, "in Elysium" (*SL*, p. 46).

But such was not always, or even predominantly, her experience. She *wanted* to see settlement without despoliation. She *wanted* to see the stands of woodland along the prairie as "fair parks, and the little log-houses on the edge, with their curling smokes, harmoniz[ing] beautifully with them" (*SL*, p. 40). "Almost always when you came near," however, that attractive vision evaporated and, in its place, "the slovenliness of the dwelling, and the rude way in which objects around it were treated" appeared "very repulsive" (*SL*, p. 46). "After seeing so many dwellings of the new settlers," Fuller was reluctantly forced to conclude that, for the most part, the settlers did not—as she did—appreciate the natural beauty surrounding them, having "no thought beyond satisfying the grossest material wants" (*SL*, p. 46). And this, she foresees, bodes ill for the future: "their mode of cultivation will, in the course of twenty, perhaps ten years, obliterate the natural expression of the country" (*SL*, p. 47).

Having ventured west prepared to encounter "mushroom growth," knowing "that where 'go ahead' is the only motto, the village cannot grow into the gentle proportions that successive lives, and the gradations of experience involuntarily give" (*SL*, p. 28), Fuller seems nonetheless to have been unprepared for her profound disappointment in "the raw, crude, staring assemblage of houses, everywhere . . . to be met in this country" (*SL*, p. 172). What she called "the natural expression of the country" had suggested other possibilities to her. "I know not when the mere local habitation has seemed to me to afford so fair a chance for happiness," she wrote (*SL*, p. 59), believing herself to have found "the very Eden which earth might still afford to a pair willing to give up the hackneyed pleasures of the world, for a better and more intimate communion with one another and with beauty" (*SL*, p. 122). Having regained something of that paradise in her own wanderings, she could not easily let it go. And so, despite a growing distaste for much of what she saw, Fuller nonetheless stubbornly fixed her "attention almost exclusively on the picturesque beauty of this region" (*SL*, p. 104).

The results were in one sense "the poetic impression" she aimed at, in another, passages that read like excerpts from a promotional tract. Naively, and without any indication of the capital necessary to purchase and then run a farm until its crops could yield a profit, Fuller insisted that "with a very little money, a ducal estate may be purchased, and by a very little more, and moderate labor, a family be maintained upon it with raiment, food and shelter." The privations of first settlement she altogether dismissed. "If the houses are imperfectly built, they can afford immense fires and plenty of covering; if they are small, who cares?—with such fields to roam in." "With plenty of fish, game, and wheat," she insisted, even displaced city-dwellers might easily "dispense with a baker to bring 'muffins hot' every morning to the door for their breakfast" (*SL*, p. 59).

If she could only ignore the sheer ugliness that greeted her worst apprehensions, she wanted to believe, she could secure her vision of a welcoming alternative to the rocky hillsides and impoverished farms of New England. From that rural poverty, which now produced only "a society of struggling men," Margaret Fuller had eagerly embraced the west, hoping to locate there a stable and contented domesticity, with a truce to the age-old struggle between the human and the natural. For on the prairies, Fuller averred, nature "did not say, Fight or starve; nor even, Work or cease to exist; but, merely showing that the apple was a finer fruit than the wild crab, gave both room to grow in the garden" (*SL*, p. 60).

It was not only a refuge for her fellow New Englanders that Margaret Fuller clung to in this vision, however. Underpinning her social and economic concerns was a commitment to a personal refuge "where nature still wore her motherly smile" (*SL*, p. 60). The phrasing was not accidental. It pointed to childhood experiences she could not abandon and, consequently, to adult dreams she would not see obliterated. For, whether "travers[ing] the blooming plain" or "the fine, parklike woods," Fuller "'found . . . where fresh nature suffers no ravage'" "such country as I have never seen, even in my dreams, although those dreams had been haunted by wishes for just such an one" (*SL*, pp. 40, 51, 73, 36). Of course, she *had* seen such a country—or at least a version of it—in childhood, in her mother's garden in Cambridgeport. But less happy rural associations, coming in later years, had blurred the earlier image, leaving the young woman "haunted by wishes" for a terrain she could not clearly identify. In Illinois, at last, the intervening "years of dullness" were once and for all "redeemed," as the bright days on the blooming prairies (*SL*, p. 36) restored to adult consciousness the palpable incarnation of a little girl's garden retreat.

Sarah Margaret Fuller was born in Cambridgeport, Massachusetts, in 1810, the descendant of two old and once-affluent New England families. Her father, Timothy Fuller, was a lawyer prominent in Massachusetts politics, several times elected to the state senate and to the Congress. Well educated, though idiosyncratic in his opinions, and an imperious, rarely affectionate man, Timothy Fuller took upon himself the early schooling of his eldest child. Almost as soon as young Margaret could speak, her father put her "under discipline of considerable severity" and began training her in the classics of antique Greece and Rome. "He was a severe teacher," she was later to write, so much so that the daily regimen of reading and recitation that he demanded made of his daughter "a 'youthful prodigy' by day, and by night a victim of spectral illusions, nightmare, and somnambulism." When she sought escape from her father's study, she retreated to "the happiest haunt of my childish years,—our little garden, . . . which was my mother's delight." There she could daydream as she pleased, gazing upon the flowers that her "mother's hand had planted" and delighting particularly in a creeping clematis vine: "How exquisitely happy I was in its beauty." At age thirty, just three years before her summer in the midwest, she recalled "thankfully . . . what I owe to that garden, where the best hours of my lonely childhood were spent."[4]

The debilitating effects of the intellectual discipline inculcated by her father in the young Margaret Fuller notwithstanding, precisely that discipline, and the enormous learning it engendered, later afforded the young woman entrance—on almost equal terms—into the (mostly male) intellectual circles in and around Cambridge and Harvard. Her geographical proximity to those circles had been enhanced by the family's move from Cambridgeport to the beautiful Dana mansion overlooking the college in 1826 and then, in 1832, removal to the pre-Revolutionary house built by Colonel Brattle in Cambridge. During this period, Fuller began what one biographer has called "a new and rich phase in her life,"[5] but a phase abruptly curtailed with the reelection of Andrew Jackson. Timothy Fuller, having backed John Quincy Adams in the election of 1832, now saw his own political future extinguished. Disappointed and disillusioned, he decided to retire from public life and, in 1833, he moved his wife and eight children to his boyhood home on the Fuller family homestead in Groton, Massachusetts, some forty miles northwest of Boston.

Habitually passive in her relations with her husband and always in frail health, Fuller's mother quietly acquiesced in the move. Fuller, then twenty-three and reluctant to part with newfound friends, bitterly opposed it, even lingering in Cambridge for a few weeks after the rest of the family had left. In the end, however, she had no choice but to follow them to her father's chosen rural retreat (a place she already knew and disliked from its association with her earlier attendance at the Misses Prescott's School for Young Ladies in Groton). Despite the town's location on a daily stagecoach route to Boston, Fuller felt lonely and isolated on the Groton farm. Trying to make the best of it, she wrote bravely to a friend in the city, "I highly enjoy being surrounded with new and beautiful natural objects," even insisting, in July, that "the evenings lately have been those of Paradise."[6] But not for long did rural Groton remain a paradise.

Upon her first arrival there, Fuller found her ten-year old brother, Arthur, feverish and in danger of losing an eye from a recent farm accident. The baby, Edward, soon sickened. Her mother was often ill, and her grandmother, who visited for extended periods, was also ailing. Under such circumstances, Margaret served as nursemaid to all who needed her, at the same time training and helping the single servant the family's now "narrowed income" permitted.[7] She sewed, saw to the daily feeding of eight or nine people and, according to her most recent biographer, "spent five to eight hours a day tutoring her sister, her brothers Arthur and Richard, and three other children" besides.[8] For all her efforts, however, she could not keep the family together. Economic strains and personal tensions drove the two older sons to leave home, and, for all her care, the youngest child finally died. "There," in Groton, Fuller wrote bitterly to one of her brothers, "your mother's health was injured and mine destroyed."[9]

A trip up the Hudson with friends from Boston proved only a brief respite. Upon her return, faced with the same crushing household drudgery, she fell seriously ill. Upon her recovery, in 1835, her father died suddenly of Asiatic cholera. "The Peterborough hills and the Wachusetts"—the hills over which the kitchen and parlor windows looked out—"are associated in my mind with many hours of anguish, as great, I think, as I am capable of feeling," she wrote her brother.[10] Timothy Fuller's dream of rural retreat had proven a disaster. And not until her trip to the middle western prairies, some eight years later, would his eldest child again be able to experience the power of such dreams as her own.

For what Fuller was able to repossess on the parklike and flowered prairies of the middle west was her unmediated pleasure in "the dear little garden" remembered from childhood. The back door of the Cambridge-port house had "opened on a high flight of steps, by which I went down to a green plot," Fuller recalled. "This opened into a little garden, full of choice flowers and fruit-trees, which was my mother's delight, and was carefully kept. Here I felt at home."[11] Her mother's garden had thus first awakened Fuller to the pleasure she would later take in "the beautiful prairie flowers" (*SL*, p. 33). So too it had given a hint of the expansiveness that would later delight her in Illinois and Wisconsin. At the far end of the Cambridgeport garden, "a gate opened thence into the fields" beyond. "This gate I used to open," the adult recalled of the child, "to see the sunset heaven."[12] On her first ride out onto the prairies from Chicago, Fuller encountered her childhood memories magnified many times over in the prairie flowers, all "in their glory the first ten days we were there," and in "the sun set[ting] with that calmness only seen in the prairies" (*SL*, pp. 33, 34).

It was this capacity to take pleasure in flowers and sunset fields, however, that the two years in Groton had threatened to destroy. The rural paradise she had hoped for, but then irrevocably lost in Groton, at last seemed possible in her newfound prairie Eden. Little wonder that "years of dullness" seemed to her "redeemed." And less wonder still that the prairies seemed to offer "such country as I had never seen, even in my dreams, although those dreams had been haunted by wishes for just such an one" (*SL*, p. 36).

In repossessing the pleasures of her childhood garden, moreover, Fuller also returned to the emotional center of that refuge: her mother. Timothy Fuller's imperious presence may have brooded over Groton, but onto the prairies Fuller projected "a scene where nature still wore her motherly smile" (*SL*, p. 60). What had made her feel at home in the Cambridgeport garden, after all, and what had forever after rendered the flowers of clematis creeper an "emblem of domestic love" for her was the presiding presence of the frail and lovely Margarett Crane Fuller, herself "one of those fair and flower-like natures." As Fuller characterized her in an autobiographical memoir, her mother was "a creature . . . bound by one law with the blue sky, the dew, and the frolic birds" and filled with "that spontaneous love for every living thing, for man, and beast, and tree, which restores the golden age."[13] If the language of the memoir transformed the woman into a kind of nature deity, the language Fuller later used to describe the prairie attempted, no less, to turn the landscape into a kind of mother bestowing "lavish love" (*SL*, p. 68).

In the poem of farewell she composed upon leaving Chicago, Fuller made explicit what she encountered in the fortnight's jaunt across De Kalb and Lee counties and, in that encounter, what she had experienced. "A tender blessing lingers o'er the scene," she wrote of the prairie landscape—

> Like some young mother's thought, fond, yet serene,
> And through its life new-born our lives have been. (*SL*, p. 68)

If the whole of the Illinois chapter of *Summer on the Lakes* generally hints at adult reversion to childhood raptures and "fairy-land exultation" (*SL*, p. 34), these lines point to the particular raptures of psychic rebirth through the mother. In Illinois, these lines suggest, the adult woman repossessed the maternal garden of childhood refuge and, in that process, healed the trauma of the rural nightmare imposed by her father's retirement to Groton.

Perhaps because she was so eager to recapture the garden of her childhood, and perhaps because she needed emotionally to restore the marred "Paradise" of Groton through the newfound "Elysium" of the prairies, the habitually tough-minded Fuller allowed herself to overlook contradictions and inconsistencies. For example, were entire families to remain on the prairies—especially on the same homestead—generation after generation, as she suggested, the press of ever increasing population density (augmented by American-born emigrants and foreign immigrants alike) would mean that, soon enough, as in New England, the western farmer, too, would be able to take only "a small slice from the landscape." And none could then afford to leave any of it "wild," as she had hoped (*SL*, pp. 59–60). Indeed, the very premise of her frontier "ducal estate" was sheer fantasy—albeit a fantasy promoted on frontier after frontier in America. "With a very little money," little good land remained to be purchased in the areas she visited; and without capital to secure the necessary equipment, seed, and labor to make a go of it, and without ready cash to support a family until the land itself could support them, even "raiment, food, and shelter" became luxuries (*SL*, p. 59). Like Holley in Texas, so too, Fuller in Illinois seemed unwilling to acknowledge hardship or poverty on "the blooming plain" (*SL*, p. 30)—even though, to her credit, Fuller accurately observed that many an emigrant, "amid the abundance of nature," could not, "from petty, but insuperable obstacles, procure, for a long time, comforts, or a home" (*SL*, p. 121).

But there was one challenge to her image of happy families on a prairie Eden that she could not overlook—because it called into question the very heart of her fantasy. Echoing the views of an earlier century, Fuller believed that the women settlers were "to render Home a Paradise,"[14] by "veil[ing] every rudeness" and exhibiting within their homes "every sylvan grace" (*SL*, p. 58). At the same time, however, echoing the prairie promotionalists of her own era, Fuller also believed that women settlers were to find a home and, as she had, a welcoming garden—in the prairie paradise. And herein, she came to discover, lay the frustrating contradiction in her fantasy. The frontier cabins, more often than not, were slovenly and repulsive to her, and the women within them revealed again and again their "unfitness . . . for their new lot" (*SL*, p. 61). In short, the experiences of the women settlers she met recapitulated no Edenic return; what they recapitulated was her own horrific residence at Groton.

Few of the women, she learned, had welcomed the move westward. That had "generally been the choice of the men, and the women follow, as women will, doing their best for affection's sake, but too often in heartsickness and weariness" (*SL*, p. 61). It was a species of suffering Fuller and her mother knew all too well. With a recognition that comes of shared experience only, Fuller immediately understood that because it was not for these women "a choice or conviction of their own minds that it is best to be here, their part is the hardest" (*SL*, p. 61). Even more appalling, along with the Provence rose or the locust tree of "old home loves" (*SL*, p. 39), these women had also transported with them "the necessary routine of small arrangements"—in other words, the exacting details of housekeeping, all of it exacerbated by the conditions of a frontier. Again, as though recalling her own gradual collapse in Groton under analogous demands, Fuller observed that the western woman "can rarely find any aid in domestic labor. All its various and careful tasks must often be performed, sick, or well, by the mother and daughters, to whom a city education has imparted neither the strength nor skill now demanded." "The wives of the poorer settlers," she added, "having more hard work to do than before, very frequently become slatterns; but the ladies, accustomed to a refined neatness, feel that they cannot degrade themselves by its absence" and so, often to the destruction of their health, keep up the "struggle under every disadvantage" (*SL*, p. 61).

In defending her vision of a frontier "ducal estate" against the lure of "the luxurious and minute comforts of a city life," Fuller had argued that if the cabins were "imperfectly built" or "small, who cares?—with such fields to roam in" (*SL*, p. 59). What she thought she was offering among those "fields," and "'amid those bowers of wild-wood, those dream-like, bee-sung, murmuring and musical plains,'" of course, were what one of her correspondents (quoted in *Summer on the Lakes*) called "'the imaginative, yet thoughtful surfaces'" of her own fantasied maternal garden (*SL*, p. 73). All who came, she hoped, would respond as she had; all would discover, as had a fellow New Englander, that, on the prairies, "'the solitudes are not savage; . . . they never repel; there are no lonely heights, no isolated spots, but all is gentle, mild, inviting,—all is accessible'" (*SL*, p. 75). In fact, for herself, a summer's tourist, Fuller discovered that it *was* all accessible. But among the new settlers, she learned, it was accessible to the men only. The women were housebound, both by necessity and by training. "The men," she wrote, "can find assistance in field labor, and recreation with the gun and fishing-rod. Their bodily strength is greater, and enables them to bear and enjoy both these forms of life." The women, by contrast, lack both the time for leisure (since they cannot find "aid in domestic labor") and the "resources for pleasure": "When they can leave the housework, they have not learnt to ride, to drive, to row, alone" (*SL*, pp. 61–62).

In a year when thousands of Americans eagerly devoured *The Lost Sister of Wyoming* (1842), the story of Frances Slocum's captivity and sixty-year sojourn among the Delaware Indians,[15] Margaret Fuller—all unwittingly—was composing yet another version of the oldest of American narrative forms. The women she met in Illinois and Wisconsin, as she made clear, had by and large, like the captivity heroine, been taken there against their will. But, in Fuller's text, no longer did the Indian stand in as symbolic substitute for the perpetrator of the deed and no longer did the landscape figure as a "howling Wilderness" emblematic of captivity.[16] The landscape, in fact, figured as an appealing and promised garden. And the frontier home—once the place of refuge—now stood as the place of imprisonment, with the small, dark, often windowless cabins isolating women from the fields without. Probably without realizing what she was about, Fuller thus managed to lay bare the emotional structures of the traditional captivity design where she had hoped to delineate her fantasy of "the very Eden which earth might still afford" (*SL*, p. 122).

It was a pattern she described first in her chapters on Illinois, and then she repeated it in her account of the carriage tour across the Wisconsin Territory. When her carriage broke down outside of Milwaukee, for example, Fuller reports that she "took refuge" in a farmhouse that at first promised to fulfill the fantasy: "Here was a pleasant scene. A rich and beautiful estate, several happy families, who had removed together, and formed a natural community, ready to help and enliven one another. They were farmers at home, in Western New York, and both men and women knew how to work." "Yet even here," she cautions in the very next sentence, "the women did not like the change." Even so, like so many others she met, they had been "willing 'as it might be best for the young folks'" (*SL*, pp. 124–25). Only once—again in Wisconsin—did Fuller report meeting "a contented woman, the only one I heard of out there. She was English, and said she had seen so much suffering in her own country that the hardships of this seemed as nothing to her." "But the others," Fuller had to admit, "found their labors disproportioned to their strength, if not to their patience" (*SL*, pp. 116–17). The recurrence forced Fuller to repeat her disheartening discovery that the garden was available to men only: "while their husbands and brothers enjoyed the country in hunting or fishing, [the women] found themselves confined to a comfortless and laborious indoor life" (*SL*, p. 117).

The problem, as she saw it, was two-fold: women had not the leisure to enjoy the prairie garden because of their burdensome domestic responsibilities; but even where leisure might be found, the city-bred women, especially, did not know how to enjoy the new landscape. "Their culture," Fuller commented ruefully, "has too generally been that given to women to make them 'the ornaments of society.' They can dance, but not draw; talk French, but know nothing of the language of flowers; neither in childhood were allowed to cultivate them, lest they should tan their complexions. Accustomed to the pavement of Broadway, they dare not tread the wildwood paths for fear of rattlesnakes!" Her most immediate response to the ensuing "joylessness, and inaptitude, both of body and mind" that she everywhere witnessed in these women, therefore, was to attack the fashionable patterns of eastern education that had so ill-fitted them for their new life (*SL*, p. 62). In this, she anticipated Eliza Farnham, whose *Life in Prairie Land* (published two years after *Summer on the Lakes*) similarly and repeatedly castigated "'the empty and worthless character of our plans of female education at the east'" as "'unfit[ting] females for everything like a natural or useful life.'"[17]

But where Farnham was content to attribute all the ills of western women to the deficiencies of (generally eastern) education, Fuller was not. Though she never stated it explicitly, she nonetheless seems to have grasped that even improved educational programs would not necessarily lead women out onto "the wildwood paths" if their domestic duties continued to confine them "to a comfortless and laborious indoor life" (*SL*, pp. 62, 177). As a result, in the process of turning the notes in her journal into the book-length record of her travels in the west, she attempted, in a way Farnham never would, to understand why the promised garden, now palpably available, as she herself had seen it in Illinois and Wisconsin, continued to remain the exclusive domain of men.

Her analysis was complicated by the fact that, in part, she was dealing with her own unacknowledged psychic needs and, in part, with the realities of other women's lives, insofar as they had revealed themselves to her. And the two—that is, her fantasy and the reality these women reported— were deeply in conflict. Without any available psychoanalytic paradigm to get at the fact that she was essentially trying to salvage a personal fantasy as public property, protecting herself thereby from the specter of its frustration, Fuller employed instead a vocabulary of "dreams" (*SL*, p. 36) and "poetry" (*SL*, p. 28) and a narrative structure that most readers have found digressive and full of apparent irrelevancies. So certain was Arthur Buckminster Fuller of the essentially "episodical nature of the work," for instance, that, when he edited *Summer on the Lakes* for reissue in 1856, he boasted of making "omissions" in the text "without in any way marring its unity." The reader, he felt confident, would not miss his sister's interpolated "extracts from books which she read in relation to the Indians; an account of and translation from the Seeress of Prevorst, a German work . . .; a few extracts from letters and poems sent to her by friends while she was in the West . . .; and the story of Marianne."[18] He was no doubt right. Still, in reducing the text mainly to Fuller's original observations of the west, he eliminated many sections—especially the Seeress of Prevorst and

Mariana stories—in and through which his sister sought "to woo the mighty meaning of the scene" and evoke "a new order, a new poetry" from the confused "chaos" of her own responses (*SL*, p. 28).

To be sure, the stories of Mariana and the Seeress of Prevorst, having no obvious relation to western travel, do not immediately identify themselves as integral to the text. But, in fact, they served Fuller as crucial thematic glosses on her larger understanding of the position of women on the frontier. The Seeress of Prevorst, an uneducated German peasant with apparently unusually developed psychic powers, may at first have fascinated Fuller because her story seemed to suggest the interpenetration of this world by other-world, or spiritual, beings. And Fuller, like Farnham, strongly suggests that she, too, has experienced almost religious raptures, perhaps even spiritual elevations (or rebirth) on the prairies. Eventually, though, the Seeress of Prevorst comes to stand not for the woman of unusual power but for the woman powerless to be understood, or even to survive with her gifts, in the world as it is. Given up as mad by family and friends, and abused by improper medical treatment, the seeress (or mystic) finds a sympathetic and believing friend in a doctor who attends her during her last few years, and she dies young.

So, too, does Mariana, although the ostensible cause is different: Mariana dies of a broken heart because Sylvain, her husband, can neither appreciate her mind and spirit, nor love as ardently as she. "Such women as Mariana are often lost," Fuller ends the story, "unless they meet some man of sufficiently great soul to prize them" (*SL*, p. 102). Mariana's story is introduced when Fuller claims to meet, in Chicago, "Mrs. Z., the aunt of an old schoolmate" (*SL*, p. 81). The conversation with the aunt precipitates the narrative, the first part of which follows Mariana through school. A number of Fuller scholars have detected autobiographical elements in this section of the story (Mariana, for example, is "a sleep-walker" [*SL*, p. 83], as Fuller said she had been as a child); and the story of Mariana's schooldays is often taken as a barely fictionalized version of Fuller's own experience at the Misses Prescott's school.[19] Certainly, some temperamental affinities suggest the author's identification with her creation. Fuller, who in 1841 passionately exclaimed, "I must die if I do not burst forth in genius or heroism,"[20] described a Mariana possessed of "a mind whose large impulses are disproportioned to the persons and occasions she meets, and which carry her beyond those reserves which mark the appointed lot of women" (*SL*, p. 103).

A similar disproportion, of course, might also be attributed to the Seeress of Prevorst. And, as well, to the women whom Fuller encountered on the Illinois and Wisconsin frontiers. Indeed, that was precisely the term

Fuller used when, a few pages later, she bewailed the fate of frontier women who "found their labors disproportioned to their strength" (*SL*, p. 117). What was significant in these stories, in effect, was not whether the women possessed capacities too large for their situation—as with the German mystic or Mariana—or found their capacities inadequate. The link at which Fuller aimed was the *disproportion* itself, the poor fit between individual ability and social role.

The final chapters of *Summer on the Lakes* deal largely with Fuller's observations of the Indians on Mackinaw Island. A sympathetic portrait of a once proud, but now deteriorating people, forced off their original homelands and thereby deprived of meaningful roles within coherent social structures, these chapters repeat thematic currents from the earlier descriptions of frontier women. It is not, however, a connection that Fuller herself ever makes. And her brother, in commending her "impressions respecting that much injured and fast vanishing race" in his preface to the 1856 edition of *Summer on the Lakes*, also pointedly ignored the connection. For him, the ruminations from Mackinaw Island offered "additional proof" of his sister's "sympathy with all the oppressed"—which, for Arthur Buckminster Fuller, meant essentially "the Indian or the African."[21] His sister recognized sexual oppression as well. If she chose not to directly link the sorry situation of the Indian in general with that of the frontierswoman, she nonetheless drew from her observations of Indian women in particular a further understanding of their white sisters. Following upon an extended discussion of the social status of Indian women, including lengthy excerpts from the works of others who had written about them, Fuller came full circle, returning to the problem of woman universally "disproportioned to the persons and occasions she meets" (*SL*, p. 103). "Has the Indian [woman], has the white woman," she asked, "as noble a feeling of life and its uses, as religious a self-respect, as worthy a field of thought and action, as man? If not, the white woman, the Indian woman, occupies an inferior position to that of man" (*SL*, p. 182).

Riding "through fields, and dells, and stately knolls, of most idyllic beauty" (*SL*, p. 114), Fuller had experienced an enrichment of her being. The prairie responded to her deepest needs, gave her back some part of herself; and on its flowered expanse she had "looked on that which matches with [my] mood, / Impassioned sweetness of full being's flood" (*SL*, p. 68). It became for her, in short, an idealized "field of thought and action" (*SL*, p. 182), a fantasy realm that seemed to respond to her capacities, and, as a result, a place that promised to erase the "disproportion" that had marked her own life. What threatened to destroy the fantasy was the specter of other women debarred from that same flowered field and attentive instead only to "the necessary routine of small arrangements" (*SL*, p. 61).

"It is not so much a question of power" (in the sense of inherent talent or natural ability), she came to understand. Women like herself, like the Seeress of Prevorst, like Mariana, like the frontier settlers she had met—all had powers, or abilities, to "carry [them] beyond those reserves which mark the appointed lot of women" (*SL*, p. 103). The "disproportion" they suffered in their lives, and which threatened always to destroy them, lay in the discrepancy between their potential power for thought and action and the actual "field of thought and action" permitted them. But it was only by means of pursuing the Indian woman's status that Fuller came, albeit circuitously, to an understanding of the white woman's as well. The inadequacy of the white woman's education to prepare her for life in the frontier west, she realized, was a symptom—a telling symptom; but it was not the root cause of the problem. "It is not so much a question of power," she understood at last, "as of privilege" (*SL*, p. 182). And with that statement she pointed her finger at *male* privilege.

By custom, law, and training, the privilege of the garden belonged to those who determined who was to live on what landscape and how they were to live there. Having "never sympathized" with her father's "liking for [the Groton] farm" (as she admitted in a letter after his death),[22] but having been forced nonetheless to live there, Fuller well understood who, in the nineteenth century, made such determinations. In *Summer on the Lakes* she never said this directly, of course. But she did acknowledge that the men who dreamed themselves Daniel Boone easily enough left behind home and hearth to hunt and fish alone amid the woods and streams, while the women, carrying with them some version of her own "emblem of domestic love" (*SL*, p. 42), the remembered garden, found instead "a comfortless and laborious indoor life" (*SL*, p. 117). Indeed, a gradual movement toward attaining these insights both structures and explains her insertion of materials otherwise irrelevant to a book of personal observations about the west. The apparent digressions, the interpolated stories, and the lengthy quotations from other writers, in other words, were all part of a larger narrative process in and through which Fuller sought a clearer picture of what she called "the defect in the position of woman" (*SL*, p. 102).

Such probings were not new to Margaret Fuller. The July 1843 issue of the *Dial*, which had gone to press just before she embarked for the Great Lakes, carried her feminist essay, "The Great Lawsuit: Man *versus* Men; Woman *versus* Women." What her tour of Illinois and Wisconsin did was to confront her, ever more urgently, with the need for more of such probings. It was not just isolated women like herself and her mother who had followed an imperious male to a rural domestic nightmare. Whole generations of women going west were now following, "as women will, doing their best for affection's sake, but too often in heartsickness and weariness" (*SL*, p. 61). And what now made that "heartsickness and weariness" insupportable was that it occurred where fantasy dictated it need not, in the newfound garden, where "the mere local habitation . . . seemed . . . to afford so fair a chance of happiness" (*SL*, p. 59).

In a sense, then, the process of struggling to put into book form the "chaos" of impressions that comprised her journal notes,[23] struggling, in effect, to "woo the mighty meaning of the scene," prepared Fuller for the work upon which, to this day, her reputation still rests. The questions first raised in the *Dial* essay, the questions to which *Summer on the Lakes* drove her once again, she began more cogently to answer in her next book, *Woman in the Nineteenth Century*, published in 1845. "Not only the Indian squaw carries the burdens of the camp," she wrote there, echoing the observations she had made on the prairie; so, too, "the washerwoman stands at her tub, and carries home her work at all seasons, and in all states of health." Most vividly in her years at Groton and then again on the prairies, she had witnessed women "go through their killing labors."[24] As a result, it was to the two great themes of privilege and the "worthy . . . field of thought and action" (*SL*, p. 182) that *Woman in the Nineteenth Century* repeatedly returned.

"I think women need, especially, at this juncture," she pleaded, "a much greater range of occupation than they have, to rouse their latent powers." The example she then offered in *Woman in the Nineteenth Century* suggests how indelibly the fate of the women on the frontier had impressed itself upon her: "A party of travellers lately visited a lonely hut on a mountain. There they found an old woman, who told them she and her husband had lived there forty years. 'Why,' they said, 'did you choose so barren a spot?' She 'did not know; *it was the man's notion.*'" The woman in the mountain hut recapitulates the women in the cabins along the prairie frontier, taken—because a man had chosen it—to a place that proves, both physically and symbolically, a barren spot. "And, during forty years," Fuller laments, "she had been content to act, without knowing why, upon 'the man's notion.' I would not have it so."[25]

In this context, *Summer on the Lakes* is no more a simple response to Charles Dickens's notorious caricature of western manners in *American Notes* (1842) than *Woman in the Nineteenth Century* is simply an expansion of the July 1843 *Dial* essay. *Summer on the Lakes* is everywhere informed, not by a desire to answer Dickens, as some critics have suggested,[26] but by the concerns for women that Fuller had so recently explored in "The Great

Lawsuit" essay; and *Woman in the Nineteenth Century*, in its turn, was informed by the new insights (and the frustrated fantasies) awakened on the
prairies but only imperfectly analyzed in *Summer on the Lakes*.[27]

Despite the "complimentary notices in the papers," of which she
boasted in a letter to a friend,[28] Margaret Fuller's *Summer on the Lakes*
earned its author nothing "but copies to give away."[29] It went through one
edition only in 1844, selling at most seven hundred copies.[30] Subsequent
to Fuller's death in 1850, her friends organized to reissue her works as part
of a memorial to her. But by then it was the general consensus that the
many so-called digressions "weighed the book down too heavily for success."[31] In consequence, as noted earlier, her brother, Arthur Buckminster
Fuller, removed large sections and issued an abridged edition in 1856.
This abridged version was then reprinted in 1860, in 1869, and yet again
in 1874, in the six-volume *Collected Works* that Fuller's brother also edited.
Never, however, did it gain either the stature of her *Woman in the Nineteenth Century* or the recognition accorded more popular women's books
about the west.

Thus, for women readers seeking from women writers some notion of
what the prairie frontier might hold for them, there remained—with the
single and singular exception of Caroline Kirkland—the better-known
promotional tracts promising one form or another of the Edenic domestic
fantasy. In works like Mary Austin Holley's *Texas* and Eliza W. Farnham's
Life in Prairie Land, the flowered garden of the prairie beckoned, apparently offering easy prosperity, familial security, genial climate, and physical
freedoms for women unheard of in the east. What had begun to happen
is clear. With the advance onto the well-watered, tree-lined, and rolling
prairies of Wisconsin, Indiana, Illinois, and Texas, during the second quarter of the nineteenth century, the American landscape became for women
what it had always been for men—a realm for the projection of gratifying
fantasies. But just as the realities of actual settlement had so often thwarted
the fantasies of men, converting an inviting feminine terrain into the specter of violated maternity and ravaged virginity, so too now—as Margaret
Fuller began to perceive—the demands of frontier life also thwarted the
fantasies of women.

The prairies might indeed be beautiful and welcoming in their appearance, with flowered meadows bespeaking "the very Eden which earth
might still afford" (*SL*, p. 122). But the landscape, as most women too late
discovered, was not their domain of action. For them, the new home constituted not any flowering garden but only a rude cabin, sometimes without even windows from which to gaze out on the surrounding beauty.
Eliza Farnham would hint at the contradiction, taking out her anger on

the female education that had so ill prepared women for their role in the west. Fuller both reported the contradiction and then anticipated Farnham in similarly castigating eastern fashions of education. But Fuller went beyond Farnham, suggesting that it was precisely woman's exclusively domestic role, and her insulation from the privilege to effect any change in that role, which was destroying her chances for realizing the fantasy. Fuller, however, unlike Farnham, was not widely read. Initially misunderstood and quickly forgotten after its first small printing, her *Summer on the Lakes, in 1843* finally did little to persuade an eagerly westering nation that, where women were concerned, their newfound frontier fantasies might, in fact, turn into domestic captivity—even in Eden.

My eastern friends who wish to find
A country that will suit your mind,
Where comforts all are near at hand,
Had better come to Michigan.

—"A Michigan Emigrant Song,"
ca. 1833

7 The Literary Legacy of Caroline Kirkland: Emigrants' Guide to a Failed Eden

Among those whom Margaret Fuller read in order to prepare herself for her summer in Illinois and Wisconsin was Caroline Kirkland. Like Fuller, Caroline Kirkland was the daughter of old and well-connected eastern families, and, also like Fuller, she ventured onto a rapidly expanding western frontier. Unlike Fuller, when Kirkland resigned her teaching post at a girls' school in Geneva, New York, in order to head out to Michigan with her husband and children in the spring of 1835, she anticipated a permanent removal. For, by this time, her husband had tired of teaching and harbored dreams of buying land and founding a settlement on the Michigan frontier. To that end, he had accepted the post of principal at the new Detroit Female Seminary and, upon his arrival, he began acquiring parcels of land in the southern part of Livingston County, along Portage Creek (about twenty miles from what is now the university town of Ann Arbor). In less than a year he owned eight hundred acres; and, having invested his father's capital in an adjoining five hundred, by 1836 William Kirkland controlled over thirteen hundred acres of prairie, forest, and swamp, some sixty miles west of Detroit.

These were the years of the great Michigan land fever, when it was said that over a thousand new emigrants a day poured into Detroit—a few to stay, most to push on into the wilderness. So quickly did immigration in these years swell the population that in 1837 Michigan changed its status from a territory to a state. Completion of the Erie Canal and steamers across the Great Lakes to Detroit had earlier made the area accessible. Reports of Michigan's rich sandy loam now made it desirable.

Hoping to capitalize on the land boom, William Kirkland set about advertising the "village of Pinckney . . . in the midst of one of the finest and best settled agricultural districts in the State."[1] In 1836, with these notices appearing in a number of Michigan papers, he resigned his post at the Detroit Female Seminary and turned in earnest to developing his holdings. Two hundred acres were roughly surveyed, a central village was laid out, and a flour mill was to be set in operation (having "just been constructed," according to his advertisements, "at a cost of from Seven to Eight Thousand Dollars").[2] Even so, it was not until the fall of 1837 that William Kirkland considered Pinckney sufficiently established to move his family out of their lodgings in Detroit and into his fledgling frontier village.

Where Margaret Fuller, in 1843, would enjoy the benefit of Caroline Kirkland's candid portrait of western life, Kirkland, in 1837, had only "pictures, touched by the glowing pencil of fancy" to prepare her for what was ahead.[3] James Hall's *Legends of the West* (1833) had promised "accurate descriptions of the scenery and population of the [southern Illinois] country in which the author resides"; but the stories and legends he offered were highly romanticized and, as he himself admitted, "entirely fictitious."[4] Charles Fenno Hoffman's *A Winter in the West* (1835) promised the perennial agricultural miracle, describing Michigan as a place where "a man can run his plough without felling a tree; and, planting a hundred acres, where he would clear but ten in the unsettled districts of New York, raise his twenty-five bushels of wheat an acre in the very first season."[5] But he neglected to mention that the "'breaking up'" of that soil would often require an immense plough, with "three or four yoke of oxen" (*ANH*, p. 134).

Having put her trust in such sources, Kirkland found herself burdened by what proved to be only "incorrect notions." "When I first 'penetrated the interior,'" she later wrote, "all I knew of the wilds was from Hoffman's tour or Captain Hall's 'graphic' delineations: I had some floating idea of 'driving a barouche-and-four anywhere through the oak-openings'—and seeing 'the murdered Banquos of the forest' haunting the scenes of their departed strength and beauty" (*ANH*, p. 12). But, on her first excursion through the woods to the site of Pinckney, she encountered neither wide pathways for her carriage nor ghostly Indians. Instead, she and her husband got stuck in one of the ubiquitous Michigan "mud-holes," from which a French-speaking deer-hunter—and not any romanticized Noble Savage—helped to extricate them (*ANH*, pp. 11, 13). With this, Kirkland began to examine the impressions gleaned from Hall and Hoffman. For the poor roads of the Michigan backwoods, she acknowledged, her "vehicle was not perhaps very judiciously chosen," being "a light high-hung carriage." Lest others make the same mistake, she "seriously advise[d] any of my friends who are about flitting to Wisconsin or Oregon, to prefer a heavy lumber-waggon" (*ANH*, p. 12).

Precisely that impulse to protect others from her own "sentimental" expectations (as she called them) provided the impetus for what was to become the first realistic depiction of frontier life in American letters. The original idea for "a veracious history of actual occurrences" grew out of Kirkland's attempts to share her new experience in letters to friends and family in the east. "Our friends in the 'settlements' have expressed so much interest in . . . our letters to them," she explained, "and have asked so many questions . . . that I have been for some time past contemplating the possibility of something like a detailed account of our experiences" (*ANH*, p. 7). In the process of composition, however, the "detailed account" grew into something more. It became, in effect, as Kirkland described it in her preface, "a sort of 'Emigrant's Guide'" (*ANH*, p. v), repeatedly measuring the reality of western life against its more popular literary incarnations.

That there was a "romance of rustic life" Kirkland never denied (*ANH*, p. 151). But what she wanted to impress on her readers was that the genuine romance bore little resemblance to "any of the elegant sketches of western life which had fallen under my notice" (*ANH*, p. 83). She therefore offered minute details of her first summer as an "inmate of a log dwelling in the wilds," describing herself fretting over the inadequate space and roasting beside "the inextinguishable fire" for cooking. And then she sardonically pointed to "Chateaubriand's Atala, where no such vulgar inconvenience is once hinted at," concluding that all her book-learned "visions of a home in the woods were full of important omissions" (*ANH*, p. 83).

What made *A New Home—Who'll Follow? Or, Glimpses of Western Life* unique among contemporary writings about the west was Kirkland's abiding perception that the "important omissions" weighed most heavily on women. Unlike their menfolk, Kirkland observed, the women along the Michigan frontier had often "made sacrifices for which they were not at all prepared" (*ANH*, p. 247). For them, removal from the "small farms in the eastward states" (*ANH*, p. 245) had brought with it dislocations the men did not suffer. "The husband goes to his work with the same axe or hoe which fitted his hand in his old woods and fields, he tills the same soil, or perhaps a far richer and more hopeful one—he gazes on the same book of nature which he has read from his infancy, and sees only a fresher and more glowing page." But his wife, by contrast, finds her world now altogether stripped "of the old familiar means and appliances":

> *She* has been looking in vain for the reflection of any of the cherished features of her own dear fire-side. She has found a thousand

deficiences which her rougher mate can scarce be taught to feel as evils. What cares he if the time-honoured cupboard is meagerly represented by a few oak-boards lying on pegs and called shelves? . . . Will he find fault with the clay-built oven, or even the tin "reflector?" His bread never was better baked. What does he want with the great old cushioned rocking-chair? When he is tired he goes to bed. (*ANH*, p. 246)

If she could alert prospective female emigrants to the enormity of these changes, Kirkland hoped, she might in some sense help to ameliorate them. At the very least, she could certainly counter—*beforehand*—the dangerous delusions "of a home in the woods . . . always in a Floridian clime, where fruits serve for *vivers*" (*ANH*, p. 83).[6]

Her intended audience, then, was essentially women—some of whom, Kirkland knew, would, like herself, "find themselves borne westward by the irresistible current of affairs" (*ANH*, p. 86). To hold the attention of those habituated by novels and popular magazines to tales of love and courtship or sentimentalized domesticity, however, required something more than the dry paragraphs of a conventional emigrant's manual or a personal journal "published entire and unaltered" (*ANH*, p. v). Practical hints like "bring[ing] with them some form of portable yeast" for baking bread (*ANH*, p. 59)—hints most emigrants' manuals omitted—were thus to be offered as part of an entertaining narrative.

Kirkland's "veritable history," her "unimpeachable transcript of reality," in other words, took on what she called "glosses, and colourings, and lights . . . for which the author is alone accountable" (*ANH*, p. v). The short tales and sentimental love stories that run through many of her chapters, therefore, should not be read, as some critics have suggested, as nascent "experiments in fiction."[7] Kirkland knew her audience, and she knew what she was about. It was not fiction she aimed at; it was "a veracious history of actual occurrences" (*ANH*, p. 7). But in order to make the sobering counsels usually reserved for emigrants' manuals palatable to readers bred on sentimental novels, she employed the two sure devices she knew would prove familiar and compelling: plot and character, with women always at the center. To understand this is to understand the organizing principle of her phenomenally popular *A New Home* (1839).

As promised, Caroline Kirkland's first book begins as a personal account of the author's own experience—though it attributes that experience to the pseudonymous "Mrs. Mary Clavers—An Actual Settler." On "the very last of April," the narrator tells us, she left her lodgings in Detroit in order to make her "first visit to these remote and lonely regions" where her husband has laid out his prospective town. The trip is at first a pleasurable excursion through the literary rhetoric of first spring, all of it reminding her "of 'the pied wind-flowers and the tulip tall'" of which Shelley sang (*ANH*, p. 10). But a "formidable gulf" (*ANH*, p. 10) soon opens between landscape reveries plucked from Shelley and Charles Lamb and the less appealing topography of a raw frontier in mud season. First, the narrator and her husband must negotiate a "ditch . . . filled with water and quite too wide to jump over" (*ANH*, p. 13). Then they spend their first night in "a wretched inn, deep in the 'timbered land,'" where the master's "horrible drunkenness" leaves his "wife and children . . . in constant fear of their lives, from his insane fury" (*ANH*, pp. 13–14). No longer can Kirkland's pseudonymous Mary Clavers claim to be even "a little sentimental" about the landscape through which she is passing (*ANH*, p. 10).

Literary allusions to pastoral splendors are forthwith dropped—except for ironic contrast—and other stories begin to replace those of the romantic poets. The first is that of the proprietress of the first night's inn, a "desolate woman" unhappily removed "from a well-stored and comfortable home in Connecticut to this wretched den in the wilderness" (*ANH*, p. 14). The second, though, recounts relative success. Mrs. Danforth, mistress of a subsequent frontier "hotel," boasts at least minimal comfort and cleanliness in her "log-house of diminutive size" (*ANH*, p. 16)—although she is quick to point out that this has not always been the case. "'We had most awful hard times at first,'" she confides to the narrator, recalling that "'many's the day I've worked from sunrise till dark in the fields gathering brush heaps and burning stumps.'" "'But that's all over now,'" she proudly boasts, "'and we've got four times as much land as we ever should have owned in [New] York-State'" (*ANH*, p. 38).

Albeit in different ways, both stories are instructive. The first challenges the image of easy success promised by writers like Charles Fenno Hoffman; the second, in modifying that theme, points to the physical labors demanded of women on a new frontier. As well, Mrs. Danforth's narrative makes clear that prosperity, as defined in the west, does not also insure "domestic comforts" (*ANH*, p. 29). Even though the acquisition of increased landholdings "forms a prominent and frequent theme of self-gratulation among the settlers in Michigan," standing in their eyes as a symbol of success, still Kirkland cautions her readers to understand that "the possession of a large number of acres" often enough "makes but little difference in the owner's mode of living." The Danforth cabin is a case in point. For, though Mrs. Danforth boasts of the acreage her husband now farms, she nonetheless continues to make do with inadequate living space and a makeshift kitchen of primitive appliances. All of which leads Kirkland to conclude that "comforts do not seem to abound in proportion to landed increase" (*ANH*, p. 38).

The six chapters in which Mrs. Danforth's personal history is unraveled are also the chapters in which Mary Clavers first visits her husband's projected townsite (a visit during which the Claverses board with the Danforths). In recounting her narrator's first view of the village, Kirkland took the opportunity to disabuse her readers of yet one more sentimental notion. The new communities springing up in the fertile and supposedly innocent west were often erected on foundations of greed and duplicity, without any eye for the intrinsic beauty of the place. Her vehicle for this lesson was Mr. Mazard, the agent in charge of overseeing the construction and design of Mr. Clavers's village.

That this "factotum" is busily swindling the proprietor is not revealed until a later chapter. Nonetheless, the man's "air of earnest conviction, of sincere anxiety for your interest, and, above all, of entire forgetfulness of his own," is clearly meant to arouse suspicion. Especially when, after inviting Mrs. Clavers to give the village a name—she chooses Montacute—he asks her opinion "as to the location of the grand esplanade" for the public square. At this, she "particularly requested that the fine oaks which now graced it might be spared when the clearing process commenced," a request with which Mr. Mazard expresses himself wholly in agreement. "'A place that's designed for a public promenade must not be divested of shade trees,'" he enthuses. "Yet I believe," Kirkland has her narrator comment in the next sentence, "these very trees were the first" victims of the clearing process (*ANH*, p. 21).

Having directed her first six chapters predominantly to the delusions women readers might harbor, Kirkland turns briefly to the fantasies of men. Upon returning to their Detroit hotel, Mr. Clavers falls in with male companions and accepts "an invitation to accompany a party of . . . men of substance literally and figuratively, who were going to make a tour with a view to the purchase of one or two cities" (*ANH*, p. 45). Kirkland then engages in a quiet mockery of those who would emulate Charles Fenno Hoffman in a ramble across Michigan or, even more pointedly, those who would follow Washington Irving in *A Tour on the Prairies* (1835). For the outing proposed by the eastern gentlemen visiting Detroit is intended not simply as a speculative venture. They also "intended to 'camp out' as often as might be desirable," and at least one of the company is said to be "as keen in his pursuit of game as of money" (*ANH*, p. 45). But the dispirited little party that returns to Detroit just four days later has seen nothing of Irving's "vast tract of uninhabited country" and even less of the "smiling openness" so pleasing to Hoffman.[8] Instead, "tired and dirty, cross and hungry, were they all," with "no word of adventures, no boasting of achievements" (*ANH*, pp. 45–46). The story that Mrs. Clavers finally draws from her "toil-worn spouse" is one of mistaken trails; poorly aimed shots that miss the intended game; bad weather and worse shelter in a "forlorn dwelling"; and, to top it off, discomfiting encounters with drunken Indians and corrupt land agents (*ANH*, pp. 46–48).

At this point, with all the relevant literary ghosts laid to rest (or to laughter), fully a third of the way into her text, Kirkland is at last ready to begin the advertised subject of her narrative: a "veracious" account of removal to a home in the wilderness. After a journey once more beset by "ruts and mud-holes" and one large marsh—but this time traveled in a sturdy "large waggon"—the Claverses arrive in Montacute. In tow are three small children, a pet greyhound, and an assemblage of what Mrs. Clavers considered "the most needful articles." "The log-house, which was to be our temporary home" (*ANH*, p. 70), has not yet been vacated by its former tenants, however, and so Mrs. Clavers and her children are obliged to board for nine days with a neighboring family. Mr. Clavers, in the meantime, returns to Detroit to secure "storage for sundry unwieldy boxes which could by no art of ours be conjured into" the modest space of their future home (*ANH*, p. 71).

Vexed by the tight quarters and lack of privacy in the neighbors' cabin and "anxious to go as soon as possible to a place where I could feel a little more at home" (*ANH*, p. 72), Mrs. Clavers eagerly takes possession of her cabin the day it is vacated, not even waiting for her husband's return from Detroit. But the "real satisfaction" she anticipates "in a removal to this hut in the wilderness" (*ANH*, p. 72) is thwarted initially by urban habits and inappropriate expectations. At first she is unable to hire domestic help for the task of cleaning the place (though a neighbor does at last volunteer her services). Then she discovers that the domestic furnishings she had naively "ranked . . . as absolutely essential" prove both superfluous and too cumbersome to fit "under one roof in the back-woods" (*ANH*, p. 73). All the while, moreover, a "blazing fire in the chimney"—needed to heat water for cleaning and cooking—has rendered the cabin "absolutely insufferable" (*ANH*, p. 74). And, after such a day, Mary Clavers must face her "first night in my western home, alone with my children and far from any neighbor" (*ANH*, p. 74).

To make the cabin comfortable for sleeping, Mrs. Clavers attempts to cool it down by extinguishing the fire and "set[ting] both doors open." But this only makes the city-bred newcomer feel "exposed." Her first night in her wilderness cabin, she declares, is therefore one that "will never fade from my memory. Excessive fatigue made it impossible to avoid falling asleep, yet the fear of being devoured by wild beasts, or poisoned by rattlesnakes, caused me to start up after every nap with sensations of horror and alarm." At length, however, sleep overcomes fear, and the narrative voice adds—almost with amusement—that, toward morning, the little family was "awakened only by a wild storm of wind and rain which drove in upon us and completely wetted every thing within reach" (*ANH*, p. 74).

The morning is understandably "doleful": What Mary Clavers awakens to is a hearth without fire (and no means of starting any), "streams of water on the floor, and three hungry children to get breakfast for" (*ANH*, pp. 74–75). Housekeeping on the frontier now begins in earnest. And the chapters that follow are thus necessarily a study in accommodation.

Again, Kirkland reminds her readers, literary-bred delusions must be dismissed. Following upon Mrs. Clavers's fond memory that she had once "dwelt with delight on Chateaubriand's Atala" (*ANH*, p. 83) is the sobering—and contrasting—reality: "The inexorable dinner hour, which is passed *sub silentio* in imaginary forests, always recurs, in real woods, with distressing iteration" (*ANH*, p. 84). In the Michigan woods, especially, that recurrence demands continuous attention. For baking, "a tin reflector" serves as the "only oven, and the fire required for baking drove us all out of doors" (*ANH*, p. 84). Washing at least provides occasion for a picnic "by the side of the creek," but ironing requires "the aid of a fire made on some large stones at a little distance from the house"—and is then successful *only* "when the wind sat in the right quarter" (*ANH*, pp. 84–85).

City-bred habits are similarly abandoned withindoors. The woman who had set out with "a nest of delicate japanned tables" (*ANH*, p. 73) and "great glass dishes" (*ANH*, p. 75) now finds her "ideas of comfort . . . narrowed down to a well-swept room with a bed in one corner, and cooking-apparatus in another" (*ANH*, p. 76). Even a treasured "tall cup-board" is turned out-of-doors—because it cannot fit the cabin's tiny space—and is praised for performing "yeoman's service long afterwards as a corn-crib" (*ANH*, p. 77). So dramatic are these shifts in attitude that the narrator declares that she "can scarcely, myself, credit the reality of the change" (*ANH*, p. 76). But the change is real, profound, and so minutely detailed that no reader could miss the lesson Kirkland would teach: "No settlers are so uncomfortable as those who, coming with abundant means as they suppose, to be comfortable, set out with a determination to live as they have been accustomed to live" (*ANH*, pp. 88–89).

What Kirkland has mapped is what westerners then called the "seasoning" process. Comprising chapters twelve through sixteen, this mapping details the minutiae of frontier housekeeping, bouts with the ague (or malarial fevers), and the apparently inescapable frontier swindle. For just as the little village of Montacute seems to be taking substantial shape in the form of a mill, a dam, and a tavern, Mr. Clavers learns that much of the money entrusted to his agent for these and other improvements has instead been expended "for his, Mr. Mazard's, private behoof and benefit"

(*ANH*, p. 93). The agent, in the meantime, "had absconded" (*ANH*, p. 92), leaving the Claverses in considerable debt.

Having taken her autobiographical narrator through most of the harder lessons to be learned on a frontier, Kirkland then follows Mrs. Clavers into a more commodious framed house within the village proper and introduces yet another newcomer. This is the young Mrs. Anna Rivers, genteel, city-bred, and—as Mrs. Clavers once had been—"fond of novels and poetry" (*ANH*, p. 109). With her appearance, the ongoing emigrants' manual takes on new life. Recounting the exchanges between the seasoned older woman and the youthful newcomer gives Kirkland the opportunity to emphasize, again, how much Mary Clavers has been changed by her sojourn in the west; while, at the same time, it allows the reader to follow another woman as she adjusts her habits and expectations to Michigan demands. As in no other emigrants' manual of the period, for example, Mary Clavers advises her friend as to the proper attire for attending a frontier wedding and the wisdom of getting there by ox-cart rather than "a more ambitious carriage" (*ANH*, p. 112). "On this and many similar occasions," Kirkland has her narrator boast, "I assumed the part of Mentor . . . considering myself by this time quite an old resident, and of right entitled to speak for the natives" (*ANH*, p. 112).

In so speaking, Mary Clavers also put prospective emigrants from the genteel middle class in possession of attitudes that would prove essential to their *emotional* survival in the west. For, in honestly exploring her protagonist's eagerness at "the idea of having a neighbour, whose habits might in some respects accord with my own" (*ANH*, p. 97), Kirkland made clear that—for all the rhetoric of Jacksonian Democracy so popular in the new settlements—class and caste, opinion and prejudice had also moved westward. Migration to the frontier, in other words, did not release Americans from the burden of history to shape society wholly anew. What the rigors of the frontier engendered, instead, were altered responses to the facts of rank and social class. And these altered responses are what the mentor diligently attempts to teach her protegée.

Thus, Mary Clavers declares herself "determined at all sacrifice to live down the impression that I felt *above* my neighbours." And what we see her teaching Anna Rivers, in object lesson after object lesson, is that "however we may justify certain exclusive habits in populous places, they are strikingly and confessedly ridiculous in the wilderness." "What can be more absurd than a feeling of proud distinction," she argues to the newcomer,

> where a stray spark of fire, a sudden illness, or a day's contre-temps, may throw you entirely upon the kindness of your humblest neigh-

bour? If I treat Mrs. Timson with neglect to-day can I with any face borrow her broom to-morrow? And what would become of me, if in revenge for my declining her invitation to tea this afternoon, she should decline to do my washing on Monday? (*ANH*, p. 111)

The exchanges between Mary Clavers and Anna Rivers are central to the book's intent for another reason, too: they highlight the special attachment that defines women's relationships on a new frontier. All along, Kirkland has suggested that removal to the frontier implies added hardships for women. Even among the happiest of the many young couples who come west, she insists, there is a sense of isolation experienced by the wife that her husband will never know. Though these women "find no fault with their bare loggeries" and manage to prepare meals with "the help of such materials and such utensils as would be looked at with utter contempt in a comfortable kitchen," still, Kirkland avers, it is a "long, solitary, *wordless* day" that they endure until their husbands return for the evening meal. Under such circumstances "in this newly-formed world," Kirkland explains, there can be little wonder that "the earlier settler has a feeling of hostess-ship toward the new-comer" (*ANH*, pp. 108–9). But "I speak only of women" here, she cautions. The men, by contrast, "look upon each one, newly arrived, merely as an additional business-automaton—a somebody more with whom to try the race of enterprize, i.e. money-making" (*ANH*, p. 109).

Anna Rivers's husband provides an example of this contrast. Foregoing Montacute society and even his wife's company, he pursues a fraudulent banking venture in the nearby town of Tinkerville. When state bank auditors disclose that the Tinkerville bank lacks the collateral Harley Rivers has claimed for it, Kirkland enjoys yet another occasion for a valuable lesson: on the frontier, she makes clear, swindlers are not only those like the oafish agent, Mr. Mazard. Fraud and deceit may also wear the garb of eastern gentility.

The revelation of the bank fraud precipitates the Riverses' removal from Montacute to "one of the Eastern cities" where they live handsomely "on the spoils of the Tinkerville Wild-cat" (*ANH*, p. 214). By this time, however, the mentor device is beginning to wear thin, and Anna Rivers's presence as a foil for the narrator is no longer necessary to Kirkland's purposes. In her place stands the village of Montacute itself. Now well enough established to afford alternate devices—like the Montacute Female Beneficent Society, a sewing circle through which all gossip flows—Montacute (and its residents) takes over as an index to local attitudes and social practices. The town's established status, moreover, helps to underpin the final feature of Kirkland's emigrants' manual: Having outlined the initial journey to the frontier and then twice detailed the necessary seasoning process, she now takes up the challenge of ongoing survival there.

For this, she turns to personal histories—approaching short stories—of exemplary neighbors. In one she offers "an absolute homily" on the delusion that the frontier is an easy paradise, free of labor; in the other, she demonstrates the rewards of "plodding industry"—especially on the frontier (*ANH*, p. 132). The "pride and indolence" of Mr. B____ leaves his wretched wife laboring "with all her little strength for the comfort of her family. She had brought up five children on little else beside Indian meal and potatoes; and at one time the neighbours had known the whole family live for weeks upon bread and tea without sugar or milk" (*ANH*, pp. 130, 131).[9] By contrast, with close affectional ties between them, and hard work on both sides, the Beckworths establish what is clearly Kirkland's fantasy ideal: "not a Michigan farm-house, but a great noble, yankee 'palace of pine boards,' . . . in these remote wilds." "Fields of grain, well fenced and stumpless, surrounded this happy dwelling," Kirkland continues, "and a most inviting door-yard, filled to profusion with shrubs and flowers" (*ANH*, p. 148).

It is in the closing story of Cora and Everard Hastings, however, that Kirkland etched her fullest portrait of a model frontier couple. The story serves as a reprise of everything that has gone before, pitting young Cora's book-learned fantasies against economic and geographic realities and once again rehearsing how the newcomer might overcome the "various deficiencies and peculiarities, which strike, with rather unpleasant force, the new resident in the back-woods" (*ANH*, p. 307). To these themes Kirkland added another: Committed as she was to seeing Michigan as an "incipient Eden" (*ANH*, p. 134), Kirkland now set about defining the appropriate Adam and Eve for her frontier paradise. The heresy she preached in that endeavor was that the American Adam and Eve could not afford their innocence. To achieve a frontier garden, they would first have to fall into experience.

Kirkland's version of the fortunate fall begins when Everard Hastings and Cora Mansfield "fall shockingly in love" (*ANH*, p. 258). The spoiled offspring of rich and prominent New York families, the two decide to forego a formal wedding and plan instead to elope to "a home in the wilderness" (*ANH*, p. 265). The plan is especially appealing to the sixteen-year-old Cora because, from much indulgence in pastoral romances, she is herself "deeply tinged with romance" (*ANH*, p. 262). In her private reveries, she is prone to imagining herself "the happy tenant of a cottage" situated on a landscape of "ever-smiling skies and ever-rippling rivulets. No thought of dinner, no concern about 'the wash,' no setting of barrels to catch rain-water" intrude upon such reveries, of course. "Only think of coming to Michigan to realize such a dream as that!," the narrator comments (*ANH*, p. 263).

But the couple does not head for Michigan—at least not immediately. Upon leaving New York, they take a carriage to Albany, where Everard pawns some of their jewelry for ready cash, and from there, newly married, the two go on to Utica. "At Utica, Everard purchased a few books; for Cora had not been able to crowd into her travelling basket more than two mignon volumes of her darling Metastasio; and to live in a wilderness without books, was not to be thought of" (*ANH*, p. 269). Had she been with them, the narrator makes clear, she would have selected *Robinson Crusoe* as "the most rational purchase," along with "Buchan's Domestic Medicine, the Frugal Housewife, the Whole Duty of Man, and the Almanac." "But, counselled only by their fantasies," she surmises that Cora and Everard instead chose "Atala, perhaps Gertrude of Wyoming, perhaps . . . some novels and poetry-books," all of it in her view, "idle gear at best" (*ANH*, p. 270).

From Utica, the couple heads toward "a small village, in the southwestern part of New York" where, inspired by the landscape of their readings, Everard examines "the face of the country; wishing to ascertain whether it was rocky, and glenny, and streamy enough to suit Cora, whose soul disdained any thing like a level or a clearing. . . . Ere long he found a spot, so wild and mountainous and woody, as to be considered entirely impracticable by any common-sense settler" (*ANH*, p. 270). And there, leasing some land from a neighboring farmer, Everard builds Cora "her 'forest sanctuary'" (*ANH*, p. 275).

Despite a nagging sense of guilt that her own and Everard's parents as yet know nothing of their whereabouts, and despite continued silence from New York even after Everard has written to his parents, Cora expresses herself delighted with "the very home of her dreams" (*ANH*, p. 275). "But she was a spoiled child, and her boy-husband the most indulgent of human beings," the narrator reminds us, "so we must excuse her if she was a little naughty as well as very romantic" (*ANH*, p. 279). Besides, the narrator continues, "the world's harshness soon cures romance" (*ANH*, p. 279). Precisely that process begins there in Cora's "much-admired glen" (*ANH*, p. 276). As the spring and summer wane, "the cold winds of autumn turned the maple leaves yellow, then scarlet, then brown." And "the whole face of the earth presented to the appalled eye of the city-bred beauty, but one expanse of mud—deep, tenacious, hopeless mud" (*ANH*, p. 280). The anticipated idyll has turned into a kind of rural imprisonment. "No walks either by day or evening; books all read and re-read; no sewing, for small change of dress suffices in the woods"; and no company save the neighboring farmer and his sister. Adding to their disappointment is the fact that Everard has received no answer to the several letters he had written to his father.

Things brighten briefly with another change of seasons, as Cora discovers that she is pregnant—a discovery that prompts her, too, "at length [to write] to her mother" (*ANH*, p. 280). "Spring came and with the flowers a little daughter." Supported by the care she receives from the friendly farmer and his widowed sister, "Cora made out much better than she deserved," the narrator notes (*ANH*, p. 280). But even if she has survived a dreary winter and begun to appreciate—rather than snobbishly shun—the many "kindnesses of her rustic friends," Cora has yet to experience the full force of "the world's harshness" (*ANH*, pp. 280, 279). She is not yet, in short, cured of romance. For that, the bitter remedy is smallpox, a disease that leaves Everard "helpless, and at times slightly delirious," and that gradually saps the infant's strength as well. Nursing both husband and child, bearing "up wonderfully for a few days," Cora finally sinks into despair at what appears to her the imminent death of her child. "With a wild cry [she] sunk senseless on the floor," at which point the narrator, like the chorus in a morality play, chimes in with, "Her punishment was fulfilled" (*ANH*, p. 281).

Happily, all survive. Cora awakens from her swoon to find herself cradled on her mother's "soft bosom" (*ANH*, p. 282). Infant and husband are nursed back to health, and Cora herself begs—and receives—forgiveness from her visiting parents. At this point, the Cora who doted over Italian pastoral romances, the Cora who naively put her faith in "the sweet little enchanting 'Isola Disabitata' of Metastasio" because it proved "that people—nay, women alone, can live in a wilderness" (*ANH*, p. 263), that Cora is no more. She has been disabused of once-cherished pastoral fantasies by "the world's harshness" (*ANH*, p. 279) and, with that, shorn of the innocence to which those fantasies appealed. "The time of this sore trial," in other words, has represented a fall from innocence into experience. And the chastened Cora, forerunner and pattern of the chastened and experienced New World Eves who would soon populate a rash of domestic fictions set in the west, is now ready to enter the garden. She is, at last, "a new creature, a rational being, a mother, a matron, full of sorrow for the past and of sage plans for the future" (*ANH*, p. 283).

It is, even so, a future "which Cora at least, had never included in her plans." For what her parents reveal is that, recently, "the long-established house of Hastings and Mansfield" has suffered heavy losses, the upshot of which is that Everard, no longer secure in his inheritance, must now "get his own living" (*ANH*, p. 283). To the parents' relieved surprise, the couple takes this news with equanimity, eagerly accepting Mr. Mansfield's proposal that they relocate to "his Michigan lands." Indeed, they confess, their time in upper New York State has given them "a taste for the wilderness." Despite the difficulties they have known there, they nonetheless share "a yearning, common to those who have lived in the free woods, 'To forsake / Earth's troubled waters for a purer spring.'" If this be "visionary still" (*ANH*, p. 284), interjects the narrator, it is a vision at least no longer tainted by Cora's "romance-ridden brain" (*ANH*, p. 266).

The proof that the meaning of the young couple's vision has changed is in the prosperity and happiness they enjoy in Michigan. If their frontier home bears little resemblance to the pastoral cots of the Pastor Fido, and if their woods do not accord with "the 'Care beate selve' of Amaryllis" (*ANH*, p. 262)—the mainstays of Cora's former fantasies—that home and their present woods are nonetheless "handsome and picturesque-looking" in their own right. The house, "built of rich brown tamarack logs, . . . looking so rural and lovely," is situated so that it looks "on the basin below the bluff on one side, and on the deep woods on the other." Withindoors, everything is "capacious and well-divided, and furnished . . . neatly" (*ANH*, p. 255). Most importantly, however, the economic realities ignored in the "glenny" dell of upstate New York are here given their due. In Michigan Cora and Everard possess "a fine large fertile tract, managed by a practical farmer and his family," all of which establishes them, in the narrator's estimation, as among "the happiest people of my acquaintance" (*ANH*, p. 284).

To be sure, in her assertion of frontier realities, Kirkland preserved a number of recognizable features from the genteel domestic fictions of her day. She took from Cora the trappings of excessive wealth (always condemned in these stories)—"neither papa's side-boards nor mamma's dressing tables" (*ANH*, p. 278)—and replaced them with a home solid in its less showy, but no less middle-class, comforts. "There was a great chintz-covered sofa . . . and some well placed lounges; and in an embayed window draped with wild vines, a reading-chair of the most luxurious proportions, with its foot-cushion and its prolonged rockers" (*ANH*, p. 278). Moreover, because class lines have not been breached, the reader is invited to imagine Cora and Everard enjoying a leisure not unlike that which marked Cora's original pastoral daydreams. In addition to many "books, new as well as old," we are informed, their home contains "a cabinet piano-forte" (*ANH*, p. 278). And the daily management of their "fertile tract," we recall, is in the hands of others.

These facts notwithstanding, it would be a mistake to underestimate Kirkland's intended gesture toward realism. The Adams and Eves of the American west, she wanted her readers to understand, could afford neither their innocence of experience nor their literary delusions. Their garden could be no "rocky . . . glenny . . . streamy" dell from European pastoral, though it might well boast "tall oaks near the cottage" (*ANH*, p. 255). And, for her women readers especially, Kirkland tried to make clear that along the agricultural frontier there would be no "'sweet white dress,' with straw-coloured kid-gloves, and a dog tied to a pink ribbon, like 'the fair Curranjel'" of romance pastoral. The American Amaryllis would wear "rational, home-like, calico" (*ANH*, p. 256)—but she need be no less happy for that.

The compensation for putting aside exaggerated expectations and pastoral delusions in *A New Home* is a concomitant awakening to an achievable "romance of rustic life" (*ANH*, p. 151)—as with the Beckworths and the Hastings—and, no less important, an awakening to the inherent "glory and splendour in grass and wild-flowers" (*ANH*, p. 251). Michigan may have offered nothing so luxuriant as the Floridian wilderness of *Atala*, but Kirkland nonetheless pictured her narrator enjoying "woods cool and moist as the grotto of Undine, and carpeted every where with strawberry vines and thousands of flowers" (*ANH*, p. 144). Indeed, on this subject Kirkland almost approached the unleavened promotionalism of Mary Austin Holley's *Texas* (1831). For, even "after allowing due weight to the many disadvantages and trials of a new-country life" (*ANH*, p. 249), Kirkland still echoed Holley in asserting an "incipient Eden" (*ANH*, p. 134) in what she saw.

What seems to have appealed to both women on their respective frontiers—as it would later appeal to Margaret Fuller and Eliza Farnham—was the alternation of closed and open landscapes, always with a view or prospect. In Michigan, Mary Clavers boasted, she could ride her horse "now through woods . . . [and] now across strips of open land where you could look through the straight-stemmed and scattered groves for miles on each side" (*ANH*, p. 144). Even "the deep woods" offered their "arched vistas" (*ANH*, p. 125).

As an autobiographical projection of her creator, of course, Mary Clavers (along with her friend, Anna Rivers) enjoyed the privileged leisure to explore the "ancient woods, which I could not help admiring" (*ANH*, p. 125). Her economic situation—insuring her ability to hire domestic help—protected her from the fate of the toil-worn and housebound women who would elicit Margaret Fuller's sympathy in Illinois and

Wisconsin. Thus, not through cabin windows alone did Mary Clavers "discern glory and splendour in grass and wild-flowers" (*ANH*, p. 251). "A bridle-path through the deep woods which lie south-west of our village, had long been a favourite walk" on summer days, she makes clear (*ANH*, p. 251). And, on several occasions, she recounts exploratory rides with her husband or with Anna Rivers.

Though Kirkland repeatedly waxes eloquent in praise of the grapevines, flowers, ferns, and "wild straw-berries" of the Michigan woodlands (*ANH*, pp. 147–48), it is not here that she has Mary Clavers locate her "incipient Eden" (*ANH*, p. 134), however. Instead, in keeping with American women's repeated habit of locating for themselves some cultivated plot in the wilderness, Caroline Kirkland too looked for the familiar features of earlier gardens. When she has Mary Clavers exclaim over discovering "'a honey-suckle! absolutely a honey-suckle on the porch!'" of a neighboring farmhouse, Kirkland makes of the moment an opportunity for Clavers further to disclose that she has suffered "a sort of home calenture at times since we removed westward" (*ANH*, p. 149). The juxtaposition of the admission of homesickness with the delighted discovery of an eastern honeysuckle is pointed. For, in that coupling, the honeysuckle comes clearly to represent a crucial emblem of fondly remembered familiarity transplanted even to "these remote wilds" (*ANH*, p. 148). What will make Michigan less remote and less wild for Mary Clavers, the scene suggests, are precisely such elements from a cultivated garden begun with "quantities of choice seeds received in a box of treasures from home" (*ANH*, p. 133).

In her own "rough, pole-fenced acre, which we had begun to call our garden" (*ANH*, p. 190), Mary Clavers even goes so far as to compare herself to "another Eve" (*ANH*, p. 137). In that voice she describes the progress of her "early [flower] bulbs . . . on the opening of our first spring," detailing "the interest with which I watched each day's development of these lovely children of the sun" (*ANH*, p. 134). And, chiding herself for digressing briefly, "wandering like another Eve from my dearly beloved garden," she returns to her main topic with an impassioned catalogue of the fruits and vegetables that do particularly well "in our rich sandy loam." Among other things, she recommends "palm-leaf rhubarb, and . . . egg plants! . . . [and] all the humbler luxuries in the vegetable way, from the earliest pea to the most delicate cauliflower, and the golden pumpkin" (*ANH*, p. 137). From all this she asks her prospective emigrant-reader to draw one "practical conclusion": "that it is well worth while to make [a] garden in Michigan" (*ANH*, p. 139).

It is a cause Kirkland pleads with no little passion because, as she reveals, she has too often been disappointed in her efforts to share her garden with current neighbors. "In answer to my enthusiastic lectures on this subject," she confesses, more than one villager has replied disdainfully, "'Taters grows in the field, and 'taters is good enough for me'" (*ANH*, p. 139). At another time, "a lady to whom I offered a cutting of my noble balm geranium . . . declined the gift, saying 'she never know'd nobody make nothin' by raisin' sich things'" (*ANH*, p. 135). The readers of *A New Home*, in other words, Kirkland is suggesting here, must themselves supply the future Eves if the "incipient Eden" is to become a Michigan reality.

If the planting of a garden in Michigan has not progressed as quickly as she might like, even so Kirkland points to its clear beginnings. Genteel eastern ladies like herself who now ventured westward would not quite find themselves—as she had—in "remote wilds." Earlier Eves had already begun "the refining process." As the dwellings in Montacute became more permanent, Mary Clavers notes, "a looking glass" might be introduced withindoors, or "a nice cherry table." And without, "eglantines and wood-vine, or wild-cucumber, are sought and transplanted to shade the windows. Narrow beds round the house are bright with Balsams and Sweet Williams, Four o-clocks, Poppies and Marigolds" (*ANH*, p. 248). By the end of her first three years there, the plantings have become even more ambitious: "a few apple-trees are set out; sweet briars grace the door yard, and lilacs and currant-bushes" (*ANH*, p. 248).

Kirkland emphasizes, however, that the garden is achieved "all by female effort—at least I have never yet happened to see it otherwise where these improvements have been made at all" (*ANH*, p. 248). Her explanation is that, "as women feel sensibly the deficiencies of the 'salvage' state, so they are the first to attempt the refining process" (*ANH*, p. 247). To be sure, men's physical strength is sometimes harnessed to help with such planting. But "hers" alone "is the moving spirit," Kirkland insists of her female pioneer. And to her only must be attributed the resolution thus "to throw over the real homeliness of her lot something of the magic of [the] IDEAL" (*ANH*, p. 248).

The cumulative effect of such statements was to place the responsibility for creating a western Eden where sentiment and habit had traditionally located it—in women's hands. More specifically, in the hands of those for whom Kirkland was writing: the genteel, solidly middle-class dreamers like Cora Hastings and the author herself in earlier times. These were the readers who needed to be disabused of their falsely "visionary" pastoral fantasies; but they were, as well, Kirkland understood, those to whom a real-world "incipient Eden" would continue to appeal. For, her candor about "the many disadvantages and trials of a new-country life" (*ANH*,

p. 249) notwithstanding, what Kirkland had managed to depict for such readers was an attractive, familiar, and, above all, *responsible* role on an unformed landscape that might yet bear their especial and *idealizing* imprint.

Having cautiously signed her first book manuscript with the pseudonym, "Mrs. Mary Clavers—An Actual Settler," Caroline Kirkland sent *A New Home* to eastern publishers, totally unprepared for the fame it would bring. Success was immediate. In a typical notice, the influential *North American Review* hailed the significance of a text that refused to spread any "romantic coloring" over the western scenes it described. "She has no paradise to offer him 'who'll follow,'" the reviewer noted, concluding that the book was unquestionably "one of the most spirited and original works which have yet been produced in this country."[10] Almost overnight, then, *A New Home* became—as Edgar Allan Poe phrased it—an "undoubted sensation."[11]

But the "fidelity and vigor"[12] for which Poe and others praised her work were causing Kirkland serious problems at home. Despite the authorial pseudonym and the fictitious names throughout the book, Kirkland's neighbors in Michigan were quick to recognize their little Pinckney mirrored in Mary Clavers's Montacute; and, worse still, some identified what seemed their own unflattering portraits in her sketches. As one of Kirkland's contemporaries recalled, "she had supposed that it was all concealed by calling the town Montacute and altering the names of the actors, and that no copies of the work would find their way to that remote settlement. But in this she was mistaken, and the result was that all the persons thus truthfully depicted, were exasperated almost to frenzy. One woman threatened to have her put under bonds, and the life of the Kirkland family in Pinckney thereafter was the reverse of agreeable."[13]

Stung by the furor and smarting from her neighbors' accusations, but withal encouraged by the success of her initial undertaking, Kirkland began a second collection of western sketches. When these appeared, however, they showed the effects of the local "whirlwind of indignation" that had greeted *A New Home*.[14] "I am credibly informed," Kirkland declared at the outset, "that ingenious malice has been busy in finding substance for the shadows which were called up to give variety to the pages of 'A New Home,'—in short, that I have been accused of substituting personality for impersonation." "I regret it," she continued, "if, in drawing on experience, I have inadvertently given offence." That apology made, she nonetheless remained "horror-stricken" that "every creation of my not very lively imagi-nation instantly becomes a living, breathing, and very angry reality."[15]

As a result, Kirkland composed the two volumes of *Forest Life* (1842) under constraints unknown to its predecessor. "A stranger . . . writes with a freedom which a friend and neighbor of several years' standing must re-nounce entirely," she explained (*FL*, 2:233). And, in closing the second volume of *Forest Life*, she made clear the editings imposed by the role of "friend and neighbor": "It is impossible to describe minutely our own per-sonal experience without giving in some degree the experience of others; and this is a matter requiring careful handling, to say the least. . . . We may describe our own log-house, but woe betide us if we should make it appear that any body else lived in one! We may tell of our own blunders, but we must beware how we touch upon the blunders of others" (*FL*, 2:233).

Her response to these constraints was twofold. First, with characteristic humor, she took the "opportunity to declare that all the naughty and un-pleasant people—all the tattlers and mischief-makers,—all the litigious,—all the quarrelsome,—all the expectorant,—all the unneat,—all the un-handsome,—have emigrated to Iowa, Wiskonsan, or Texas, or some other far distant land . . . and that there is not . . . one single specimen of any of these classes remaining in this wide peninsula." Therefore, she insists, "any description of such characters which I may hazard in future must be mere phantoms of the brain, and cannot have been drawn from real life within these bounds" (*FL*, 1:34).

Her second response was the more serious—for it suggested a change in narrative focus. Where *A New Home* had promised "an unimpeachable transcript of reality" (*ANH*, p. v), *Forest Life* offered only "such general sketches of life and its chances and changes, as shall exempt me from any charge of being too correct or too sincere." To avoid "thus the sour glances of the conscious and the critical" (*FL*, 1:34), in other words, Kirkland had chosen now to sketch only "a general outline of truth, with a saving veil of acknowledged fiction" (*FL*, 2:232). Eschewing the immediacy of a single (perhaps identifiable) village, in *Forest Life* Kirkland describes "rambles . . . all over our beautiful state" (*FL*, 1:15); and rejecting the device of a narra-tor whose daily accommodations to western life necessarily involve inter-actions with real-world neighbors, Kirkland here uses her narrative voice to introduce interpolated love stories with western settings and clearly fic-titious personages—as with the Sibthorpes, a couple newly arrived from England, who have "purchased a farm about twenty miles from our cot-tage" with a view toward enjoying "the delights of American forest life" (*FL*, 1:207).

Even so, Kirkland presented her new volumes as "a continuation . . . to the sketches offered to the public" in *A New Home* (*FL*, 1:3). To be fair, *Forest Life* did attempt to continue patterns first introduced in that earlier volume. Identifying itself as an emigrants' manual, *Forest Life* repeated the generalized wisdom of "accommodat[ing] our ideas and habits to . . . present condition[s]" (*FL*, 2:147). It followed the romantically inclined Sibthorpes as they surmounted the incessant difficulties that recur "at every turn, in the country" (*FL*, 2:82). It described in minute detail the Michigan custom for tapping maple trees on the grounds that such details would be of interest to a reader who "is among those who are about emigrating to these fruitful wilds" (*FL* 2:212). And, as with *A New Home*, it directed itself especially to women of Kirkland's class. They, she warned, must learn how to tune their piano-forte on their own, before bringing it—or any instrument—"into the wilds" (*FL*, 2:122). And they would do well to outfit themselves with "a pair of very stout shoes, water proof," if they plan to enjoy a Michigan spring (*FL*, 2:142).

At the same time, *Forest Life* continued Kirkland's habit of measuring literary fabrications against frontier realities. Donning a pair of "magic glasses" in the first volume, she beholds a landscape of "poetical paradises" (*FL*, 1:17, 22). In making "a tour of observation" while wearing these "glorification spectacles" (*FL*, 1:17, 16), she relives the fantasies of books and operas. Amid the newly discovered "Arcadian simplicity, . . . cottages now appeared, roofed with golden thatch, . . . every casement . . . curtained with veined ivy, satin-leaved, and every door surrounded with its group of lovely mothers, and children" (*FL*, 1:21–22). The offspring of rough pioneers become "youths and maidens . . . of Arcadia" (*FL*, 1:20). When the glasses are broken, however, another picture comes into view. The pioneer women have "dingy locks" and "shoeless feet," while, in place of a pastoral cottage, they inhabit "a tumble-down log house, with its appropriate perfumes of milk-emptins, bread, and fried onions" (*FL*, 1:23).

It is, in effect, a playful reprise of lessons hard-won in *A New Home*. And no less pointedly than in *A New Home*, the breaking of the "magic glasses" in *Forest Life* is intended to shift the reader's focus from literary daydreams to the genuinely appealing features of the real "rural beauty" of "our green peninsula" (*FL*, 1:129). For, if in place of "girl[s] of seraphic beauty," Kirkland now encounters—without her glasses—"rustic maidens, looking coarse," the point to be learned is that these frontier damsels look "coarse only by contrast with the illusions of the past" (*FL*, 1:23–24). The danger of such illusions, she emphasizes, is that they inevitably blind one to the "ordinary beauty" that otherwise might be appreciated. Ruefully, then, the narrator turns her horses homeward, temporarily abandoning her proposed tour, and "resolutely closing my eyes upon prospects of merely ordinary beauty, which I knew would be, for the present, divested even of their real charms" (*FL*, 1 : 24).

But if the details of tapping maple trees or the admonitory fable of the "glorification spectacles" seem clearly directed at prospective emigrants from the east, *Forest Life*—in contrast to *A New Home*—appears at times as eagerly directed at Kirkland's western neighbors. Disappointed that too many of these do not "set some value on education for its own sake" (*FL*, 1 : 235), for example, she purposefully digresses from a story she is telling in order to argue for better schools. "If I can cheat some of my Western friends into a moment's attention to a subject so important to us" by thus digressing, she explains, "I shall rejoice" (*FL*, 1 : 236).

Elsewhere, Kirkland berates "the prevailing taste of the country" that insists on levelling all the trees in any area, thereby leaving "not a tree of the dense forest . . . to shade" home or schoolhouse "from the burning sun" (*FL*, 1 : 159). She points particularly to Pinckney's "'public square,'" once "intended to become . . . the glory of our village," now standing instead denuded, a "bare, open space" marked by the "blackened stumps" of girdled trees (*FL*, 1 : 42–43). What she fears, in short, is "the total extirpation of the forest." "The Western settler," she complains, looks upon the trees "as 'heavy timber,'—nothing more. He sees in them only obstacles which must be removed," and so intent is he on the clearing process that "not one tree, not so much as a bush, of natural growth, [can] be suffered to cumber the ground, or he fancies his work incomplete" (*FL*, 1 : 43).

In this appeal to western readers, *Forest Life* swerved dramatically from themes initiated in *A New Home*. For in trying to "cheat some of my Western friends" into attending to her disappointments, *Forest Life* revealed an author struggling, less and less certainly, with the problem of living on a landscape increasingly resistant to her more hopeful visions. To be sure, *A New Home* depicted "writhing serpents of living fire" (*ANH*, p. 190) invading the "incipient Eden" of the author's pole-fenced garden. Nonetheless, that first book had also closed with a catalogue of "progressive improvements" (*ANH*, p. 297). Precisely that progress, however, is what *Forest Life* cannot sustain. Following upon "the great commercial revulsion which succeeded the land-mania"—that is, the closing of the frontier banks and the depression that succeeded the Panic of 1837—in Kirkland's view, "every thing . . . has dwindled and looked blighted" (*FL*, 1 : 30).

Where *A New Home* boasted that "many of our ladies wear silk dresses on Sunday" (*ANH*, p. 317), *Forest Life* tells us that "the men wear their old coats; the women turn and alter their faded dresses; and the children are taught that it is wholesome to go barefoot" (*FL*, 1 : 30). Where *A New Home* announced that "loggeries are becoming scarce within our limits" and pointed to several Montacute women who could finally afford "as many as three cows; some few, carpets and shanty-kitchens; and one or two, piano-fortes and silver tea-sets" (*ANH*, pp. 317, 313), *Forest Life* assaults us again with the "uncomfortable though strictly neat and decent poverty" of an original log cabin (*FL*, 1:90). Where *A New Home* welcomed the construction of a local school and "a new meeting-house" with "a settled minister" (*ANH*, p. 317), *Forest Life* deplores the fact that "efforts . . . toward intellectual advancement" along the frontier are as yet "few and feeble" (*FL*, 1:215–16). And, finally, where *A New Home* praised "the roses and honey-suckles" with which frontier women adorned their homes (*ANH*, p. 316), *Forest Life* "wish[es] our people cared more for the beautiful!" (*FL*, 1:41).

Undercutting the purported simple "continuation . . . to the sketches offered to the public more than two years ago" (*FL*, 1:3), in other words, was a subtext of radically different implications. The "incipient Eden" of the earlier work had not been realized, and, with palpable impatience, in *Forest Life* Kirkland declares, "we ought all to have good gardens by this time" (*FL*, 1:52).

What she apparently came to accept as she composed her chapters for *Forest Life* was that the very appeal of early pioneering precluded the Edenic cultivated garden of her desire. "For our neighbors seem bit with the strange madness of ceaseless transit, flitting mostly westward," she observed. "They purchase a lot or two of 'government land;' build a log-house, fence a dozen acres or so, plough half of them, girdle the trees, and then sell out to a new comer. . . . The pioneer is then ready for a new purchase, a new clearing, and a new sale" (*FL*, 1:27). The consequence of this "nomadic life" (*FL*, 1:28) was that the early pioneer necessarily abandoned "all the dear delights of home; all idea of providing domestic comforts, all interest in public improvements; [and] all local attachments and neighborly sympathies" (*FL*, 1:27). In short, by always believing "that he can get twice as much good land . . . where the country is quite new" (*FL*, 1:37), the farmer along the agricultural frontier gave up the settled commitments that tended to allow a landscape to be marked by the signs of women's presence. Frequent removals denied his wife the leisure to seek out "eglantines and wood-vine, or wild-cucumber . . . to shade the windows"; nor was she in one place long enough to want to set out "a few apple-trees . . . lilacs and currant-bushes" (*ANH*, p. 248). The fact was, as Kirkland sadly understood, "the universal freshness and newness of [this] world" (*FL*, 1:213) had been preempted by those for whom "the alluring prospects held forth by the 'West'" included either high romantic adventure or else the endless pursuit of "grass growing higher than a giant's head, and fields of corn through which a mounted horseman might gallop unobserved" (*FL*, 1:35). Of a more modest Eden cultivated with fruits and flowers, they did not dream.

With something approaching desperation, therefore, Kirkland nonetheless attempted to offer versions of a frontier Eve. "'To rove in the summer woods and read or gather wild flowers'" is said to make "'a paradise for'" Florella Sibthorpe (*FL*, 1:207). And a neighbor, Mrs. Ainsworth, is said to have been converted by a visit to relatives in the east from "a desperate utilitarian" (*FL*, 1:49) into the happy designer of flower beds and flowered walkways. Echoing Mary Clavers's enthusiasms in *A New Home*, Florella Sibthorpe delights in "the early bulbs . . . and a beautiful perennial, here called the Ohio bluebell," which decorate the Michigan woodlands in early spring (*FL* 2:142). Mrs. Ainsworth, by contrast, gathers "acres of happiness" (*FL*, 1:54) by planting her own garden. Having brought back with her from New York State "a load of treasures" of seeds and bulbs, Mrs. Ainsworth persuades her grumbling spouse to "delay his wheat-sowing until roses and honey-suckles, and peonies and tulips, with multitudes of their fair or fragrant brethren, were duly committed to the bounteous soil" (*FL*, 1:51–52).

The anecdotes about her good neighbor offered Kirkland a pretext for inserting two pages of practical gardening advice into her text—advice, we may now suppose, addressed to westerners and prospective eastern emigrants alike. Quite pointedly, Kirkland pictures Mrs. Ainsworth as an "excellent example" who would, "it is to be hoped, wake up the whole village" to the advantages of planting gardens (*FL*, 1:52). In that statement, however, lay the admission that Michigan as yet harbored too few Eves for Kirkland's incipient visions. Even Florella Sibthorpe—whose name suggests the fantasies her presence would imply—returns permanently to the manicured parks of an English manor house in the second volume.

There is, then, a dying fall to the cadence of *Forest Life*. Writing in these volumes as "one whose lot is cast in, for better for worse, with the settlers of the backwoods" (*FL*, 1:5), Kirkland nonetheless betrayed "the yearning with which the dweller in the far distant wilderness looks back upon the land of his early love; the land of society, of conversation . . . the land of churches, of books, of music, of pictures" (*FL*, 1:10). While trying to hold fast to the image of "the calm, contemplative quiet of a country life" (*FL*, 2:230), she revealed instead her own "lingering mental martyrdom" (*FL*, 1:122) in a frontier society that expressed only "a strong prejudice against educated people" (*FL*, 1:215). Affecting still the tone of the emigrants' manual, she continued to invite her readers to "this great, growing Western country" (*FL*, 2:232). But no longer could she pretend that the hardships and crudities of western life might "prove very enticing to the educated and refined" (*FL*, 2:234).

Not surprisingly, *Forest Life* was the last collection she would publish as "one whose lot is cast in . . . with the settlers of the backwoods" (*FL*, 1:5). Disaffected, disappointed, and having lost much of their initial investment, the Kirklands left Michigan for New York City in 1843. By then, Caroline Kirkland had spent eight years in Michigan—two in Detroit and six in the frontier village of Pinckney.

Her literary reputation having been established by the success of *A New Home* and then secured by good sales (if not unqualified critical acclaim) for *Forest Life*, Kirkland continued to capitalize on her western associations by contributing miscellaneous "Western sketches" to popular magazines and to giftbook anthologies. Increasingly, however, her sketches turned to fiction—mostly love stories and moralizing domestic tales—and the western material was moved from center stage to backdrop. To be sure, this pattern was already evident in the two short stories that fleshed out the second volume of *Forest Life*. One of these gave voice to yet another plea for increased educational opportunities along the frontier; the other described the method of boiling syrup in a "sugar-bush." But while both contained accurate details of fire-prone log cabins and frontier housekeeping, none of this western material was finally intrinsic to the plot structures of misunderstandings, family feuds, and lovers' quarrels. The characters were stock figures from the popular ladies' magazine fiction of the day, and the story lines could as easily have been set among the farms of western New York State or rural New England. Whereas in *A New Home*, the story of Cora and Everard Hastings was very much a fable of the frontier Adam and Eve learning to identify their proper landscape, in *Forest Life* the western setting for the two love stories is merely a given. The young couples of that second collection are never required to grapple with its meaning.

Still, *Forest Life*, with its portrait of a blighted Eden, was not wholly without the fidelity for which *A New Home* had been so justly praised. The sketches composed after *Forest Life*—those written for magazine publication and, most especially, those printed in Kirkland's third collection, *Western Clearings* (1846)—cannot lay claim to that same fidelity, however. Though its chapters were, she claimed, "all written at the West,"[16] for the most part, *Western Clearings* turned away from marshes and mudholes, fire-prone cabins, and neglected town squares to offer, in their place, a disconnected assemblage of romantic nature descriptions, humorous character sketches, stories of young love, and thinly veiled morality tales. The voice of Mary Clavers recurs in the recapitulation of the oddities of western dialect, in a fleeting nod toward the social and physical adjustments demanded of a population "contriving to live under the pressure of extreme difficulties" (*WC*, p. vii), and in an opening chapter on the land fever and its accompanying unscrupulous speculators. (This gave Kirkland an opportunity to vent her personal anger at those she blamed for her family's financial misfortunes in Michigan.) Only in her prefatory remarks did Kirkland locate the mood of this text in relation to its predecessors. For what she inadvertently acknowledged there was her sense that her first book's "incipient Eden" was now a dream whose time had passed irrevocably. The stories in *Forest Life*, Kirkland made clear, were meant to be "illustrative of a land that *was once* an El Dorado" (*WC*, p. vi, my emphasis).

Readers, of course, continued to expect western sketches from her pen, and, for her part, Kirkland asserted that she might write about the west "for years to come, without fear of exhausting its peculiarities" (*WC*, p. vi). But, in fact, the longer she resided in the urban east, the less she harkened back to the agricultural west. Increasingly she moved into the field of domestic sentimental fiction, and only now and again did she return to the disillusionments of western life as subject matter. In a magazine article published in January 1848, she acknowledged the human and economic devastations of a "hard winter" on the frontier.[17] That June, she reworked materials from *A New Home* to offer yet another catalogue of primitive arrangements within a frontier "log-house."[18] And, in 1850, called upon to review Edward Bulwer-Lytton's paean to emigration to Australia, *The Caxtons*, she made of it an occasion to question the "heartiness of approval which makes light of the roughness of life in the wilderness."[19]

Censuring Bulwer-Lytton for his romanticized portrayal of British emigration to the Australian frontier in much the same way she had once quarreled with James Hall and Charles Fenno Hoffman, Kirkland reminded readers that "wolf-hunts, and bear-fights, and deer-shooting" might make "charming books," but they offered only "a poor preparation for the reality of life in the wilderness." Repeating the urge to correct such faulty images—the urge that had once proven the impetus for *A New Home*—she proceeded to offer her readers "a practical notion of forest life," warning them of the "wearisome" and "daily cares for mere subsistence" that marked most new settlers' experience of a frontier.[20]

Although she continued to write and publish actively until her death in 1864, never again did Caroline Kirkland strike a note of such gritty realism. The note she no longer sang, however, was to become the resounding chord of an American literary realism that would emerge after her death, in the decades following the Civil War. And, though the fact is not often enough remarked, Caroline Kirkland was the direct progenitor of that bold new direction in American letters. For, in attempting to follow "the path marked out by his mother," emulating *A New Home* and parts of *Forest Life* in his desire to tell "the truth, unadorned, and unvarnished,"[21] Joseph Kirkland composed *Zury: The Meanest Man in Spring County*

(1887). A milestone in the rise of American realism, Joseph Kirkland's "novel of Western rural life"[22] echoed its inheritance on almost every page. With buildings "glar[ing] under the pitiless sunshine, asking in vain for the shadows of trees which had been on the ground before any houses intruded, but which had been unwisely sacrificed, leaving only ugly stumps where they had stood,"[23] Joseph Kirkland's fictional Wayback recalled Caroline Kirkland's pseudonymous Montacute. It was a portrait of the harshness of western life that was to have no little impact on Howells, just as it was the power of what he had learned from his mother that gave Joseph Kirkland the authority to urge Hamlin Garland to leave off journalism and take up the cause of realism in fiction.

Had she lived to see that legacy, it is doubtful Caroline Kirkland would have recognized it as her own. When she began *A New Home*, after all, she thought herself following the model of the "charming sketches of [English] village life" (*ANH*, p. vi) composed by Mary Russell Mitford in her five successive volumes, *Our Village* (London, 1824–32). What Kirkland discovered was that the fixed social hierarchy and settled countryside of rural England did not easily translate to a fledgling frontier outpost with "common-place people" (*ANH*, p. 193). Despairing of successfully imitating her chosen model, therefore, she excused herself by explaining of Michigan: "Here are neither great ladies nor humble cottagers. I cannot bring to my aid either the exquisite boudoir of the one class, . . . nor yet the cot of the other more simple but not less elegant, surrounded with clustering eglantine and clematis" (*ANH*, pp. 193–94).

Yet she never entirely gave up such images. That she found many of her neighbors more rude than charming and, in place of a thatched cottage, went visiting in "an ordinary log house" that was often "dilapidated" (*ANH*, p. 195), Kirkland never hid. But she was also quick to depict, when she could, the "handsome and picturesque-looking" domestic arrangements of Cora and Everard Hastings (*ANH*, p. 255) or "a honeysuckle on the porch" of some improbable farmhouse in the wilds (*ANH*, p. 149). No less eagerly, she included the kinds of humorous character sketches and sentimental love stories that had helped to make Mitford's volumes so enormously popular on both sides of the Atlantic.

From the outset, however, Kirkland's intentions had differed somewhat from Mitford's. Where Mitford sought merely to entertain, Kirkland sought also to enlighten. Reacting against the fallacious expectations invited by "Hoffman's tour, . . . Captain Hall's 'graphic delineations,'" and Chateaubriand's fantasy wilderness "always in a Floridian clime" (*ANH*, pp. 12, 83), she had embarked on "a sort of 'Emigrant's Guide'" (*ANH*, p. v) to prepare others for the intractable realities that these books suppressed. As with its contemporaneous incarnations in England and France, then, American literary realism—in the hands of Caroline Kirkland—derived from a commitment to measure the verisimilitude "of common-place occurrences" (*ANH*, p. 8) against the delusions of romantic exaggeration.

What distinguished this first sustained expression of American realism from its European cousins was that it derived, as well, from a *woman's* need to reject (for herself and for others of her sex) the available *male* fantasies. "I have never seen a cougar—nor been bitten by a rattlesnake," she warned at the outset of *A New Home* (*ANH*, p. 8). And then continuing the theme in *Forest Life*, she declared that "no wild adventures,—no blood-curdling hazards,—no romantic incidents,—could occur within my limited and sober sphere" (*FL*, 1 : 10). What her "limited and sober sphere" did embrace were the daily "homely toils"[24] about which men's writings had remained so consistently silent. In offering to explore the housekeeping chores and social habits of a frontier village, however, Kirkland saw herself not as any innovator but as a writer simply extending the concerns of eastern ladies' magazines to western neighborhoods. The conventions of contemporary women's literature, we must remember, Kirkland did not question and never discarded.

These facts of her literary genesis perhaps explain why Kirkland's legacy took such different shape in the male realists and the female sentimentalists who followed her lead to western materials. In her early volumes, especially, the male tradition of high romantic western adventure had been challenged at its very core, and in response that tradition eventually rejected its inherited exaggerations and turned to realism. Women writers, by contrast, saw in Kirkland's work only an invitation to turn their attention from eastern townhouses and New England farmhouses to "a home on the outskirts of civilization" (*ANH*, p. 8). In the view of her female contemporaries, Kirkland had provided the kinds of details that would enable them now to locate the plots of domestic piety in a log cabin on a far frontier.

Thus, the most immediate impact of Kirkland's success was not that it introduced an element of realism to the literary depiction of the west, but that it made the west available for literary treatment by women. Until the publication of *A New Home*, even those women with literary aspirations who resided in the west, for the most part, had shied away from it as subject matter.[25] But after the enthusiastic notices for *A New Home* in 1839 and the brisk sales of *Forest Life* in 1842, Margaret Fuller felt encouraged to compose *A Summer on the Lakes* (1844) to stand beside Charles Fenno Hoffman's *A Winter in the West* (1835). And Eliza Farnham, befriended and encouraged by Kirkland in New York, was emboldened thereby to let her own experience of *Life in Prairie Land* (1846) compete with Washington Irving's *A Tour on the Prairies* (1835) for some share of the public's attention.

In a period when most Americans' ideas of the west were molded by male writers, these were not insignificant contributions. But the decade that followed upon Kirkland's last attempt to persuade readers that "bushlife lacks the pleasant stimulant with which the imagination is apt to invest it"[26]—the decade that Fred Lewis Pattee has forever denominated "the feminine fifties"[27]—that hothouse antebellum decade saw the full flowering of Kirkland's influence in the pages of the sentimental fictionists who relocated their domestic fantasies westward. Like Kirkland, they offered heroines schooled in the world's harshness. And like Kirkland, they too claimed "accuracy and fidelity" for what they composed.[28] Nonetheless, in the progressive blunting of rude frontier realities that transpired between Alice Cary's *Clovernook* (1852) and Caroline Soule's *The Pet of the Settlement* (1860), these writers replicated the essential pattern of Kirkland's career by once again retreating from the burden of fidelity. Their reasons, of course, were not the same as Kirkland's. Kirkland fled a blighted western Eden; the domestic fictionists, in their turn, fled a slavery-tainted south and an industrializing northeast. For them, the frontier was the only "incipient Eden" left to imagine. And so, following Kirkland—albeit from different motives—the domestic fictionists, too, moved inexorably from realism to sentiment and from "an unimpeachable transcript of reality" (*ANH*, p. v) to "a saving veil of . . . fiction" (*FL*, 2:232).

> *They carry their carpetbags and trunks*
> *with clothes, dishes, the family pictures;*
> *they think they will make an order*
> *like the old one, sow miniature orchards,*
> *carve children and flocks out of wood*

> —Margaret Atwood,
> *The Journals of Susanna Moodie*

Book Three
Repossessing Eden, 1850–1860

The first locomotive across the Alleghenies, about 1840. Courtesy Library of Congress

I am lost
near home

—Marie Harris,
Interstate

8 The Domestic Fantasy Goes West

In 1852 the Ohio-born writer Alice Cary pictured herself at a window in Cincinnati, looking out across the Ohio River toward the Kentucky shore. "I cannot see the blue green nor the golden green of the oat and wheat fields, that lie beyond these infant cities, nor the dark ridge of woods . . . along their borders," she complained, "for . . . the soaked earth this morning sends up its coal-scented and unwholesome fogs, obscuring the lovely picture that would else present itself."[1] In that image she captured the anxiety of a nation.

By the middle of the nineteenth century, Americans had to struggle to preserve their shared self-image as a nation of independent yeoman farmers. Everywhere there was the inescapable evidence of an increasingly industrial urbanization made possible by a technology forged of steam and iron. Though the collective mind's eye anxiously looked toward an expanding agrarian west, as though in confirmation of the original eighteenth-century dream, contemporary reality betrayed a growing centripetal movement toward the town, the factory, and the city. To be sure, the great bulk of the population remained on the land. Even so, by 1840, the structures of self-subsistence agriculture, organized around commercial towns and household industries, were already yielding before the beginnings of a capitalistic and industrial economy.

Small farmers in the northeast who had been hurt by the financial Panic of 1837 now poured into the cities and factory towns, there joining recent European immigrants to form a new class of urban poor. Fortunes made in manufactures and railroads bought up once productive farmland, converting it into summer homes or grand resorts for the urban rich.[2] And, linking eastern and western markets through a proliferating network of railroads and canals, steam and iron created "infant cities" whose effluvia threatened to obscure even "the oat and wheat fields" of the agricultural west.

Popular resistance to these changes resulted in a wave of anti-urbanism that first surfaced at the tail end of the 1830s. James Fenimore Cooper perfectly caught the mood in *Home as Found* (1838) when he pictured Eve Effingham, "with a feeling of delight, . . . escap[ing] from" a New York City that, in her view, "contains so much . . . that is unfit for any place, in order to breathe the pure air, and enjoy the tranquil pleasure of the country."[3] With the 1840s and 1850s that initial response grew into "a sizeable body of journalistic fiction depicting the modern city as a place of lurid sin and crime, economic debasement, and heartless chicanery," while, as Janis Stout points out, the countryside remained, at least imaginatively, "the chief stronghold of sobriety and virtue."[4]

In 1859 Nathaniel Hawthorne incomprehensibly reiterated outdated Jacksonian delusions to declare that the United States was "a country where there is . . . [not] anything but a commonplace prosperity, in broad and simple daylight."[5] In fact, the early statistical data coming out of official commissions and benevolent societies suggested otherwise. A Philadelphia report of 1854 showed 700 professional beggars in that city and 1,800 vagrant children. An official New York State report a year later counted one pauper, living on state charity, for every seventeen persons. In 1853 Massachusetts had 26,000 on relief rolls, one tenth of them under fourteen years of age.[6] And in the cities of the northeast generally, where $1,000 a year represented an average middle-class income, only 1 percent of the population earned over $800.

If these newly emergent signs of industrial growing pains left no perceivable imprint on Hawthorne's fiction, they did nonetheless become the subject matter of that "mob of scribbling women" whom Hawthorne had earlier damned.[7] Ann Sophia Stephens followed the influx of rural people to the city in her 1854 novel, *Fashion and Famine*.[8] A year later, in her most popular work, *The Old Homestead*, she depicted, first, family life eroded by the destructive forces of the city—including official corruption, callous institutions, and the patronage system—and then, in the second part of the novel, she focused on a countryside devastated by the impact of big-city life and wealth, its population absorbed by urban industry and its farms turned into summer playgrounds for vacationing New Yorkers.[9] Novels such as these belied Hawthorne's sanguine optimism.

These novels also contributed to the rabid anti-urbanism by anatomizing the city as a place where the awful realities of class division simply could not be overlooked. Their casts of characters typically included both the very rich and the very poor, with few novels missing the opportunity for scenes of dramatic, intentionally sentimental contrast. In her 1857 novel, *Mabel Vaughan*, for example, Susanna Maria Cummins had her heiress heroine encounter "a little boy, ragged, dirty, and bending beneath the weight of an old basket filled with half-burnt coals," which he accidentally spills onto the cold and wintry New York street.[10] Later that evening, as Mabel Vaughan warms herself before "a brilliant fire" in her elegant mansion, she hears "the cold wind whistle round the corner of the house, [and] she thought again of the little boy and the spilt coals." "Painful visions," we are told, "rose before her of dreary garrets, where half-starved children and despairing mothers crouched beneath scanty coverings, and cried and shivered with the cold" (*MV*, pp. 128, 131).

The frequency of such episodes notwithstanding, it would be a mistake to conclude that the so-called "domestic sentimentalists" of mid-nineteenth-century America were thereby agitating, through their fiction, for radical social change. The manipulation of a reader's sentiments, to be sure, represented a genuine political tool for writers otherwise disenfranchised. Indeed, in some respects, mid-nineteenth-century sentimental fiction may be seen as *the* political strategy of the disenfranchised, moving its readers to tears in hopes that the sight of those tears might then move husbands and fathers, sons and brothers, to more public forms of responsiveness. Be that as it may, however, the writers of domestic fictions tended toward amelioration rather than solution. Though they elaborated the evil effects of the transformation from decentralized agrarian to industrial capitalistic structures—and often with a brutal realism—they did not analyze the transformation itself.

Their focus, instead, was on what they perceived to be the moral challenge to the heart of their fictional vision. The corrupting superfluities of city life or, conversely, the unremitting poverty of the rural or urban poor seemed to these writers to threaten their vision of the American home that, ideally, was to function as the moral, ethical, and spiritual center of family and nation alike, the nursery of republican virtue, and the haven from the masculine competitiveness of the marketplace. Thus, although 1848 saw the first Paris Commune, the publication of the Communist Manifesto and, in the United States at Seneca Falls, the first women's rights convention, the women who composed the enormously popular domestic fictions of the 1850s, for the most part, continued to concern themselves with consequences rather than underlying causes. Caroline Kirkland probably voiced the views of most in this sisterhood when she attacked George Sand for being the misguided "flatterer of all who are discontented with their own lot, and who find gratification in shifting the responsibility from themselves to society and its institutions and abuses."[11]

Because they did not choose to analyze "society and its institutions and abuses," these writers inevitably turned toward the romantic in inventing solutions to the difficulties elaborated in their fictions. A young girl's pious patience might, in the end, win some curmudgeonly authority figure to kindness; a religious conversion might salvage a sinking brother and thereby recover the family's farm or business; some other fortuitous reversal of fortune or even the advent of a virtuous hero could move a plot toward happy resolution. But by the 1850s these no longer seemed sufficient solutions where whole communities were being disrupted and uprooted. And so a number of novelists began to look toward what Ann Sophia Stephens called "the green west,"[12] as though seeking a geographical locale in which the social ills evident in the northeast might forever be evaded.

Removing a heroine to the west was nothing new in women's fiction, of course. As early as 1837, Catharine Maria Sedgwick delivered one young married couple from New York "to the land of promise—the indefinite *West*" in *Live and Let Live; Or, Domestic Service Illustrated.*[13] The fictional removals of the 1850s, however, had about them an urgency that Sedgwick never hinted at; and they portrayed, in vivid detail, as she did not, the idealized "Western home . . . the blessed haven of rest, which afforded . . . a safe and welcome shelter from the storm of adversity and trial" (*MV*, p. 505). During the antebellum decade, the "prairie home," with "its bare white walls, its plain brick hearth, its low-roofed rooms," thus became the emblematic moral counterweight to impoverished country homesteads or city mansions and tenements alike, teaching its inhabitants "that happiness is independent of ornament; [and] that contentment brings joy to the humblest fireside" (*MV*, p. 505).

Decades of eager western promotionalism—composed both by women and by men—had had their intended effect. The domestic fictionist who relocated her characters to Illinois or Iowa essentially accepted Charles Fenno Hoffman's earlier assurance of "the ease with which a man can here support a family as a farmer."[14] And not a few of these writers followed Mary Austin Holley in depicting a physical terrain "literally flowing with milk and honey," its bounty generating a social Eden where "there are no poor people . . . and none rich."[15] Indeed, one of the characters in Cummins's *Mabel Vaughan* repeats a favorite refrain from these promotional tracts when she insists of Illinois that "'every effort is sure to find its reward in a land which makes such a rich return for the labor bestowed on it'" (*MV*, p. 355).

It was not only writers dismayed at the increasing industrialization of the northeast who relocated their characters westward, however. The agricultural frontier held an equivalent imaginative appeal for novelists appalled at the dissolution of family bonds (for both blacks and whites) under the chattel slavery system then dominant in the plantation south. Especially following the 1849 formation of the Free-Soil party, pledged to keep slavery out of the territories and newer states, Emma D. E. N. Southworth and Mary Hayden Pike repeatedly showed their native southerners "mak[ing] a new home for themselves in the West." A west that, as

Nina Baym notes, stood in their novels "for salvation from the feudal South."[16] Typically, the hero of Southworth's *India: The Pearl of Pearl River* (1856) frees his slaves in Mississippi and then goes west to establish a newspaper called "The True Freeman."[17] The heroine of Pike's *Ida May* (1854) similarly frees her slaves and then heads west with the intention of establishing a center for the training and education of former slaves.[18] In each story, moreover, the free west is credited with making possible what the slaveholding south could not: here the characters' "home is a very happy one" (*I*, p. 401), and loving relationships thrive.

Still, it must be emphasized that, for most of these writers, their commitment to the frontier west derived from an ideology that was inherently nostalgic. At the heart of their western vision was a fantasy of home that, though they did not acknowledge it, harked back to an earlier era. For, as a newly industrializing nation was fast eroding the economic functions of the home and consequently narrowing the scope of women's activity in general, the domestic novel of western relocation still suggested that the home, and particularly women's traditional role within it, held tangible significance. The fact was, by the middle decades of the nineteenth century, the middle class woman—the main consumer of domestic fiction—was undergoing what Susan Phinney Conrad calls "a status revolution." Her "social status prohibited [the middle-class woman] . . . from wage work in the new cottage industries and sealed her off from that female world of mill and factory," while, at the same time, "the professional training and certification becoming essential for work in medicine, law, and higher education denied her access to these fields." As a result, Conrad concludes, "in direct and ironic contrast to tenets of equality and increased opportunity voiced by Jacksonian America, her opportunities were dwindling."[19]

A number of women spoke out against the shift from the earlier division of labor according to sex to the increasing allotment (or even elimination) of labor according to class. As early as 1835, for example, in her *The History of the Condition of Women, in Various Ages and Nations*, Lydia Maria Child criticized social attitudes that looked down upon middle-class women's gainful employment, insisting that "active industry" implied no "bar to gentility."[20] By 1852, feminist activist Paulina Wright Davis was telling audiences that, where the middle class was concerned, the contemporary woman had no real "function" because "manufactures" had usurped her traditional duties, removing these from home to factory.[21]

Catharine Beecher's solution to the dwindling status of middle-class women was to raise housewifery to "woman's distinctive profession" and to inveigh against an increasing tendency to turn over household chores "to hirelings."[22] Summarizing two decades of speaking and writing on these subjects for an 1865 article in *Harper's New Monthly Magazine*,

Beecher defined the new domestic professionalism as "includ[ing] three departments—the training of the mind in childhood, the nursing of infants and of the sick, and all the handicrafts and management of the family state."[23] Beecher's emphases, however, only served to rationalize—and by rationalizing, reinforce—the pervasive *sentimental* domestic ideology of the day.

Addressing a largely comfortable and highly literate middle-class readership, editors of fashionable ladies' magazines and domestic novelists alike suggested that, by eschewing the world of trade and commerce, the home had become something better: a kind of moral and spiritual "beacon-light" in a crass and materialistic world. In one of the more successful novels of 1846, a happy husband writes to a friend that "'when I am absent during the day, and perplexed with the multitudinous cares of an extensive mercantile concern, my home rises before my mind's eye, like a beacon-light to the tempest-tossed mariner. The sweet, consoling thought, that I have such a haven of peace and love soothes and hushes my perturbed spirit.'"[24]

The woman within that home was no less sentimentalized. Catharine Beecher might see her as a "professional," with necessary practical tasks to perform; but the more popular view rendered her the leisured repository for the culture's morals, emotions, and spiritual well-being. Indeed, from the 1830s on, as Americans experienced what Nancy Cott has noted as an accelerated "shift of production and exchange away from the household,"[25] middle-class women were simultaneously enjoined to shift their attention away from "money-making." "Our men are sufficiently money-making," announced Sarah Josepha Hale in the Boston *Ladies' Magazine* of 1830.[26] By 1850, now the editor of *Godey's Lady's Book*, Hale continued the theme by asking that her reader forego complaints regarding her diminished economic status and realize that "hers is the empire of the affections."[27] The influential *North American Review* employed a similar vocabulary when it asked women to "leave the rude commerce of camps and the soul-hardening struggling of political power to the harsher spirit of men," while taking up, instead, "the domain of the moral affections [and] the empire of the heart."[28]

Clearly, it was a rhetoric designed to reconcile middle-class and wealthy women to the fact that they had essentially lost their traditional functions and, in their place, been relegated to largely ornamental roles. "If there be any thing likely to banish the fiend *ennui* from the dwellings of women of fortune," recommended Caroline Kirkland in 1854, "it is the habit of assuming a moderate share of the daily cares which go to make home home. To do every thing by proxy, . . . deputing our duties and privileges to hirelings," she warned, "is to deprive ourselves of a thousand wholesome, cheerful, innocent interests."[29]

The problem was that the very design of home was also undergoing rapid change. The capacious fireplace traditionally associated with making "home home" and the hearth traditionally associated with women's tasks within the home—these were now disappearing amid the new technology. In an age when popular magazines, even in their titles, continued to link *Hearth and Home*,[30] there was a peculiar distress attached to the fact that the hearth and fireplace were slowly giving way before the gas furnace. Catharine Beecher railed against the change, ostensibly for health reasons, complaining that "as wealth and luxury have increased . . . fire-places have been shut up, and closed stoves and furnaces introduced."[31] The writers of domestic fiction, on the other hand, appreciated the symbolic meanings of household arrangements and so found alternate ways of rejecting the innovation. Associating it with the cold pretensions of excessive wealth, they always made clear that, for them, "a furnace in the cellar" did not a home make.

One of Caroline Kirkland's rare longer fictions, for example, follows a young woman's progress from the happy but simple home of the aunt and uncle who raised her to the elegant mansion of her wealthy and indulgent husband. For her first Christmas as a new wife she insists on inviting her aunt and uncle to dinner, rather than allowing them to orchestrate the festivities, as usual, at "their own board crowned with good cheer." In the end, Kirkland writes, the young bride "prevailed," and the aunt and uncle "exchanged their comfortable dining-room, with sprigs of box stuck in the window-panes, branches of hemlock and wreaths of green forest fringe about the pictures, and a bright, hospitable Christmas fire burning in the grate, for their niece's too magnificent *suite*, curtained with satin and lace till one could not distinguish the snow falling thick through the air without, and warmed by a furnace in the cellar till you felt uncertain whether a fan or a fire were most desirable."[32] In this passage, there is no doubt as to which is the house and which the home; or what pertains to either.

"The story of feminine trials and triumphs," which Nina Baym observes "dominated woman's writing in the 1850s,"[33] must therefore be seen as a literary response born of the anxiety attendant upon rapidly changing role expectations and accelerating technological transitions. In the face of increasingly restricted employment opportunities for middle-class women, "slave wages" for working-class women,[34] quickened industrialization, spreading urbanization, and still carrying with it the memory of the economic upheavals following the Panic of 1837, the domestic fiction of mid-century America sought solace and security in the image of the home "as a moral repository in an immoral society . . . [and] a bastion of stability in a changing, fragmentary world."[35]

The very factors that produced such a fiction also conspired to make the frontier west an attractive setting for its fantasy. To begin with, current wisdom pictured the west—and especially the frontier—as largely agricultural. For most Americans, this implied not only the absence of mills and factories but the absence of those glaring disparities in wealth that had begun to mark the northeast; for novelists like E.D.E.N. Southworth and Mary Hayden Pike, moreover, the small farms of the frontier promised a society untouched by the blot of slavery.³⁶ In an age that looked with suspicion on the phenomenal fortunes apparently made overnight by factory and mill owners, the west suggested an escape from superfluity, an escape from wealth gained only by investment, and an escape from the exploited labor of the poor. In an era when fewer than 2 percent of the rich were not born rich, the raw frontier could still be fantasized as a realm that might nurture that quintessential American hero, the self-made man.

Above all else, however, the frontier west gave these novelists the chance to displace the gilded mansions and sordid tenements of New York, the dormitory dwellings of the New England mills, and the columned plantation houses of the south with the "very comfortable and pleasant . . . log cabin home." No novel missed the chance to extol its virtues or ignored the opportunity to picture the happy family gathered cozily "about the hearthstone." "Yes, very comfortable and pleasant was that log cabin home," these novels all averred, "and seldom in the splendid parlors of our Atlantic cities does a happier [family] gather about the hearthstone, than that which, after the supper was over, drew around that ample fire-place." In this scene from Caroline Soule's *The Pet of the Settlement* (1860), the daughter of the house is pictured "knitting" clothes that are essential—not merely ornamental—for the family, while her father tends both the fire and a baby, "trotting [the child] on his foot 'to Banbury Cross.'"³⁷

It is an image of relaxed domesticity. But it is an image with a point. The domesticity that these novelists pictured in the new west was a domesticity in which women and men alike played important (if different) roles. The father who once spent all his evenings away from home in the counting houses of the city now delights in entertaining children by the hearthside and in taking his family for picnics on the flowering prairies. At the same time, the women in these cabins are given real, but never arduous, work to perform. Theirs is a role that keeps them happily and usefully "busy from early dawn to twilight" (*PS*, p. 196).

Significantly, the "three departments" that Catherine Beecher had entrusted to women are only played out in these novels once the family removes to the west. While the family remains in the east, by contrast, we rarely see the women characters work (unless they are poor), and more often than not, we see them wasting their time in frivolous social pursuits. To the functioning of the log cabin home, however, the woman is essential—as essential as the "ample fire-place" where she does her cooking or boils water for washing, and around which (like herself) the family gathers. Thus, in an age when many middle-class women experienced themselves increasingly displaced from any real responsibility in running a household, the domestic novel of western relocation claimed contemporaneity through the frontier setting, but all the while harked back to patterns symbolic of earlier times—patterns that reestablished women's meaningful centrality in the domestic scene.

No less important, the supposedly unformed frontier settlements offered these novelists a chance to project their idealized notions of community itself. It was, needless to say, a community informed by the domestic ethos in which the values of home and hearth, rather than the market economy, organized the larger social structure. When a small child is found abandoned on the Iowa prairie in Caroline Soule's *The Pet of the Settlement*, for instance, it is not a single household but the settlement as a whole that adopts her, with all the "men, women and children" crying out, "'I'll do my part, I'll do my part'" (*PS*, p. 58). Older widows and single men in these novels are similarly adopted by neighboring families who offer them not only a room of their own but the affectionate appellation of "grandmother" or "uncle." Exploiting the familial metaphors inherent in women's promotional writings, novelists like Caroline Soule thus sought to portray communities in which the inhabitants gave palpable meaning to Farnham's description of westerners acting together as "the sons and daughters of this land"; and the characters in these novels repeatedly bear out Holley's description of pioneer Texans as "universally kind and hospitable."[38]

The urgent need for such fantasies, of course, explains these writers' penchant for ignoring what Caroline Kirkland had earlier tried to teach, or what the daily newspapers everywhere declared about the west. Land speculators, absentee landlords, or moneylenders charging anywhere from 30 to 60 percent annual interest do not appear in the westernized domestic fictions.[39] Their representations of the west are never informed by the fact that, as early as 1836, President Andrew Jackson was expressing his alarm at the growing "monopoly of the public lands in the hands of speculators and capitalists, to the injury of the actual settlers in the new States, and of emigrants in search of new homes."[40] Nor did they hint that Jackson's alarm had been well grounded: of the 38,000,000 acres of public lands sold between 1835 and 1837, 29,000,000—that is, almost three-quarters of the whole—were acquired by speculators.[41] Absentee landlords and exploited tenants became the rule, rather than the exception, in places like the prairie counties of central Illinois. And by 1846 an Indiana farmer observed that one-third of the voters in his state were "tenants or day laborers or young men who have acquired no property."[42] In the novels of the domestic fantasists, by contrast, the families relocated westward are universally prosperous, and most characters reap "golden harvests" (*MV*, p. 378).

Refusing also to acknowledge the stark reality of a crude first cabin, constructed of "logs and nothing else, the fire made on the ground, or on a few loose stones, and a hole in the roof for the escape of the smoke,"[43] these writers instead adhered to the further fantasy of the "very comfortable and pleasant . . . log cabin home" (*PS*, p. 102). Lydia Hunt Sigourney captured its essence in her enormously popular, "The Western Home" (a poem which first saw magazine publication at the beginning of the decade and then titled a collection of her poems in 1854). Here, Kirkland's reports of tight quarters and rough puncheon floors are superseded by the prettier picture of a "new home in greenwood fair":

> [The] humble roof was firmly laid,
> Of jointed logs the building made,
> Yet more of space, and comfort too,
> Was there than met the careless view;
> For well these walls the storm could quell,
> And tyrant cold or heat repel.[44]

Discounting Kirkland's descriptions of the sheer drudgery of first settlement, these novelists joined with Sigourney to picture the frontier housewife working "with harmonizing will," finding only "pleasure in her duties." Discounting Kirkland's anger at the dishonest practices of western bankers and land speculators, the novelists asserted, along with Sigourney, that the western home implied "an Eden refuge, sweet and blest." And, like her, they asked their readers to believe that the western "home's secluded bound" (*WH*, p. 31) offered a sure haven from the exploitations of a capitalist economy and the uncertainties of the marketplace. Caroline Soule, for example, portrayed moneylending as a local affair based wholly on benevolence. In *The Pet of the Settlement*, her displaced easterner, Mr. Belden, recoups the fortune earlier lost in the counting-houses of New York by virtue of "patient, honest industry, and not by skin-flint usury," she insists (*PS*, p. 237). In turn, as Soule depicts him, Belden helps others to prosper in Iowa. "'If ye ever happen to get hard up for cash and need a loan to lift ye,'" one of the older pioneers boasts to a prospective newcomer to the settlement, "'there's Belden'll help you along, and won't ask you forty per-cent either, and if he sees ye'r industrious and steady-like, he'll wait till the heavens open before he'll foreclose any mortgage he may have agen ye'" (*PS*, p. 205).

If Soule's portrait of the honorable Belden bore little resemblance to the actuality of eastern-financed moneylending on the western frontier, it nonetheless testified to the underlying motives of her story. In *A New Home*, Kirkland may have aimed at "a veracious history of actual occurrences" (*ANH*, p. 7). The women who followed her lead to western materials, however, wanted only to escape the circumstances that gave rise to what Margaret Fuller had described as "those painful separations, which already desecrate and desolate the Atlantic coast." The domestic fictionists, in short, wanted to believe—as Fuller had wanted to believe—that on the uncrowded and fertile tracts of the western prairies "whole families might live together" in a kind of extended domestic Eden, the sons returning "from their pilgrimages to settle near the parent hearth" and the daughters finding "room near their mother."[45] As a result, though their novels never shied away from depicting the squalor of the urban poor or the mind- and body-numbing labor of an impoverished New England farm,[46] only rarely did these women even approach Kirkland's description of "the tenant of a log-cabin whose family, whatever be its numbers, must burrow in a single room, while a bed or two, a chest, a table, and a wretched handful of cooking utensils, form the chief materials of comfort" (*ANH*, p. 311).

Precisely because these writers were committed to a fantasy and not to any specific geography or agrarian economic organization, moreover, their novels exhibit a peculiar tension that goes beyond the purposeful masking of historical reality. The reversion to familial configurations from an earlier period, made possible by the isolated border setting, stands side by side in their texts with assertions of development and centrality. For, without ever owning up to the contradiction, the domestic fictionists who turned to western materials generally applaud the change "from a straggling, border village into a populous and central town" (*PS*, p. 235). The point must therefore be made that just because writers like Maria Susanna Cummins and Caroline Soule chose to regenerate their broken and ruined city families in the agricultural west did not mean that they were inveterately opposed to cities, manufacturing, or even to class distinctions. It was only the squalor and corrupting influences of the city, the meaner exploitations of poor laborers by factories, and the vicious disparities of class to which these writers objected. They wanted to evade certain consequences attendant upon an accelerated industrialized urbanization because they saw those consequences ravaging families and destroying the domestic ideals to which they held; but industry and urbanization themselves they did not reject. (Only Mary Hayden Pike and E.D.E.N. Southworth actually rejected on ideological and philosophical grounds the plantation society premised on slavery.)

Needless to say, to preserve the fantasy, the domestic fictionists took great pains to distinguish their fictional western towns from the "crowded, cramped and choked" environments of the older settlements. *This* town, they assure readers, is "spacious, broad and airy." Caroline Soule declares that the fifteen-year period of development she catalogues in *The Pet of the Settlement* represents "only a bright, beautiful change" (*PS*, p. 236). But her language subtly suggests otherwise:

> Years have come and gone . . . changing [the little Settlement] from a straggling, border village into a populous and central town; not crowded, cramped and choked though, but spacious, broad and airy. The arching trees that line each avenue, giving it a picture-look, with their cool and waving shadows, while the ample parks, with their green and tasteful hedges, their closely shaven lawns, their clustering shrubs, their gorgeous flowers, their sparkling fountains, singing birds, tame forest pets, and chattering, dancing little children, are a sweet relief to the dim [*sic*: din] and bustle of its thoroughfares, and give to its busiest denizen a taste of that dear country life for which his heart is panting. (*PS*, p. 235)

Now so disassociated is the town from its frontier origins that, within its precincts, the busy "denizen" *pants* for even a "taste of that dear country life" that had gone before. To a genre originally conceived in nostalgia, that sentiment is here again introduced—though, again, it is never named as such.

The reason such contradictions go unacknowledged is that most of these novelists did not so much want to abandon the east as to offer an idealized alternative by which it might be regenerated. The west merely provided an appropriate stage set for elaborating the ideal. Thus, though many a heroine is said to be "held . . . spell-bound" by "the sudden glory of the extended landscape" (*I*, p. 194), none of these writers invoked either irony or regret when they pictured "hundreds of glorious old forest trees falling only to rise again, not as the green and leafy bowers of singing birds, but . . . as the spacious marts of trade, [or] the dusty, noisy workshop" (*PS*, p. 191).

The point, after all, was not to suggest that the informing values of hearth and home could only take hold in the relatively unsophisticated settlements at the edges of society. The reformist impulse of this fiction needed to demonstrate that such values could flourish even in the face of accelerating development and thus serve as a model by which the nation as a whole might be transformed. Displacing the uglier realities of the older regions, the idealized fictional west was to become central to a new national self-image. And to that end, even the new technology might be useful. As one of the Iowa pioneers in Soule's *The Pet of the Settlement* confidently predicts, in the near future "'there'll come puffin' and blowin' and snortin' along, that . . . iron horse . . . and then ye see, why we shan't be out west a bit, but jist in the very centre of creation, with all the world a-coming in to see how we git along'" (*PS*, p. 205).

Though the bulk of its story line is usually played out on some prairie frontier, the domestic novel of western relocation was nonetheless a response to eastern—and not western—concerns. And although the fantasy demands of the genre produced an idealized west onto which women readers might project otherwise threatened visions of home and hearth, writers like Cummins, Southworth, and Soule did not conceive themselves as promotionalists for westward migration. Even so, constrained by the need to make their western idylls persuasive as well as attractive, the domestic fictionists had to offer palliative resolutions to the fears and anxieties that their women readers traditionally associated with westward migration. As a result, following promotionalists like Mary Austin Holley and Eliza Farnham, and adapting many of their happier metaphors as plot structures, the domestic fictionists (even if inadvertently) succeeded in creating a sort of collective "emigrants' guide" that spoke specifically to women.

When Elisabeth Adams wrote from Iowa to her sister in Ohio, in 1846, complaining that "if I could only have mother or a sister here I should be very glad,"[47] she testified to women's general distress at family separations— and to their particular distress at isolation from female relatives. The domestic fictions set in the west, which began to appear just a few years after Adams's arrival in Davenport, responded to this familiar complaint by inventing an ingenious pattern of surrogates. In *Mabel Vaughan*, Cummins provided her heiress heroine with a surrogate sister in the person of a neighboring minister's daughter. And when the Widow Symmes becomes ill in Soule's *The Pet of the Settlement*, the motherless Margaret Belden took her home and "nursed her as a daughter would a mother" (*PS*, p. 244). Upon her recovery, the old woman is urged to remain on in the Belden household and is given a room that, thereafter, all "called . . . affectionately, grandmother's room" (*PS*, p. 245).

Responding to women's reluctance to exchange comfortable household arrangements for primitive conditions—"I miss many of the conveniences of home," Elisabeth Adams admitted in a letter to her sister[48]—the domestic fictionists hinted at a speedy transition from original log cabin to framed house or charming cottage. The fear of geographical isolation to which Elisabeth Adams gave voice soon after her arrival in Iowa—"I am alone tonight, the wind sounds so mournful and the house is so still that I am almost sad"[49]—called forth other devices. To these plaintive chords the domestic fictionists responded with promises of "'the iron horse'" putting their western settlements, soon enough, "'jist in the very centre'" of things (*PS*, p. 205). Even the rigors of the journey were minimized, as most of these novelists depicted their characters traveling in relative comfort on steamboats, canalboats, and railroads; and since they generally restricted their settings to frontiers well east of the Missouri River, arduous travel by wagon only rarely figured in their pages.

Perhaps the most tenacious anxiety to which these books responded was the lingering suspicion that women became dessicated or masculinized (or both) on the frontier. Writing from Kansas in 1859, Sarah Everett thanked a sister-in-law in western New York State for sending dress trimmings. She then added: "It was two or three weeks before I could make up my mind to wear anything so gay as that lining and those strings." "I am a very old woman," Sarah explained, "my face is thin sunken and wrinkled, my hands bony withered and hard—I shall look strangely I fear with your nice undersleeves and the coquettish cherry bows."[50] The Sarah Everett who wrote those lines was twenty-nine years old. Whether we take her protests as exaggerations or, more probably, as accurate assessments of the physical toll of pioneering, one crucial fact emerges: Sarah Everett's fear of growing old before her time, of losing the capacity for feminine coquetry, was a fear that most women (and men) associated with westward emigration.

With unerring precision, Cummins directed herself to these fears in *Mabel Vaughan*. To the dread of physical dessication, Cummins offered categorical denials. At twenty-five, now having spent six years in Illinois, Mabel is said to enjoy a "complexion [that] has lost nothing of its fairness; the full brown eye glows with as soft a light; the smile which plays around the mouth is as spontaneous and attractive; and the chestnut hair . . . is as rich and glossy as ever" (*MV*, p. 397). To the fear "that Mabel's manners would lose something of their delicacy . . . [or] her mode of expression, would become masculine and harsh" (*MV*, p. 396), Cummins opposed fully one-third of her novel. Portrayed throughout the book as stereotypically patient and passive, though always acutely sensitive to the needs of those around her, Mabel's capacity for "unfailing cheerfulness and sympathy with others' joy" (*MV*, p. 398) is especially emphasized once she removes to Illinois.

These novels exhibited their greatest ingenuity for altering contemporary belief and perception, however, in their strategies for making the prairie landscape seem both inviting and familiar. Only Southworth, in *In-*

dia, played upon American women's habitual fear of entrapment within an isolated wooded landscape. She allowed her heroine one fearful night in a log cabin located within an "old primeval forest" (*I*, p. 270), where she is menaced by a pack of hungry wolves. Denominated "'a small, cowardly race'" (*I*, p. 290), though, the wolves are quickly dispatched by the heroine's husband and, thereafter, the young bride is pictured wandering safely and happily in a wilderness garden where, like a latter-day Eve, she gathers "a rich harvest . . . of ripe fruit" (*I*, pp. 294–95). For the most part, however, the landscapes of these novels involve the open spaces of the prairies. And even Southworth describes the prairie stands of trees as "dotted groves" or "like oases in [a] desert" (*I*, p. 294).

In fact, by 1850, the cutting edge of settlement had for so long been identified with the prairie that heavily wooded landscapes no longer figured prominently as emblems of the frontier. Instead, Americans imagined the parklike expanses made famous by Holley and Farnham: unimpeded prospects across rolling and flowered prairies with, here and there, a river and a stand of trees. By the end of the decade, when *The Pet of the Settlement* appeared, the alternations of closed and open spaces had become almost schematic. Soule's characters encounter "on the one side a ten-mile prairie stretching its emerald hues to the golden horizon, . . . on the other, a dense forest" (*PS*, p. 16). And everywhere in these novels, the prairies are said to be carpeted with wild strawberries and "multitudes of roses and pinks" (*PS*, p. 23).

If the prairie frontier was thus made inviting, it was also denuded of its strangeness. "'Well, really now,'" declares a maiden aunt, newly arrived in Illinois, "'I don't see such a great difference, after all, between this country and what I've been used to at the East.'" The domestic novels of western relocation were full of such statements, though none as fully articulated as that of Aunt Sabiah in Cummins's *Mabel Vaughan*:

> "That 'ere great field, prairie, or whatever you call it, is pretty much like our meadows at home, only it ain't fenced off; and rivers are rivers anywhere, and always will run down hill, and trees are trees, and sky's sky, and as to the people, you say they're most all New England settlers so I don't see there's anything heathenish about the place after all." (*MV*, p. 390)

The comparison of prairies to meadows—a frequent comparison in these novels—without any acknowledgment of the tall prairie grasses unique to the west is trivializing and inadequate, as are the statements about rivers, trees, and sky. But then this was precisely the purpose of the passage: it was intended to trivialize real topographical differences. The closing reference to "New England settlers" then successfully completes the imputation of the customary. And a recognizable social community is thereby transposed to a landscape that has now been reclaimed as familiar.

With strategies such as these, aided by a vocabulary and a symbolic system evocative of Eden, the westernized domestic fictions encouraged women readers to claim the new frontier as a garden of their own—as men had always done—but, at the same time, they followed the promotionalists in redefining what the garden signified. No longer the realm of the isolate Adamic male adventurer, the frontier in these novels came to embrace home, family, and a social community informed by their values. If few pioneer women actually encountered such idealized configurations as daily reality, this does not diminish the fact that the novelists' domesticated western fantasy represented a historically important creative act. For it provided prospective female emigrants with a set of images through which to forge some kind of acceptable anticipatory relationship to an unfamiliar landscape.

To fully appreciate the crucial significance of that contribution, we need only recall that it was not simply deteriorating conditions in the east that made the domestic novel turn westward in the 1850s. The nation as a whole had turned its eyes and imagination in that direction. As financial institutions recovered from the Panic of 1837, the two decades preceding the Civil War counted American emigrants and European immigrants, in unprecedented numbers, pushing out to the borderlands along the Missouri River. Beyond the Missouri, lengthening wagon trains began crossing the Great American Desert, heading overland to a fabled Pacific paradise. What made the domestic novel unique in this context was its single-minded insistence upon *women's* participation in the westward movement.

Of course, as the historian Elizabeth Fries Ellet pointed out, women had always been part of these migrations, even if her 1852 *Pioneer Women of the West* was among the first studies devoted to demonstrating that fact.[51] The promotional writings of Mary Austin Holley and Eliza Farnham and Caroline Kirkland's successive volumes on her experience in Michigan notwithstanding, the emigrants' guides upon which most families depended for their dreams and facts about the west still largely continued to ignore women's presence. Almost as an afterthought, following paragraphs of detailed advice concerning clothing and gear for men and boys, one popular overland guide of 1846 commented briefly, "All [women and girls] can do, is to cook for camps . . . nor need they have any wearing apparel, other than their ordinary clothing at home."[52] It was an inaccurate statement of women's many trail duties, and it was bad advice.[53] Worse than that, it all but edited women out of the great westward adventure.

In the face of this kind of repeated refusal to formally prepare women for their role in the westering process, the domestic novels of western re-location fulfilled a vital—if unintentional—function. As always in women's fiction, they offered their readers practical advice about housekeeping on a frontier (since some of these authors knew the west firsthand), and they provided symbolic constructs where more conventional sources of information were lacking. These westernized domestic fictions thus represented unique guide-books to uncharted territories and, as such, they offered comforting and familiar image systems that could serve as templates for the organization of experience. Ten years after her arrival in Iowa, for example, Elisabeth Adams still clung to images lifted directly out of the domestic fictionists' pages. "Sometimes," she wrote her husband, "a vision of a pleasant home with a garden and flowers and creeping vines, and children and husband dear all at home, no more to roam, comes over me, and I confess I look forward to its reality with anticipated pleasure."[54]

Once by a bitter candle
of oil and braided
rags, I wrote

—Margaret Atwood,
The Journals of Susanna Moodie

9   Alice Cary and Caroline Soule: Book Ends

Alice Cary never accepted the judgment of those who claimed that the sketches and short stories comprising her *Clovernook; Or Recollections of Our Neighborhood in the West* (1852) were "of too sombre a tone." In her view, the problem derived from the fact that most other writers of her day—including "nearly all indeed of those writers of my sex who have essayed to amuse or instruct society—have apparently been familiar only with wealth and splendor."[1] They therefore offered, as Cary did not, "descriptions of the gay world." As a result, Cary believed, readers were unprepared for the fictionalized reminiscences of a writer who had spent her days "with the humbler classes"—in this case, the struggling farm families like her own who had only slowly worked their way from indebtedness to prosperity in the fertile Ohio valley. Knowing that world as intimately as she did, Cary protested, she had sketched "Western rural life" as neither "less lovely [n]or more exposed to tearful influences than it is." (*CL*, 2d ser., p. 363).

Even so, in portraying the world of debt-encumbered farms, the daily penalties of pinched circumstances and pinched lives, and the frustrations of a lifetime in which there is "never rest nor respite from labor,"[2] Alice Cary forced her readers to acknowledge struggle and toil in a region where the popular imagination had decreed only a bountiful garden. Thus, the writer whom Edward Eggleston would later call "the founder of the tradition of honest interpretation of the West"[3] succeeded in unmasking some of the period's prettier notions of the agricultural heartland, following Caroline Kirkland in a realistic portrayal "of what occurred in and about the little village" of her childhood (*CL*, 2d ser., p. 364). The difference was that where Kirkland wrote about the difficulties of settling a raw frontier, Cary—a full two generations removed from the pioneers of her grandfather's generation—described the struggles of permanent settlement, insisting upon the presence of "the armies of the poor" even where "the wheat-field stand[s] smiling" (*CL*, 2d ser., p. 362). Cary's subject, then, even as she detailed abundant harvests and "barns . . . full of new hay" (*CL*, p. 138), was always "poverty, . . . with whom none of us voluntarily mate ourselves" (*CL*, 2d ser., p. 362).

It was a subject for which she was uniquely qualified, having felt, for the first fourteen years of her life, "as if there was actually nothing in existence but work."[4] Cary's paternal grandfather, a native of Lyme, New Hampshire, had received a warrant for land in Hamilton County, Ohio, in payment for his service in the continental army. Her father, Robert Cary, was fifteen years old when his family finally crossed the mountains by emigrant wagon and then floated down the Ohio on a flat-boat to Fort Washington in 1803. When, in 1814, Robert Cary married Elizabeth Jessup, he took up farming on a quarter section of the original Cary purchase. But, as the land had not been a gift and the equipment necessary to sustain a farm was expensive, the newly married couple faced years of sacrifice before they could pay off their considerable debts.

His indebtedness and the fact that most of his neighbors still contented themselves with log cabins notwithstanding, Robert Cary built his bride a small, unpainted, one-and-a-half-story framed house, around which she planted "several fruitful apple and cherry trees; and a luxuriant sweet-briar."[5] Here, eight miles north of Cincinnati, near the village of Mount Healthy, Alice Cary was born on the 26th of April, 1820. She was the fourth child in a family of seven daughters and two sons.

The relative affluence suggested by their framed house and the "luxuriant sweet-briar," however, did not bespeak a life of either ease or comfort. Indeed, as a younger sister, Phoebe Cary, later commented, the sweet-briar was "the only thing near that seemed designed solely for ornament."[6] All else was practical and utilitarian. In such an atmosphere, Alice Cary and her imaginative, high-spirited sisters "pined for beauty; but there was no beauty about our homely house," she remembered bitterly. Nor was there much to satisfy girls who "hungered and thirsted for knowledge." "There were not a dozen books on our family shelf," Alice Cary later complained, and "not a library within our reach." Even had there been, though, farm chores would have left the girls "little time to study." What book learning the Cary children received, therefore, came from "the district school-house, down the road." "I never went to any other," Alice Cary noted in an autobiographical fragment composed in her adult years, and "not very much to that."[7]

To compensate, Alice Cary and her beloved older sister, Rhoda, spun stories of faraway romance as they walked to and from school and shared their imaginings of a wider world in whispers, late at night, in their low-ceilinged tiny bedroom under the eaves. And they looked to their mother who, despite the fatigues of the day, still found the time to read a weekly religious newspaper, "often at night, after every other member of the household was asleep."[8] For the most part, however, Alice Cary recalled a childhood in which, "for the first fourteen years of my life, it seemed as if there was actually nothing in existence but work. The whole family struggle was just for the right to live free from the curse of debt. My father worked early and late; my mother's work was never done."[9]

Then, in 1832, at last cleared of his debts, Robert Cary erected a new, more commodious dwelling for his large family. The change, unfortunately, was not unattended by sorrow. Within a year of moving into the new house, Rhoda—to whom Alice was ardently attached—and a three-year-old sister both succumbed to tuberculosis. Two years later, when Alice was just fifteen, the same disease claimed her mother. In the daughter's view, her mother had been "taxed far beyond her strength and died before her time."[10]

The relaxation of economic strains thus did not bring unalloyed happiness, nor did it really bring any concomitant relaxation in the chores required of the children. When her father remarried two years later, Alice found herself at odds with a stepmother who expected her to scrub, sweep, milk cows, wash dishes, make beds, and tend to the vegetable garden during the day,[11] but who saw no profit in the girl's wasting valuable candles in order to scribble at night. The literary career of the writer whom Henry Nash Smith cites as "the first native of the Ohio Valley who attempted to interpret the region in fiction" therefore began by the smoky light of "a saucer of lard with a bit of rag for wick."[12]

Though their stepmother could never see any value in it, Alice and her younger sister, Phoebe, persisted in writing poetry. Phoebe secretly submitted a poem to a Boston newspaper when she was fourteen, only learning of its acceptance when she saw it reprinted in a Cincinnati newspaper. At about the same time, Alice—now eighteen years old—had a poem entitled "The Child of Sorrow" accepted by the *Sentinel*, a Universalist paper published in Cincinnati. For almost the next ten years, the sisters continued to contribute poetry to both eastern and western journals and newspapers, always without recompense. Not until 1847 did the Washington-based *National Era*—the paper in which *Uncle Tom's Cabin* was first serialized (1851–52) and for which William Dean Howells composed some of his earliest pieces—pay Alice Cary $10 for poems and sketches previously published in its pages under the pseudonym, "Patty Lee."[13]

The sisters' work had begun to appear in the more fashionable eastern magazines like the Boston *Ladies' Repository* and *Graham's Magazine*. So prolific was their output that it caught the attention of Horace Greeley and

Rufus W. Griswold. Greeley made a point of visiting the Carys when he toured the west in 1849, and Griswold included selections from the work of both sisters in his 1849 compendium, *The Female Poets of America*. These connections helped the Cary sisters to locate a Philadelphia publisher who paid them $100 to issue their first volume, *Poems of Alice and Phoebe Cary* (1849), a collection of previously published pieces.[14]

Encouraged by the friendly notices their poetry collection was receiving, the two embarked on a brief pilgrimage to the east in 1850, visiting New York, Boston, and stopping over in Amesbury, Massachusetts, to pay a call on their favorite poet, John Greenleaf Whittier (who was to become a close friend to the women and a strong supporter of their work). Shortly after her return to Ohio, Alice decided to remove permanently to New York, determined to try to earn a living there from her writing. Biographers have speculated that the unhappy termination of her courtship with an Ohio businessman (whose wealthy family opposed the match) prompted her decision, or that she was encouraged to make the move by hints of marriage from Rufus Griswold (who later married someone else).[15] It is equally likely that Alice Cary simply realized that in New York she could find what had always eluded her in Ohio: an environment sympathetic to her literary aspirations. "I know how lonesome I used to be in the country," she confided many years later in a letter to a friend, "and alone. Alone, I mean, so far as the society to which one belongs is concerned. For we all need something outside of ourselves and our immediate family."[16] In Ohio, after all, an older brother to whom she submitted her poems for approval generally responded by "teas[ing] her by some such remark as 'I can't bother with your poetry, I must go feed the hogs;' or, 'Well, I 'spose I'll have to stand it—read away.'"[17]

Whatever her motives, Alice Cary arrived in New York in November 1850 and was joined there by Phoebe the following spring. As Horace Greeley recalled it, "they hired two or three modest rooms, in an unfashionable neighborhood, and set about to work resolutely to earn a living by the pen."[18] With the 1852 publication of *Clovernook; Or Recollections of Our Neighborhood in the West*, the gamble paid off. The sketches and stories depicting what one reviewer called "rural occupations, in the interior of Ohio" became a minor best-seller, and Alice Cary herself was compared with "Poe or Hawthorne."[19] A second collection, which proved even more successful, was issued the next year, and the success of these gave rise to yet a third Clovernook volume—this one aimed specifically at children.[20]

Avowedly autobiographical, the Clovernook stories are all shaped by the places and events that shaped their author. Many of Cary's characters inhabit dwellings that bear a striking resemblance to the original Cary homestead, with "the little branches of . . . sweet-brier . . . [growing] close under the window," and "the cherry trees, beside the house" (*CL*, p. 104). Sisters dream together of faraway places; beautiful children die young; young women are abandoned by faithless lovers; poor farm girls gifted with "a superior intellect" find themselves "hedge[d] . . . round with circumstances that prevent its recognition"; and everywhere there is the sense that farm life leaves "never rest nor respite from labor" (*CL*, pp. 328, 94).

What ameliorates the otherwise straitened circumstances of "the poor and humble" among "the farming class" (*CL*, pp. vi, vii)—and what saves Cary's chapters from the lachrymose in what Fred Lewis Pattee has labeled "the decade of tears"[21]—is her insistence on a surrounding landscape in which "every thing betokened plenty" (*CL*, p. 138). Indeed, more than half the chapters of the first Clovernook volume open on an autumnal setting marked by the abundance of harvest. "It was the time of the full moon of the harvest," begins one story, when "winrows of sweet-smelling hay ridged the meadows, and the golden waves of the wheat fields rose and fell as the winds ran in and out. The flocks, shorn of their heavy fleeces, . . . bleated along the hill sides, while the heifers buried their sleek flanks in great beds of clover, and the oxen . . . bowed their necks to the yoke, for the ingathering of the dry hay and the bound sheaves" (*CL*, p. 93). Full of the details of the countryside she knew so well, still another chapter opens in "the middle month of the autumn," when "loaded wains were driven slowly homeward from orchards and cornfields, heaped high with bright apples or yellow corn" (*CL*, p. 138).

Against this background of plenty, the unremitting labors of her characters are at least granted material reward. And, with the passage of time in the fertile Ohio valley, she quietly suggests, even the hardships will pass. A young woman whose family poverty had once deprived her of books and education, for example, is pictured later, "in the sober prime of womanhood," gazing out upon an autumn landscape "ridged with furrows, and plenteous in milk and wool." If the narrowed possibilities of her earlier years have left her "habitually sad, and discontented, and embittered," it is nonetheless the case that her father has moved her into a large and comfortable home and that she has long ago left behind "the old homestead, where passed her childish years, with its hard experiences" (*CL*, pp. 302–3). She even contemplates studying to become a schoolmistress now. A younger sister, significantly, raised in more prosperous times, knows nothing of the deprivation that blighted the older sister's childhood, nor does she suffer from the bitterness that marks the elder's adulthood. If the first two generations must struggle and sacrifice, Cary seems to be telling her readers, the third may then begin to enjoy the consequent bounty of a land "ridged with furrows, and plenteous in milk and wool." Her faith in the inevitability of this progress, in fact, underlies the abiding optimism with which she details the generational changes "in the interior of my native state, which was a wilderness when first my father went to it, and is now crowned with a dense and prosperous population" (*CL*, p. v).

The progress from the first to the third generation, then, marks the time span of Cary's Clovernook reminiscences. And the end result of that progress is an idealized landscape emancipated from its frontier origins but not yet significantly urbanized. By the time in which most of these stories are set, Uncle Dale, one of "the pioneer settlers of Clovernook" (*CL*, p. 260), has been in his grave for ten years. His sons enjoy "beautiful mansions" and prosperous farms, "reaping the harvest in peace which was sown long ago amid perils and difficulties" (*CL*, p. 83). The pioneer who now earns Clovernook's respect is Mr. Harmstead, "the pioneer of elegance and refinement among the people" (*CL*, p. 320). Eastern-bred and educated, the Harmsteads have been forced by financial misfortunes to remove from "their native city" in the east to rural Clovernook, where they set about "transform[ing] Mr. Hinton's brier-smothered farm into Willow Dale" (*CL*, pp. 311, 310). That their efforts have been a success is borne out by the fact that "Willowdale, with its level meadows, nicely trimmed groves, picturesque gardens, winding walks and shrubberies, would not be recognized by the proprietor, who, twelve or fourteen years ago, ploughed around blackened stumps, and through patches of briers and thistles" (*CL*, p. 320).

In the process of improving his own grounds, moreover, Mr. Harmstead has also exerted "a refining and elevating influence" on the entire neighborhood. Cary thus portrays what Caroline Kirkland had only hoped for when, in *A New Home*, she had urged genteel easterners to migrate west. "Chiefly through his instrumentality, in the course of a few years," Cary's narrator boasts, "the neighborhood of Clovernook had been changed from a thinly inhabited and ill-cultivated district to one abounding with green lawns and spotted with vineyards and orchards, ridged with clipt hedges, and sparkling with public edifices" (*CL*, p. 320). If Cary shies away here from suggesting anything more urban than "sparkling . . . public edifices," she nonetheless makes clear that the agricultural west has been embraced by city interests. Since many of the Harmsteads' friends "have been led to build houses and cultivate grounds" in the area, Clovernook now "may boast of as many attractions in point of taste and utility as the pleasantest summer retreat in the vicinity of any of the cities" (*CL*, p. 320).

This embrace of the rural by the urban, which Cary celebrates in the first of the Clovernook volumes, begins to imply an unwanted intrusion in the second. And the landscape whose progressive cultivation she has applauded here comes, in the second volume, to seem threatened by the very success of its "dense and prosperous population" (*CL*, p. v). What Cary could not ignore as she continued her reminiscences was the fact that the same expansive development that saved a later generation from the sacrifices of the first might, as well, make "the head sick and the heart ache as we entered city limits" (*CL*, 2d ser., p. 24).

In an era when sequels rarely achieved the success of the original volume, Alice Cary's second series of Clovernook tales proved a unique exception. Issued in 1853, with the same title as the first collection, the second volume quickly outstripped its popular predecessor in sales. The subject matter and setting, ostensibly, were the same—"the 'hilly country' that overlooks" the Ohio (*CL*, 2d ser., p. 13). And the narrative tone remained determinedly nostalgic, traveling "oftener to the days that have been, than to those that are to come" (*CL*, 2d ser., p. 10). But what distinguished the second volume from the first, and perhaps accounted for its unusual success, was Cary's ambivalent recognition of industry and manufacture within the "fair dominions" of her "pastoral" garden (*CL*, 2d ser., p. 13; *CL*, p. v). "Young cities" have now made their way to the Ohio and, with them, "hot furnaces where swart labor drives the thrifty trades, speeding the march to elegance and wealth." As a result, as she tries to gaze out upon the oat and wheat fields for reminders of the world she knew as a child, "a dense column of smoke . . . rises" to obscure her view. Thus momentarily denied the vision she would have, Cary articulated the thwarted fantasies of an entire nation, as more and more Americans blanched before "coal-scented and unwholesome fogs, obscuring the lovely picture that would else present itself" (*CL*, 2d ser., p. 13).

The settings for the second Clovernook collection, therefore, could not retain the unalloyed rusticity of the first. In acknowledging the rapidity of change in the Ohio valley, Cary not only admitted industry to the garden but, in so doing, she mapped a landscape increasingly demarcated as urban, suburban, or rural.[22] Similarly, her tone in the second volume could not retain the innocence of pure nostalgia only. In looking back at the changes already taking place during her childhood years near Mount Healthy, she must now acknowledge their ultimate consequences. When she does this, however, Cary betrays her suspicion that the speedy "march to elegance and wealth" is extracting a toll she would rather evade. The outcome is a book that yearns toward an arrested agrarian past, even as it identifies the irrevocable seeds of change sown in that past.

Thus, an opening meditation on the imaginative capacity to "woo back the visions of departed joys" is essentially undercut by the first story in the collection, which reveals a past in which spreading urbanization is already threatening the world of one who is "thoroughly a country woman" (*CL*, 2d ser., pp. 10, 16). And the rural "May grass" of the opening (*CL*, 2d ser., p. 10) is replaced by a landscape subdivided into agricultural farming areas, suburbs, and city, with the last two threatening to spread out and overwhelm the first.

The first story in the collection, "Mrs. Wetherbe's Quilting Party," is a rambling narrative of some seventy pages, loosely cohering around the love and courtship of Jenny Mitchel and Helph Randall. The emotional parameters of the story, however, derive from the responses of Mrs. Wetherbe, "a plain old lady . . . good and simple-hearted as a child," who is "thoroughly a country woman," and the narrator, recalling incidents from her girlhood. The two were once neighbors. What brings the young girl and the elderly Mrs. Wetherbe together is Mrs. Wetherbe's request for a ride "to the city on the morrow in my father's wagon" (*CL*, 2d ser., p. 16). For the narrator, "these goings to the city" are held out as "among the most delightful recollections" of her young life. "They were to my young vision," she explains, "openings of the brightness of the world" (*CL*, 2d ser., p. 20). Mrs. Wetherbe, by contrast, "would just as soon, she said, put her head in a hornet's nest, any time, as go to town." What has prompted the older woman's exceptional request, then, is the obligation "to visit her niece, Mrs. Emeline Randall," and the equally pressing need to purchase "some cap stuff and some home-made linen" (*CL*, 2d ser., p. 17).

Retrieving youthful impressions, the narrator makes clear that, for her, the approach to the city implied a transition from poorer and outlying farming districts to affluent and attractive suburbs. "Distinctly fixed in my mind," she asserts, "is every house, its color and size, and the garden walks and trees with which it was surrounded, and by which the roadsides between our homestead and that dim speck we called the city, were adorned; and nothing would probably seem to me now so fine as did the white walls, and smooth lawns, and round-headed gate-posts, which then astonished my unpractised eyes" (*CL*, 2d ser., p. 20). But once the wagon reaches the outskirts of the city, Mrs. Wetherbe's reactions come to dominate.

To begin with, the city is quickly identified as the place of commerce and manufacture. Here, only the farmers who have come to sell their produce remind the narrator of the bucolic countryside recently left behind. "Now and then a little market-cart, with empty boxes and barrels that had lately been filled with onions, turnips, or radishes, went briskly by us," the narrator recalls. Or else she sees "countrymen who had ridden to market on horseback . . . already returning to their farms. The basket which had so lately been filled with the yellow rolls of butter, and covered with the green broad leaves of the plaintain, was filled now, instead, with tea and sugar, with perhaps some rice and raisins, and possibly a new calico gown for the wife at home" (*CL*, 2d ser., p. 25). But all too soon, these benign images of commerce and exchange are replaced by what Mrs. Wetherbe character- izes as "'a dreadful sight!'"

To approach the city more closely is to enter a realm where "the slant rays of the sun" must "struggle through the black smoke that blew against our faces, [as] the candle and soap factories of the suburbs began to thicken." To continue on that course is to risk revulsion. Indeed, as the narrator herself admits, "the bleating of lambs and calves from the long, low slaughter-houses which ran up the hollows opposite the factories, made the head sick and the heart ache as we entered city limits" (*CL*, 2d ser., p. 24).

Antedating by more than half a century Upton Sinclair's exposé of the Chicago stockyards in *The Jungle* (1906), Alice Cary described "fat and red-faced butchers, carrying long whips . . . driving back from the market great droves of cattle, that, tired and half maddened, galloped hither and thither, lashing their tails furiously, and now and then sharply striking their horns against each other, till they were forced through narrow pas- sages into the hot and close pens—no breath of fresh air, nor a draught of water between them and their doom" (*CL*, 2d ser., pp. 24–25). Mrs. Wetherbe points to "a cart filled with sheep and lambs, on the top of which were thrown two or three calves, with their feet tied together, and reach- ing upwards, their heads stretched back, and their tongues hanging out" (*CL*, 2d ser., p. 26). Finally, the fictional Mrs. Wetherbe and the author's own youthful persona both agree that what they have witnessed represents only "'wicked and useless cruelty.'"

After scenes such as these, the young girl's initial enthusiasm is damp- ened, and Mrs. Wetherbe's suspicions of city life take on greater authority. The girl who had once looked forward to her rare excursions to the city now considers that, "after all, the independent yeoman, with his simple rusticity and healthful habits, is the happiest man in the world." And Mrs. Wetherbe concludes that "'it stands to reason that it hardens the heart to live in cities, and makes folks selfish too'" (*CL*, 2d ser., p. 25).

The older woman's conclusions are affirmed as the narrative moves into the city proper and details Mrs. Wetherbe's visit to the home of her niece. The narrator eagerly accompanies her on this visit, only to discover that, despite its wealth, the Randall family is nonetheless ill-mannered, stingy, and ungenerous. The children are vicious and unmannerly; the husband begrudges food shared with guests and is too often drunk; and his wife, Emeline Randall, takes unfair advantage of Jenny Mitchel, a girl of fifteen who, under the ruse of having been adopted by the Randalls, is in fact being used by them as an unpaid servant, "'an underling and a drudge'" (*CL*, 2d ser., p. 33). To leave the "perfect bedlam" (*CL*, 2d ser., p. 26) of the city for the quiet of the country, then, is to abandon not simply a world of modern conveniences but a world of noise, greed, cruelty, and affectation.

The country, however, proves no permanent refuge in this story. For, one day, some weeks later, just before Mrs. Wetherbe's old-fashioned quilting party is to take place, "Mrs. Randall suddenly made her appearance." Her stated purpose is "to assist" in the arrangements, but her actual impact is to threaten a traditional quilting bee with the affectations of modern urban society. "She gave accounts of all the balls, dinners, and suppers, at which she had been, and tried to impress us with the necessity of having our country quilting as much in the style of them as we could," the narrator recalls. Cary then offers examples of the niece's suggestions: "'We must graduate our ginger-cakes,'" Mrs. Randall proposes, "'and so form a pyramid for the central ornament of the table; the butter must be in the shape of pineapples, and we must either have no meats, or else call it a dinner, and after it was eaten, serve round coffee, on little salvers, for which purpose we should have pretty china cups'" (*CL*, 2d ser., p. 38). Happily, Mrs. Wetherbe's original plans prevail, so that "before the appointed day every thing was in readiness—coffee ground, tea ready for steeping, chickens prepared for broiling, cakes and puddings baked, and all the extra saucers filled with custards or preserves" (*CL*, 2d ser., p. 39). But that temporary triumph does not entirely expel the larger threat, of which Emeline Randall is only an emblem.

The city and the country are again pitted in the love story that occasions the narrative. Young Helph Randall, alienated from his drunkard father and his pretentious mother, has long ago left the city in order to live in the country with the Wetherbes and there learn farming and apprentice himself as a blacksmith. When he falls in love with Jenny Mitchel, he must confront the snobbish disapproval of his parents and save his Jenny from the drudgery that is hers within city limits. Except for its subtext of country ingenuity vanquishing urban rapacity, the story of how young Helph, with his aunt's aid, manages to overcome parental disfavor and win Jenny's hand is, in gross outline, a fairly conventional tale of stalwart devotion on the young man's part and, on Jenny's, of submissive virtue.

What arrests the attention here is the physical locale of the predictable happy ending. "Nowhere among all the suburban gardens of this basin rimmed with hills," insists the narrator, "peeps from beneath its sheltering trees a cozier home" (*CL*, 2d ser., p. 15). What precedes this remark is a pastiche of conventions, all of it organized into a "very pretty" cottage in a gardenlike setting, its "cream-white walls, overrun with clematis and jasmine, and the clambering stalks of roses":

> The white-pebbled walk, leading from the gate to the doorway, is edged with close miniature pyramids of box, and the smoothly-shaven sward is shadowed by various bushes and flowers, and the gold velvet of the dandelion shines wherever it will, from the fence close beneath the window sending up its bitter fragrance out of dew, while sheaves of green phlox stand here and there, which in their time will be topped with crimson blossoms. (*CL*, 2d ser., p. 14)

Within, Jenny is happily employed at her housewifery. Singing as she molds her pastry, the "rosy-cheeked Jenny" croons lullabies to a "rosy-faced baby . . . in his white willow cradle" (*CL*, 2d ser., pp. 14–15). The only thing that distinguishes this attractive domesticity from its prototype in the pages of the domestic fictionists is that, unlike their New England or western New York farm settings, Alice Cary has placed her heroine in a suburb of Cincinnati.

On practical grounds, it might be argued that a suburban dwelling was the most suitable for a blacksmith—who must ply his trade in country and city alike. But Cary herself makes no such suggestion, only noting that, at the end of each day, Jenny's "honest husband will come from healthful labor" (*CL*, 2d ser., p. 15). The key to the location of the couple's idealized habitation, therefore, must lie within the geography of the story's symbolic contours. And in this regard Helph and Jenny serve as mediators between the opposing realms of city and country, being, as they are, "plain common-sense people" who care "little for the great world" (*CL*, 2d ser., p. 15). Having apprenticed himself in the country, despite his city origins, Helph represents the enduring qualities of rural virtue, even as his trade helps to sustain intercourse between city and country. As keeper of the garden home, Jenny symbolically stands guard against the extension of city vanities to outlying districts. They are, in short, a human bulwark against the spread of the city's "'wicked and useless cruelty.'"

In this sense, the suburbs have come to represent both access and buffer. They are at once the passageway between city and country, where elements of both intermingle; and they are, as well, the defining boundary beyond which neither realm is to impinge on the other.

But it was, of course, in nineteenth-century fiction—as in our twentieth-century reality—a precarious compromise. Indeed, what gives "Mrs. Wetherbe's Quilting Party" its startling edge is the author's implicit admission that her fictive equilibrium will not hold. Framing the story, after all, are the adult perceptions of a narrator now seated at a window in Cincinnati and looking out, with difficulty, toward the old "familiar shapes . . . of the landscape" she had known in earlier years. Only when "the mists" lift is she able to discern the neighborhood where Jenny and Helph reside (*CL*, 2d ser., p. 14). Until that clearing, however, the "goodly city" in which she currently finds herself sends out "a dense column of smoke" that mingles with "coal-scented and unwholesome fogs" and, together, these blot out "the lovely picture that would else present itself." In that prolonged opening image, Cary made clear the urban future that was fast overtaking the "fair dominions" of her beloved "hilly country." These "infant cities" of the west, she suggests—like the older cities of the east—will perforce grow and reach out into the countryside, first sending their mists and smokes as harbingers of the transformations to follow (*CL*, 2d ser., p. 13). And against the inevitability of this progress, the suburb will prove no bulwark.

Finally, then, the urban "march to elegance and wealth" seems shabby and unattractive beside a fondly recalled day in "early . . . July, when the bitter of the apples began to grow sweet, and their sunward sides a little russet; when . . . blackberries were ripening in the hedges, and the soft silk was swaying beneath the tassels of the corn" (*CL*, 2d ser., pp. 13, 16). So begins the story proper. But lest the reader find in this scene a seemingly secure refuge from the effluvia of the opening, "this was years ago," the narrator reminds us (*CL*, 2d ser., p. 17). And, with that reminder, we understand anew the nostalgia that has motivated the Clovernook tales, as we understand also that the scene upon which we would imaginatively rest for solace is, in all probability, no more.

In 1852, Alice Cary distinguished carefully between the prose and the poetry she would compose about Ohio. The former, in her view, commanded "fidelity" (*CL*, p. vii), while the latter permitted license to embellish and romanticize. "There were no bird songs to cheer the haymakers," she noted at one point in the first of her Clovernook volumes, "and as I am not writing poetry, I don't feel at liberty to say there were" (*CL*, p. 189). By the end of the decade, depictions of the agricultural frontier in the works of the domestic fictionists included birdsong everywhere. At times approaching the romantic woodland pastorals of which Caroline Kirkland's Cora Hastings had once been so fond, novels like Caroline Soule's *The Pet of the Settlement* (1860) habitually pictured some lovely young heroine "upon the threshold of their cabin, her lap full of brier-buds, which she was stringing into a necklace for the little [child] who sat beside her, cuddling a snow-white dove to her heart and singing a baby song."[23]

The surrounding prairies are uniformly brilliant with flowers and "the golden air . . . fragrant with balmy winds." And to the heroine, the world about her "seemed . . . like Eden, . . . as she daily wandered about and drank in the living loveliness" (*PS*, p. 79).

Insofar as Caroline Soule's *The Pet of the Settlement* typifies what finally became of the domestic novel of western relocation, it illustrates how few of Cary's concerns (or Kirkland's, for that matter) were adapted by the genre. Poverty carries no penalty in Soule's "poor man's Canaan" (*PS*, p. 207). Nor do class divisions prove anything other than beneficial to the less fortunate. The "border land," Soule insists, is "the only spot we have yet found where the brotherhood of men is recognized as an actual as well as an ideal thing" (*PS*, p. 56). Changes that came to disturb Alice Cary are unquestioningly applauded—and delineated as beautiful. According to Soule, the ten-mile Iowa prairie, which, when her novel opened, "was but a beauteous blending of grasses, violets and strawberry blossoms," is now, after fifteen years in her story, "a series of fine farms, with snow-white cottages nestling in the fresh foliage of young locust trees, with ample barns, fair gardens, thrifty orchards, and rich fields." Even industry, "costly dams," trains, and telegraph wires herald "only a bright, beautiful change" (*PS*, pp. 235–36).

Had *The Pet of the Settlement* been written from Soule's native New York, it would simply have substantiated Caroline Kirkland's opinion that "people who have only heard or read of life in the wilderness have but crude notions of its actual characteristics."[24] But the fact is, Caroline Augusta White Soule composed her first novel in a log cabin in Boonsboro, Iowa, where she had resided since 1854.[25] And she prefaced her story with the assurance that it contained "truthful transcripts from my own pioneer joys and sorrows, while the actual scenery is the same that gladdens my eyes every time I look from my cabin window" (*PS*, p. iii). As such, the novel marks the triumph of a fantasy in the face of observation and experience. For, by 1859, when Soule began to write, the promotionalists' prairie Eden had melded with the fictionists' domestic Eden to encode a new subset of literary conventions for representing the west.

To be sure, Soule's sumptuous descriptions of the landscape "in the valley of the Upper Des Moines" River (*PS*, p. iii), her catalogues of "the varied notes of bird-music" there (*PS*, p. 16), and her evocations of "the fresh morning air, so deliciously flavored with the breath of blue violets, and so sweetly dampened with the dew of wild roses" (*PS*, p. 17), are not without reference to a terrain she knew firsthand. But in generating her fictionalized portrait of the kind of society that such a landscape might sustain, Soule demonstrated how literally the domestic fictionists had taken the suggestive metaphors of the promotionalists. Indeed, melodramatic and full of improbable coincidences as it is, Soule's novel seems less an integrated narrative than a pretext for exploring how "pure water, deep soil, rich harvests and heavy timber" might cohere into "a model town" (*PS*, p. 201).

The main plot is precipitated by an evil villain who has lured a young couple with their two-year-old daughter out to the Iowa frontier. The villain has designs on the beautiful wife. After shooting the husband, and leaving him for dead, the villain abandons the child on the prairie and then kidnaps his drugged victim. Partnering the white man in these crimes is a Sioux chieftain who soon discovers that the white man has tried to cheat him. At this discovery, the Sioux imprisons his former partner, making a slave of him, and takes the kidnapped white woman into his lodge, where he begins to woo her for a bride.

Meanwhile, back on the prairie, the abandoned child is discovered by the picnicking Belden family and by "Uncle Billy," an ancient hunter and one of the original pioneers of the settlement. Some moments later, fourteen-year-old Harrie Belden shoots and wounds a young Indian boy whom he thinks intends the child harm. When Uncle Billy recognizes the Indian as the son of a friendly Sac chief, he rejoices that the boy has only been grazed and, with the help of Margaret Belden, Harrie's older sister, he dresses the wound. The infant and the wounded Indian are then brought into the Belden wagon, and everyone heads back to the settlement.

As they approach the village, neighbors greet them with the news that a stranger has been discovered nearby, mortally wounded. Before dying, he had uttered, "'I am murdered—my wife—my little child carried off'" (*PS*, p. 39). This, they surmise, explains the mystery of the abandoned child—a surmise that the child confirms at the man's funeral when, peering into the coffin, she cries out, "'Da-da; da-da'" (*PS*, p. 60). All attempts to follow the trail of the murderer and his kidnap victim prove fruitless.

Since the infant is now without either parent, the populace as a whole decides to adopt her, with "all, men, women and children" crying out, "'I'll do my part, I'll do my part.'" On the afternoon following her father's funeral, then, the child is formally christened "'Allie—Allie, the Pet of the Settlement,'" a name taken from the father's dying words and intended, as well, to "'give us all a claim upon her love'" (*PS*, p. 58). The child is to make her home with the Beldens—but, the text assures us, "there was not one, young or old, in the whole settlement, but had done some kindness for her" (*PS*, p. 94).

Officiating at the funeral and the christening is a newcomer to the settlement, a "hunter priest," whose voice at once thrills and disturbs Margaret Belden. Some months later, on a stormy winter's night, when Margaret is alone in the cabin with little Allie, the half-frozen stranger knocks at the door for succor. Taking him in from the blizzard and reviving him, Margaret saves his life and learns the secret of his identity. Beneath his artificially darkened "'olive skin, this long Indian hair, and this heavy raven beard,'" the stranger reveals that he is really Edward Somers, the lover Margaret has not seen in "seven long, weary years" (*PS*, pp. 133, 109).

At this point, the novel pauses for a lengthy flashback. The Beldens, it turns out, were once wealthy New Englanders. But the death of Mrs. Belden, followed by Mr. Belden's considerable investment losses, have induced the father to relocate to Iowa to start anew. Edward Somers, we learn, had earlier met and wooed Margaret "in the May of her life and in the May of the year" (*PS*, p. 110). Unfortunately, his prior attachment to another led to their eventual separation. And a series of improbable errors (he thinking her dead and she believing herself abandoned by him) continued that separation until, all unexpected, "on a wild prairie of Iowa, they . . . again clasped hands; again [spoke] their holy betrothal vows; met, to part no more" (*PS*, p. 109). The novel's central love story is thus happily concluded, and on "a brilliant June morning" Margaret Belden and Edward Somers are "married in the open air" in "a picturesque green spot on the edge of the woodland" (*PS*, p. 135).

The embedded Indian captivity story then takes over. For, amid the wedding festivities, little Allie is briefly kidnapped by a Sioux. She is pursued and safely returned by White Cloud, the Indian boy whom Harrie Belden had earlier wounded. While being nursed back to health in the Belden household, we learn, White Cloud became attached to Margaret and sought her instruction in the teachings of Christianity. As a result, White Cloud has broken with his father and chosen not to go on the annual warpath with his tribe. His heroic deed, instead, will be the rescue of Allie's mother. Concluding from the attempted kidnapping of the child that her mother is being held by Sioux, White Cloud tells Margaret that he will be taking a long journey, at the end of which he hopes to "'steal by night into the lodges of the bad Sioux'" (*PS*, p. 150).

To help in this rescue, White Cloud enlists the aid of "Bright-eyed," daughter of the Sioux chieftain who holds the white woman captive. The chief's earlier mistreatment of Bright-eyed's mother, which eventually led to her mother's death, has turned the daughter against her father. She has even proven resourceful in helping Allie's mother ward off the chief's marital imperatives. Now, Bright-eyed eagerly helps to engineer the white woman's escape. When White Cloud returns to the Iowa settlement with Alice Merton, therefore, he also brings with him Bright-eyed; and she, too, becomes a member of the Belden household, continuing to minister to the needs of the former captive.

Though more traditional forms of the captivity narrative continued to be published and popular throughout the 1850s,[26] women's domestic fictions about the west tended either to avoid them altogether or, as in the case of *The Pet of the Settlement*, incorporated them only to subvert their original implications. The genocidal tendencies inflamed by such narratives are here muted by the fact that the initial kidnapper is a white man, while the ultimate rescuer is an Indian. Functioning once as a symbolic projection of women's resistance to the wilderness frontier, traditional captivities ended with the heroine's return to some established urban center (like Boston in Mary White Rowlandson's narrative). Soule, however, returns Alice Merton to the Iowa frontier, making clear that the prairie settlement is now a safe and true haven. Here Alice Merton and her little Allie are joyfully reunited. And here the mother gradually regains her strength, nursed by Margaret and by Bright-eyed, until she is well enough to become the teacher in the village school.

At the same time, the village itself grows stronger. "The winter that succeeded the rescue of Allie's mother was a very pleasant and profitable one to the little prairie settlement," we read, because "Mr. Belden and Mr. Somers had formed a co-partnership, and were intending to build a fine saw and grist mill, . . . the rare business talent of the former balancing the capital which the latter had raised from his eastern funds." The mill "it was hoped would stimulate the tide of emigration and centre it at this particular site" (*PS*, p. 190).

Margaret Belden (now Mrs. Edward Somers), meanwhile, continues her sway over White Cloud. The result is that the young Sac puts aside his former "ambition to be a mighty chief" and, instead, asks "only to be an humble preacher of that new religion which he had first learned of Margaret—not a preacher to the white men, but to his own poor, ignorant Indian friends" (*PS*, p. 195).

The only sorrow to mar this western idyll is Alice Merton's eventual decline. Wasting away from tuberculosis, she gradually weakens and, on her deathbed, she consigns the care of "'my little Allie, my only child,'" once more, "'to the Settlement'" (*PS*, p. 217). Her death is followed by a kind of retribution. The man who had first kidnapped her escapes from his own Indian captivity and happens to make his way to this very place. After years of enslavement to the Sioux chief, the villain has been reduced to an incoherent snarling "maniac" who must be chained "as wild beasts are chained." He then begins to weaken and die. His physical deterioration, though, brings the "human look . . . back to his face" (*PS*, p. 232), and, at his death, he at last utters a prayer for forgiveness. "They buried him in the church yard, in a lonely little dell, where the shadows lay all day long" (*PS*, p. 234).

Having terminated the Indian captivity story and having seen the villain to his grave, the closing chapters of the novel skip ahead fifteen years, noting the settlement's change "from a straggling, border village into a populous and central town" (*PS*, p. 235). The Beldens' log cabin is replaced by "a quaint, rambling cottage, with picturesque terraces . . . pleasant bay-windows . . . porches draped all over with scented vines" and, within-doors, it is "furnished with taste and elegance" (*PS*, p. 237). Mr. Belden remains spry and youthful, having become the "richest man" in the town that now bears his name. Margaret and Edward Somers reside with him— "for he would never hear of their making a separate home" (*PS*, p. 238)— along with their three children. Uncle Billy, too, is "hale and hearty" despite his "eighty winters" (*PS*, pp. 241, 240). And he also has a room within the Belden cottage, as does "Old Grandmother Symmes," a widow who happily plies her herbal cures for the good of her newfound family. White Cloud is betrothed to Bright-eyed, but "their wedding has been deferred till he should have accomplished the arduous task he has taken upon himself,—the erection of a series of mission houses between the Missouri river and the Rocky Mountains, and the furnishing of each with a native minister" (*PS*, pp. 247–48).

In the final chapter, Harrie Belden returns to Iowa. "For the past ten years," we are informed, he had "been a resident of the far North West" where, plying the hunting skills taught him by Uncle Billy, he has been engaged in "the fur trade." By the time he returns to Iowa, however, he does so not as a mere trapper but as the owner of "one of the most important [fur trading houses] in the States, having agencies not only in the Atlantic cities, but in all the prominent ones of the Old World." "Now," the text tells us, "he is a richer man than his father even" (*PS*, p. 249). With the closing pages, White Cloud returns to claim Bright-eyed; Harrie proposes to and is accepted by a grown-up Allie; and Edward Somers officiates at the double wedding.

In addition to exposing the weaknesses of a text overburdened by melodramatic subplots and improbable coincidences (only a few of which have been included here), this brief plot summary should also suggest that the contemporary appeal of *The Pet of the Settlement* lay in something other than its style or story line. In fact, the real drama of the novel resides in the human appropriation of a landscape "ankle-deep in roses and cluster pinks" (*PS*, p. 18). Eclipsing the love story of Margaret Belden and Edward Somers, the rescue of Alice Merton, or the Christianizing of White Cloud, is the fantasy of an original prairie Eden converted into a human social garden. The agents of *this* drama are the landscape itself and Margaret Belden.

The novel opens by focusing on their separate roles. For its part, the surrounding landscape provides both beauty and sustenance. Margaret Belden is showered "with the strange, fairy-like blossoms that hide in the dim nooks of the forest" when her brother returns from fishing one morning, while her father displays a straw hat "lined with oak leaves, and filled to the brim with freshly gathered strawberries" (*PS*, p. 9). These, combined with "a string of fine fish" caught in the nearby river, then provide a sumptuous meal for the little family newly arrived from New England. For her part, Margaret Belden turns a "rude" scene into one of homey cheer. The Beldens' windowless log cabin has been transformed by her "snow white sheets," her "rose-blankets and calico quilts"; and the fare provided by raw nature is complemented by her addition to the table of two goblets "filled . . . with the choicest of the gathered flowers" (*PS*, pp. 10–11).

The abundance of nature thus allows the little family's physical survival, especially after the father has been "'so suddenly and fearfully too, . . . ruined'" in the counting-houses of the east. Equally important is Margaret's role in supporting the family's domestic happiness, despite their now "'humbled life.'" Having once feared that his daughter might shrink from "'the every day annoyances of our limited means; the household drudgery; the menial tasks,'" Mr. Belden, delighted at the breakfast he has just been served, assures her, "'believe me, dearest, never did I reverence you more than just now, when I saw you so quietly serve up this meal—the sweetest I have tasted for many a long year. We shall be happy now, daughter,'" he concludes (*PS*, p. 13).

The structuring dynamic of this opening is repeated throughout the novel. A family picnic to gather wild grapes along the banks of the Des Moines, for example, results in a "hunter-feast." There are "the plump partridges, which Uncle Billy had broiled; the little fat quails which Harrie had roasted on a stick; the chowder Mr. Belden had stewed up from the four-foot-long fish he had been so lucky to catch." For this feast Margaret spreads "a snowy cloth on the sand . . . taking from her travelling basket sundry little delicacies to complete it" (*PS*, p. 90).

No doubt, Soule intended some of these scenes as practical manuals for those like Margaret Belden, inexperienced in frontier ways. The graping expedition, after all, follows upon the narrative's comment that Margaret was "a novice in the art of preserving, and had therefore been troubled a good deal during the past summer to keep her sweet-meats from fermenting." In response, Uncle Billy announced that "'the whole river is black'" with ripe grapes and proceeds to instruct Margaret in the means of preserving them "'for winter pies and *sarse*'" (*PS*, p. 84). This kind of cookbook practicality, however, cannot fully account for eating as the single activity most often detailed in the text, nor does it embrace the symbolic function of the novel's unending feasting.

Both of these derive from the fact that Soule wanted her cornucopia of prairie plenty to suggest the foundation for a new kind of human community—a human community where the very abundance of the landscape invites sharing instead of competition, generosity instead of greed. Margaret's wedding to Edward Somers perhaps best symbolizes these impulses because, to it, "all the settlers" have been invited. And there, together, they enjoy "a bridal feast" that requires a full page for the listing of the "almost endless variety and quantity of food" (*PS*, p. 136). The feast thus marks not only the forging of a private marital relationship but the communal sharing of the newfound bounty.

Complementing that bounty is the influence of Margaret Belden. Her presence, we are meant to believe, somehow permeates the community, linking natural abundance to human (and Christian) sympathy. She helps her father bear the loss of his fortune; she nurses—one after the other— White Cloud, little Allie, Alice Merton, and, finally, the Widow Symmes; she converts the Indian boy from the warpath to the Bible; and, as Uncle Billy insists, she has even gentled him, "'the very sight of whom would make some white folks screech and swoon away'" (*PS*, p. 206). But she functions beyond her own door as well, visiting each newcomer to the settlement and, in Uncle Billy's words, "'mak[ing] her feel settled-like right off'" (*PS*, p. 206). If Iowa "seemed to Margaret like Eden" (*PS*, p. 79), the text suggests, she is also responsible for making it so.

An achieved social Eden, then, is what *The Pet of the Settlement* attempts to delineate. In small, the changes in the Belden residence measure the analogous changes in the community at large. When first we see it, the Belden cabin is "one of the rudest the emigrant ever inhabits," with leaky roof and rough puncheon floors. Margaret's efforts alone have converted it into "a rude, yet cheerful scene" (*PS*, pp. 9–10). When next we see the cabin, it resembles Lydia Sigourney's idealized "Western Home." "The cabin had been repaired early in the autumn," the text informs us. "A good tight roof . . had been laid on, the sides had been thoroughly and neatly 'pointed' outside and in, a window had been cut, doors hung, a new floor laid, and a loft of black walnut." Once more, however, it is Margaret's touches that appeal. She has disposed of "a bale of furs . . . with an eye not only to warmth and comfort but to picturesque effect" (*PS*, pp. 100–101).

By the end of the novel, the cabin is displaced altogether, and the Beldens enjoy a "rambling cottage" (*PS*, p. 237). Characteristically in the domestic novel of western relocation, the cabin was important as a place where the relocated family might be regenerated, but it was not an end in itself. Yet another home must mark the characters' reconstituted prosperity. Like other practitioners of the genre, though, Soule was careful to limit the implications of that prosperity, making clear that the final residence bears no resemblance to the urban superfluities earlier rejected. "It is no stately city mansion, nor modern Grecian villa" that now houses the Beldens but, rather, "a neat, commodious and cheerful home, furnished with taste and elegance," and surrounded by the mandatory "orchards, and gardens, shrubs and flowers" (*PS*, p. 237).

These transitions are narratively linked to the improvement of the surrounding village. Thus, the Beldens' final removal from cabin to cottage is seen as part of that process whereby "a straggling, border village" grows "into a populous and central town" (*PS*, p. 235). Indeed, the Beldens' activities in the village are, in large part, responsible for that growth. The combination saw-and-grist mill constructed by the Belden-Somers partnership initiates the transition from village to town. And, after fifteen years, just as the Beldens have advanced from cabin to cottage, so too the town—again, thanks to Horace Belden—advances to greater development. "The splendid Agricultural College that stands to the south-west of the town . . . owes its existence" to his "generous purse," we are told, as does "the pretty school-house" and several churches (*PS*, p. 237).

We are, in short, no longer on the frontier landscape with which the novel opened. The original woodland has been "cleared" and "is now a shaded Common of the town." "The river . . . now ripples . . . over costly dams," providing power for "the whirling wheels" of the mills. "The whistle of starting and stopping trains echoes now where resounded once the war whoop of contending Sioux and Sacs. News from Atlantic and trans-Atlantic cities glides noiselessly along the silent wires . . . while the gossip of the day is read at morning and at evening from the fresh papers of the East" (*PS*, p. 236). And all this has been accomplished, apparently, without either numbing toil or greedy exploitation.

The mill that is to make Horace Belden's fortune, for example, is presented as a kind of community project, built amid "joyous shouts and cheery whistling." Although the text acknowledges "the hands he employed," in fact, the economics of hired labor is deemphasized, as Belden's woodcutters take their place "in the timber" alongside "the head of every family, all being anxious to make many improvements the next season" (*PS*, pp. 190–91). The impression for which Soule seems to be striving here is that of an extended family, its members all voluntarily sharing the labors of common purpose. "There were no idlers in the settlement that winter," we are told, "for while the men were all industriously driving the saw or swinging the axe, and the boys hauling the logs, the women and girls were as busy indoors, doing up chores, getting ready the substantial and abundant meals which the hearty appetites of the wood-men craved, and making and mending the heavy garments which their severe labors required" (*PS*, p. 192).

Once completed, moreover, the mill serves community interests before it begins to earn profits for its owners. "Mr. Belden had said, when the project of a mill was started, that the first lumber sawed should be reserved for a church, and the next for a school-house, and he kept his word too" (*PS*, p. 202). The result of Belden's community-spirited generosity, combined with his willingness to lend money to newcomers, is that emigrant families happily end their travels in this particular settlement, sending "closely written letters to old neighbors back in Indiana or Ohio, telling them to pack up and come on, for they had found the poor man's Canaan" (*PS*, p. 207).

It was a dream with ancient antecedents. Ever since the earliest explorers found themselves in what seemed to them an untouched garden, America had promised a fertile and giving natural world that would harbor a new order of society. For Hector St. John de Crèvecoeur, in the eighteenth century, the "boundless continent," with its "anticipated fields of future cultivation," assured a place where humankind could be changed for the better, "entertain[ing] new ideas, and form[ing] new opinions."[27] What the domestic fictionists of the nineteenth century added to the dream was the guiding spirit of a womanly Eve as essential to the realization of the New World garden. Male capital may be required for development, these writers hint, but Eve's presence—and her presence alone—makes a *home* of paradise. "Even Uncle Billy, half-Indian as he was in all his ways," comes to appreciate her refining and domesticating influence. "'Who else ever'd a-thought of fixing things so purty out here?'" he comments of Margaret Belden (*PS*, p. 20).

Powerful though it was—combining ancient paradisal dreams with current domestic aspirations—the fantasy nonetheless could not contain the intractable realities of an economy motivated by profit. As long as Horace Belden lives, the text assures, "the poor, the suffering, and the sad, [will] find ever in him a trusty, faithful guardian." As the sentence goes on to explain—adding a quietly ominous note—"his pure life restrains by its example the excesses of his wealthy friends" (*PS*, p. 238). Buried though it is in a paragraph-long encomium on the now silver-haired Belden, the clause is devastating. Not everyone, the text tacitly admits, shares in the novel's closing fantasy; some require restraining influences. What, then, we are left to wonder, will restrain "the excesses of [the] wealthy" once Horace Belden forever departs "that cottage home [that] seem[ed] like fairy land" (*PS*, p. 253)? Is another Eden to be blighted and a "poor man's Canaan" lost to greed?

These were questions that Soule never answered: not in *The Pet of the Settlement* nor in anything she composed after it. Never again, in fact, did Soule turn to the west as a subject for fiction.[28] In this, too, she typified the form. No domestic fictionist before her had grappled with the contradictions inherent in the western relocation story; and after her, the domestic novel itself went into a decline. The Civil War effectively shattered what was left of the nation's innocence and, with that, the ragged remnants of the domestic fantasy found their way into books aimed at young girls, or they became part of the consolation fiction that flourished after 1865.[29] The west, too, receded as a subject for fiction, so that, "as late as 1870," according to James D. Hart, "fewer than 3 percent of America's new books dealt with the West."[30] In a nation that now spread across the continent, its population securely established on both coasts, the frontier could no longer promise an untouched garden in which the human community might still organize itself anew. Not until a later era would the frontier reassert its fantasied possibilities, emerging then as nostalgia for yet another vanished dream.

The Pet of the Settlement thus marks the last expression of a sub-genre that resolutely rejected the harsher realities of a Caroline Kirkland and the ambivalent anxieties of an Alice Cary, remaining to the end committed to what had become, by 1860, the nation's most cherished shared mythology. As that mythology went, an uncorrupted and fertile west had "brought hundreds of struggling, debt-ridden, homeless and hungry men and women from the crowded cities of older States, and given them peace and plenty, houses and lands, while they in grateful return have 'made the wilderness and the solitary place glad for them; and the desert to rejoice, and blossom as the rose'" (*PS*, p. 236). It was a myth the nation would not surrender, even as competing northern and southern interests increasingly focused on the new territories and thereby introduced cacophony into what Abraham Lincoln, in his first inaugural, called "the chorus of the Union."

*Whether the wilderness is
real or not
depends on who lives there.*

—Margaret Atwood,
The Journals of Susanna Moodie

10 E.D.E.N. Southworth and Maria Susanna Cummins: Paradise Regained, Paradise Lost

In a blunderingly anachronistic scene, Nathaniel Hawthorne pictured Hester Prynne begging her lover to flee the settlement and, with her, follow "'yonder forest-track . . . deeper . . . and deeper, into the wilderness.'"[1] In seventeenth-century Massachusetts, the setting for *The Scarlet Letter*, no Puritan woman would have urged such a course. But by 1850, the year the novel appeared, Hawthorne could take advantage of over two decades of publication, during which American women had increasingly written themselves back into the wilderness garden. If Hawthorne invested his Puritan woman with feminist sentiments taken from Margaret Fuller's *Woman in the Nineteenth Century*, he also attributed to her Fuller's eager willingness to "tread the wildwood paths."[2] Hester's resolve to find her way "'along the forest-path'"[3] derived not from Mary Rowlandson (nor even from a rebellious Anne Hutchinson, departing Massachusetts), but from nineteenth-century women's gradual readjustment of their imaginative relationship to the New World landscape.

That readjustment was accelerated in the decade that followed Hester Prynne's aborted fictional escape into the forest, as Hawthorne's scribbling contemporaries pursued their own historicizing impulse. Where Hawthorne looked backward to imagine a Puritan woman capable of choosing the "forest-track," so too women like Elizabeth Fries Ellet looked to history to prove that, after all, women had always "penetrated the wilderness, plunging into trackless forests." "Afford[ing] a picture of the . . . progressive settlement of the whole country, from Tennessee to Michigan," Ellet's *Pioneer Women of the West* (1852) offered sketches of sixty-one "American women who followed the earliest adventurers into the unknown forests of the West."[4]

In fiction, Ann Sophia Stephens invented the magnificent and tragic—albeit like Hester Prynne, anachronistic—Catharine Montour, "cast out, by her own free will, from civilized life" and seeking refuge "'in the broad, deep forests of a new world.'" Where Hawthorne's guilt-ridden Dimmesdale thwarted Hester's woodland fantasy, Stephens's Catharine Montour knows no such check. Set in pre-Revolutionary days in the Wyoming valley of Pennsylvania, Stephens's *Mary Derwent* (1858) portrayed a white woman who boasted proudly of living "'in the heart of an American forest, where civilized foot had never trod.'" Making her home with the Shawnee, Catharine Montour declares that "'for the first time in my life I felt the force of liberty and the wild, sublime pleasures of an unshackled spirit. Every new thought which awoke in my heart in that deep wilderness, was full of sublimity and wild poetic strength.'"[5]

Even Lydia Sigourney, "the sweet singer of Hartford," looked to history to confirm the white woman's place in the wilderness. Turning also to the Wyoming valley of Pennsylvania "in days long past," her 1853 poem, "The Lost Lily," retold the captivity story of Frances Slocum, captured as a small child by the Delawares, adopted by them, and then late in life rediscovered by her white brothers and sisters.[6] Loosely adapted from John Todd's bestseller of 1842, *The Lost Sister of Wyoming*,[7] Sigourney's verses emphasized the "pagan sister's" continuing commitment to a life "deep in the wilderness." Following thematic patterns first popularized in Seaver's rendering of Mary Jemison's life, Sigourney shows her heroine firmly refusing to return with her white siblings to "'the home, the grassy bank / Where we have played.'" Instead, the old woman twice affirms—both of her Indian lodge and of the wilderness surrounding it—"'Here is my home.'"[8]

The exploits of contemporary women suggest that such attitudes were not figments of the literary imagination only. The same year that introduced readers to Stephens's fictional Catharine Montour, twenty-one-year-old Julia Archibald Holmes ascended Pike's Peak—while the wagon train with which she was traveling to the gold fields of Colorado remained encamped below. In a letter to her mother, written from the summit and dated August 5, 1858, Holmes boasted, "In all probability I am the first woman who has ever stood upon the summit of this mountain and gazed upon this wondrous scene, which my eyes now behold." For three days, attired in the bloomer costume of the suffragists, toting a seventeen-pound backpack, and resolutely ignoring those who "tried to discourage me from attempting it,"[9] Holmes (in the company of her husband and brother) made her way up the treacherous slopes. At one point, she recorded in her journal, footing became so difficult that the little company was "obliged to take off our moccasins that we might use the toes and balls of our feet in clinging to the asperities of the sidling rock." But these difficulties seem not to have daunted her. Emboldened by the arguments of the feminists, Julia Archibald Holmes felt that she "possessed an ownership in all that was good or beautiful in nature," and an equivalent right to take an "interest in any curiosities" she might encounter on the journey as much as if she had been "one of the favored lords of creation."[10]

Anecdotes like this and Elizabeth Ellet's historical evocation of women "plunging into trackless forests" notwithstanding, in the popular imagination mountain peaks and wooded wildernesses still remained the domain of men. Even the fictional Catharine Montour confessed to "'feeling . . . as if I were treading, unauthorized, upon the confines of a darker world.'"[11] At one level, her statement suggests that she has somehow stepped beyond the proper bounds of both her race and sex to enter a morally degraded realm. And, in fact, this is the view to which the novel finally accedes. At another level, however, the statement emphasizes the character's *unauthorized* presence on a landscape where she does not belong. If this reading is admitted, then the buried pun in the sentence also suggests the author's discomfort at having so boldly altered the conventions of contemporary western romance. For the most part, in that antebellum decade, only literature's Indians and Indianized white men eagerly sought entrance into the dark and "'deep hush of the forest.'" By voluntarily choosing "the broad, deep forests of a new world," enjoying there the "'sublime pleasures of an unshackled spirit,'"[12] Stephens's Catharine Montour represented a unique—and, for the period—atypical image of a white woman: an unwonted and morally ambiguous Eve at home in a wilderness usually reserved for the isolate American Adam.

The more common rendering of the white woman on the frontier involved wives and daughters of spotless virtue settling themselves on flowered prairie expanses. An extended white family, rather than Shawnee, keep these women company. And a charming log cabin supplants Catharine Montour's exotic fur-lined lodge. For, the fact is, by adhering to conventions that preserved (rather than challenged) contemporary notions of female propriety, and by locating its story in the present (or quite recent past), the domestic novel of western relocation—and not the reconstructed historical wildernesses of Stephens, Sigourney, or Ellet—provided the major vehicle through which a decade of American Eves imaginatively took their place in Eden.

The phrasing is not rhetorical. The two most able practitioners of the form—Emma Dorothy Eliza Nevitte (E.D.E.N.) Southworth and Maria Susanna Cummins—clearly intended to portray the removal from east to west as the rejection of a blighted garden and the attainment of one "'not only undiminished, but almost untouched.'" "'It seems to me that here, the age, the weariness, and the sorrow of the old world has been left behind,'" one of Southworth's heroines exclaims during her first ride across the prairies. "'That this is a breaking out in a new place, or rather that this country and people, and we ourselves, are a new creation, fresh from the hand of God, and with a new promise!'"[13]

At least part of that promise, these novelists also suggest, was the reconstitution of the American Adam. If, as R. W. B. Lewis argues, American fiction written by men often concerns itself with "an Adamic person . . . at home only in the presence of nature and God,"[14] the fiction composed by nineteenth-century American women stubbornly returned that figure to the human community. The familiar "young and powerfully-built man, dressed in a simple hunting-suit," with a "rifle . . . slung over his shoulder, and [a] string of prairie-fowl suspended from his horse's neck,"[15] is not, in their pages, a Daniel Boone or Natty Bumppo. In Cummins's *Mabel Vaughan* (1857), he is a pioneer farmer, lawyer, rising politician and, most important of all, a man "'[un]likely to forget [the] simple, every-day duties'" of home and hearth (*MV*, p. 442).

E.D.E.N. Southworth's most accomplished projection of the new American Adam is Mark Sutherland, a principled son of the plantation south who frees his slaves and reestablishes himself westward in *India: The Pearl of Pearl River*. Serialized first in 1853 under the title, *Mark Sutherland*, and then issued as a book in 1856, Southworth's ninth novel breaks the usual pattern of domestic fictions by placing a male—rather than a female—at the center of the story line. *India* is unusual, too, in granting its hero two successive love attachments. Two quite different Eves, in other words, find a home in Mark Sutherland's "garden of Eden" (*I*, p. 345). What is most startling about the novel, however, is its anticipation of southern literature's postbellum requiem for a lost "Elysium of the sunny south" (*I*, p. 37).

As the novel opens, Mark Sutherland is graduating from Yale (where he has studied law) and is preparing to return to Mississippi to take over the plantation he has inherited from his father. There he expects to marry his beautiful half-Creole cousin, India Sutherland. But a week's attendance at antislavery meetings in New York convinces him of the inherent evil of "the 'peculiar institution'" (*I*, p. 36). And he now heads home with the intention of emancipating his slaves, confident that his intended bride will share his impulse for "'a simple act of justice'" (*I*, p. 121). When he reaches Mississippi, however, he finds that his plans are universally opposed. Still, he persists, even though his widowed mother withdraws from him, and, pressured by her father, Clement Sutherland (Mark's uncle), India breaks their engagement. Only the frail young Rosalie, then visiting the Sutherlands in the company of her stepmother, sympathizes. When no one else at Cashmere, the seat of Clement Sutherland's plantation, will communicate with Mark or respond to his notes of appeal, Rosalie sends him her little ladies' Bible, inscribed "*with . . . deep respect*" (*I*, p. 151).

Having freed his slaves and settled what is left of his inheritance upon his mother, Mark Sutherland is left with "only ninety dollars . . . his wardrobe and his law books" (*I*, p. 154). With these, he turns his back upon "that Eden of the valley where the Pearl river" runs (*I*, p. 38) and "embark[s] in a steamboat up the Mississippi," headed toward the new prairie west. As this new phase of his life commences, Southworth makes clear the associations she intends by quoting from John Milton's *Paradise Lost*:

> "The world was all before him, where to choose
> His place of rest, and Providence his guide."
>
> (*I*, p. 160)

Providence, however, does not at first seem a kindly guide. After eighteen months of failed efforts to establish a legal practice in the Rock River country of Illinois, Sutherland winds up in Cincinnati, "quite penniless, and nearly hopeless" (*I*, p. 162). There, in desperation, he answers a newspaper advertisement and accepts a position as tutor to the two young sons of Colonel Ashley in (West) Virginia.[16]

At the Ashley plantation, Sutherland again meets up with Rosalie and her stepmother. The pale, blonde, sixteen-year-old Rosalie, it turns out, is a distant relative of Colonel Ashley's and has been visiting at his estate for some months. Though she is clearly happy to see Mark Sutherland, she nonetheless upbraids him for abandoning his earlier ambitions. "'I thought you were going to open a glorious career for yourself, and achieve a great name,'" she explains. "'I thought you were going to be a statesman'" (*I*, p. 191). Mark's demurrals evoke only her impatience. "'And even if there *were* difficulties,'" she retorts, "'what then? We have no royal road to distinction in our country. We have no ready-made great men. . . . If any would be great, he must 'achieve greatness.' Nearly *all* of our heroes and statesmen have struggled up from the humblest places,'" she insists (*I*, p. 192). With this lesson on the virtues of the self-made man, the youthful Rosalie begins to inspire new courage in her listener, and their courtship begins.

Overcoming Colonel Ashley's concern that Mark Sutherland is as yet a young man without either fortune or position, and overcoming the stepmother's fear that the frail, tubercular girl has not the "'strength to endure the hardships of a Western life'" (*I*, p. 245), Mark and Rosalie obtain permission to marry. Before they can leave Ashley Hall, however, they once more encounter the darkly sensuous India. She has recently married St. Gerald Ashley, the colonel's oldest son and a rising politician in Washington. She and her new husband have come to Ashley Hall for a celebratory visit. But once arrived, India (who is still in love with her cousin) faints at Mark's approach. And later, in the privacy of her bedroom, she cries out, "'False to Mark! false to my husband! falser than all, to myself!'" From that moment on, she rebuffs the "manly, trusting love" of her adoring spouse (*I*, p. 217), in consequence of which her husband's political career begins to decline.

Unaware of what India suffers, Mark and Rosalie happily depart for their "log cabin in the West" (*I*, p. 249). What distinguishes this journey up the Mississippi from Mark's earlier remove westward is that the American Adam is no longer alone. On his arm is "'a source of strength and joy'" (*I*, p. 250) necessary to the establishment of another Eden.

Debarking at "the new village" of Shelton, "in the Northwest Territory," the two find themselves "at the very outskirts of pioneer civilization" (*I*, pp. 253, 254). Here Mark leaves Rosalie for the day in a crude hotel, while he attends to securing a home and an office. In the meantime, Rosalie gazes out the hotel window to survey her new domain. What she sees spread before her is "a high, level, and limitless prairie, its flat and green monotony broken, at wide intervals, by groves . . . and relieved by countless millions of wild flowers" (*I*, pp. 256–57).

The interlude that follows neither furthers the plot nor anticipates anything that Rosalie will actually encounter. Nonetheless, in her conversation with the hotel landlord's wife, Rosalie receives a grim picture of women's daily drudgery on a new frontier. In between cooking, cleaning, and tending to her infant, the woman prophesies to Rosalie, "'If ever you have a house of your own, and a baby of your own, and no one to tend to nyther but yourself—*mark my words*—just exactly when the loaf of bread is burning up in the oven, and the tea-kettle is boiling over, and the fat is catching afire in the frying-pan, that very time the baby's going to . . . squall you deaf'" (*I*, p. 258). She then concludes by telling a somewhat discouraged Rosalie, "'You may thank goodness if, on top of all that, your man aint down with a spell of sickness, and the cow lost in the woods, and the well dry!'" (*I*, p. 259). With these dire predictions still fresh in her mind, Rosalie at last retires to her bedroom, only to look out toward a landscape that now seems "strange, wild, lonely," with "the full moon" appearing as "the only familiar object that met her eyes" (*I*, p. 263).

The next day, after a ride across flowered prairies, which Rosalie hails as "'a new creation'" (*I*, p. 269), she and Mark embark in earnest upon what Southworth terms "*cabin*-keeping" (*I*, p. 291). Though there are difficulties to be encountered, Rosalie never suffers the drudgery outlined by the hotel's landlady. She finds herself in "a large log cabin . . . in good repair" (*I*, p. 265), and the text suggests that she has brought ample furnishings with her. The cabin is located, however, within an arm of forest that stretches out onto the prairies, ominously named "Wolf's Grove." And, true to its name, here Rosalie is menaced by a pack of hungry wolves prowling outside. So begins her first night in her new home, facing these terrors alone since Mark has temporarily returned to town for additional supplies. When he comes back, he easily routs the wolves with a pistol and reassures Rosalie that the animals will never again frequent the grove. Thereafter, the novel pictures Rosalie surrounded by a wild garden fruitful with "woodland treasures" (*I*, p. 295). Among other delicacies for her table, she discovers "wild plum" and "a profusion of wild raspberries, of unusual size and richness" (*I*, pp. 294, 295).

Having herself lived in Prairie du Chien, Wisconsin from 1841 through 1844, Southworth was apparently incapable of altogether masking the realities of her characters' situation. Their "first day of housekeeping in the forest log cabin taught them" the difference, she insists, between generalized impressions of such a life and the dailiness of its "irritating and exhausting details." "They had no garden," she explains, "no cow, no poultry, and there was no market where to procure the necessaries that these should have supplied." In consequence, "their first breakfast consisted of coffee without cream or milk, and biscuits without butter" (*I*, p. 292). Still, committed as she was to the Edenic associations already invoked, Southworth could not entirely evade the requirements of her chosen fantasy. The cabin is said to enjoy "a wild, woodland air," with "nothing to offend the most aesthetic taste." Rosalie sets her table with "damask table linen" and "delicate china," while the narrative voice assures us that "there was nothing mean, poor, or squalid, in [her] surroundings" (*I*, p. 295). (Quickly enough, moreover, a neighbor appears who offers Rosalie the freedom of her garden and dairy, so that the Sutherlands are not long without cream for their coffee or vegetables for their table.)

A snowfall early in December puts an end to this woodland idyll. With three feet of snow on the ground, the Sutherlands find themselves "nearly blockad[ed] . . . in their log cabin." Mark is barely able to walk the three miles to his office in town, while Rosalie becomes "a close prisoner in her house." At "the earliest opportunity," therefore, the two decide to leave Wolf's Grove, "and Mark accordingly sought a house in Shelton" (*I*, p. 305).

Having thus discharged her obligation to the convention of the log-cabin home, Southworth now proceeded to identify what, in her view, comprised the substance of paradise regained. It did not entail log cabins or even agriculture. "Indeed," when "many of his best-meaning neighbours strongly advised [Mark Sutherland] to take up government land, and turn his attention to agriculture," Southworth's Eve opposes this "with all her might, encouraging him to be constant to his profession" (*I*, p. 305). For Southworth, then, the paradise promised by the new west emanates not from any renewing relationship with the American landscape but from a morally renewed human community, untouched by the blot of slavery. In Shelton, Rosalie finds each citizen acting to "benefit . . . his individual self and the community" alike. Here she urges Mark to "edit an independent newspaper" (*I*, p. 306), and she herself opens a school for young girls.

After four years in Shelton, "their paper, '*The True Freeman*,' and their school, had both greatly prospered" (*I*, p. 308). Mark has become "the most popular, the busiest, as he was also considered the most able lawyer in the West." And, "though but twenty-five years of age," he is "the presiding Judge of the court . . . [and] had been named as a candidate for Governor" (*I*, p. 309). The surrounding community has similarly prospered, having "more than doubled in population and importance" (*I*, p. 307).

The emblem of the newfound garden, appropriately enough, is Rose Cottage, the Sutherland home "on the outskirts of the town, embosomed in a grove of trees" and surrounded by "every variety" of rose bush. In a set piece far more elaborate than her earlier presentation of the log cabin in Wolf's Grove, Southworth here details "this sweet home." It boasts "a kitchen-garden and young orchard" behind, and "in front and at the sides a spacious yard, where single great forest trees were left standing, with rural seats fixed under their shade." And, most important, there are the roses that give the cottage its name. "Rose-trees adorned the yard, rose-bushes hedged the parterres, rose-vines shaded the arbours and climbed the pillars of the piazza and gracefully festooned the eaves, and the fragrance of roses filled the air" (*I*, pp. 344–45).

It is to this richly detailed scene that Mark Sutherland returns after his first trip back to Mississippi in seven years. What he had encountered in Mississippi was a blighted garden. What he returns to in the west, Southworth will have us understand, is "his garden of Eden" (*I*, p. 345). The phrasing gains special strength from the contrast it enforces.

Only seventeen when she married, Rosalie has reached twenty-one, the age when she is to collect her considerable inheritance. To effect "a final settlement" of these monies, Mark has traveled back to Mississippi to meet with his uncle and Rosalie's guardian, Clement Sutherland. But upon entering "once more the 'Beautiful Valley of the Pearl,'" he finds "all . . . changed!" "Now late in a dry and burning September," it seems to Mark that "the beauty and glory had departed from the vale. . . . All the vegetation—forests, and shrubberies, and grasses—was dry and parched in the sun, and the very earth beneath seemed *calcined* by the dry and burning heat" (*I*, p. 311). Even the grounds around Cashmere appear ravaged. In the orchards, the trees are "untrimmed; some broken down with their loads of over-ripe fruit, some blighted—a prey to vermin—and some dying or dead." Once-beautiful gardens are now "a wilderness where thousands of the most lovely flowers and most noxious weeds dried and decayed together under the burning sun of September" (*I*, p. 313). What was formerly the "elegance and luxury" of the plantation house is given over to "rust and must, mildew and canker" (*I*, p. 329). Both within and without, "all was cheerless, hopeless, desolate" (*I*, p. 330).

Mark quickly discovers that India and her husband live as strangers at Cashmere, he given over to drink and adultery, she secluded in her darkened boudoir. Only a few elderly slaves and India's mulatta attendant remain; the rest have all been sold in a futile attempt to recoup Clement Sutherland's many investment losses. Indeed, so desperate and so greedy has the old man become that—as Mark finally learns to his dismay—Clement Sutherland has even forged Rosalie's name to a document and embezzled, and lost, "the orphan's funds" (*I*, p. 249). It is with this disheartening news, therefore, that Mark first returns to "his garden of Eden."

When Mark informs his wife of what has become of her inheritance, he also asks whether she wishes to prosecute her former guardian. But the magnanimous Rosalie takes pity on Clement Sutherland and, instead, urges Mark to travel yet once more to Mississippi to help. By the time Mark returns to Cashmere, however, Clement Sutherland has died, a wrecked and broken man. Soon afterward, St. Gerald Ashley also dies, falling from a second-story balcony in a drunken stupor. Preparing himself to help put in order what remains of his cousin's estate, Mark at last confronts his former fiancée "with the words of bitter truth and stern rebuke upon his lips" (*I*, p. 362). Among other things, he admonishes India to sell the property still under her control in order to pay off her father's and her husband's debts; he asks her to provide for "a poor girl who lives in the pine forest" with her child, explaining that "'when you estranged [St. Gerald Ashley] from your bosom, he sought sympathy and affection'" elsewhere (*I*, p. 363). And, returning to the novel's single most insistent theme, Mark entreats his cousin to emancipate her remaining slaves. To all of this, India agrees, even though it will impoverish her. Mark then remains "three weeks longer in the neighborhood of Cashmere," working with local lawyers to reduce "the chaos of the Cashmere accounts" (*I*, p. 367).

If his first return represented a passage from paradise lost to paradise regained, Mark's second return to Rose Cottage is a return to sorrow. The frail, tubercular Rosalie, exhausted from helping to run the newspaper and from teaching her girls' school, is dying. Advised by a local doctor to "spend the fall and winter in the South" (*I*, p. 376), Rosalie writes to her stepmother. Within a week that good woman arrives in Shelton to take

Rosalie to Louisiana. Mark accompanies them, though he knows his absence will jeopardize his chances for election to the United States Senate (to which he has recently "been nominated by the Human Rights" party [*I*, p. 371]). At Rosalie's deathbed, Mark is at last reconciled with his mother.

Rosalie's passing coincides with the announcement that Mark has won the election and is to go off to Washington, "the goal of his young ambition" (*I*, pp. 383–84). Grief-stricken, he can serve only desultorily at first. But after a time, aroused to action by issues that Southworth dimly hints pertain to the slavery question, he emerges as "among the foremost, most earnest and strenuous" in Congressional debates (*I*, pp. 386–87).

"At the close of his first senatorial term,"—that is, six years later—political business calls Mark to New York. There he once more meets India who now supports herself by teaching drawing and music to the children of New York society. Again, he woos "his boyhood's passion" (*I*, p. 402), but, as the text makes clear, the woman he now pursues, unlike the selfish and indulged India of the opening, is "disciplined and chastened by sorrow." She has spurned the "life of luxurious dependence" offered her by wealthy friends in the south, preferring instead "the honest independence of labour" (*I*, p. 390).

After "a quiet marriage ceremony performed before the altar of Grace Church" in New York and a honeymoon in Europe, Mark and India Sutherland take up residence in "Mr. Sutherland's elegant country seat on Lake Crystal, in one of the most thriving of the Western States" (*I*, p. 399). Beyond emphasizing its elegance, the text offers no further details about this "exquisite" mansion (*I*, p. 400). We are told merely that two children soon share it and that their "home is a very happy one" (*I*, p. 401). Lest we think that Rosalie has been forgotten amidst this newfound happiness, the novel concludes by assuring us that "her name was a sacred, sacred name," indelibly etched on a chamber deep in Mark Sutherland's heart (*I*, p. 402).

Judged by the conventions that governed domestic fiction at mid-century, *India* is at once satisfying and innovative. The characteristic moralizing is clearly articulated, but it is never obtrusive. By offering Clement Sutherland ("'a monomaniac on the subject of money-getting'" [*I*, p. 60]) as a dramatic foil against whom Mark Sutherland may be measured, Southworth effectively damns the value system of the plantation south while simultaneously hinting that the nephew's fall from grace with his family is ultimately a *felix culpa*. Because Southworth was a better writer than most other practitioners of the form, moreover, the many characters (only a few of whom have been included in the foregoing plot summary) are distinctive and affecting; the pacing is brisk; and the accustomed set pieces involving houses and their surrounding scenery are particularly vivid.

Even the informing antislavery position is offered so discreetly as to sustain the well-mannered gentility of the genre. Indeed, as the publisher's opening sheet approvingly announces, "It is one great merit in her fictions, that they faithfully delineate life and manners, without entering on vexed social, religious, or political issues" (*I*, n.p.). The publisher intended the statement as ameliorative, of course. With the Compromise of 1850, slavery had in fact become an increasingly volatile and "vexed" issue.[17] Nonetheless, the statement was not without accuracy. For those who held antislavery views of any stripe, Mark Sutherland's plan to send his emancipated slaves to Liberia would not offend. Nor would the novel, as a whole, offend any who still held to the merits of the "peculiar institution." For *India* was no *Uncle Tom's Cabin*, and the real evils of slavery are only hinted at, but never fully delineated in its pages.

In the presentation of its hero and heroines, by contrast, the novel at least tampered with domestic formulas—even if it never broke with them entirely. Unsurprisingly, Southworth's publisher stressed the formulaic. In his view, "the heroic spirit in which [Mark Sutherland] goes west, abandoning the luxuries he has been accustomed to," represents "the true type of a self-relying American" (*I*, n.p.). What is left unstated is that, unlike the heroes of most contemporary western romances, "the planter's son" (*I*, p. 27) goes west—but not to hunt or till the garden. Fulfilling in that journey the novel's thematic imputation of a new creation, Mark Sutherland does not, as it were, labor in the fields. Not even the roses that adorn "his garden of Eden" come from his hand. Instead, they "were all love-offerings from the young girls and children" who attended Rosalie's school (*I*, p. 345). As a result, once he has quit "the beautiful vale" of his youth (*I*, p. 159), Sutherland is identified only with a generalized "west," never with its forests or prairies. The effect of these strategies—strategies that radically challenged the forest intimacies of Daniel Boone or Leatherstocking—was to disengage Southworth's conception of the New World Adam from any *defining* relationship with the landscape around him.

In her presentation of two distinct Eves, Southworth was no less daring. If contrasting dark and fair women were a staple of nineteenth-century novels, they were not often both accorded the role of heroine, and rarely were both permitted a happy marital access to the novel's hero. Especially not in domestic fictions, which generally granted their heroes and heroines only one (usually happy) marriage apiece. But, in *India*, Southworth was less interested in adhering to domestic formulas than in elaborating a lesson first taught by Caroline Kirkland. Because Southworth distinguishes the western Eden from the fallen southern garden on ethical and moral—

rather than geographical—grounds, she appropriately designates as its first Eve the virginal Rosalie, "fair [and] pale" (*I*, p. 56). Hers is the role of "angel wife," inspiring her husband to "'be faithful to our part of the covenant'" (*I*, pp. 402, 269). Thus is Eden restored. For Eden to be sustained, however, another Eve entirely is required—an Eve like Kirkland's Cora Hastings, who has been shorn of her innocence and forcibly confronted with the harsher truths of some prior pastoral idyll. This is India, the dark-complected Creole who has learned to reject the "life of luxurious dependence" that had once been hers in the plantation south (*I*, p. 390).

Among other things, India's physical vigor and voluptuous sensuality introduce libidinal possibilities to the garden. But precisely because she has paid so high a price for the former indulgences of her "costly form of Oriental beauty" (*I*, p. 47), the text subtly suggests, she may yet prove no less a protectoress of the garden than her innocent predecessor. For, "disciplined and chastened . . . in the trials of her life" (*I*, p. 396), India now embodies knowledge born of experience, knowledge that can ward off future error. And it is she, appropriately, having inherited her Creole "mother's graceful harmony of form and complexion, and her father's strength and vigour of constitution" (*I*, p. 40), who brings children to the garden. By bending the conventions of dark and fair to suit her own purposes, then, Southworth made clear the kinds of seeds she would see sown in her idealized west. Rosalie's girls' school, we know, has "'sow[n] good seed, that will bring forth fruit long after'" she is dead (*I*, p. 349). Whereas India's "strength and vigour" provide "two fine children—a beautiful boy . . . and a lovely girl" (*I*, p. 401).

Where Southworth seems unable to make the conventions work for her is in her depiction of the novel's competing gardens. For, although we never doubt that Cashmere has become a blighted Eden, no other landscape in the course of the novel attains anything like its initial appeal. The fact is, nothing that Southworth shows us of the west has the force to dispel the declaration in the second chapter that, "the sun shines on no more beautiful and entrancing region than the vale of Pearl River" (*I*, p. 37). As a result, the novel veers dangerously close to defeating its explicit intentions.

"The Elysium of the sunny south," according to Southworth, contains "birds of the most brilliant plumage and enchanting melody, . . . flowers of countless varieties, . . . [and breezes] charged with music and fragrance" (*I*, pp. 37, 38). The "one spot more favoured than all the rest . . . in this garden . . . is 'Cashmere,' the beautiful seat of Clement Sutherland" (*I*, p. 38), upon which Southworth lavishes all her considerable descriptive skill. The plantation house is a graphic rendering of Ionic colonnades, open verandas, and "elegant" Venetian balconies (*I*, pp. 41–42); while withindoors are bay-windowed and satin-draped comforts. The grounds surrounding the house are almost "narcotic" in their beauty, everywhere suggesting "luxurious repose" (*I*, pp. 42–43). "So various, beautiful, and aromatic" is a nearby grove, for example, "that one is lost and entranced amid [its] luxuriating wealth" (*I*, p. 43).

The passages describing western scenery—the profusion of prairie wild-flowers or the picture-pretty Rose Cottage—pale by comparison. To begin with, they are never as elaborate as the descriptive passages marking the opening chapters in Mississippi. And they are not, as are the Mississippi landscapes, reified and reinforced by repetition. Thus, the single description of Rose Cottage does not as indelibly etch itself upon our imagination as do the several pages of varied views of Cashmere.

In choosing to subtitle the book *The Pearl of Pearl River*—dispensing with *Mark Sutherland*, the title of the first magazine serialization—Southworth (or her publisher?) tacitly acknowledged the powerful appeal of the opening chapters set in Mississippi. In the wake of these chapters, we are made to sympathize with Mark Sutherland—like a latter-day Adam—lifting up his voice and weeping as "from the beautiful vale he turned" (*I*, p. 159). And, even as the novel progresses westward, we nonetheless sense that, for all its decadent sensuality and the unholy institution that sustains it, the Pearl River valley plantation remains the most beautiful garden we have encountered. Not even its blasted and blighted ruin can erase the earlier appeal. If anything, in a peculiarly modern way, these later passages suggest not so much just retribution as nostalgia for a lost magnificence.

At the time she was composing the serialized *Mark Sutherland*, Southworth was living in her birthplace, Washington, D.C., and from there visiting friends and relatives on plantations in Maryland, Virginia, and the deeper south. The immediacy of the southern landscape may perhaps explain something of the vividness of her Mississippi settings.[18] By comparison, it had been at least eight years since she had last lived in the west. Indeed, several of the western passages betray either the inevitable mistakes attendant on hasty composition or, more probably, a faulty memory of specific sites and their unique geography.[19]

What should not be overlooked, however, is the possibility that Southworth's use of the *idea* of the west conflicted with what had been her own firsthand experience in Prairie du Chien. Unfortunately, too little is known about Southworth's four years in Wisconsin. She went there with her husband, the inventor Frederick Hamilton Southworth, in 1841, a year after their marriage. She gave birth to a son and taught school in nearby Platteville. Then, in 1844, pregnant with a second child, Southworth separated from her husband and returned permanently with her son to Washington, where she gave birth to a daughter.

Southworth never revealed the reason for the separation. Even so, odd passages in a number of her novels lead one to speculate that, at least in part, Southworth was separating herself from the hard life of the west as much as she was separating from her husband. Tightly plotted and briskly paced as they are, Southworth's novels rarely engaged in extraneous materials that did not, in one way or another, further her central story. And yet in every one of her novels of western relocation, there are lengthy passages describing the toils of "the hard-working pioneer woman" (*I*, p. 257)—even when none of her central characters ever fulfill such a role. The landlady at the crude frontier hotel, for example, prepares Rosalie for a life that, in fact, the novel never grants her. Similarly, while the cabin in Wolf's Grove honored the log-cabin conventions of westernized domestics, it also veered from the fantasy sufficiently to portray the genuine difficulties of preparing a meal without benefit of a garden, a cow, some poultry, or a convenient market. Cutting against the grain of the western fantasy her novel implied, in other words, there may well have been a bitter Wisconsin memory of having no time to rest "half an hour before it was time to get up, fire up the cooking-stove once more, and prepare supper" (*I*, p. 261).

If, in fact, Southworth's memories of Prairie du Chien countered the fictional fantasy to which she was otherwise committed, this could explain her inability to portray a western Eden as inviting as the southern Eden she had known since childhood. It might also explain why her work so early anticipated the literature of the postbellum south. For, whatever the moral virtues of the west in *India*, the "beautiful and entrancing . . . vale of Pearl River" (*I*, p. 37) nonetheless stands as one of the first of many Edens that generations of southern writers would portray as blighted and destroyed, even as they allowed its lost beauty to continue to seduce and haunt the imagination.

Framing Maria Susanna Cummins's 1857 novel, *Mabel Vaughan*, are two scenes in which a woman sits at a window and gazes out upon an open landscape. In the first, a New England widow named Mrs. Herbert looks toward "a green and sloping orchard, now fragrant with new-mown hay," where Mabel Vaughan, a little girl "between eleven and twelve years of age," is seated "at the foot of an old apple-tree" (*MV*, pp. 5, 6). By the end of the novel, Mabel herself—now a mature woman on the eve of her wedding—sits "in front of the familiar window which commanded a view of the wide-spreading prairie" (*MV*, p. 502) and composes a letter to her old friend and teacher, Mrs. Herbert. As she does, she watches her nephews at play out by the barn, just as Mrs. Herbert had once watched her. Although there are no suggestive quotes from Milton between these two scenes, the structure of the novel suggests an American Eve's expulsion from Eden, her fall into temptation, and her eventual repossession both of an alternate garden and an appropriate Adam.

The first part of Mabel Vaughan's history is told in flashback. The youngest "daughter of a New York merchant" and his "beautiful and fashionable" wife (*MV*, p. 12), Mabel spends her earliest childhood years in the nursery in company with her brother, Harry, and both are cared for by hired help. Her mother pursues a busy social life, while her father, disappointed at his wife's lack of interest in "those fireside and domestic joys which had always figured in his dreams of married life" (*MV*, p. 13), turns from his home to his counting-house. Only the education of the eldest, a daughter named Louise, is supervised by her mother. But, under her mother's tutelage, Louise becomes little more than "a complete mistress of all the arts of coquetry," lacking in both "mental and moral discipline" (*MV*, p. 13).

The closeness of the bond that develops in the nursery between Mabel and Harry is broken when Harry turns nine and is sent away to boarding school. When, a year or so later, her mother dies (presumably a victim of her own social excesses), Mabel too is sent from home. Having "reflected upon the disappointment he could not but feel in Louise, and resolved that a wholly different course should be pursued with Mabel's education" (*MV*, p. 16), John Vaughan decides to place his youngest daughter under the care of Mrs. Herbert, a well-educated and religious widow who lives in rural New England. And it is here, in the apple orchard of Mrs. Herbert's pretty "country home" (*MV*, p. 6), that the novel opens.

During her ten years with Mrs. Herbert—from ages eight to eighteen—Mabel receives visits from her father, her brother Harry, and from her older sister, now a fashionable young matron married to the wealthy Mr. Leroy. At eighteen, her education completed, Mabel leaves the "plain but well-ordered New England homestead" (*MV*, p. 18) to take up the role of mistress in her father's newly renovated and refurbished New York mansion, with all its "display of luxury and elegance" (*MV*, p. 29). In New York, she encounters the temptations of what her sister terms "society." Her beauty, intelligence, and grace of manner so captivate that city's wealthy partygoers that almost overnight—just as her brother Harry had predicted—Mabel becomes *the* belle of the season and gets caught up in a constant whirl of balls and entertainments.

Mrs. Herbert's influence is not entirely lost on her, however. Gradually, Mabel tires of "the endless repetition of ball-room nonsense, which constituted the conversation of Mrs. Leroy's set" (*MV*, p. 96). But she does not give up that set because she is now drawn to it by the arrival of Lincoln Dudley, "cosmopolitan in his habits, artistic in his tastes, [and] completely versed in the knowledge of society" (*MV*, p. 101). To the young and inexperienced Mabel, the dilettantish and wittily cynical Dudley appears attractively unlike anyone else she has met in New York.

Their flirtation has the effect of drawing Mabel more and more often away from her father's fireside. Without her warm, domesticating presence, her father reverts to earlier habits, staying late at his counting-house. His sister, Sabiah, Mabel's kindly and shy maiden aunt, spends her evenings alone in the empty mansion. And Harry, also missing his sister's company, himself embarks on a round of undisciplined social activity. Finally, Harry's erratic behavior brings Mabel to the shocked discovery that her beloved older brother has become an alcoholic, drinking and gambling his nights away with other dissipated young men of his class.

At this juncture, help comes in the form of the appropriately named Hope family—a poverty-stricken widow with three children, all living in a sunless "cellar-like apartment" in another part of the city (*MV*, p. 109). Mabel becomes acquainted with the Hopes through their eldest daughter, Lydia, who is employed by Louise Leroy as a nurse for her two small sons. Jack Hope, Lydia's younger brother, reminds Mabel of her own beloved Harry. Like Harry, Jack has fallen into bad company and is in danger of running afoul of the law. What saves Jack is the devotion of his younger sister, Rosy. With a "depth of sisterly love" that bespeaks the "power of self-sacrifice" (*MV*, p. 184), little Rosy Hope keeps her brother at home with her in the evenings, or else waits up for him when he is out, and thus effectively curtails his time on the street. Framed in the identical sentimental mold that produced Harriet Beecher Stowe's Little Eva, or even Southworth's angelic Rosalie, Rosy Hope—enfeebled and dying of tuberculosis—is credited with special access to "that knowledge of things divine, in which [she] was the thoroughly-gifted teacher" (*MV*, p. 253). A special bond develops between the dying Rosy and Mabel Vaughan, and, through that bond, Mabel determines to follow Rosy's example and aim toward "the reformation" of her own "prodigal brother" (*MV*, p. 188).

The test of Mabel's resolve comes when her father asks her to accompany Harry to a New England town where (without consulting his son) John Vaughan has arranged for Harry to be apprenticed in the law under a local Judge. While in "the town of L. . . . in the country" (*MV*, p. 272), the brother and sister are to reside with their widowed aunt, Mrs. Ridgway (John and Sabiah Vaughan's older sister). At the same time, Mr.

Vaughan proposes to close the New York house, while he accompanies Mr. Leroy to the west in order to look after their large investments there.[20]

At first, Mabel resists her father's wishes, having set her heart on other plans. Guided by Lincoln Dudley, she and her sister, and others of Mrs. Leroy's set, were to have made a trip to Trenton Falls. It is an excursion to which Mabel has been looking foward—not just for the scenery, but because she fully hopes that, on such an excursion, Dudley might propose to her. But, of course, Mabel does at last acquiesce to her father's wishes, foregoing the anticipated excursion. In this decision, Mabel is strengthened by the timely discovery of a Bible that Mrs. Herbert had earlier tucked away in her traveling trunk and by the example of little Rosy Hope. Now "armed with a Christian resolution" and sensing herself "led by the hand of a little child," Mabel feels the reawakening of her "sleeping conscience" (*MV*, pp. 243, 244).

Despite their father's good intentions, removal to "the town of L." proves a disaster. The widowed Mrs. Ridgway is a pretentious social climber who forces her fashionable niece and nephew into the "centre of a whirl" of unwanted social "excitement" (*MV*, p. 272). Harry discovers he has no aptitude for the law and again falls in with a crowd of fast young men from "a neighboring university" (*MV*, p. 273). And Mabel receives word that, on the Trenton excursion, she had not only not been missed but that Lincoln Dudley had been "perfectly devoted" to another (*MV*, p. 274). Finally, forced by their aunt to a party they have no desire to attend, a humiliated Mabel must depend upon the good offices of a young stranger named Bayard to maneuver the sodden Harry and their carriage safely home.

A few days later, Harry is again brought home unconscious and inebriated—this time after falling from his horse. When a fever sets in, only Mabel sits at his bedside, their aunt having been too embarrassed by his behavior to wish any longer to encourage his presence in her house. During his feverish delirium, Harry confesses to Mabel "his past folly, extravagance, and dissipation" (*MV*, p. 305). When the fever at last breaks, a chastened and regenerated Harry awakes. Mabel, we are told, "felt herself repaid for every trial, every sacrifice, every suffering. She had watched, and waited, and hoped, and prayed. In spite of weariness, alienation, disgrace, and sin, led by patience, fortitude, and holy love, she had sought and found her brother" (*MV*, p. 307).

As Harry convalesces, he and his sister are struck by news of yet another misfortune. A newspaper story informs them that both Mr. Vaughan and Mr. Leroy have been in a train accident in the west, the former injured, the latter killed. Harry proposes to go west immediately to look after his father, while Mabel takes off for New York to comfort her now-widowed sister. In Illinois, Harry finds himself "'inspire[d] with new energy'" in what he calls "'a glorious country'" (*MV*, p. 318). In New York, Mabel faces a sister prostrated not by grief but by the news that her husband has died insolvent, leaving her penniless.

When Louise Leroy dies from the shock of her impoverishment, Mabel takes responsibility for the care of her two nephews. At first, she considers reopening her father's New York mansion. But she now learns that it was not just Mr. Leroy who had been ruined by his western land speculations. John Vaughan, too, has lost everything, and the New York house and its furnishings have gone to auction. Undaunted, Mabel determines to take her nephews and join her father and brother in the west. Once again, the Hope family comes to her aid. Owen Dowst, a young workman from their neighborhood, has decided "to seek his fortune at what was then termed the far West" (*MV*, p. 329), and the Hopes propose that he travel with Mabel as a protective escort to her and the boys. This proposal she gladly accepts.

En route, Mabel meets another helpful traveling companion, the venerable and kindly Madame Percival. Having previously seen the philanthropic widow in New York society, Mabel now learns that Madame Percival is traveling to a destination in eastern Illinois not far from her own in order to visit a son who has been farming there for some years. Because she already knows the area, Madame Percival encourages Mabel not to "'feel discouraged by its rough and undeveloped character.'" "'Take part in [its] progress,'" she urges Mabel and, appealing to what were then considered distinctively female inclinations, she counsels the newcomer to help the region "'advance in moral and spiritual growth.'" Espousing the notion of woman's separate and special sphere, a notion that all the domestic fictions supported, Madame Percival adapts it to the west. "'It is woman's peculiar privilege and province to exert that softening, elevating, purifying spirit, which sanctifies the ruder labors of life,'" she tells Mabel, "'and sheds abroad in the community a nobler ambition than that of building cities in the wilderness, and subduing the elements to human will'" (*MV*, p. 355).

Having thus established women's responsibility for civilizing (or "softening") the raw frontier, Madame Percival then voices the western relocation novels' fond hope that their imagined communities might yet serve as models for reality. The geographic centrality of these fictive western townships molded by women's "purifying spirit" was to translate itself into a like centrality of moral influence. "'Above all,'" warns this "benevolent and Christian matron," "'do not consider your life in the West a period of exile; this is but a part of our mother country, destined, in time perhaps, to become in its influence, what it already is in its locality,—the centre and heart of the republic'" (*MV*, pp. 353, 355).

For the next one hundred pages—or, in terms of the novel's chronology, for the next six years—we watch Mabel follow Madame Percival's advice. She brings "harmony and order" and an "unwonted sense of comfort" to the rude farmhouse that Harry had previously termed "'this bivouac in the wilderness'" (*MV*, pp. 366, 367, 360). She serves as surrogate mother and as teacher to her nephews. She makes a place in the household for her maiden aunt, Sabiah. She encourages Harry in his plan to take up farming on the "large tracts of arable land" that their speculating father has left "lying waste" (*MV*, p. 378). And, after nursing her father through an illness, Mabel sees her influence finally help to reconcile the old man to his loss of fortune. The financial ruin of the father in the counting-houses of the east, in short, has released the daughter to a western landscape upon which she may—for the first time in the novel—exercise the full range of her abilities.

In all of this, Mabel fulfills the "three departments" prescribed by Catharine Beecher. That enactment of mid-nineteenth-century women's special "profession" takes on added significance here, however, because it is used to mark women's distinctive contribution to the redemption of the American "waste land." Rejecting the notion of a found or waiting paradise, Cummins instead asserts the garden that must be *made*; and to that process, she insists, women have always been essential. "Mabel Vaughan was not the first among the women of this fair land who have suddenly waked from a dream of luxury to the homely realities of Western life," we are reminded. And, as a consequence, what must not be forgotten is that, "while manly enterprise and vigor have been put forth with unparalleled energy, the success which has redeemed the waste land, and made the wilderness glad, is no less due to the cheerful sacrifices, the patient toil, and the sympathising heart of woman" (*MV*, p. 363).

When she had done elaborating that theme, Cummins needed only to tie up the loose ends of her several characters' stories in order to bring the novel to a satisfying close. In that last fifty pages, then, Cummins allows Harry to marry. His bride is a local minister's daughter who has also been an affectionate surrogate sister to Mabel. The Hope family reappears (though without Rosy, who has died). Lydia is now happily married to a thriving Owen Dowst; and her brother Jack, once the wayward son, is now his mother's pride, earning "'a handsome living'" as the "'foreman of some [machine] works not far from'" the "spacious and substantial barns and granaries" that surround the family's "comfortable two story dwelling" in Illinois (*MV*, pp. 460, 456).

Most important of all, with Lincoln Dudley long forgotten, Mabel Vaughan finds a more suitable partner. This turns out to be Bayard Percival, son of the same Madame Percival who had assisted Mabel on her journey westward and, as well, the same "Bayard" who had once helped Mabel and a drunken Harry to return safely from a party in "L." By the time Mabel and Percival again meet in Illinois, he is a prosperous farmer and (having earlier earned a degree from Harvard) a successful lawyer and rising politician also. In fact, his election to a two-year term in Congress precipitates his proposal of marriage, as Percival pleads, "'O Mabel! Must I go alone?'" (*MV*, p. 498).

As the novel concludes, the Vaughans' "humble . . . Western home" is dismantled. Mabel and her husband take her father with them to Washington, after which the three return to Percival's beautiful Lake Farm estate in eastern Illinois. Harry and his wife invite Aunt Sabiah to lodge with them on their adjacent farm. And Madame Percival takes the two Leroy nephews with her to Cambridge, where, in company with her two grandsons at Harvard, they will complete their schooling. This dispersal of the Vaughan household does not, however, diminish the symbolic importance of the "humble . . . Western home." To the contrary, in "'bid[ding] farewell to that Western home, which, humble as it is, has become to us a dear and honored spot,'" Mabel makes clear its crucial role as a "'blessed haven of rest, which afforded us a safe and welcome shelter from the storm of adversity and trial.'" Her closing letter to Mrs. Herbert thus assures her old teacher that the lessons once taught in a humble New England farmhouse have now been reified by its western counterpart. "'Blessings on its bare white walls, its plain brick hearth, its low-roofed rooms!'" Mabel concludes her encomium to "'our prairie home.'" These humble surroundings, she writes, "'have taught us that happiness is independent of ornament; that contentment brings joy to the humblest fireside; and that love knows no limits and often expands the widest in the narrowest space'" (*MV*, p. 505).

Perhaps because Maria Susanna Cummins had never been west or herself followed Mabel's trail beyond Buffalo,[21] her passages of scenic description lack the vividness and startling detail achieved by those who had seen the west firsthand—including Alice Cary, Caroline Soule, and E.D.E.N. Southworth. But then what Cummins seems to have understood better than any other writer of the western relocation novel was that its intrinsic appeal derived not from the actual physical details of the prairie landscape but from the fantasy with which that landscape might be invested. What distinguished *Mabel Vaughan* among its contemporaries, therefore, was the novel's gesture in the direction of explaining the particular appeal of a western locale.

New York, obviously, could not serve the fantasy requirements: corrupt and corrupting, it besets Mabel and Harry with temptations on every hand, luring them away from home and fireside. But the return to New England, to John Vaughan's boyhood "town of L. . . . in the country" (*MV*, p. 272), does at first seem to promise some kind of curative refuge. What defeats that refuge is its vulnerability to city designs. "New York was not so far distant but that reports of [John Vaughan's] wealth, standing, and fashionable alliance had reached the ears of those who remembered him in his boyhood" (*MV*, p. 271), the text explains, thus suggesting that the same shallow pretensions that had marked New York society are now making their way into the countryside. The presiding genius of the place, after all, is no longer Mrs. Herbert but the social climbing Mrs. Ridgway, currying favor with the town's elite by catering to their eagerness to meet her fashionable niece and nephew. As a result, the values Mrs. Herbert represents must flourish elsewhere—someplace (as Bayard Percival puts it) "'where life is plain, simple, and robbed of all conventionalities'" (*MV*, p. 281). Within the terms of the westernized domestic, this can only be the agricultural frontier.

The *domestic* possibilities of a place "'where life is plain, simple, and robbed of all conventionalities'" is what the westernized women's fictions aimed at, of course. Those possibilities could only be realized, however, by asserting an Adam and Eve who encompass the symbolic implications of the western garden and, together, make clear the import of the established western home.

At the center of Cummins's story, moving from childhood to maturity and from adversity to happiness, is Mabel Vaughan. In relocating from New York to Illinois, Mabel discards her silks and satins to put on "a simple lilac print . . . with a snowy collar" and becomes "the fair mistress" of a cozy prairie farmhouse (*MV*, p. 433). She has lost nothing of her beauty in that translation, the narrative insists, nor have her manners lost anything "of their delicacy." On the contrary, we are assured, in the removal to a raw frontier, "the soul of Mabel became more and more imbued with sweet, womanly tenderness" (*MV*, p. 396). That, after six years in Illinois, she has indeed become accommodated to and mistress of her new domain, the text signals by literally "'crown[ing] her queen of the prairie.'" As she and her nephews are driving their wagon across the prairie after an overnight visit to Harry and his wife in their new home, the youngest boy makes "a collection of brilliant wild flowers, which, as they continued their drive, he busied himself . . . in wreathing into a tasteful garland." "Placing the wreath, with an air of playful homage, on the uncovered head of Mabel," the boy calls out, "'I crown her queen of the prairie'" (*MV*, pp. 410–11).

At precisely this moment, with a regal Mabel atop her wagon, seated "in her elevated position, in the midst of an unbroken prairie," her appropriate consort is reintroduced. "A young and powerfully-built man, dressed in a simple hunting-suit," rides up, his "rifle . . . slung over his shoulder, and [a] string of prairie-fowl suspended from his horse's neck" (*MV*, p. 413). But while Mabel's first view of Bayard Percival in Illinois may suggest his identification with a western Adam derived from Daniel Boone or Leatherstocking—so that their prairie meeting seems symbolically realized—the text itself has already begun to dress him in other garb. Harry, we have been informed, had earlier met Percival while out hunting. There, "the manners and bearing" of the man whom Harry first takes to be only an "expert hunter . . . proclaimed him to be a gentleman, and his knowledge and cultivation proved him to be one of no ordinary attainments." The hunter thus turns out to be an educated gentleman, and the educated gentleman, further, turns out to be a farmer, equally conversant "on a question of foreign policy, or the details of Western farming." In fact, it is "the young stranger's animated account of his own successful experiments in agriculture, and the almost fabulous crops which the rich soil was capable of yielding" (*MV*, pp. 377–78) that finally influences Harry to take up farming on his father's land.

Clearly, Cummins was attempting to refine the traditional male images of the yeoman farmer and the isolate hunter in such a way as to forge a new kind of western Adam. Writers like Southworth and Soule also shared that ambition, variously casting their male protagonists as frontier lawyers or hunter-priests. What they did not always communicate was the fantasy underlying those refinements. On this, as on everything else, Cummins was explicit. Bayard Percival may woo "the queen of the prairie," she makes clear, not only because, as a hunter, he can provide game for her table, and not only because, as a farmer, he has learned to cultivate her garden, but because, as a new kind of western hero, he has also turned the garden into a home. His mother applauds that fact when, once again visiting her son in Illinois toward the end of the novel, she boasts to Mabel of Percival's efforts to domesticate his frontier holdings. "'I am always ready to congratulate my son anew on the patience with which he occupied a most primitive dwelling,'" she tells Mabel, "'until he had acquired the means to build a house to his own taste, and on the spot of his choice'" (*MV*, p. 453).

Because the Lake Farm estate is to become Mabel's new home and, as such, culminates the fantasy, Cummins takes great pains to describe it. In an "ecstasy of pleasure," Mabel first approaches the house by means of a road "now winding like a thread amid corn and wheat fields . . . and now leading the traveller beneath the refreshing shade of grand primeval forests" (*MV*, p. 452). Situated on "a higher point of land," the house offers views that continue that standard alternation of closed and open spaces, looking out over "an open expanse of prairie, grain land, and forest, with here and there a little collection of farm-houses and a village church" (*MV*,

p. 453). The house itself, "built of the pale yellow stone peculiar to the region," is "long and low, being only a story and a half in height, but covering a wide extent of ground, having wings on either side, and including all the principal rooms on the lower floor" (*MV*, p. 453). Across its front runs "a light verandah, festooned with the graceful American woodbine." But, as attractive as these external views certainly are, it is within-indoors that Cummins locates the symbolic key to the significance of Lake Farm.

At once a satisfying alternative to the luxurious New York mansion and a fulfillment of the sentimental obligations of the humble "Western home" that it will soon replace, the Lake Farm house boasts tasteful and comfortable appointments even as it groups its inhabitants "round the wide hearth . . . while the flickering flames cast a subdued, but cheerful light round the room." When the flames from "the wide hearth" are said to be "reflected in the polished furniture and the old family tea-urn under the antiquated sideboard" (*MV*, p. 454), however, the text is doing something more than merely establishing an ambience of cozy domesticity. It is also articulating what other western relocation novels had only dimly hinted at.

It is not only "the rough, new, and undeveloped character of almost every thing pertaining to Western life" (*MV*, p. 454) that appeals, Cummins wants us to understand. What makes the west attractive for the purposes of the domestic fictionists is its putative capacity to hallow and maintain "such ancient, and time-honored tokens" of domesticity "as everywhere pervaded the [Lake Farm] establishment." To Mabel's eyes, "even the heavily-carved chairs and tables, the Turkey carpet, the antique fire-set, and the quaint, old family plate, which were here preserved as ancestral heirlooms, all bore their part in giving to the place the secluded and familiar air of a cherished home" (*MV*, p. 455). All of which stands in stark contrast to the fashionable refurbishings of her father's New York mansion, in which the returning Mabel had recognized nothing from her earlier years there. What Mabel has recovered in the new west, in other words, is a quality of familial continuity that the unstable old east no longer affords. The artifacts of that continuity—the hearth, the old family plate, and the dated furnishings—which would be sacrificed to fashion in New York, become in the west cherished "tokens" of a past to which the domestic fictionists looked with eager nostalgia.

The nostalgia that pervades the Lake Farm interiors is palpable. But it is precisely that combination of the "quaint" and the "antique" withindoors, coupled with the cultivated prairie garden without, that makes Lake Farm the Eden to which the novel aspires. Echoing what had been Margaret Fuller's earlier observations of frontier women, Cummins now acknowledges that her heroine has, after all, "been taxed with a responsibility disproportioned to her years, and had well nigh sunk beneath the burden of recent labors." Feeling herself "sheltered" and protected within the Lake Farm house, however, Mabel at last finds "sweet and welcome repose." "Thus," the text continues, "the first evening of her visit proved one of unmixed satisfaction, and the night that followed, brought with it sweet and dreamless rest" (*MV*, p. 455). Mabel Vaughan has recovered paradise.

In surveying a half century of domestic fictions composed between 1820 and 1870, Nina Baym observes that "the men in this fiction are less important to the heroine's emotional life than women."[22] While the statement is generally accurate for the vast majority of writing in this category, it is not so for that small sub-genre of western relocation novels that emerged between 1850 and 1860. Unlike their counterparts set in the east, these westernized domestics paid as much attention to the fathers, brothers, and suitors of their potential Eves as they did to the relationships between the women. As though tacitly acknowledging that the domestic Eve could not survive without an Adam properly adapted to home and community, these novels repeatedly depict male characters rehabilitated by frontier hardships and boys who point to their western experience as bracing and improving. As young Harrie Belden phrases it in Caroline Soule's *The Pet of the Settlement*, the west is a place where a boy might "'grow to be a man'" not the dandified gentleman of New York society, but "'a man with hands that could do something else beside twirl a moustache or gold-headed cane; with feet that could follow the plough.'"[23]

On the one hand, this unusual attention to male characters catered to the domestic fictionists' dream that a new order of society might be modeled in the frontier west—a society in which masculine competition in the marketplace would be subordinated to masculine participation in a community governed by the values of hearth and home. On the other hand, the frequency of the characterizations—coupled with the willingness to make a male the central figure in a fiction otherwise focused on the female (as in Southworth's *India*)—strongly suggests that these writers shared a discomfiting awareness of powerful prior male images that needed to be tamed and refined.

When, in the 1850s, writers like Southworth and Cummins recast the heroine of domestic fiction, dressing her "in a simple lilac print" (*MV*, p. 433) and sending her off for excursions across the prairie, they virtually *invented* the first coherent and recurrent image of a frontier Eve. Earlier incarnations had either been too Indianized (as was Mary Jemison) or too indistinct (as was Rebecca Bryan Boone in the shadow of her husband) to take hold in the popular imagination. The image that had taken hold, and the figure whom most Americans associated with the frontier, was "the solitary, Indian-like hunter of the deep woods."[24] Derived from Daniel Boone, reified by Cooper's Leatherstocking, and now identifiable in the mountain men who trapped and traded across the Continental Divide, the hunter's image all but obliterated that of the yeoman farmer and, in so doing, established the frontier as the exclusive domain of the individual alienated from or cast out of the community, hostile alike to settlements and petticoats. The problem facing the domestic fictionists when they took up their western relocation stories, therefore, was that the terrain into which they wanted to insert a domesticating Eve was the same terrain already imaginatively appropriated by "the most significant, most emotionally compelling myth-hero" of American culture, the isolate American Adam.[25]

Their solution was to bring Adam out of the woods and into the town, carefully redrawing his image, novel by novel. If his identification with the hunt was too powerful to be altogether suppressed, it could nonetheless take on different meaning. Thus, Harrie Belden becomes a wealthy businessman as a result of his years of hunting and trapping in the Pacific northwest, and, with that wealth to sustain him, he returns permanently to Iowa to claim his bride in *The Pet of the Settlement*. Harry Vaughan and Bayard Percival both hunt and fish in *Mabel Vaughan*, but their activity is shown directly contributing to the maintenance of the Vaughan household. And Edward Somers, the "hunter-priest" of *The Pet of the Settlement*, is intended to express the ruggedness of the hunter joined to the gentleness of a community's spiritual adviser—the first a holdover from traditional male images, the second an acknowledgment of the religious impulse behind so much of this fiction. Only E.D.E.N. Southworth's Mark Sutherland completely evades the hunter's trappings (as he also evades the farmer's)—except, of course, for his routing of the prairie wolves.

Perhaps because the Jeffersonian yeoman farmer had always been identified with home and community, if not with the frontier, his is the most frequent vocation of the domestic fictionists' western Adam. Even so, while all of these novels emphasize the flowering prairies and cultivated farmlands that surround their Eves, they do not mandate that their Adams be tillers of the soil. Bayard Percival and Harry Vaughan establish themselves as successful farmers, of course, but Edward Somers, Harrie Belden, and Mark Sutherland never do. What these men share instead—whether as lawyer, newspaper editor, or partner in a local gristmill—is principled involvement in the community around them and demonstrated commitment to home and family life. What established the locales of western fictions as Edenic, in other words, was not so much their fertile expanses as the pos-

sibility that, supported by the wealth of the landscape, all the characters—
male and female alike—might participate in what Catharine Maria Sedgwick termed "a zealous devotion to '*home missions*.'"[26]

Looking back over American literary history, however, the Adams and
Eves of the domestic fictionists appear anomalous. Their figures are no
longer familiar to us, and—except in the degraded version of the cowboy
reluctantly tamed and married by a civilizing schoolmarm—their story
seems to have left no lasting imprint on our shared cultural imagination.
An Eve who would cheerfully and, on her own, make a home of a "'bivouac in the wilderness'" (*MV*, p. 360) and an Adam who would just as
eagerly seek to create a home in that same wilderness—these are the figures of an American paradisal myth that never took hold. In part, this may
derive from the domestic fictionists' incapacity to firmly enough embed
their new American Adam in a defining relationship with the landscape
itself. But, in recovering Adam for home and community, it was precisely
his traditional (and often erotic) ties to the land that had to be severed. In
part, too, the figure of the American Eve was anchored to an intrinsically
nostalgic ideology that would not survive the assaults of an increasingly
public feminist movement. Then, again, there is the inescapable fact that,
without any abiding commitment to an exclusively agrarian west, the domestic fictionists virtually prophesied that their fantasied gardens would
eventually be invaded by the identical urbanizing forces that had earlier
blighted the east. (And, as Southworth well knew, slavery was already riding the wagon trains to Oregon.)[27]

It should not be left unstated, however, that at least in part, the failure of
the domestic fictionists' western idyll to last much beyond 1860 may be
due as well to the fact that "the process of mythogenesis," as Richard
Slotkin points out, demands "continuous activity."[28] But continuous activity is what the writers of these western relocation novels never enjoyed.
By the 1850s, when women's novelists first seriously began to focus their
attention on the west, Daniel Boone and his fictional successors had already reigned for more than a half century in the wilderness paradise,
whereas the American Eve—with generations of unwilling captives behind
her—was just learning to claim the garden as her own. With the advent of
the Civil War, moreover, the domestic fictionists' engagement with western themes all but disappeared.[29] A single decade of western relocation
novels had been sufficient to establish their initiating conventions. Indeed,
as *The Pet of the Settlement* warns, it had been sufficient even to threaten
that the hardening of those conventions might render the form moribund.
But a single decade had not offered these writers enough time to experi-
ment with their new material. No daring rejection of conventions so newly
forged could yet occur, nor any uniquely memorable character or story

emerge. In one brief decade, there was not time either to leave a mark on literary history or to alter the cognitive character of the culture. As a result, the mid-nineteenth-century American Adam and Eve, turning wilderness or prairie into a communal garden of domesticity, remained only uncompleted mythic possibilities, the short-lived victims of discontinuous images and unreconciled symbolic inheritances.

Even so, their impact on the women then making their way across 2,400 miles of unmarked terrain to "a terrestrial paradise" in Oregon[30] or California was profound and immediate. Paradise, these novels declared, was now to be claimed by Adam and Eve alike. And a raw frontier might yet sustain viable images of home.

At a deepening
of the Isinglass River
I lie down in stones and
*   tea-colored water.*
I think: be careful. Do not say
home. The bones
of that word mend slowly.

—Marie Harris, *Interstate*

Epilogue
A New Frontier Beckons:
A Transitional Meditation

A pioneer family in Illinois, about 1855. Gift from Lynda Koolish to the author

"At the time of which we write," explained Maria Susanna Cummins in *Mabel Vaughan* (1857), "the States which form the eastern and western boundaries of the Mississippi were the chief theatre of emigration" (*MV*, p. 361). Since the action of the novel takes place within the eight years following the Panic of 1837, Cummins was correct in locating the Mississippi valley as the goal of most western emigrants. In those years, the Missouri River roughly demarcated the extreme edge of the agricultural frontier, so that, in the 1840s, along "the main highway" that ran from Peoria to Pekin, Illinois, residents reported "long lines of covered wagons . . . in Spring and Summer, laden with the crude belongings of emigrants, bound for Missouri, at that time the anticipated goal of the restless path breakers who left their homes in Kentucky, Indiana and Illinois to plant for themselves new habitations in a newer West."[1]

In the 1850s, as Cummins glanced backward toward an earlier, sparsely settled Illinois, railroads began to link the Ohio and Mississippi rivers with the Great Lakes, thus precipitating yet another wave of emigration into the Mississippi valley and, virtually for the first time, making areas like northern Michigan accessible to settlers. Throughout the 1850s, in other words—despite our habit of identifying that period exclusively with the overland migration to the Pacific west—areas well east of the Missouri River continued to be newly settled and to demand adaptation to what one relocated New Englander called "the wilderness, . . . the wild pioneer life of those times."[2]

As late as 1859, for example, the forty-eight-year-old Nicolas Stott Shaw accompanied her children on a week-long trek "through a dense and often trackless forest," nervously making her way from the railroad station in Grand Rapids to a waiting cabin about ten miles from present-day Big Rapids, Michigan. Sustained by the belief "that we were going to a farm, . . . [with] some resemblance at least to the prosperous farms we had seen in New England," Nicolas was shocked to discover at the end of her journey only "the four walls and the roof of a good-sized log-house, standing in a small cleared strip of the wilderness, its doors and windows represented by square holes, its floor also a thing of the future, its whole effect achingly forlorn and desolate." To be sure, Nicolas Shaw and her children succeeded in making a home of the cabin some "one hundred miles from a railroad, forty miles from the nearest post-office, and half a dozen miles from any neighbors save Indians, wolves, and wildcats." But in the first shock of recognition "that this was really the place father had prepared for us," she could only bury "her face in her hands, and in that way she sat for hours without moving or speaking." Indeed, as her daughter would insist many years later, Nicolas's "face never lost the deep lines those first hours of her pioneer life had cut upon it."[3]

That scenes like this recurred throughout the 1850s all along the Mississippi valley and around the Great Lakes, however, does not diminish the pointedness of novelist Maria Susanna Cummins's explanatory remark. For, while the domestic fictionists resolutely confined their western fantasies to territories on either side of the Mississippi, as if trying to consolidate imaginatively the meaning of what had already transpired, the rest of the nation—as Cummins herself was well aware—watched with rapt fascination the progress of those who would now set "foot upon every inch of ground between the Atlantic and the Pacific shores" (*MV*, p. 361). By the time Cummins was composing *Mabel Vaughan*, women had for twenty years been a part of that progress.

In 1836, the year Eliza Farnham was married in Illinois and the year that Mary Austin Holley's expanded edition of *Texas* appeared, two white women crossed the continent from western New York to Oregon. Setting out in mid-February with their husbands, Narcissa Prentiss Whitman and Eliza Hart Spaulding rode by wagon to Pittsburgh over what was now a well-traveled route across the Alleghenies. From Pittsburgh they went by riverboats, via St. Louis, to Liberty, Missouri, then the western extreme of the American frontier. At Liberty, the women mounted side-saddle, occasionally resting by riding in one of the two light wagons that carried their supplies. Their destination was Fort Walla Walla on the Columbia River. On July 4, 1836, guided by a caravan of mountain men and fur traders, they became the first white women to cross the Continental Divide through the South Pass of the Rockies (in what is now western Wyoming).

Two years later, in 1838, four more women—also accompanied by their husbands and guided by fur traders—followed that same overland route to Old Oregon. Sent out by the American Board of Commissioners for Foreign Missions (which represented both Congregationalists and Presbyterians), the six newly married couples were to set up missions and embark on the conversion of the Pacific coast Indian tribes. Missionary zeal had thus motivated these women to take on what Narcissa Prentiss Whitman referred to in her diary as "the difficulties of an unheard of journey for females."[4]

Only two years later, however, the women of the Walker family went overland as the first avowed homeseekers to Oregon. But, when Oregon did not live up to expectations, Joel Walker guided his wife, their children, and his wife's sister south to California, where the two Walker women became the first American white women to reach California by the overland route. By the summer of 1843, as Margaret Fuller observed the continuing influx of newcomers to Illinois and Wisconsin, more than one thousand prospective settlers were completing their journey to Oregon by the overland route. And, with the success of that 1843 emigration heralded in the newspapers, covered-wagon caravans began yearly to assemble at Independence and St. Joseph, Missouri, ready to make their way across the Great American Desert to the promised Eden beyond. In less than a decade, the frontier had jumped nearly two thousand miles, and Americans had been promised yet another garden in which to enjoy "strawberries as well as wheat, and green peas picked on Christmas day."[5]

The great obstacles to overland emigration in previous decades had been fear of the so-called Great American Desert east of the Rockies and the belief that wagons—so necessary for transporting a family westward—could not be taken across the mountains.[6] But when, in 1830, the American Fur Company sent provision wagons to the Pacific through the South Pass (where, previously, only pack animals had been used) and William L. Sublette returned safely from the Pacific side of the Continental Divide with wagons heavily laden with pelts, newspaper accounts were quick to celebrate the venture and to predict the eventual migration of entire families across that same route. It was a response consciously invited by Sublette and his partners, Jedidiah S. Smith and David E. Jackson. Their report to the secretary of war, widely quoted in the press, emphasized, "This is the first time that wagons ever went to the Rocky Mountains; and the ease and safety with which it was done prove the facility of communicating over land with the Pacific ocean."[7]

What Henry Nash Smith has called "the forbidding image of an American Sahara"[8] was less easily countered. As John D. Unruh, Jr., has noted, "until the beginning of the Civil War virtually all maps of these regions in school textbooks and governmental reports were labeled the 'Great American Desert.'"[9] The image had probably first been fixed by the phenomenal success of James Fenimore Cooper's *The Prairie* (1827), with its unrelentingly "bleak and solitary" landscape of "meagre herbage" and "hard and unyielding soil."[10] In later decades, the notion of an uninhabitable arid region stretching for hundreds of miles east of the Rockies was retained for other reasons. Throughout the 1840s, newspapers in the Mississippi valley, especially, editorialized against venturing too far west of the Mississippi's fertile fields. In one memorable series of articles during those years, the St. Louis *Daily Missouri Republican* insisted that the overland route was too treacherous for family groups, exposing "wives and children to all degrees of suffering," and urged that California and Oregon were inferior to Missouri anyway. The editorial advice, accordingly, was that readers should "not . . . move one foot" beyond Missouri.[11] Even Horace Greeley—better remembered for more optimistic sentiments about going west—used the pages of his New York *Daily Tribune* to inveigh against the growing "Oregon fever." As reports reached New York that eight of those who set out in the 1843 emigration had died even before reaching the Rockies, Greeley editorialized "that it is palpable homicide to tempt or send women and children over this thousand miles of precipice and volcanic sterility to Oregon."[12]

In the face of this kind of resistance, the best evidence for the feasibility of the overland route remained the sheer fact of those who had done it. From the first, therefore, groups with an interest in fostering emigration to the Pacific made much of Narcissa Prentiss Whitman's and Eliza Hart Spaulding's comparatively uneventful crossing of 1836. The Oregon Provisional Emigration Society, headquartered at Lynn, Massachusetts (and comprised of Methodist ministers and lay persons), used its monthly magazine, *The Oregonian and Indian's Advocate*, to publicize the women's accomplishment. The first issue of October 1838 referred to the missionaries as "the first white women who have traversed these mountains" and then suggested that the fact that "delicate females" had successfully crossed the continent meant that, in future, whole families might do the same. "Thus has vanished the great obstacle to a direct and facile communication between the Mississippi valley and the Pacific ocean," the editor concluded (no doubt intentionally echoing Sublette).[13] The magazine's express goal, of course, was to encourage speedy "Christian" settlement of Oregon in order to effect the conversion of the "heathen."

If the pious Massachusetts editor of *The Oregonian and Indian's Advocate* was impelled by religious ideals to urge "the feasibility of this route for ladies, and even children,"[14] a growing industry of hucksterism on behalf of Pacific emigration operated out of quite different motives. With the tacit approval of a Congress eager to wrest California from Mexico and Oregon from the British, private land speculators circulated allegedly firsthand reports of a Pacific paradise and appealed to imperial impulses to extend American hegemony across the continent. But above all, they appealed to Americans' continuing land hunger. Investors with interests in California's Central valley, for example, sent booster letters to newspapers in Missouri, Arkansas, and elsewhere in the Mississippi valley, lavishly describing the healthfulness, beauty, and fertility of the region and setting forth the favorable terms on which land might be obtained there. As often as not, this kind of boosterism proved exaggerated or even altogether false and misleading.

In 1842, one such letter appeared in a St. Louis newspaper, claiming that Americans could obtain liberal land grants in California on the sole conditions that they take an oath of allegiance to Mexico and adopt Roman Catholicism. But, as Frederick Merk has pointed out, "the article ignored the fact that in 1842 the Mexican Congress enacted a law forbidding further land acquisition or settlement by foreigners in California except by special permission of the authorities in Mexico City." Nonetheless, he continues, "the St. Louis article was widely copied in newspapers of the Mississippi Valley, though it was denounced by the Mexican minister in Washington as false propaganda of land speculators."[15]

The popular emigrants' guides to California and Oregon were less coy about their imperial designs. After describing California's seacoast as "very fertile," with "plains produc[ing] an abundance of oats and clover spontaneously," J. M. Shively's *Route and Distances to Oregon and California* (1846) advised readers to "seek a good location for your farm," adding only: "The Spaniards may molest you — but be firm, and soon the destiny of California will be governed by yourselves."[16]

In a sense, the government was also responsible for the growing California and Oregon fevers. By publishing reports like Lieutenant Charles Wilkes's *Narrative of the United States Exploring Expedition* (1844), with its detailed descriptions of a flowering and fertile land beyond the Rockies, government printing presses effectively added the stamp of official approval to the quest for a Pacific garden. And, finally, under pressure from speculators and restive emigrants alike, the government acted to dispatch the legal barriers to emigration. In June 1846, Congress ratified a treaty with an England unwilling to go to war over the disputed territory between the Columbia River and the forty-ninth parallel. All of the Oregon Territory—which comprised much of what we call the Pacific Northwest, including Oregon, Washington, Idaho, and smaller sections of Montana and Wyoming—was now in American hands. A year later, the chief clerk in the State Department, Nicholas P. Trist (whose grandmother had traveled the Ohio and Mississippi rivers to an earlier west in 1784), negotiated the Treaty of Guadalupe Hidalgo with Mexico. When the treaty was ratified in 1848, the war with Mexico ended and the United States took control of California.

The hucksterism and the governmental encouragement aside, motives for emigration to so far a frontier were many and complex. At bottom, of course, was the lure of fertile land that might be cheaply acquired, along with the ubiquitous fantasy of yet another waiting paradise. Economic gain seemed assured. Preparing to leave Independence, Missouri, in 1846, Tamsen Donner expressed as much in a letter to her sister when she explained, "I am willing to go & have no doubt it will be an advantage to our children & to us."[17] But the times may also have had something to do with it.

The Panic of 1837 and the long depression that followed had made credit unavailable to those newly attempting to establish themselves in the

Mississippi valley. The prospect of even cheaper land in the Pacific west, and the promise of available credit there, may thus have lured many families farther west than they had originally intended to go. Still, those who suffered most from the bank failures and ensuing depression in the middle western states could not afford the journey, because the cost of properly equipping a family for the overland trail was not insubstantial. As one observer of the 1845 migration noted, "They brought large herds of cattle, and judging from their appearance, they seem with few exceptions to have been in easy circumstances in their own Country."[18]

To emigrants from New England or the Ohio valley, the new frontier held special appeal. Advertised as well-watered and wooded, with a mild climate, California and Old Oregon seemed to promise improved versions of already familiar environments. Where the tough sod of the prairies demanded steel plows and altered methods of farming, the Pacific west called for the familiar technology of the wooden plow, the scythe, the ox, and the horse. As one Missourian who had spent four unhappy winters in Oregon, only to return to the prairies, put it, "Eastern men are more generally pleased with the country than those of the west."[19]

For families seasonally prostrated by the malarial fevers (or "agues") that still plagued the Ohio and Mississippi River valleys, the Pacific west was hailed as a healthy, even curative climate. Indeed, as Sarah J. Cummins (no relation to the novelist) recalled, it was precisely a bout with the "lung fever" that had driven her family from their new home in St. Joseph, Missouri, to Oregon in 1845.[20] The Missouri doctor who attended her and her sickly parents and siblings warned, "'Don't you stay here another winter . . . you can't brave it.'" "'Go to Oregon,'" the doctor advised her father, "'where are Pine and Fir trees and grouse.'" For the sixteen-year-old Sarah, newly married the next year and "bound for the far West" with her husband and family, the trip itself proved salutary. After only a few weeks on the trail, "the first taste of buffalo meat marked a decided improvement in our health and for the first time in my life," Sarah recorded in her diary, "I began to enjoy fairly good health" (*AAR*, pp. 22, 24).

Paradisal possibilities, cheap land, and a healthy climate notwithstanding, unquestionably the most dramatic impetus to Pacific migration came in 1849 with the news of the discovery of gold along the American River, about forty miles from Sutter's Fort. Within a year, some eighty thousand "forty-niners" poured into California—most from the States, but some from Europe, Asia, and Australia. By contrast, only about fifteen thousand had traveled overland in the years before 1849.

Many women, of course, objected to the prospect of a two thousand-mile trek across desert and mountains—often with small children in tow—to some unknown terrain, no matter what its advertised attractions. Having once followed her spouse from North Carolina to Illinois, Elizabeth Cress would be moved no further. As a result, in August of 1851, she anxiously wrote to her parents for help, explaining, "my old man has left me & has gon to Californa and took my wagon and left me and my Children in a bad situation."[21] What she wanted was a temporary loan so that she and her children might stay on in Illinois and try to make a go of the farm on which her husband had left her. Other women, even when "dazed with dread" at the challenge of such a journey, nonetheless recorded "wiping away my tears, lest they betray me to my husband" and, like one 1849 emigrant to California, "prepared to continue my trip."[22]

While this California-bound pioneer steeled herself for the journey by holding on, as best she could, to "the reputed perpetual sunshine and wealth of the promised land,"[23] still others professed only enthusiasm for what "now lay before our venturesome and adventurous feet" (*AAR*, p. 23). Like Julia Archibald Holmes, the first white woman known to have climbed Pike's Peak, a good many diarists on the overland trail eagerly noted the details of the changing landscape and, like Holmes, declared themselves "possessed [of] an ownership in all that was good or beautiful in nature . . . as much as if I had been one of the favored lords of creation."[24] It is tantalizing to speculate that, to some degree, these expressions of eagerness derived not only from the impact of the current feminism (as was clearly the case with Holmes) but, as well, from the cumulative inheritance of women's published writings about the west. It is after all the case that the women who ventured to California and Oregon in the 1840s and 1850s (along with those who traveled only as far as the Mississippi valley) enjoyed the advantage of two decades in which a variety of women writers had named the frontier Eden and extolled the virtues of "the Western home." For women relocating to a wooded Pacific coast in the 1850s, especially, Elizabeth Fries Ellet had collected authentic accounts of earlier "American women" who had ventured "into the unknown forests of the West."[25] While, for all, the domestic fictionists popularized the image of a frontier Eve and quieted fears of what such dislocations entailed.

The adventure of removing to a Pacific Eden "full of unexplored wonders and beauties" was never the subject of Elizabeth Ellet or the domestic fictionists, however. Their stories all took place well east of the Missouri. Instead, the earliest public suggestion that the Rockies and their environs might appeal to women came first from the published letters of the missionary women of 1836 and 1838, and then again in Eliza Farnham's *Life in Prairie Land* (1846). Steaming across the rivers that crisscross the Mississippi valley, Farnham declared herself entranced by the notion that the waters upon which she traveled probably had originated, either as rain or snow, in the mountainous region west of the Great Plains. There is a "sublimity" in the notion, she avers, and "in the association—the idea that the water which ripples at your side has come from a far land, a land full of unexplored wonders and beauties. The reflection opens an immense field of thought and inquiry," she continued, "and makes you long to be transported to the region where all these exist" (*PL*, pp. 208–9).

In 1849, Farnham's longing was fulfilled. Her husband's death in San Francisco that year impelled her to California (not overland but on the more expensive route, via a clipper ship around Cape Horn). Within a year of her arrival in San Francisco, she purchased land in Santa Cruz, donned the bloomer costume for its convenience and ease of movement, and "enter[ed] upon 'agricultural operations.'" By 1851, she had completed most of a manuscript that recorded, among other things, her attempts to introduce fruit-bearing trees to her California ranch and "the great labor of seed-time, . . . the potato planting."[26] Finally completed and published in 1856, Farnham's *California, In-doors and Out* appeared just a year before Cummins's *Mabel Vaughan*. Both authors were aware, though, that the frontier landscape about which they wrote was fast disappearing. Whether a fictional Illinois or a remembered California—each had already undergone what Farnham called a "revolution in progress."[27]

Looking back on her family's 1845 overland trek to Oregon, Sarah J. Cummins later remarked on the little group's general ignorance of what they were about. "Wagon loads of people and goods had left Missouri river the year previous to cross the same plain that we were preparing to cross, but none of them had ever returned to tell us of their adventures," she recalled. "And, as I now think of it," an older Sarah mused, "we were surely taking a wild and inconsiderate step for we had no definite knowledge of their fate, and yet we were willing and anxious to plunge into the same wild and risk the dangers that were so numerous with no definite knowledge of what might lie at the other extreme" (*AAR*, pp. 23–24).

The Cummins party was not alone in its ignorance. Indeed, what repeatedly struck the experienced mountain men who encountered the covered-wagon caravans was the emigrants' "uncertain information" as to what lay ahead. Traveling east after a winter of trapping in the Rockies, James Clyman met up with three small companies of emigrants along the North Platte in June of 1846. Eagerly questioned by them about the country from which he was just returning, Clyman noted it as "remarkable" in his journal "how anxious thes people are to hear from the Pacific country." To his mind, it was decidedly "strange that so many of all kinds and classes of People should sell out comfortable homes in Missouri and Elsewhere pack up and start across such an emmence Barren waste to settle in some new Place of which they have at most so uncertain information."[28] A week earlier, on June 15, 1846, Francis Parkman rode into Fort Laramie with similar sentiments. On June 19, he wrote his mother in Boston that "we have passed on the road eight or ten large companies . . . bound for Oregon or California, and most of them ignorant of the country they are going to, and the journey to it."[29]

What neither Parkman nor Clyman could assess was the motive power of the imagery that drove the emigrants onward. Though theirs was a difficult physical journey destined for a real geographical terrain, nevertheless, as Sarah J. Cummins so well understood, "the hearts and minds" of the travelers were "striving to reach the 'Land of Promise'" (*AAR*, p. 25). Even the emigrants' guides played to these metaphorical motifs, asking readers to see themselves as embarked on a kind of secular Pilgrim's Progress, at the end of which awaited paradisal rewards. "Be of good cheer," one such guide echoed Bunyan, for "though there are many unforseen difficulties to beset you, . . . you will find a country in Oregon that will fill your desires, and repay you for all your toil."[30]

For women on the overland trail, paradisal images became inextricably associated with images of home, and images of home embraced not only the cabin and landscape at the end of the trail but also the elements of former houses and former gardens that could be introduced there. To be sure, since almost all women on the overland trail traveled as part of family groups (or went as the servant to such a group), and since most domestic responsibilities at the end of the journey would fall to them, it was clearly incumbent upon the women, as Sarah Cummins put it, to be "well equipped for setting up a new home in a far off land" (*AAR*, p. 26). That said, it does not explain what, in fact, the women chose to take with them.

Repeatedly warned "that on such a journey one should take only the bare necessities of life," most, like Sarah Cummins, insisted also on those "treasures that are most valuable for their associations than for their intrinsic value or usefulness" (*AAR*, p. 50). Seeds and dried root cuttings from the wildflowers or cultivated ornamentals of a previous homesite were packed in as carefully as the more obviously utilitarian seeds and cuttings from vegetable and herb gardens. What the newly married Sarah Cummins could not leave behind included "my little chair made of sugar maple wood, a chest of books, . . . calicoes bought during the Revolutionary war and . . . used to make my stock of spare quilts, also many rare bits of needlework, . . . my sheetings, pillow covers, towels and all other household linen," most of it packed in a "great walnut-wood sea chest that had been sent to me from Massachusetts" (*AAR*, p. 50). The attachment to items with old family associations (like "calicoes bought during the Revolutionary war") illustrates how well the novelist Maria Susanna Cummins had understood women's need to put the stamp of some domestic past on the new west. Lifelong New Englander though she was, the author of *Mabel Vaughan* accurately identified "time-honored tokens" as crucial to the western woman's ability to take comfort in the "familiar air of a cherished home" (*MV*, p. 455).

Many such tokens could not survive the journey overland. On a route still marked in some places by the imprint of wagon wheels, travelers followed a trail of recent gravesites or, especially along the Platte, passed "the shattered wrecks of ancient claw-footed tables, well waxed and rubbed, or massive bureaus of carved oak." In order to save oxen parched by the sun and spent by the long haul across the desert, emigrants were often forced to lighten their loads, abandoning these time-honored tokens "to scorch and crack upon the hot prairie."[31] However necessary to survival, though, few women easily accepted the discarding of treasured family heirlooms. As Francis Parkman observed to his mother, many tended to "get impatient and cry to go home again."[32]

Some families, of course, did turn back. But what is more often remarked upon by those who observed the overland emigrants are the repeated instances of women persevering even in the face of a husband's death or else taking over when a "husband's will and energies failed." In *California, In-doors and Out*, Eliza Farnham paid homage to one such pioneer. When her husband broke "under the tremendous sufferings of that terrible journey," she became "the efficient care-taker of him and their three sons; yoked and unyoked the oxen, gathered fuel, cooked their food," and the statements in the emigrants' guides to the contrary, also "drove the team, hunted wood and water . . . and for months performed all the coarser offices that properly belong to the other sex."[33]

If the statements in the diaries composed along the route may be taken at face value, what seems to have sustained such women—whether their overland crossing proved easy or difficult—was an appreciation of the changing beauty of the scenery, coupled with a firm capacity to hold on to some happy image "of our anticipated home" (*AAR*, p. 46). The image might be domestic or geographic; often enough, it derived from literary sources. To dispel her own "rueful thoughts and dim forebodings" along the way, Sarah Cummins "recall[ed] lines of prose and verse, descriptive of Evergreen Firs, soughing Pines, and flowing rivers that mingled their placid waters with the rolling turbulent waters of the great Pacific" (*AAR*, p. 26). During times of crisis, these imaginative strategies could betoken survival itself.

Sarah J. Cummins's *Autobiography and Reminiscences*, compiled for her grandchildren in 1908 but largely "copied from my diary as written in years long since gone by" (*AAR*, p. 7), offers a vivid illustration. When, in late September of 1845, her family and others in their wagon train reached the snow-peaked Cascade Mountains, prudence dictated that most in the company hire boats to take them "down the [Columbia] river, together with the household goods" (*AAR*, p. 40). Only a small contingent remained behind to lead the cattle over the mountains into the Willamette valley beyond. Sarah Cummins, her husband, and her two brothers were part of that contingent.

By now it was late September and, as Sarah recorded in her diary, "the travelling was slow and toilsome. Heavy fall rains were coming on and the steep slopes were almost impassable for man and beast." The inexperienced little party misread the trails and, within a few days, admitted that they had somehow lost the track "on the slopes of Mount Hood." Thus they continued for several days more, their food supply perilously low, until "one morning we awoke in a blinding snowstorm." By nightfall, "it seemed we must all perish," Sarah recalled. Even "the strongest horses had given out" (*AAR*, p. 44).

Because the snow had fallen "all day long and had melted and thoroughly drenched every garment we wore," the little company was not only exhausted and hungry but wet and suffering from cold and exposure, too. Still, they trudged on in search of wood, leading their "riding nags" (*AAR*, p. 44) and keeping what stock they could. Finally, when their "situation was each moment becoming more desperate, . . . the welcome sound of 'we have found wood'" echoed from those ahead. But when Sarah and her husband who were at the rear of the company "at last reached the assembled group," there was "no sign of a fire . . . and most of the men and all the boys were shedding tears. We were told that not a man could be found whose hands had strength to fire a gun, and not a dry thread of clothing for kindling" (*AAR*, pp. 44, 45).

In the end, however, one man's coat provided some dry inner lining for kindling and, "with almost super-human effort," another man "succeeded in firing the gun." "In an instant the flames burst forth." Exhausted to the point of indifference, Sarah had to be led "to the fire side" by her husband. But "no sooner had the warmth penetrated my wet and freezing garments," she recalled, than she felt the full force of the exposure and frost that had numbed her limbs. "Such extruiciating [*sic*] pains seized me that I was wild with pain and could not forbear the scream that rent the air on that wild mountain." Even so, "there was nothing to be done and I had to endure this suffering until the clothing on my body was dry and the chill of frost drawn out of my limbs" (*AAR*, p. 45).

Sarah and her companions all survived the harrowing snowstorm on the peaks of Mount Hood and, after a night huddled by their fire, they awoke to cleared skies. The adult men who were able went off to look for lost stock, while Sarah and her brothers were left to tend the campfire. At this point, though still weak with hunger and fatigue, the young girl could not rest content until she had taken in the beauty of the scenery surrounding her and looked toward "the land of our adoption" (*AAR*, p. 45). She therefore proposed to her brothers that "we go to the summit of a near ridge and look beyond and in the direction of our anticipated home" (*AAR*, p. 46). Her brothers, however, did not share these imaginative compulsions, and so Sarah climbed alone.

The passage that describes what she saw suggests that in some way the "wonderful view" may have begun to compensate the young woman for her sufferings:

> The sky was cloudless. The storms of the previous day had so cleared the air of dust and impurities that my horizon was boundless, and this, my first, prospect of everlasting green forests and their wonderful vividness, green on all the near approaches and changing with wonderful blend from green to etheral [*sic*] blue, and on the distant margin rested the shade of blue, so intense, so indescribably beautiful that no power of words can express the wonderful panorama of beauty with which my soul was entranced. Seated on eternal snow, looking from over these mountains and hills, across wide valleys into dark glens, above the roar of wind or of water, I was lost in infinity. (*AAR*, p. 46)

It is a rhapsody that echoes the awed stillness that came over Daniel Boone when, three-quarters of a century earlier, he "gained the summit of a commanding ridge" and first gazed "round with astonishing delight" upon "the ample plains" and "beauteous tracts" of Kentucky.[34] Albeit with none of the eroticism that marked Boone's language, it is, even more significantly, a rhapsody that recapitulates much of the spirit of John Filson's original figure. For, as Filson had first represented him in 1784, Boone too was looking "in the direction of our anticipated home," contemplating eventual settlement in Kentucky as he gazed out over its splendors. The point must therefore be made that in the diaries composed along the overland trail, women's private voices—for the first time—begin to recall *the* avatar of the westering process. Not the isolate Boone of myth and legend, to be sure, but the contemplative Boone of Filson's original, exploring with wonder in anticipation of relocating home and family in paradise.

The domesticating Eve, her calicoes and root cuttings safely tucked away within the wagon, was now asserting the voice of an earlier and almost forgotten Adam. With the advent of homestead laws that protected women's—as well as men's—right to take up new land in the far west, in fact, the postbellum Eve of California and Oregon, the Dakotas and the high plains, soon spoke in the voice of *both* adventurer *and* domesticator, asserting a garden wholly her own. Indeed, just as Eve had once been edited out of the wilderness paradise, so now Adam would become superfluous to the homestead Eden. Another volume is required, however, to trace how the fantasy thus came full circle.

For Sarah J. Cummins, suffice it to say, her anticipatory dreams were fulfilled at trail's end. "The environs of our new home, surrounded by giant fir trees, the healthful sea breezes," she wrote, "precluded any form of home sickness [for our old home in the Mississippi valley] and our united efforts were wholly set upon the building of a home" in the Oregon Territory (*AAR*, p. 49). In this regard, thirteen-year-old Virginia Reed, scabrous and emaciated survivor of the Donner party, probably spoke for many when, in the spring of 1847, she wrote to a cousin in Illinois: "We are all very well pleased with California. . . . it aut to be a beautiful Country to pay us for our trubel in geting there."[35]

Notes

Prologue. Dispossessed of Paradise

1. Quoted in John Seelye, *Prophetic Waters: The River in Early American Life and Literature* (New York: Oxford University Press, 1977), p. 43.

2. "The First Voyage Made To The Coasts Of America With Two Barks, Wherein Were Captains M. Philip Amadas And M. Arthur Barlowe Who Discovered Part Of The Country Now Called Virginia, Anno 1584. Written By One Of The Said Captains [probably Barlowe, who kept the daily record], And Sent To Sir Walter Raleigh, Knight, At Whose Charge And Direction The Said Voyage Was Set Forth," in David Leroy Corbitt, ed., *Explorations, Descriptions, and Attempted Settlements of Carolina, 1584–1590* (Raleigh: State Department of Archives and History, 1948), p. 13; quoted from Walter Raleigh's "Discovery of Guiana" (1595), in Howard Mumford Jones, *O Strange New World, American Culture: The Formative Years* (1952; reprint, London: Chatto and Windus, 1965), p. 48.

3. Quoted in Seelye, p. 43.

4. Robert Mountgomry, "A Discourse Concerning the design'd Establishment of a New Colony To The South of Carolina In The Most delightful Country of the Universe" (London, 1717), p. 6, in Peter Force, comp., *Tracts and Other Papers, Relating Principally to the Origin, Settlement, And Progress of the Colonies in North America, From The Discovery Of The Country To The Year 1776*, 3 vols. (Washington, D.C., 1836–38), vol. 1 (hereafter cited as *Force's Tracts*). All of the tracts and pamphlets collected in *Force's Tracts* are facsimile reprints, paginated separately.

5. Robert Johnson, "Nova Britannia: Offering Most Excellent fruites by Planting in Virginia. Exciting all such as be well affected to further the same" (London, 1609), p. 11, in *Force's Tracts*, vol. 1; John Smith, "A Description of New England; or, The Observations, and Discoueries of Captain John Smith (Admirall of that Country) in the North of America, in the year of our Lord 1614" (London, 1616), p. 9, in *Force's Tracts*, vol. 2.

6. From Roger Wolcott's *Poetical Meditations* (1725), quoted in Seelye, p. 332.

7. Quoted in Henry Nash Smith, *Virgin Land: The American West as Symbol and Myth* (1950; reprint, New York: Random House, Vintage Books, 1961), p. 298.

8. J. Hector St. John de Crèvecoeur, *Letters from an American Farmer* (1782; reprint, New York: E. P. Dutton, 1957), p. 39.

9. J. Hector St. John de Crèvecoeur, *Crèvecoeur's Eighteenth-Century Travels in Pennsylvania and New York*, trans. and ed. Percy G. Adams (Lexington: University

of Kentucky Press, 1961), p. 42; Hector St. John de Crèvecoeur, *Sketches of Eighteenth-Century America*, ed. Henri L. Bourdin, Ralph H. Gabriel, and Stanley T. Williams (New Haven: Yale University Press, 1925), p. 48.

10. Crèvecoeur, *Sketches of Eighteenth-Century America*, pp. 230–32.

11. Annette Kolodny, *The Lay of the Land: Metaphor as Experience and History in American Life and Letters* (Chapel Hill: University of North Carolina Press, 1975), p. 7.

12. John Hammond, "Leah and Rachel; or, The Two Fruitfull Sisters Virginia and Mary-Land" (1656), in Clayton Colman Hall, ed., *Narratives of Early Maryland, 1633–1684* (New York: Charles Scribner's Sons, 1910), p. 300.

13. Bayard Taylor, *At Home and Abroad: A Sketch-Book of Life, Scenery, and Men* (New York: G. P. Putnam, 1862), p. 155.

14. Thomas Cole, "Lecture on American Scenery, Delivered Before the Catskill Lyceum, April 1st, 1841," *Northern Light* 1 (May 1841): 26.

15. Richard Slotkin, *Regeneration through Violence: The Mythology of the American Frontier, 1600–1860* (Middletown, Conn.: Wesleyan University Press, 1973), p. 21.

16. John Filson, *The Discovery, Settlement And present State of Kentucke . . . To which is added, An Appendix, Containing, The Adventures of Col. Daniel Boon, one of the first Settlers . . .* (Wilmington, Del.: James Adams, 1784), p. 57.

17. For an analysis of this figure, see Kolodny, pp. 89–115.

18. James Fenimore Cooper, *The Pioneers* (1823; reprint, New York: Holt, Rinehart and Winston, 1959, 1964), p. 474.

19. R. W. B. Lewis, *The American Adam: Innocence, Tragedy, and Tradition in the Nineteenth Century* (Chicago: University of Chicago Press, 1955), p. 89.

20. Frederick Jackson Turner, *The Frontier in American History* (New York: Henry Holt and Company, 1920), p. 4.

21. John Winthrop, "A Modell of Christian Charity. Written on Boarde the Arrabella, On the Attlantick Ocean" (1630), in *Winthrop Papers*, 5 vols. (Boston: Massachusetts Historical Society, 1927–32), 2:295.

22. Winthrop, "General Conclusions and Particular Considerations: Early Draft" (1629), in *Winthrop Papers*, 2:127; "John Winthrop to His Wife" (1630), in *Winthrop Papers*, 2:320.

23. Anne Bradstreet, "To my Dear Children," in Anne Bradstreet, *The Works of Anne Bradstreet in Prose and Verse*, ed. John Harvard Ellis 1867; reprint, New York: Peter Smith, 1932), p. 5.

24. Joan White's 1645 conversion testimony is recorded in John Fiske, *The Notebook of the Reverend John Fiske, 1644–1675*, ed. Robert G. Pope, Publications of the Colonial Society of Massachusetts, vol. 47 (Boston: The Society, 1974), p. 30.

25. Mary Rowlandson, *A True History Of The Captivity and Restoration of Mrs. Mary Rowlandson, A Minister's Wife in New-England* (London: Joseph Poole, 1682), p. 4.

26. Eliza Lucas Pinckney, *The Letterbook of Eliza Lucas Pinckney, 1739–1762*, ed. Elise Pinckney (Chapel Hill: University of North Carolina Press, 1972), p. 185.

27. Ibid.

28. [Caroline M. Kirkland], *Forest Life*, 2 vols. (New York: Charles S. Francis and Co.; Boston: J. H. Francis, 1842), 1:43.

29. The best discussion of this to date is Lee Clark Mitchell's fascinating *Witnesses to a Vanishing America: The Nineteenth-Century Response* (Princeton: Princeton University Press, 1981).

30. Lydia H. Sigourney, "Fallen Forests," in *The Western Home, and Other Poems* (Philadelphia: Parry and McMillan, 1854), p.85.

31. Ibid., pp. 83, 84.

32. Mary Austin Holley, *Texas. Observations, Historical, Geographical and Descriptive, In a Series of Letters, Written during a Visit to Austin's Colony, with a view to a permanent settlement in that country; in the Autumn of 1831* (Baltimore: Armstrong and Plaskitt, 1833), p. 14 (hereafter cited in the text as *T*).

33. S.M. Fuller, *Summer on the Lakes, in 1843* (Boston: Charles C. Little and James Brown; New York: Charles S. Francis and Co., 1844), p. 122 (hereafter cited in the text as *SL*).

34. Eliza W. Farnham, *Life in Prairie Land* (New York: Harper and Brothers, 1846), pp. iii–iv (hereafter cited in the text as *PL*).

35. [Caroline Kirkland], *A New Home—Who'll Follow? Or, Glimpses of Western Life. By Mrs. Mary Clavers. An Actual Settler* (1839; reprint, New York: Garrett Press, 1969), p. 247 (hereafter cited in the text as *ANH*).

36. Quoted in John Mack Faragher, "History from the Inside-Out: Writing the History of Women in Rural America," *American Quarterly* 33, no. 5 (Winter 1981): 548–49.

37. Pat. Tailfer, Hugh Anderson, Da. Douglas, and others, "A True and Historical Narrative of the Colony of Georgia, in America, From the First Settlement thereof until this present Period" (Charles Town, South Carolina, 1741), p. 18, in *Force's Tracts*, vol. 1.

38. Typescript of the "Diary of Mrs. Nicholas [Elizabeth House] Trist (1783–1784)," undated May 1784 entry, p. 11, in Mrs. Nicholas Trist Papers, Southern Historical Collection, University of North Carolina Library, Chapel Hill.

39. Mrs. Benjamin Ives Gilman, Cincinnati, Ohio, to Elizabeth H. Gilman, New York, October 30, 1823, in Mrs. Charles P. Noyes, ed., *A Family History in Letters and Documents, 1667–1837*, 2 vols. (St. Paul, Minn.: Privately Printed, 1919), 1:446.

40. Ibid.

41. Elisabeth Adams, Davenport, Iowa, to Ephraim Adams, Grinnell, Iowa, May 5, 1856, in Ephraim Adams Papers, Manuscript Collection, Iowa State Historical Department.

42. Eliza Johnston Wiggin, *Impressions of Early Kansas* (Wichita: Grit Printery, 1915), p. 1; her reference here is to Waverley, Kansas, ca. 1855.

43. Mollie Dorsey Sanford, *Mollie: The Journal of Mollie Dorsey Sanford in Nebraska and Colorado Territories, 1857–1866*, ed. Donald F. Danker (Lincoln: University of Nebraska Press, 1959), p. 33.

1. Captives in Paradise

1. "To my Dear Children" in Anne Bradstreet, *The Works of Anne Bradstreet in Prose and Verse*, ed. John Harvard Ellis (1867; reprint, New York: Peter Smith, 1932), p. 5; in John Fiske, *The Notebook of the Reverend John Fiske, 1644–1675*, ed. Robert G. Pope, Publications of the Colonial Society of Massachusetts, vol. 47 (Boston: The Society, 1974) p. 30, there appears an account of the conversion declaration of "Joan White from the church at Salem," dated February 10, 1645.

2. Mary Rowlandson, *A True History of the Captivity and Restoration of Mrs. Mary Rowlandson, A Minister's Wife in New-England* (London: Joseph Poole, 1682), p. 4 (hereafter cited in the text as *ATH*). No copy exists of the first New England edition, printed under the title, *The Soveraignty and Goodness of God, Together with the Faithfulness of His Promises Displayed: Being a Narrative of the Captivity and Restauration of Mrs. Mary Rowlandson*. A second edition, utilizing this same title, appeared in 1682 (Cambridge, Mass.: Samuel Green), but extant copies are damaged and incomplete. Many subsequent American editions were reprinted from the English edition, and so the work has come to be best known under the title, *A True History*.

Although first published some years after her death (which probably occurred in 1678), Mary Rowlandson's narrative nonetheless had to confront Puritan resistance to women making public statements (the same resistance that motivated reaction against Anne Hutchinson). It did this by proclaiming itself a document of orthodox Puritan piety and by declaring on the title page that it had been released for public view only "*for the Benefit of the Afflicted*." An anonymous "Preface to the Reader" corroborates this by assuring readers that "this Gentlewomans modesty would not thrust [the manuscript] into the Press, yet her gratitude unto God, made her . . . perswadable to let it pass, that God might have his due glory, and others benefit by it as well" (*ATH*, n.p.).

3. The title page of *A True History* reads: "Whereunto is annexed, A Sermon of *the Possibility of God's Forsaking a People that have been near and dear to him*. Preached by Mr. *Joseph Rowlandson*, Husband to the said Mrs. *Rowlandson*: It being his Last Sermon."

4. Sacvan Bercovitch, *The Puritan Origins of the American Self* (New Haven: Yale University Press, 1975), p. 117.

5. Richard Slotkin, *Regeneration through Violence: The Mythology of the American Frontier, 1600–1860* (Middletown, Conn.: Wesleyan University Press, 1973), p. 109.

6. Rowlandson acknowledges that she "never saw one [Indian] die with hunger" (*ATH*, p. 28), but she attributes that survival not to the raw wilderness's capacity to sustain life or to the Indians' survival skills but, instead, to "the wonderful power of God, in providing for such a vast number of our Enemies in the Wilderness, where there was nothing to be seen, but from hand to mouth" (*ATH*, p. 29).

7. Francis Higginson, "Some brief Collections out of a letter that Mr. Higginson sent [from New England] to . . . Leicester" (1629), quoted in Peter N. Car-

roll, *Puritanism and the Wilderness: The Intellectual Significance of the New England Frontier, 1629–1700* (New York: Columbia University Press, 1969), p. 11. Carroll's discussion, pp. 7–25, has been especially helpful to me here.

8. Cotton Mather's "Humiliations, follow'd with Deliverances" was first preached "At Boston Lecture . . . 1697. The Week before a General FAST" and that same year was published as *Humiliations follow'd with Deliverances. A Brief Discourse On the Matter and Method, Of that Humiliation which would be an Hopeful Symptom of our Deliverance from Calamity. Accompanied and Accommodated with A Narrative, Of a Notable Deliverance lately Received by some English Captives, From the Hands of Cruel Indians. And some Improvement of that Narrative. Whereto is added A Narrative of Hannah Swarton, containing a great many wonderful passages, relating to her Captivity and Deliverance* (Boston: B. Green and J. Allen, 1697) (hereafter cited in the text as *HFD*).

9. Once alerted to the Indians' presence in the neighborhood, Thomas Dustin was able to flee, with his seven other children, to a hiding place in the woods.

10. Slotkin, p. 114.

11. John Seelye, *Prophetic Waters: The River in Early American Life and Literature* (New York: Oxford University Press, 1977), p. 289.

12. Although Swarton's time in the wilderness stretched from May 1690 through mid-February, 1691, her narrative almost exclusively details the winter hardships.

13. Swarton's narrative is unusual for the period because it does not end with a reunited family: her children still remain in captivity as her narrative closes.

14. Cotton Mather, *Decennium Luctuosum. An History of Remarkable Occurrences, In the Long War, Which New-England hath had with the Indian Salvages, From the Year, 1688. To the Year, 1698. Faithfully Composed and Improved* (Boston: B. Green and J. Allen, 1699), p. 220 (hererafter cited in the text as *DL*). With only slight alterations, *Decennium Luctuosum* was incorporated into Mather's *Magnalia Christi Americana; or, The Ecclesiastical History of New England from Its First Planting* (London, 1702).

15. Ann Eliza Bleecker, *The History of Maria Kittle* (1790; Hartford: Elisha Babcock, 1797), p. 25 (hereafter cited in the text as *MK*).

16. John Filson, *The Discovery, Settlement And present State of Kentucke . . . To which is added, An Appendix, Containing, The Adventures of Col. Daniel Boon, one of the first Settlers . . .* (Wilmington, Del.: James Adams, 1784), pp. 64–65. For an excellent discussion of Filson's Boone narrative, to which I am largely indebted here, see Slotkin, pp. 268–312.

17. John Trumbull, comp., *The Adventures of Colonel Daniel Boon, One of the first Settlers at Kentucke: Containing The Wars with the Indians on the Ohio, from 1769 to 1783, and the first Establishment and Progress of the Settlement on that River. Written by the Colonel himself. To Which Are Added, A Narrative of the Captivity, and Extraordinary Escape of Mrs. Francis Scott An Inhabitant of Washington-County Virginia; who after the Murder of her Husband and children, by the Indians, was taken Prisoner by them; on the 19th of June, 1785* (Norwich, Conn.: John Trumbull, 1786) (hereafter cited in the text as Trumbull).

18. Slotkin, pp. 323–24.

19. It was a contrast for which American readers seemed eager. That same year, a Boston printer, E. Russell, paired the Scott narrative with yet another male exploration and adventure narrative in his *Narative of Mrs. Scott and Capt. Stewart's Captivity. A True and Wonderful Narrative Of the surprising Captivity and remarkable Deliverance of Mrs. Frances Scott* (Boston: E. Russell, 1785), to which he appended, "A true and faithful Narrative of the surprizing Captivity and remarkable Deliverance of Captain Isaac Stewart, who was taken Prisoner by the Indians near Fort-Pitt, in the Year 1764" (p. 19).

20. The Scott cabin was probably located in what is now West Virginia, near settlements on the Clinch River, on the road to Kentucky through the Cumberland Gap.

21. The 1786 pamphlet printed by E. Russell of Boston contains an "Editor's Preface . . . To the serious and pious READER," which identifies the narrative's events as "among the many remarkable and surprising Instances of the Infinite Goodness of DIVINE PROVIDENCE" (p. 4), followed by a two-page sampling of "Passages of Sacred Writ." Several later editions, beginning with *A Remarkable Narrative of the Captivity and Escape of Mrs. Frances Scott, An Inhabitant of Washington County, Virginia* (N.p.: Chapman Whitcomb, ca. 1800) include the following pious conclusion, tacked on by editors and printers: "She expresses her thankfulness to divine Providence, for its kind interposition in her favor, in aiding and assisting her escape from the Indians, in supporting her, when she leaped from the precipice; in preserving her from the poison of the venomous snake, and sending the birds to direct her course" (p. 16).

22. Quoted in Henry Nash Smith, *Virgin Land: The American West as Symbol and Myth* (1950; reprint, New York: Random House, Vintage Books, 1961), p. 236.

23. Mary H. Emery, Exeter, New Hampshire, to "My dear brother," January 14, 1852, a typed copy of which is in the Gilman Family Papers, Massachusetts Historical Society. The letter quotes, "in her own language," the reminiscences of an "aunt Margaret."

24. Mary H. Emery to her brother, January 14, 1852.

25. Joseph Gilman, Marietta, Ohio, to Hon. Nicholas Gilman, New York, August 21, 1789, in Gilman Family Papers, Massachusetts Historical Society.

26. Joseph Gilman, Marietta, Ohio, to Hon. Nicholas Gilman, New York, February 23, 1790, in Gilman Family Papers, Massachusetts Historical Society.

27. Mary H. Emery to her brother, January 14, 1852.

28. [Caroline M. Kirkland], *Forest Life*, 2 vols. (New York: Charles S. Francis and Co., 1842), 1:37–38.

2. Gardens in the Wilderness

1. Mrs. Benjamin Ives Gilman, Cincinnati, Ohio, to Elizabeth Hale Gilman, New York, October 30, 1823, in Mrs. Charles P. Noyes, ed., *A Family History in Letters and Documents, 1667–1837*, 2 vols. (St. Paul, Minn.: Privately Printed, 1919), 1:446.

2. See, for example, the title page of E. Russell, comp., *Narative of Mrs. Scott and Capt. Stewart's Captivity* (Boston: E. Russell, 1786), which promises, among other things, that the ensuing narrative will depict a woman who "was often surrounded in her melancholy and solitary Journey, by Buffaloes, Serpents, Elks, Wolves, Bears, and a Variety of other hideous, shocking and frightful Beasts who inhabit the Wilderness of America." Such narratives were widely circulated in England and often stylized European expectations of the New World.

3. Diary of Mrs. Eliza [Carolina Burgwin] Clitherall (1784–1863), Typed vol. I: MSS vol. 4, typed p. 30, in the Southern Historical Collection, University of North Carolina Library, Chapel Hill. The diary consists of seventeen manuscript volumes and a three-volume typescript. Notes here refer to vol. I of the typescript, which comprises vols. 1–6 of the original manuscript diaries; the typescript is divided into separate sections, following the original diaries, each section individually paginated.

4. Mrs. Benjamin Ives Gilman, Cincinnati, Ohio, to Elizabeth Hale Gilman, New York, October 30, 1823, in Noyes, ed., *A Family History*, 1:446.

5. Hannah Robbins Gilman, Marietta, Ohio, to Dr. Peter G. Robbins, Lynn, Massachusetts, January 5, 1811, in Gilman Family Papers, Massachusetts Historical Society.

6. Mrs. Benjamin Ives Gilman, Cincinnati, Ohio, to Elizabeth Hale Gilman, New York, October 30, 1823, in Noyes, ed., *A Family History*, 1:446.

7. In November 1788, Hannah's fiancé, Benjamin Ives Gilman, had removed with his parents from Exeter, New Hampshire, to what is now Marietta, Ohio. The next year, Benjamin Ives Gilman returned to New England, marrying Hannah Robbins in February 1790. The couple remained in New England until the following June, when they began their journey across the mountains and then traveled down the Ohio to Fort Harmar. By the time the couple set out for Ohio, Hannah Robbins Gilman was already three months pregnant. She was then 22 years old, her husband 24.

8. See "Diary of Sarah White Smith, March 1838 to September 1839," in Clifford Merrill Drury, ed., *First White Women Over the Rockies: Diaries, Letters, and Biographical Sketches of the Six Women of the Oregon Mission Who Made the Overland Journey in 1836 and 1838*, 3 vols. (Glendale, Calif.: Arthur H. Clark Co., 1966), 3:66.

9. See Joseph Gilman, Marietta, Ohio, to Hon. Nicholas Gilman, Philadelphia, February 12, 1797, in Noyes, ed., *A Family History*, 1:217.

10. Benjamin Ives Gilman, Marietta, Ohio, to Hannah Robbins Gilman, Plymouth, Massachusetts, April 25, 1795, in Gilman Family Papers, Massachusetts Historical Society; also reprinted in Noyes, ed., *A Family History*, 1:209.

11. Diary of Mrs. Eliza Clitherall, Typed Vol. I: Mss vol. 4, typed p. 30.

12. Ibid., pp. 37–38.

13. See Benjamin Ives Gilman, Marietta, Ohio, to Hannah Robbins Gilman, Plymouth, Massachusetts, April 25, 1795, in Gilman Family Papers, Massachusetts Historical Society; also reprinted in Noyes, ed., *A Family History*, 1:206–10.

14. Diary of Mrs. Eliza Clitherall, Typed Vol. I: MSS vol. 4, typed p. 37.

15. Ann S. Stephens, *Mary Derwent* (Philadelphia: T.B. Peterson and Brothers, 1858), p. 181.

16. Typescript of the "Diary of Mrs. Nicholas [Elizabeth House] Trist (1783–1784)," in Mrs. Nicholas Trist Papers, Southern Historical Collection, University of North Carolina Library, Chapel Hill, undated May, 1784 entry, pp. 11, 10 (hereafter cited in the text as Trist). The first twelve pages of the typescript describe the journey by horseback from Carlisle, Pennsylvania, to Pittsburgh, in a running narrative with dates included; only one lengthy entry, clearly composed sometime toward the end of her stay in Pittsburgh, in May, 1784, has no separate datings for the various events it records (pp. 9–11). The last eleven pages, unpaged, are separately dated entries in the manner of a daily journal; these describe her journey from the Ohio into the Mississippi River, ending on July 1, 1784, just short of her expected arrival in Natchez. See also Elizabeth House Trist, "The Travel Diary of Elizabeth House Trist: Philadelphia to Natchez, 1783–84," edited and with an introduction by Annette Kolodny, in *Journeys in New Worlds: Early American Women's Narratives*, ed. William L. Andrews, Sargent Bush, Jr., Annette Kolodny, Amy Shrager Lang, and Daniel B. Shea (Madison: University of Wisconsin Press, 1990), pp. 181–232.

17. Margaret Van Horn Dwight, *A Journey to Ohio in 1810*, ed. Max Farrand (New Haven: Yale University Press, 1912), pp. 46–47, 32.

18. John filson, *The Discovery, Settlement And present State of Kentucke . . . To which is added, An Appendix, Containing, The Adventures of Col. Daniel Boon, one of the first Settlers . . .* (Wilmington, Del.: James Adams, 1784), pp. 55, 54.

19. Ibid., p. 57.

20. A later entry in the "Diary of Mrs. Nicholas Trist" makes clear how essential "good Society" was to her during the winter in Pittsburgh: "The number of strangers resorting thither on their way to the Cumberland &cc made the winter pass a way much more agreeable than it otherwise wo'd[.] we were at several dances at which there would be fifteen or twenty ladies and as many Gentlemen—if there had not been those little recreations I shou'd certainly have been very miserable" (Trist, May 20, 1784).

21. Quoted in Howard Mumford Jones, *O Strange New World, American Culture: The Formative Years* (1952; reprint, London: Chatto and Windus, 1965), p. 356.

22. From David Humphreys's *A Poem on Industry* (1794), quoted and discussed in Cecilia Tichi, "The American Revolution and the New Earth," *Early American Literature* 11 (Fall 1976): 206.

23. The conversion declaration of "Joan White from the church at Salem" is recorded in the February 10, 1645, entry in John fiske, *The Notebook of the Reverend John fiske, 1664–1675*, ed. Robert G. Pope, Publications of the Colonial Society of Massachusetts, vol. 74 (Boston: The Society, 1974), p. 30.

24. Richard Slotkin, *Regeneration through Violence: The Mythology of the American Frontier, 1600–1860* (Middletown, Conn.: Wesleyan University Press, 1973), p. 267.

25. Hore Browse Trist was appointed revenue collector in the Mississippi Territory by President Jefferson; his 1802–3 letters from the Territory to various family members in Virginia are collected in the Nicholas Philip Trist Papers, Southern Historical Collection, University of North Carolina Library, Chapel Hill.

26. Cornelia Greene, Cumberland Island, Georgia, to Margaret Cowper, Baron Hill Plantation, Rio Bueno, Jamaica, August 6, 1800, in Mackay-Stiles Papers, Southern Historical Collection, University of North Carolina Library, Chapel Hill.

27. Greene to Cowper, October 10, 1800, ibid.

28. Philip Vickers Fithian, *Journal and Letters of Philip Vickers Fithian, 1773–1774: A Plantation Tutor of the Old Dominion*, ed. Hunter Dickinson Farish (Williamsburg, Va.: Colonial Williamsburg and Princeton University Press, 1943), pp. 42, 59.

29. In Fithian's view, the "Method of farming" at the Nomini Hall plantation (and its neighbors) was "slovenly, without any regard to continue their Land in heart, for future Crops." He described local agricultural practices as follows: "They plant large Quantities of Land, without any Manure, & work it very hard to make the best of the Crop, and when the Crop comes off they take away the Fences to inclose another Piece of Land for the next years tillage, and leave this a common to be destroyed by Winter & Beasts till they stand in need of it again to plough" (p. 118).

30. Fithian, pp. 85, 105, 58.

31. See Anne B. Shteir's "Linnaeus's Daughters: Women and British Botany," in *Women and the Structure of Society: Selected Research from the Fifth Berkshire Conference on the History of Women*, ed. Barbara J. Harris and Jo Ann McNamara (Durham, N.C.: Duke University Press, 1984), pp. 67–73.

32. Deposition of Ann McGinty, Mercer County, Kentucky, taken November 10, 1801, in the Archibald Woods Papers, 1777–1893, Earl Gregg Swem Library of the College of William and Mary in Virginia.

33. For details of the conversion of "nettles and other weeds" into "an acceptable substitute for flax," see Helen Deiss Irvin, *Women in Kentucky* (Lexington: University Press of Kentucky, 1979), pp. 13–14.

34. See, for example, Pat. Tailfer, Hugh Anderson, Da. Douglas, and others, "A True and Historical Narrative of the Colony of Georgia, in America, From the First Settlement thereof until this Present Period" (Charles Town, South Carolina, 1741), reprinted in *Force's Tracts*, vol. 1, in which disgruntled colonists listed as second among "the REAL Causes of the Ruin and Desolation of the Colony," "The Restricting the Tenure of Lands . . . [and] cutting off Daughters" from the right to inherit land from their fathers (p. 79). Originally planned simply as a military outpost, Georgia had initially excluded women from title to land, but, under pressure from the settlers, this soon changed.

35. Eliza Lucas Pinckney, *The Letterbook of Eliza Lucas Pinckney, 1739–1762*, ed. Elise Pinckney (Chapel Hill: University of North Carolina Press, 1972), p. 8 (hereafter cited in the text as *Pinckney*). According to n. 8, "Lucerne is an alfalfa. 'Casada' is probably *cassava*, a plant with a fleshy rootstock which was cultivated in the tropics where it was a staple food."

36. Elizabeth House Trist, Birdwood [Virginia] to President Thomas Jefferson, Washington, D.C., June 13, 1801, in Nicholas Philip Trist Papers, Southern Historical Collection, University of North Carolina Library, Chapel Hill.

37. In his *Life of Daniel Boone* (Boston: Charles C. Little and James Brown, 1847), John M. Peck explains that "*Cabin* is the name, throughout the west,

for a plain, rough log house, constructed in the cheapest and simplest form" (p. 147). Trist would certainly have known this from her own earlier trip across the Alleghenies.

38. Elizabeth House Trist to President Thomas Jefferson, June 13, 1801, Nicholas Philip Trist Papers.

39. See Leo Marx, *The Machine in the Garden: Technology and the Pastoral Ideal in America* (New York: Oxford University Press, 1964), p. 130.

40. Diary of Mrs. Eliza Clitherall, Typed Vol. I: MSS vol. 3, typed p. 14.

41. Susanna Rowson, "Rights of Women" in *Miscellaneous Poems* (Boston: Gilbert and Dean, 1804), p. 100; for evidence that this poem was composed earlier than its publication date and contained much of Mrs. Rowson's pedagogical theory, see Dorothy Weil, *In Defense of Women: Susanna Rowson, 1762–1824* (University Park: Pennsylvania State University Press, 1976), p. 49.

3. The Lady in the Cave

1. John Seelye, *Prophetic Waters: The River in Early American Life and Literature* (New York: Oxford University Press, 1977), p. 291.

2. Mrs. Benjamin Ives Gilman, Cincinnati, Ohio, to Elizabeth Hale Gilman, New York, October 30, 1823, in Mrs. Charles P. Noyes, ed., *A Family History in Letters and Documents, 1667–1837*, 2 vols. (St. Paul, Minn.: Privately Printed, 1919), 1:446.

3. The origins and implications of this white European fear of being "taken over" by the wilderness is the subject of Frederick Turner's eloquent *Beyond Geography: The Western Spirit against the Wilderness* (New York: Viking Press, 1980).

4. J. Hector St. John de Crèvecoeur, *Letters from an American Farmer* (1782; reprint, New York: E. P. Dutton, 1957), p. 47.

5. Quoted in Page Smith, *Daughters of the Promised Land: Women in American History* (Boston: Little, Brown, 1979), p. 222.

6. Ibid.

7. Crèvecoeur, *Letters from an American Farmer*, p. 48.

8. Quoted in Mary Sumner Benson, *Women in Eighteenth-Century America: A Study of Opinion and Social Usage* (1935; reprint, New York: AMS Press, 1976), p. 284.

9. Crèvecoeur, *Letters from an American Farmer*, p. 49.

10. John Filson, *The Discovery, Settlement, and Present State of Kentucke . . . To Which is Added an Appendix, Containing, The Adventures of Col. Daniel Boon, One of the First Settlers . . .* (Wilmington, Del.: James Adams, 1784), p. 81.

11. See John Trumbull, comp., *The Adventures of Colonel Daniel Boon, One of the first Settlers at Kentucke . . . To Which are Added a Narrative of the Captivity, and Extraordinary Escape of Mrs. Francis Scott An Inhabitant of Washington-County Virginia* (Norwich, Conn.: John Trumbull, 1786).

12. "A Surprising account of the Discovery of a Lady who was taken by the Indians in the year 1777, and after making her escape, She retired to a lonely Cave, where She lived nine years," in *Bickerstaff's almanack, for the year of our*

Lord, 1788 (Norwich, Conn.: John Trumbull, 1787), unpaged; reprinted (along with a later reprinting) in the Garland Library of Narratives of North American Indian Captivities, comp. Wilcomb E. Washburn (New York: Garland Publishing, 1978), vol. 17. All subsequent quotes are from this facsimile reprint. For a brief publishing history of this narrative, see Richard Slotkin, *Regeneration through Violence: The Mythology of the American Frontier, 1600–1860* (Middletown, Conn.: Wesleyan University Press, 1973), p. 256.

13. Boone states that in 1769, along with some male companions, he first "wander[ed] through the wilderness of America, in quest of the country of Kentucke," proceeding "through a mountainous wilderness, in a westward direction"; in addition to the "myriads of trees, some gay with blossoms, others rich with fruits," Boone reports that he and his companions "were diverted with unnumerable animals presenting themselves perpetually to our view," and he repeatedly details his hunting successes, in Filson, pp. 50–51, 52.

14. Ibid., p. 55.

15. Ibid., p. 56.

16. See, for example, "A Narrative of the Captivity and Escape of Mrs. Francis Scott, an Inhabitant of Washington County, Virginia," in *The Adventures of Colonel Daniel Boon* (Norwich, Conn.: John Trumbull, 1786), pp. 16–24; and Cotton Mather, *Humiliations follow'd with Deliverances. A Brief Discourse On the Matter and Method, Of that Humiliation which would be an Hopeful Sympton of our Deliverance from Calamity. Accompanied and Accommodated with a Narrative, Of a Notable Deliverance Lately Received by Some English Captives, From the Hands of Cruel Indians* . . . (Boston: B. Green and F. Allen, 1697), pp. 41–47.

17. See Trumbull, comp., "A Narrative of the Captivity and Escape of Mrs. Francis Scott," p. 22.

18. See Mather, *Humiliations,* p. 31.

19. At the close of the Revolutionary War both state and federal governments sold off (or exchanged for notes of indebtedness) their public lands to the west in an effort to clear the debts they had incurred during the war years.

20. See Ann Eliza Bleecker, *The History of Maria Kittle* (1790; Hartford: Elisha Babcock, 1797), and Trumbull, comp., "A Narrative of the Captivity and Escape of Mrs. Francis Scott," p. 23.

21. For an excellent discussion of the origins and implications of Jefferson's agrarianism, see Leo Marx, *The Machine in the Garden: Technology and the Pastoral Ideal in America* (New York: Oxford University Press, 1964), esp. pp. 98, 126–27.

22. Slotkin, pp. 258–59.

23. Ibid., p. 259.

24. I use the term "command" here so as to include the lady's father who, while never depicted with a weapon in the narrative, is nonetheless directly responsible for their use: if he was, in fact, a merchant at Albany, then his fur-trading investments certainly supported the activities of hunters; moreover, he hires (presumably armed) men to pursue his eloped daughter. The single exception to the chain of males wielding weaponry is, of course, the young clerk, of whom the lady is enamored; but, within the story, he figures less as a character in

his own right and more as a pretext for precipitating the lady out into the wilderness.

25. Slotkin, p. 259. For a discussion of the way in which Norwich, Connecticut, printer, John Trumbull, edited John Filson's original Boone narrative in such a way as to delete the original "passages of melancholy or philosophical meditation . . . leaving only the image of an Edenic Kentucky and an adventurous, uncontemplative Daniel Boone," see Slotkin, p. 324. As Slotkin points out, Trumbull's version outstripped Filson's in popularity, his "pirated version of Filson's Boone narratives . . . copied and reprinted in popular periodicals, pamphlets, and anthologies for the next fifty years" (p. 323).

4. Mary Jemison and Rebecca Bryan Boone

1. Colonial observations on the successful adoption of whites by Indians are quoted and discussed in Frederick Turner, *Beyond Geography: The Western Spirit Against the Wilderness* (New York: Viking Press, 1980), p. 244.

2. Ibid.

3. Ibid. For an excellent discussion of the successful adoption of whites by Indians, see also James Axtell's "The White Indians of Colonial America," *William and Mary Quarterly*, 3d ser. 32 (January 1975): 55–88.

4. See James Fenimore Cooper's "Preface to the Leather-Stocking Tales, New York, 1850," in *The Last of the Mohicans* (1826), ed. William Charvat (Cambridge, Mass.: Houghton Mifflin, 1958), p. 12.

5. See John Filson, *The Discovery, Settlement And present State of Kentucke . . . To which is added, An Appendix, Containing, The Adventures of Col. Daniel Boon, one of the first Settlers . . .* (Wilmington, Del.: James Adams, 1784), p. 65; Alexander Henry, *Travels And Adventures in Canada and The Indian Territories, Between The Years 1760 and 1776* (New York: I. Riley, 1809), p. 161; Cooper, *The Last of the Mohicans*, p. 284.

6. The details of the 1704 raid on Deerfield were preserved by John Williams, Eunice's father, who, upon being ransomed in 1706, composed a narrative of his captivity experience, *The Redeemed Captive Returning to Zion: Or, A Faithful History of Remarkable Occurrences in the Captivity and Deliverance of Mr. John Williams, Minister of the Gospel in Deerfield*, first published in Boston in 1707 and many times reprinted thereafter.

7. For a full discussion of the Eunice Williams captivity and the gossip aroused by her subsequent visits to Massachusetts, see Dawn Lander Gherman, "From Parlour to Tepee: The White Squaw on the American Frontier," Ph.D. dissertation, University of Massachusetts, 1975, pp. 70–91.

8. James Fenimore Cooper, *The Pioneers; or, The Sources of the Susquehanna: A Descriptive Tale* (1823; reprint, New York: G. P. Putnam's Sons, 1893), p. 475.

9. See Susan Phinney Conrad, *Perish the Thought: Intellectual Women in Romantic America, 1830–1860* (New York: Oxford University Press, 1976), p. 105.

10. Lydia Maria Child, *Hobomok. A Tale of Early Times* (Boston: Cummings,

Hilliard and Co., 1824; facsimile reprint, New York: Garrett Press, 1970), pp. 186, 182, 187, 187–88.

11. James Everett Seaver, *A Narrative of the Life of Mrs. Mary Jemison, Who was taken by the Indians, in the year 1755, when only about twelve years of age, and has continued to reside amongst them to the present time* (Canandaigua, N.Y.: J. D. Bemis and Co., 1824), p. 44 (hereafter cited in the text as *MJ*).

12. Richard Slotkin, *Regeneration through Violence: The Mythology of the American Frontier, 1600–1860* (Middletown, Conn.: Wesleyan University Press, 1973), p. 450.

13. Slotkin finds the Jemison narrative "revolutionary" because its unconventional ending radically diverged from the "restoration scene that concluded the captivity tales of the Puritans" (p. 450). That the Jemison narrative did not offer the conventional restoration scene is true, but it was hardly the first captivity narrative to abandon the convention.

14. At the close of the Revolution, Jemison turned down yet another opportunity to be repatriated to the white community, preferring to remain near her Indian relations and on the Gardau flats. The reason she gives in Seaver, *Narrative*, is "that I had got a large family of Indian children, that I must take with me; and that if I should be so fortunate as to find my relatives, they would despise them, if not myself; and treat us as enemies; or, at least with a degree of cold indifference, which I thought I could not endure" (p. 93).

15. See Filson; also "A true and faithful Narrative of the surprizing Captivity and remarkable Deliverance of Captain Isaac Stewart," in E. Russell, comp., *Narative of Mrs. Scott and Capt. Stewart's Captivity* (Boston: E. Russell, 1786), pp. 19–24.

16. See Frank Luther Mott, *Golden Multitudes: The Story of Best Sellers in the United States* (New York: Macmillan Co., 1947), pp. 97, 96–97, 305.

17. James Everett Seaver, *Life of Mary Jemison: Deh-He-Wä-Mis* (New York and Auburn: Miller, Orton and Mulligan; Rochester, N.Y.: D. M. Dewey, 1856), p. 9.

18. Cooper, *The Last of the Mohicans*, pp. 364, 172.

19. Gherman, p. 193.

20. [Catharine Maria Sedgwick], *Hope Leslie: Or, Early Times in the Massachusetts*, 2 vols. (New York: White, Gallaher, and White, 1827), 2:262.

21. Timothy Flint, *Biographical Memoir of Daniel Boone, The First Settler of Kentucky: Interspersed with Incidents in the Early Annals of the Country* (Cincinnati: N. and G. Guilford and Co., 1833), p. 247 (hereafter cited in the text as *DB*).

22. Filson, p. 60.

23. Ibid., p. 72.

24. See *The Adventures of Colonel Daniel Boon, One of the first Settlers at Kentucke . . . Written by the Colonel himself* (Norwich, Conn.: John Trumbull, 1786). In Daniel Bryan, *The Mountain Muse: Comprising the Adventures of Daniel Boone; and the Power of Virtuous and Refined Beauty* (Harrisonburg, Va.: Davidson and Bourne, 1813), Rebecca Bryan Boone makes her most dramatic appearance when she attempts to dissuade her husband from first going off to explore Kentucky,

crying "My Boone! / How can you leave your Home, your Wife and Babes" (p. 56).

25. *Life and Adventures of Colonel Daniel Boon, The First White Settler of the State of Kentucky* (Providence, R.I.: H. Trumbull, 1824), pp. 19, 27, 22.

26. I am indebted in this discussion to materials in John Bakeless, *Daniel Boone: Master of the Wilderness* (New York: William Morrow, 1939), esp. pp. 26–30, 38, 347.

27. Timothy Flint, *A Condensed History and Geography of the Western States, Or the Mississippi Valley*, 2 vols. (1828; reprint, Gainesville, Fla.: Scholars' Facsimiles and Reprints, 1970).

28. *Life and Adventures of Colonel Daniel Boon* (H. Trumbull, 1824), p. 15.

29. See Slotkin, p. 300; and Bakeless, pp. 26–27.

30. Henry Nash Smith, *Virgin Land: The American West as Symbol and Myth* (1950; New York: Random House, Vintage Books, 1961), p. 59; also see Mott, p. 318.

31. See Elizabeth Fries Ellet, *The Pioneer Women of the West* (1852); facsimile reprint, Freeport, N.Y.: Books for Libraries Press, 1973), pp. vii, 43. Although John Frost did not acknowledge Flint as his source, his debt to both Filson and Flint is clear enough in his remarks on Rebecca Boone in *Heroic Women of the West: Comprising Thrilling Examples of Courage, Fortitude, Devotedness, and Self-Sacrifice, Among the Pioneer Mothers of the Western Country* (Philadelphia: A. Hart, 1854), pp. 26–31.

32. Ellet, p. 49.

33. Ibid., p. 56.

5. Mary Austin Holley and Eliza Farnham

1. Timothy Flint, *Biographical Memoir of Daniel Boone, The First Settler of Kentucky: Interspersed with Incidents in the Early Annals of the Country* (Cincinnati: N. and G. Guilford and Co., 1833), p. 115.

2. Margaret Van Horn Dwight, *A Journey to Ohio in 1810*, ed. Max Farrand (New Haven: Yale University Press, 1912), pp. 36–37.

3. Sarah Ann J. Goodmand, [no postmark] to Mrs. Elizabeth Garth, Charlottesville, Virginia, February 14, 1837, in Jesse Garth Family Papers, Earl Gregg Swem Library of the College of William and Mary in Virginia.

4. Quoted in "Poems of Rebecca (Wilkinson) Street, 1798–1833," p. 11, Anonymous typed MS, Southern Historical Collection at the University of North Carolina Library, Chapel Hill.

5. See Jane Robbins, Plymouth, Massachusetts, to Hannah Gilman, Marietta, Ohio, October 5, 1792–January 26, 1793, in Gilman Family Papers, Massachusetts Historical Society.

6. Jane Robbins, Plymouth, Massachusetts, to Mr. and Mrs. Benjamin Gilman, Marietta, Ohio, May 13, 1799, in Gilman Family Papers, Massachusetts Historical Society.

7. M. W., Philadelphia, Pennsylvania, to Maria McKean, Washington, Pennsyl-

vania, May 6, 1803, in Archibald Woods Papers, 1777–1893, Earl Gregg Swem Library of the College of William and Mary in Virginia.

8. Christiana Holmes Tillson, *A Woman's Story of Pioneer Illinois*, ed. Milo Milton Quaife (Chicago: Lakeside Press, R. R. Donnelley and Sons, 1919), p. 31.

9. Mrs. Francis Le Baron Goodwin, Plymouth, Massachusetts, to Mrs. Hannah Gilman, Marietta, Ohio, June 12, 1790, in Gilman Family Papers, Massachusetts Historical Society.

10. Mrs. Chandler Robbins, Plymouth, Massachusetts, to Mrs. Joseph Gilman, Marietta, Ohio, June 6, 1790, in Gilman Family Papers, Massachusetts Historical Society.

11. Mrs. Francis Le Baron Goodwin to Mrs. Hannah Gilman, June 12, 1790, Gilman Family Papers.

12. Mrs. Peter Gilman, Plymouth, Massachusetts, to Mrs. Benjamin Ives Gilman, Marietta, Ohio, November 29, 1790, in Mrs. Charles P. Noyes, ed., *A Family History in Letters and Documents, 1667–1837*, 2 vols. (St. Paul, Minn.: Privately Printed, 1919), 1:177.

13. Jane Robbins, Plymouth, Massachusetts, to Hannah Gilman, Marietta, Ohio, October 13, 1797, in Gilman Family Papers, Massachusetts Historical Society.

14. Dwight, p. 34.

15. Eliza Paull, St. Clairsville, Ohio, to Ann Woods, Wheeling, [West] Virginia, January 12, 1823, in Archibald Woods Papers, 1777–1893, Earl Gregg Swem Library of the College of William and Mary in Virginia.

16. Mrs. Benjamin Ives Gilman, Cincinnati, Ohio, to Elizabeth Hale Gilman, New York, October 30, 1823, in Noyes, ed., *A Family History*, 1:46.

17. Pat Jones, "Solitude" Plantation, Tennessee, to Mary E. Thweatt, Colesville, Chesterfield County, Virginia, September 25, 1833, in Berkeley–Thweatt Papers, Earl Gregg Swem Library of the College of William and Mary in Virginia.

18. Dwight, p. 63.

19. Henry Nash Smith, *Virgin Land: The American West as Symbol and Myth* (1950; reprint, New York: Random House, Vintage Books, 1961), pp. 202–3.

20. Eliza W. Farnham, *Life in Prairie Land* (New York: Harper and Brothers, 1846), p.75.

21. Tillson, pp. 51, 69, 52, 53–54.

22. Ibid., pp. 104, 56–57.

23. Quoted in Dorothy Anne Dondore, *The Prairie and the Making of Middle America: Four Centuries of Description* (Cedar Rapids: Torch Press, 1926), p. 241.

24. Mary Austin Holley, *Texas. Observations, Historical, Geographical and Descriptive, In a Series of Letters, Written during a Visit to Austin's Colony, with a view to a permanent settlement in that country, in the Autumn of 1831* (Baltimore: Armstrong and Plaskitt, 1833), p. 62.

25. In *Discoverers, Explorers, Settlers: The Diligent Writers of Early America* (Chicago: University of Chicago Press, 1979), Wayne Franklin defines "promotional tracts" as a form of "literature which aims at persuading the reader to move, to

make a commitment and thus realize the ideal journey of the text" (p. 79); see also p. 94.

26. See John Filson, *The Discovery, Settlement And present State of Kentucke . . . To which is added, An Appendix, Containing, The Adventures of Col. Daniel Boon, one of the first Settlers . . .* (Wilmington, Del.: James Adams, 1784), p. 81.

27. Flint, pp. 12, 74, 78. The identification of Boone as "Adamic" derives from R. W. B. Lewis, *The American Adam: Innocence, Tragedy, and Tradition in the Nineteenth Century* (1955; reprint, Chicago: University of Chicago Press, 1965).

28. In 1821 Stephen F. Austin introduced into Texas (then a Mexican province) a colony of emigrants from the United States. Although the Austins were New Englanders, most of the immigrants to the colony were southern yeoman farmers and small slaveholders. The open abrogation of Mexico's antislavery laws (which permitted only limited terms of indenture, but not lifelong or inherited servitude) drove the Mexican government to drastic measures by 1830: that year, the Mexican government attempted to prohibit further emigration from the States; it stopped the importation of slaves; it levied heavy duties on most American goods brought into the colony; and it dispatched troops to the province to see that these laws were enforced. When Holley arrived in 1831, she heard talk of open rebellion and rumors of foreign intervention, and many Texans, she came to understand, feared further, harsher measures from the Mexican government. Trying to minimize the danger in her promotional tract, and sidestepping the slavery issue that was at the core of the problem, she wrote only that "nothing . . . is wanting but a liberal system of policy, on the part of the government, with regard to emigration on the one hand, and a population of industrious mechanics and farmers and intelligent planters on the other" (*T*, p. 62).

29. See the conversion statement of Joan White as recorded in the February 10, 1645, entry in John Fiske, *The Notebook of the Reverend John Fiske, 1644–1675*, ed. Robert G. Pope, Publications of the Colonial Society of Massachusetts, vol. 47 (Boston: The Society, 1974), p. 30.

30. In selecting a site for his colony, Stephen F. Austin had purposefully chosen that portion of Texas that resembled the more fertile regions of the Mississippi valley. Thus, he sought the timbered and well-watered environments along the Brazos and Colorado rivers, rather than the plains areas.

31. This was the mother's way of making certain that her daughter was fashionably dressed.

32. See Rebecca Smith Lee, *Mary Austin Holley: A Biography* (Austin: University of Texas Press, 1962), p. 218.

33. "I have been fortunate in enjoying the conversation of some of the oldest colonists and most intelligent men of the country," Holley stated in *Texas*, "from whom I have gathered much valuable information respecting the history and geography of Texas" (*T*, pp. 51–52). "From copious notes taken" during these conversations, she says she later composed her passages describing the general terrain and prospects of the country.

34. Holley had been married to the New England-trained minister, Horace Holley, who later became the first head of Transylvania University in Lexington,

Kentucky. Her first book, published in 1828, had been a paean to his memory: *A Discourse on the Genius and Character of the Reverend Horace Holley.*

35. In a diary kept during a visit to Texas during the winter of 1837–38 (a year after her cousin's death), Holley for the first time visited the land that Stephen F. Austin had promised to set aside for her, land adjacent to his own. "Mounted on Cousin Stephen's favorite pony," Holley viewed the area, calling it her cousin's "chosen spot on this Earth, where he & I were to have our paradise," in Mary Austin Holley, *The Texas Diary, 1835–1838*, ed. James P. Bryan (Austin: University of Texas Press, 1965), p. 52.

36. For a full discussion of the relationship between the two cousins, see Lee, esp. pp. 225–95; see also Holley, *The Texas Diary*, p. 52.

37. Caroline Howard Gilman, *Recollections of a Southern Matron* (New York: Harper and Brothers, 1838), p. 24.

38. Nina Baym, *Woman's Fiction: A Guide to Novels by and about Women in America, 1820–1870* (Ithaca: Cornell University Press, 1978), p. 27.

39. Mary Kelley, "The Sentimentalists: Promise and Betrayal in the Home," *Signs* 4 (Spring 1979): 436–37.

40. Baym, p. 27.

41. Kelley, p. 436.

6. Margaret Fuller

1. See Rebecca Smith Lee, *Mary Austin Holley: A Biography* (Austin: University of Texas Press, 1962), p. 254; and Mary Austin Holley, *The Texas Diary, 1835–1838*, ed. James P. Bryan (Austin: University of Texas Press, 1965), p. 43.

2. S. M. Fuller, *Summer on the Lakes, in 1843* (Boston: Charles C. Little and James Brown; New York: Charles S. Francis and Co., 1844), p. 67.

3. Eliza W. Farnham, *Life in Prairie Land* (New York: Harper and Brothers, 1846), p. 408.

4. Margaret Fuller, "On her childhood [1840]," in Bell Gale Chevigny, *The Woman and the Myth: Margaret Fuller's Life and Writings* (Old Westbury, N.Y.: Feminist Press, 1976), pp. 37, 41–42.

5. Paula Blanchard, *Margaret Fuller: From Transcendentalism to Revolution* (New York: Delacorte Press/Seymour Lawrence, 1978), p. 54.

6. Margaret Fuller, Groton, Massachusetts, to Frederick Henry Hedge, Boston, July 4, 1833, quoted in Thomas Wentworth Higginson, *Margaret Fuller Ossoli* (1890; reprint, New York: Greenwood Press, 1968), pp. 43, 44.

7. See Higginson, p. 60.

8. Blanchard, p. 76.

9. Quoted in Higginson, pp. 59–60.

10. Ibid., p. 60.

11. Fuller, "On her childhood [1840]," in Chevigny, p. 42.

12. Ibid.

13. Ibid., pp. 42, 36.

14. Diary of Mrs. Eliza [Carolina Burgwin] Clitherall (1784–1863), Typed

Vol. I: MSS vol. 3, typed p. 14, in Southern Historical Collection, University of North Carolina Library, Chapel Hill.

15. John Todd, *The Lost Sister of Wyoming. An Authentic Narrative* (Northampton, Mass.: J. H. Butler, 1842).

16. See, for example, Mary Rowlandson, *A True History of the Captivity and Restoration of Mrs. Mary Rowlandson, A Minister's Wife in New-England* (London: Joseph Poole, 1682), p. 10.

17. Farnham, p. 353.

18. Margaret Fuller Ossoli, *Summer on the Lakes*, ed. Arthur B. Fuller, 2d ed. (1856; reprint, New York: Haskell House Publishers, 1970), p. ix.

19. See Higginson, pp. 198–99.

20. Quoted in Ann Douglas, *The Feminization of American Culture* (New York: Alfred A. Knopf, 1977), p. 279.

21. Ossoli, *Summer on the Lakes*, ed. Fuller, p. v.

22. Quoted in Blanchard, p. 93.

23. See Higginson, pp. 194–95.

24. Margaret Fuller Ossoli, *Woman in the Nineteenth Century and Kindred Papers Relating to the Sphere, Condition and Duties, of Women*, ed. Arthur B. Fuller (1855; reprint, New York: W. W. Norton, 1971), pp. 34–35. This statement first appeared, in somewhat altered form, in Margaret Fuller, "The Great Lawsuit. Man *versus* Men. Woman *versus* Women," *Dial* 4, no. 1 (July 1843): 12.

25. Ossoli, *Woman in the Nineteenth Century*, p. 174.

26. See, for example, Chevigny, p. 316.

27. My remarks here largely complement Chevigny's observation, p. 215, that *Woman in the Nineteenth Century* "represented two sorts of advances in [Fuller's] development: a quickened sense of independence and of *psychological integrity* and a new attention to the claims of society and politics" (my emphasis).

28. Quoted in Higginson, p. 198.

29. This is Higginson's assessment, p. 199.

30. See Higginson, p. 200.

31. Higginson expresses this view, p. 197.

7. The Literary Legacy of Caroline Kirkland

1. Quoted in William S. Osborne, *Caroline M. Kirkland* (New York: Twayne Publishers, 1972), p. 24.

2. Quoted in ibid., p. 24.

3. [Caroline M. Kirkland], *A New Home—Who'll Follow? Or, Glimpses of Western Life. By Mrs. Mary Clavers. An Actual Settler* (1839; reprint, New York: Garrett Press, 1969), p. 12.

4. James Hall, Author's preface to *Legends of the West* (Philadelphia: Key and Biddle, 1833), n.p.

5. Charles Fenno Hoffman, *A Winter in the West*, 2 vols. (New York: Harper and Brothers, 1835), 1:183–84.

6. Kirkland here refers to Francois René de Chateaubriand's *Atala* (Paris,

1801), allegedly based on the French author's five-month visit to America in 1791, but actually set in a lush flowering Floridian jungle that Chateaubriand had never seen (as he probably traveled no farther south than Maryland). As one of the great works of French romantic literature, *Atala* enjoyed enormous success across Europe and in the United States—both in its original French and, later, in translation.

7. Henry Nash Smith, *Virgin Land: The American West as Symbol and Myth* (1950; New York: Random House, Vintage Books, 1961), p. 264.

8. Washington Irving, *A Tour on the Prairies*, ed. James Playsted Wood (1835; reprint, New York: Pantheon Books, 1967), p. 3; and Hoffman, p. 183.

9. For similar remarks, see S. M. Fuller, *Summer on the Lakes, in 1843* (Boston: Charles C. Little and James Brown; New York: Charles S. Francis and Co., 1844), p. 61.

10. Review of "*A New Home; Who'll Follow? or, Glimpses of Western Life* by Mrs. Mary Clavers—An Actual Settler," *North American Review* 50 (January 1840): 206–23 passim.

11. From Edgar Allan Poe's "The Literati of New York City," quoted in Introduction to Caroline M. Kirkland, *A New Home—Who'll Follow? Glimpses of Western Life*, ed. William S. Osborne (New Haven: College and University Press Publishers, 1965), p. 24.

12. Ibid.

13. Quoted in Osborne, p. 44.

14. From a contemporary account quoted in ibid.

15. [Caroline M. Kirkland], *Forest Life. By the Author of "A New Home"*, 2 vols. (New York: Charles S. Francis and Co.; Boston: J. H. Francis, 1842), 1:4, 33 (hereafter cited in the text as *FL*).

16. Caroline M. Kirkland, *Western Clearings* (1845; reprint, New York: Garrett Press, 1969), p. viii (hereafter cited in the text as *WC*).

17. Caroline Kirkland, "The Hard Winter," *Union Magazine of Literature and Art* 2 (January 1848): 43.

18. Caroline Kirkland, "The Log-House," *Union Magazine of Literature and Art* 2 (June 1848): 274–75.

19. Caroline Kirkland, "Bush-Life," *Sartain's Union Magazine of Literature and Art* 6 (January 1850): 70.

20. Ibid., p. 71.

21. Joseph Kirkland to Louise C. Schuler, July 15, 1887, quoted in Clyde E. Henson, *Joseph Kirkland* (New York: Twayne Publishers, 1962), p. 89. Henson's discussion of Joseph Kirkland's career, pp. 87–92, has greatly influenced my analysis here.

22. Ibid.

23. Joseph Kirkland, *Zury: The Meanest Man in Spring County* (1887; reprint, Urbana: University of Illinois Press, 1956), p. 123.

24. Caroline Kirkland, "Bush-Life," p. 72.

25. A case in point is Caroline Lee Hentz. Although her first novel, *Lovell's Folly* (Cincinnati: Hubbard and Edmonds, 1833), was probably composed in 1832, the year the Hentzes moved to Cincinnati, its setting was "a beautiful

valley in New England" (p. 5). Her play, "Lamorah, or the Western Wild," was also probably written in 1832 (and then produced early in 1833), but although its setting was the Ohio River valley, its Indian maiden heroine showed nothing of local custom and instead betrayed Hentz's debt to the sentimentalized noble savages of Rousseau and Chateaubriand.

26. Caroline Kirkland, "Bush-Life," p. 72.

27. Fred Lewis Pattee, *The Feminine Fifties* (New York: D. Appleton-Century Co., 1940).

28. Caroline A. Soule, *The Pet of the Settlement. A Story of Prairie-Land* (Boston: A. Tompkins, 1860), p. iii.

8. The Domestic Fantasy Goes West

1. Alice Carey [*sic*], *Clovernook; Or, Recollections of Our Neighborhood in the West*, 2d ser. (New York: Redfield, 1853), p. 13.

2. Caroline Lee Hentz describes "a beautiful valley in New England . . . gradually becoming a favorite summer retreat of some of the metropolitans, who, debilitated or disgusted by the heat and confinement of a city, longed for the chartered air and liberal shade," in *Lovell's Folly. A Novel* (Cincinnati: Hubbard and Edmonds, 1833), pp. 5–6.

3. James Fenimore Cooper, *The Works of James Fenimore Cooper*, 10 vols. (New York: P. F. Collier, 1892), 6:58.

4. Janis P. Stout, *Sodoms in Eden: The City in American Fiction before 1860* (Westport, Conn.: Greenwood Press, 1976), pp. 4, 21.

5. Nathaniel Hawthorne, preface to *The Marble Faun, or The Romance of Monte Beni* (1860), in *The Complete Novels and Selected Tales of Nathaniel Hawthorne*, ed. Norman Holmes Pearson (New York: Random House, 1937), p. 590. Hawthorne, of course, had for some years been residing in Europe when he made this statement.

6. See Russel Blaine Nye, *Society and Culture in America, 1830–1860* (New York: Harper and Row, 1974), p. 43, n. 18.

7. For the context of this incident, see James D. Hart, *The Popular Book: A History of America's Literary Taste* (1950; reprint, Berkeley: University of California Press, 1963), p. 93.

8. Ann Sophia Stephens, *Fashion and Famine* (New York: Bunce and Brother, 1854).

9. Ann Sophia Stephens, *The Old Homestead* (New York: Bunce and Brother, 1855). For a more extensive discussion of this novel, see Nina Baym, *Woman's Fiction: A Guide to Novels by and about Women in America, 1820–1870* (Ithaca: Cornell University Press, 1978), pp. 186–87.

10. [Maria Susanna Cummins], *Mabel Vaughan* (Boston: John P. Jewett and Company; Cleveland: Henry P. B. Jewett, 1857), p. 127 (hereafter cited in the text as *MV*).

11. Kirkland's 1853 remark is quoted in William S. Osborne, *Caroline M. Kirkland* (New York: Twayne Publishers, 1972), p. 123.

12. Ann Sophia Stephens, *Mary Derwent* (Philadelphia: T. B. Peterson and Brothers, 1858), p. 181.

13. [Catharine Maria Sedgwick], *Live and Let Live; Or, Domestic Service Illustrated* (New York: Harper and Brothers, 1837), p. 184.

14. Charles Fenno Hoffman, *A Winter in the West*, 2 vols. (New York: Harper and Brothers, 1835), 1:191.

15. Mary Austin Holley, *Texas. Observations, Historical, Geographical and Descriptive, In a Series of Letters, Written during a Visit to Austin's Colony, with a view to a permanent settlement in that country, in the Autumn of 1831* (Baltimore: Armstrong and Plaskitt, 1833), pp. 14, 127–28.

16. See Baym, p. 122.

17. Emma D. E. N. Southworth's *India: The Pearl of Pearl River* (Philadelphia: T. B. Peterson and Brothers, 1856) was first serialized in 1853 under the title, *Mark Sutherland* (hereafter cited in the text as *I*).

18. [Mary Hayden Green Pike], *Ida May: A Story of Things Actual and Possible. By Mary Langdon* [pseud.] (Boston: Phillips, Sampson and Co., 1854). See also Baym, pp. 268–69.

19. Susan Phinney Conrad, *Perish the Thought: Intellectual Women in Romantic America, 1830–1860* (New York: Oxford University Press, 1976), pp. 99–100.

20. Mrs. D. L. Child, *The History of the Condition of Women, in Various Ages and Nations*, 2 vols. (Boston: John Allen and Cox, 1835), 2:260–61.

21. These remarks, first offered at an 1852 Women's Rights Convention, were published by Paulina Wright Davis as "Remarks at the Convention," in *Una* (September 1853): 136–37.

22. Catharine Beecher, "How to Redeem Women's Profession from Dishonor," *Harper's New Monthly Magazine* 31 (November 1865): 710; and Catharine Beecher, *Letters to the People on Health and Happiness* (New York: Harper and Brothers, 1855), p. 183. Of inestimable value to me in this discussion was Kathryn Kish Sklar's *Catharine Beecher: A Study in American Domesticity* (New Haven: Yale University Press, 1973).

23. Beecher, "How to Redeem Women's Profession from Dishonor," p. 710.

24. From Louisa C. Tuthill's *My Wife* (Boston: William Crosby and H. P. Nichols, 1846), quoted in Baym, p. 80.

25. Nancy F. Cott, *The Bonds of Womanhood: "Woman's Sphere" in New England, 1780–1835* (New Haven: Yale University Press, 1977), p. 199.

26. Quoted in ibid., p. 68.

27. Sarah Josepha Hale, "Editor's Table," *Godey's Lady's Book* 40 (January 1850): 76.

28. From "The Social Condition of Woman," *North American Review* 42 (1836): 513, quoted in Conrad, p. 36.

29. Caroline M. Kirkland, "The Island Story," in *Autumn Hours, and Fireside Reading* (New York: Charles Scribner, 1854), p. 196.

30. *Hearth and Home* was published in New York from December 1868 through December 1875; its original editors were Donald G. Mitchell and Harriet Beecher Stowe, although Stowe left the editorial staff after the first year.

Under its front-page title, the magazine featured a woodcut of a rustic cottage with children playing around the door.

31. Beecher, *Letters to the People on Health and Happiness*, p. 91.

32. Caroline M. Kirkland, "The Island Story," p. 110.

33. Baym, p. 231.

34. Paulina Wright Davis complained that women who had to earn their own living were forced to enter the "factory and the schoolroom at *slave* wages," in "Remarks at the Convention," p. 136. Catharine Beecher echoed this theme when, after a visit to the much-heralded Lowell, Massachusetts, mills, she wrote that "work of all kinds is got from poor women, at prices that will not keep soul and body together. . . . And then the articles thus made," she continued, "are sold for prices that give monstrous profits to the capitalist, who thus grows rich on the hard labors of our sex," quoted in Sklar, pp. 172–73.

35. Mary Kelley, "A Woman Alone: Catharine Maria Sedgwick's Spinster-hood in Nineteenth-Century America," *New England Quarterly* 51, no. 2 (June 1978): 209.

36. Of course, as Henry Nash Smith has pointed out in *Virgin Land: The American West as Symbol and Myth* (1950; New York: Random House, Vintage Books, 1961), p. 151, "by 1830," there were already "two agrarianisms" contesting "for control of the territories beyond the Mississippi. Each of these new agrarianisms found expression in imaginative and symbolic terms: that of the South in a pastoral literature of the plantation, that of the Northwest in the myth of the garden of the world with the idealized Western yeoman as its focal point."

37. Caroline A. Soule, *The Pet of the Settlement. A Story of Prairie-Land* (Boston: A. Tompkins, 1860), p. 102 (hereafter cited in the text as *PS*).

38. Eliza W. Farnham, *Life in Prairie Land* (New York: Harper and Brothers, 1846), p. 74; and Holley, p. 127.

39. See Paul W. Gates, *Landlords and Tenants on the Prairie Frontier: Studies in American Land Policy* (Ithaca: Cornell University Press, 1973), pp. 239, 60.

40. Quoted in ibid., p. 59.

41. See ibid., p. 56.

42. Ibid., p. 240; the entry of March 23, 1846, from the Diary of Calvin Fletcher, is quoted in Gates, p. 62.

43. Caroline M. Kirkland, *A New Home—Who'll Follow? Or, Glimpses of Western Life* (1839; reprint, New York: Garrett Press, 1969), p. 48.

44. Lydia H. Sigourney, "The Western Home" in *The Western Home, and Other Poems* (Philadelphia: Parry and McMillan, 1854), p. 29 (hereafter cited in the text as *WH*).

45. S. M. Fuller, *Summer on the Lakes, in 1843* (Boston: Charles C. Little and James Brown; New York: Charles S. Francis and Co., 1844), p. 60.

46. See, for example, Julia Caroline Ripley Dorr's *Farmingdale. By Caroline Thomas* [pseud.] (New York: D. Appleton, 1854); and for a discussion of the novel, see Baym, pp. 237–38.

47. Elisabeth Adams, Davenport, Iowa, to Emeline M. Robinson, Cleveland, Ohio, July 14, 1846, in Ephraim Adams Papers, Manuscript Collection, Iowa State Historical Department.

48. Elisabeth Adams, Davenport, Iowa, to Emeline Robinson, Cleveland, Ohio, March 17, 1846, in Ephraim Adams Papers.

49. Ibid.

50. "Letters of John and Sarah Everett, 1854–1864: Miami County Pioneers," *Kansas Historical Quarterly* 3, no. 4 (November 1939): 354. Sarah Everett and her husband immigrated to the Kansas Territory in the spring of 1855, along with other eastern "free staters." She died in 1864.

51. Elizabeth Fries Ellet, *The Pioneer Women of the West* (1852; facsimile reprint, Freeport, N.Y.: Books for Libraries Press, 1973). To be sure, isolated articles, especially in the literary magazines published in the west, also acknowledged women's participation in the pioneer experience. The July 1836 issue of the *Western Literary Journal and Monthly Review*, for example, published an anonymously authored poem entitled, "The Mothers of the West," which castigated Americans for failing to appreciate women's contribution to the settlement of the west; and an anonymously authored article, entitled "The Pioneer Mothers," praised women for going forth as "volunteers to act as hand-maids in rearing a nation in the wilds of the West . . . with a devotedness and singleness of purpose" (pp. 106, 101). Unfortunately, isolated pieces like these did not enjoy much cumulative impact.

52. J. M. Shively, *Route and Distances to Oregon and California, With a Description of Watering-Places, Crossings, Dangerous Indians, &c. &c.* (Washington, D.C.: William Greer, Printer, 1846) appears as an appendix to Dale Morgan, ed., *Overland in 1846: Diaries and Letters of the California-Oregon Trail*, 2 vols. (Georgetown, Calif.: Talisman Press, 1963), 2:736.

53. For accurate assessments of women's many tasks on the overland trail, see John Mack Faragher, *Women and Men on the Overland Trail* (New Haven: Yale University Press, 1979); Julie Roy Jeffrey, *Frontier Women: The Trans-Mississippi West, 1840–1880* (New York: Hill and Wang, 1979); and Lillian Schlissel, *Women's Diaries of the Westward Journey* (New York: Schocken Books, 1982).

54. Elisabeth Adams, Davenport, Iowa, to Ephraim Adams, Grinnell, Iowa, May 5, 1856, in Ephraim Adams Papers. A native of New Hampshire, Elisabeth Adams had removed to Iowa with her husband who was a Congregationalist minister; his many church-related administrative duties kept him—and his family—constantly on the move in Iowa.

9. Alice Cary and Caroline Soule

1. Alice Cary made these defensive remarks in her second collection of Clovernook tales, *Clovernook; Or Recollections of Our Neighborhood in the West*, 2d ser. (New York: Redfield, 1853), p. 363 (hereafter cited in the text as *CL*, 2d ser.).

2. Alice Carey [*sic*], *Clovernook; Or Recollections of Our Neighborhood in the West* (New York: Redfield, 1852), p. 94 (hereafter cited in the text as *CL*).

3. Quoted in Henry Nash Smith, *Virgin Land: The American West as Symbol and Myth* (1950; New York: Random House, Vintage Books, 1961), p. 268.

4. Quoted in Mary Clemmer Ames, *A Memorial of Alice and Phoebe Cary, With Some of Their Later Poems* (Boston: Houghton Mifflin and Co., 1882), p. 19.

5. From the reminiscence of Phoebe Cary, quoted in ibid., p. 2.

6. Ibid.

7. From the reminiscence of Alice Cary, quoted in ibid., p. 19.

8. From the reminiscence of Phoebe Cary, quoted in ibid. p. 9.

9. From the reminiscence of Alice Cary, quoted in ibid., p. 19.

10. Ibid.

11. See W. H. Venable, *Beginnings of Literary Culture in the Ohio Valley. Historical and Biographical Sketches* (1891; reprint, New York: Peter Smith, 1949), p. 484.

12. Smith, p. 168; and Ames, p. 21.

13. See Venable, p. 487.

14. Alice and Phoebe Cary, *Poems of Alice and Phoebe Cary* (Philadelphia: Moss and Brothers, 1849).

15. See Ames, pp. 28–29; and Margaret Wyman Langworthy, "Alice Cary," in *Notable American Women, 1670–1950: A Biographical Dictionary*, 3 vols. (1971; reprint, Cambridge, Mass.: Harvard University Press, Belknap Press, 1975), 1:296.

16. Dated New York, September 3, 1866, the letter is quoted in Ames, pp. 86–87.

17. See Venable, pp. 507–8.

18. Quoted in Ames, p. 32.

19. These remarks from a review in the *Illustrated News* are quoted in the endsheet to *CL*, n.p.

20. Alice Cary, *The Clovernook Children* (New York: International Book Co., 1854).

21. Fred Lewis Pattee, *The Feminine Fifties* (New York: D. Appleton-Century Co., 1940), p. 63.

22. In *Woman's Fiction: A Guide to Novels by and about Women in America, 1820–1870* (Ithaca: Cornell University Press, 1978), Nina Baym credits Maria Susanna Cummins's novel, *The Lamplighter* (1854), with giving "America one of its early fictional representations of the suburb" (p. 166). In fact, Cary's depiction of the suburbs in "Mrs. Wetherbe's Quilting Party," *CL*, 2d ser., pp. 24–26, is the earlier and far more realistic portrait.

23. Caroline A. Soule, *The Pet of the Settlement. A Story of Prairie-Land* (Boston: A. Tompkins, 1860), p. 79.

24. Caroline Kirkland, "Bush-Life," *Sartain's Union Magazine of Literature and Art* 6 (January 1850): 71.

25. Caroline Augusta White Soule was a native of Albany, New York; marriage to a Universalist minister brought her to New England. When her husband died of smallpox in 1852, he left her with four small children to raise, $300, and a few hundred books. She was then twenty-seven years old. Although she tried to remain in New England, financial difficulties finally forced her to remove to a log cabin in Boonsboro, Iowa, where she was able to support herself and her family by teaching and writing. After ten years in Iowa, and increasing success as a

writer, Soule returned to her native Albany in 1864 and three years later moved to New York City.

26. See, for example, John Frost, *Heroic Women of the West: Comprising Examples of Courage, Fortitude, Devotedness, and Self-Sacrifice, Among the Pioneer Mothers of the Western Country* (Philadelphia: A. Hart, 1854), which contains forty narratives by or about women, most of them captivity narratives.

27. J. Hector St. John de Crèvecoeur, *Letters from an American Farmer* (1782; reprint, New York: E. P. Dutton, 1957), pp. 7, 40.

28. After Soule returned to the east, in 1864, she gave herself to activities that benefited the Universalist church, the temperance cause, and the Association for the Advancement of Women; her subsequent writing reflected these commitments.

29. Baym comments that, "in many ways," Louisa May Alcott's *Little Women* (1868) "is the most technically accomplished work to rise from the genre of woman's fiction," but notes that it is nonetheless "a children's book rather than a woman's book" (p. 197); probably the best example of the consolation fiction to follow the Civil War, Elizabeth Stuart Phelps's novel, *The Gates Ajar* (1869), offers images of heavenly mansions that are essentially middle class and domestic, clearly derived from the ideals propounded by the domestic fictionists of the preceding decade.

30. James D. Hart, *The Popular Book: A History of America's Literary Taste* (1950; reprint, Berkeley: University of California Press, 1963), p. 141.

10. E.D.E.N. Southworth and Maria Susanna Cummins

1. Nathaniel Hawthorne, *The Scarlet Letter and Other Tales of the Puritans*, ed. Harry Levin (Boston: Houghton Mifflin, 1961), p. 196.

2. S. M. Fuller, *Summer on the Lakes, in 1843* (Boston: Charles C. Little and James Brown; New York: Charles S. Francis and Co., 1844), p. 62.

3. Hawthorne, *The Scarlet Letter*, p. 196.

4. Elizabeth Fries Ellet, *The Pioneer Women of the West* (1852; facsimile reprint, Freeport, N.Y.: Books for Libraries Press, 1973), pp. 14, vi, 13.

5. Ann Sophia Stephens, *Mary Derwent* (Philadelphia: T. B. Peterson and Brothers, 1858), pp. 135, 137, 74, 137.

6. Lydia H. Sigourney, "The Lost Lily," in *The Western Home, and Other Poems* (Philadelphia: Parry and McMillan, 1854), p. 342.

7. John Todd, *The Lost Sister of Wyoming. An Authentic Narrative* (Northampton, Mass.: J. H. Butler, 1842).

8. Sigourney, "The Lost Lily," pp. 349, 346, 347, 348.

9. The letter is quoted in Julia Archibald Holmes, *A Bloomer Girl on Pike's Peak, 1858*, ed. Agnes Wright Spring (Denver: Denver Public Library, 1949), p. 39. I am indebted to Margaret Solomon for alerting me to the existence of the Holmes materials and for providing an advance copy of her paper, "A Study of Feminism as a Motif in 'A Journey to Pike's Peak and New Mexico' by Julia Archibald Holmes," in *Women and Western American Literature*, ed. Helen Win-

ter Stauffer and Susan J. Rosowski (Troy, N.Y.: Whitston Publishing Co., 1982), pp. 28–39.

10. Holmes, pp. 33–34; 17.

11. Stephens, *Mary Derwent*, pp. 74–75.

12. Ibid., pp. 75, 137.

13. Emma D.E.N. Southworth, *India: The Pearl of Pearl River* (Philadelphia: T. B. Peterson and Brothers, 1856), p. 269.

14. R. W. B. Lewis, *The American Adam: Innocence, Tragedy, and Tradition in the Nineteenth Century* (Chicago: University of Chicago Press, 1955), p. 89.

15. [Maria Susanna Cummins], *Mabel Vaughan* (Boston: John P. Jewett; Cleveland: Henry P. B. Jewett, 1857), p. 413.

16. Internal evidence leaves no doubt that the Ashley plantation is located in what we now call West Virginia; but it was not until 1863, some ten years after the novel was composed, that West Virginia became an independent state, and so the novel simply shows its hero traveling "to Virginia" (*I*, p. 164).

17. California's petition to enter the union as a free state in 1849 had re-awakened regional divisions over the slavery issue. The Compromise of 1850, designed to placate southern interests and, it was hoped, stave off threats of se-cession, admitted California as a free state but placed no restriction on the intro-duction of the "peculiar institution" into the territories newly created from the Mexican cession, New Mexico and Utah. At the same time, under the compro-mise, while slave-trading was prohibited in the District of Columbia, a more severe fugitive-slave act replaced the old one of 1793. All in all, it was a compro-mise that pleased no one, and Abolitionists and Free-Soilers, especially, de-nounced it and refused to be bound by its terms.

18. At the time Southworth was writing the serialized *Mark Sutherland*, her sister Charlotte was residing with their uncle, Captain J. B. Nevitte, at Clermont Hall, Mississippi; the sisters presumably visited during this period, in which case Clermont Hall may well have been the prototype for Clement Sutherland's Cash-mere. For related biographical material, see Regis Louise Boyle, *Mrs. E.D.E.N. Southworth, Novelist* (Washington, D.C.: Catholic University of America Press, 1939), p. 7.

19. When Mark Sutherland first goes west, Southworth writes that "he ap-proached the fine 'Rock River country'" (*I*, p. 161); this places him in Illinois, an identification further confirmed by "this gigantic scene—Rock River, Rock Is-land, with the opposite shores of the Mississippi, widening here into a lake-like expanse" (*I*, p. 161). Here Sutherland is said to embark at "the village of S——, . . . [a] young city . . . but two years old" (*I*, p. 161). Upon returning to the west with Rosalie, Sutherland is again said to debark "at the new village of S——, in the Northwest Territory," on the eastern shore of the Mississippi (*I*, p. 253). Indeed, when Mark first proposes to Rosalie, he tells her that he intends to go "'back to the village of S——, to take possession of an established [law] office about to be vacated" (*I*, p. 238). Presumably, then, we are to believe that he returns to the same place. Certainly the physical descriptions are identical, with both landings emphasizing the high bluffs and woods along the Mississippi shore line (see *I*, pp. 161 and 254). But the chronology of the novel strongly

points to a Shelton located in Wisconsin. A letter composed by Mark's mother, written shortly after his return from Yale, is dated "June 184__" (*I*, p. 70). This (combined with other internal historical references) clearly places the novel in the 1840s and 1850s, and the only midwestern territory east of the Mississippi to achieve statehood during that period was Wisconsin, which joined the Union in May of 1848 (Illinois having achieved statehood in 1818). Since the text states that, during Mark and Rosalie's first four years of "residence in the village of Shelton, . . . the Territory had been erected into a state" (*I*, p. 307), we must assume that Shelton is in Wisconsin and that it therefore cannot be the same S____ to which Mark Sutherland had originally journeyed—the identical physical descriptions notwithstanding.

20. Until the advent of the modern corporation, the principle opportunity for investment was land; thus, throughout its history, the American frontier attracted eastern speculators like John Vaughan.

21. Though biographical information is scant, we know that Maria Susanna Cummins was educated in the Young Ladies School in Lenox, Massachusetts (run by a sister-in-law of the novelist, Catharine Maria Sedgwick); after that, she seems to have lived out the remainder of her life, unmarried, in the family homestead in Dorchester, Massachusetts, where her father served as a judge of the court of common pleas in Norfolk County. Internal evidence in *Mabel Vaughan*, combined with what we know of accustomed excursions for young women of her class, suggest that Cummins had enjoyed at least one trip to Niagara Falls, but probably ventured no further. Within the novel, the first part of Mabel's journey—from New York City to Buffalo (including a visit to the falls)—is clearly outlined: Mabel takes a steamboat up the Hudson River to Albany and from Albany, a night train to Buffalo. The description of Niagara Falls (*MV*, p. 350) also suggests firsthand knowledge. But after Mabel returns to Buffalo to take a steamboat on the Erie Canal, destined for some unnamed "bustling Western city" (*MV*, p. 356), the rest of her route becomes impossible to follow.

22. Nina Baym, *Woman's Fiction: A Guide to Novels by and about Women in America, 1820–1870* (Ithaca: Cornell University Press, 1978), p. 39.

23. Caroline A. Soule, *The Pet of the Settlement. A Story of Prairie-Land* (Boston: A. Tompkins, 1860), p. 20.

24. Richard Slotkin, *Regeneration through Violence: The Mythology of the American Frontier* (Middletown, Conn.: Wesleyan University Press, 1973), p. 21.

25. Although the quoted phrase is from Slotkin, p. 21, the original definition of the figure must be credited to Lewis's *The American Adam*.

26. [Catharine Maria Sedgwick], *Live and Let Live; Or, Domestic Service Illustrated* (New York: Harper and Brothers, 1837), p. vi.

27. California had outlawed slavery in 1850 in deference to miners who feared the competition of slave labor.

28. Slotkin, p. 4.

29. Because the novels first published between 1850 and 1860 continued to be reprinted, the western relocation novel did not disappear entirely, but it ceased as a form that continued to interest writers. Even so, the postbellum longevity of these books should not be discounted. *Mabel Vaughan*, for example, was re-

printed in the United States in 1858, 1877, 1885 and again in 1896; other editions appeared in England, including reprints of the first 1857 English edition, edited by Mrs. Gaskell.

30. As early as 1834, one traveler to the Oregon Territory described a soil "rich beyond comparison" and declared "the willamet valley is a terrestrial paradise," quoted in Lillian Schlissel, *Women's Diaries of the Westward Journey* (New York: Schocken Books, 1982), p. 20. Similar accounts were also being sent back from California.

Epilogue. A New Frontier Beckons

1. Abigail Scott Duniway, *Path Breaking: An Autobiographical History of the Equal Suffrage Movement in Pacific Coast States* (2d ed., 1914; reprint, New York: Source Book Press, 1970), p. 4.

2. Anna Howard Shaw, *The Story of a Pioneer* (New York: Harper and Brothers, 1915), p. 20.

3. Ibid., pp. 21, 24–25, 27–28, 25, 26.

4. "Mrs. Whitman's Diary, March to July 1836," in Clifford Merrill Drury, ed., *First White Women Over the Rockies: Diaries, Letters, and Biographical Sketches of the Six Women of the Oregon Mission Who Made the Overland Journey in 1836 and 1838*, 3 vols. (Glendale, Calif.: Arthur H. Clark Co., 1966), 1:47.

5. The promotional reports from recent pioneers to Oregon in the 1840s are summarized by Earl Pomeroy in *The Pacific Slope: A History of California, Oregon, Washington, Idaho, Utah, and Nevada* (1965; reprint, Seattle: University of Washington Press, 1973), p. 27.

6. Throughout the first half of the nineteenth century, the ocean route to the west coast, sailing around Cape Horn, had been used by traders (in the hide and tallow trade or in search of sea-otter pelts); but only profitable commercial ventures made such an expensive route feasible. The costs were too high for most families with their household goods.

7. Quoted in John D. Unruh, Jr., *The Plains Across: The Overland Emigrants and the Trans-Mississippi West, 1840–1860* (Urbana: University of Illinois Press, 1979), p. 29.

8. Henry Nash Smith, *Virgin Land: The American West as Symbol and Myth* (1950; New York: Random House, Vintage Books, 1961), p. 207.

9. Unruh, p. 30.

10. James Fenimore Cooper, *The Prairie: A Tale*, Introduction by Henry Nash Smith (1827; reprint, New York: Holt, Rinehart and Winston, 1950), p. 4.

11. Quoted and summarized in Unruh, p. 42.

12. Quoted in ibid., p. 39.

13. Quoted in Drury, ed., *First White Women Over the Rockies*, 3:315.

14. Ibid.

15. Frederick Merk, *History of the Westward Movement* (New York: Alfred A. Knopf, 1978), p. 355.

16. J. M. Shively, *Route and Distances to Oregon and California, With a Descrip-*

tion of Watering-Places, Crossings, Dangerous Indians, &c. &c. (1846) republished in Dale Morgan, ed., *Overland in 1846: Diaries and Letters of the California-Oregon Trail*, 2 vols. (Georgetown, Calif.: Talisman Press, 1963), 2:742.

17. This letter is published in Morgan, ed., *Overland in 1846*, 1:116.

18. Quoted in Pomeroy, p. 34.

19. Ibid., p. 36.

20. Sarah J. Cummins, *Autobiography and Reminiscences* (Walla Walla, Wash.: Walla Walla Bulletin, 1914), p. 22 (hereafter cited in the text as *AAR*). The author was born in Sangamon, Sangamon County, Illinois; her family removed to Missouri in 1843.

21. Elizabeth Cress, Montgomery County, Illinois, to Mr. and Mrs. Henery Ludwick, Cabarrus County, North Carolina, August 17, 1851 in Ludwick-Ritchie Papers, Southern Historical Collection, University of North Carolina Library, Chapel Hill.

22. Catherine Haun, "A Woman's Trip Across the Plains in 1849," in Lillian Schlissel, *Women's Diaries of the Westward Journey* (New York: Schocken Books, 1982), p. 169.

23. Ibid.

24. Julia Archibald Holmes, *A Bloomer Girl on Pike's Peak, 1858*, ed. Agnes Wright Spring (Denver: Denver Public Library, 1949), p. 17.

25. Elizabeth Fries Ellet, *The Pioneer Women of the West* (1852; facsimile reprint, Freeport, N.Y.: Books for Libraries Press, 1973), p. 13.

26. Eliza W. Farnham, *California, In-doors and Out; Or, How We Farm, Mine, and Live Generally in the Golden State* (New York: Dix, Edwards and Co., 1856), pp. 177, 205.

27. Ibid., p. vi.

28. Quoted in Morgan, ed., *Overland in 1846*, 1:57–58.

29. Ibid., p. 107.

30. Shively, *Route and Distances to Oregon and California*, quoted in Morgan, ed., *Overland in 1846*, 2:741.

31. Francis Parkman, *The Oregon Trail* (1849; reprint, New York: New American Library, Signet Books, 1950), p. 72.

32. Quoted in Morgan, ed., *Overland in 1846*, 1:108.

33. Farnham, *California, In-doors and Out*, pp. 298–99.

34. John Filson, *The Discovery, Settlement And present State of Kentucke . . . To which is added, An Appendix, Containing, The Adventures of Col. Daniel Boon, one of the first Settlers . . .* (Wilmington, Del.: James Adams, 1784), p. 55.

35. Quoted in Morgan, ed., *Overland in 1846*, 1:287.

Bibliography

Manuscript Collections

Boston, Massachusetts
  Massachusetts Historical Society
    Gilman Family Papers.
Chapel Hill, North Carolina
  The Southern Historical Collection, University of North Carolina Library
    Diary of Mrs. Eliza [Carolina Burgwin] Clitherall, 1784–1863.
    Ludwick-Ritchie Papers.
    Mackay-Stiles Papers.
    "Poems of Rebecca (Wilkinson) Street, 1798–1833," anonymous typed manuscript.
    Mrs. Nicholas Trist Papers.
    Nicholas Philip Trist Papers.
Iowa City, Iowa
  Manuscript Collection, Iowa State Historical Department
    Ephraim Adams Papers.
Williamsburg, Virginia
  The Earl Gregg Swem Library of the College of William and Mary
    Berkeley-Thweatt Papers.
    Jesse Garth Family Papers.
    Archibald Woods Papers.

Published Works

Ames, Mary Clemmer. *A Memorial of Alice and Phoebe Cary, With Some of Their Later Poems*. Boston: Houghton Mifflin, 1882.

Appleton, Jay. *The Experience of Landscape*. London and New York: John Wiley and Sons, 1975.

Axtell, James. "The White Indians of Colonial America." *William and Mary Quarterly*, 3d ser. 32 (January 1975): 55–88.

Bakeless, John. *Daniel Boone: Master of the Wilderness*. New York: William Morrow, 1939.

Baym, Nina. *Woman's Fiction: A Guide to Novels by and about Women in America, 1820–1870*. Ithaca: Cornell University Press, 1978.

Beecher, Catharine. "How to Redeem Women's Profession from Dishonor." *Harper's New Monthly Magazine* 31 (November 1865): 708–15.

————. *Letters to the People on Health and Happiness.* New York: Harper and Brothers, 1855.

Benson, Mary Sumner. *Women in Eighteenth-Century America: A Study of Opinion and Social Usage.* 1935. Reprint. New York: AMS Press, 1976.

Bercovitch, Sacvan. *The Puritan Origins of the American Self.* New Haven: Yale University Press, 1975.

Blanchard, Paula. *Margaret Fuller: From Transcendentalism to Revolution.* New York: Delacorte Press / Seymour Lawrence, 1978.

Bleecker, Ann Eliza. *The History of Maria Kittle.* 1790. Hartford: Elisha Babcock, 1797.

Boyle, Regis Louise. *Mrs. E.D.E.N. Southworth, Novelist.* Washington, D.C.: Catholic University of America Press, 1939.

Bradstreet, Anne. *The Works of Anne Bradstreet in Prose and Verse.* Edited by John Harvard Ellis. 1867. Reprint. New York: Peter Smith, 1932.

Bryan, Daniel. *The Mountain Muse: Comprising the Adventures of Daniel Boone; and the Power of Virtuous and Refined Beauty.* Harrisonburg, Va.: Davidson and Bourne, 1813.

Carroll, Peter N. *Puritanism and the Wilderness: The Intellectual Significance of the New England Frontier, 1629–1700.* New York: Columbia University Press, 1969.

Cary, Alice. *Clovernook; Or, Recollections of Our Neighborhood in the West.* New York: Redfield, 1852.

————. *Clovernook; Or, Recollections of Our Neighborhood in the West.* 2d ser. New York: Redfield, 1853.

————. *The Clovernook Children.* New York: International Book Company, 1854.

————, and Cary, Phoebe. *Poems of Alice and Phoebe Cary.* Philadelphia: Moss and Brothers, 1849.

Chevigny, Bell Gale. *The Woman and the Myth: Margaret Fuller's Life and Writings.* Old Westbury, N.Y.: Feminist Press, 1976.

Child, Mrs. D. L. [Child, Lydia Maria]. *The History of the Condition of Women, in Various Ages and Nations.* 2 vols. Boston: John Allen and Cox, 1835.

———— [anon.]. *Hobomok. A Tale of Early Times.* Boston: Cummings, Hilliard and Co., 1824. Facsimile reprint. New York: Garrett Press, 1970.

Cole, Thomas. "Lecture on American Scenery, Delivered Before the Catskill Lyceum, April 1st, 1841." *Northern Light* 1 (May 1841): 26.

Conrad, Susan Phinney. *Perish the Thought: Intellectual Women in Romantic America, 1830–1860.* New York: Oxford University Press, 1976.

Cooper, James Fenimore. *The Pioneers; Or, The Sources of the Susquehanna: A Descriptive Tale.* 1823. Reprint. New York: G. P. Putnam's Sons, 1893.

————. *The Pioneers.* 1823. Reprint. New York: Holt, Rinehart and Winston, 1959, 1964.

————. *The Prairie: A Tale.* 1827. Reprint. Introduction by Henry Nash Smith. New York: Holt, Rinehart and Winston, 1950.

————. "Preface to the Leather-Stocking Tales, New York, 1850." In *The Last of the Mohicans* (1826), edited by William Charvat, pp. 11–14. Cambridge, Mass.: Houghton Mifflin, 1958.

——. *The Works of James Fenimore Cooper*. 10 vols. New York: P. F. Collier, 1892.

Corbitt, David Leroy, ed. *Explorations, Descriptions, and Attempted Settlements of Carolina, 1584–1590*. Raleigh: State Department of Archives and History, 1948.

Cott, Nancy F. *The Bonds of Womanhood: "Woman's Sphere" in New England, 1780–1835*. New Haven: Yale University Press, 1977.

Crèvecoeur, J. Hector St. John de. *Crèvecoeur's Eighteenth-Century Travels in Pennsylvania and New York*. Translated and edited by Percy G. Adams. Lexington: University of Kentucky Press, 1961.

——. *Letters from an American Farmer*. 1782. Reprint. New York: E. P. Dutton, 1957.

——. *Sketches of Eighteenth-Century America*. Edited by Henri L. Boudin, Ralph H. Gabriel, and Stanley T. Williams. New Haven: Yale University Press, 1925.

Cummins, Sarah J. *Autobiography and Reminiscences*. Walla Walla, Wash.: Walla Walla Bulletin, 1914.

[Cummins, Susanna Maria.] *Mabel Vaughan*. Boston: John P. Jewett; Cleveland: Henry P. B. Jewett, 1857.

Davis, Paulina Wright. "Remarks at the Convention." *Una* (September 1853): 135–37.

Dondore, Dorothy Anne. *The Prairie and the Making of Middle America: Four Centuries of Description*. Cedar Rapids: Torch Press, 1926.

[Dorr, Julia Caroline Ripley.] *Farmingdale*. By Caroline Thomas [pseud.]. New York: D. Appleton, 1854.

Douglas, Ann. *The Feminization of American Culture*. New York: Alfred A. Knopf, 1977.

Drury, Clifford Merrill, ed. *First White Women Over the Rockies: Diaries, Letters, and Biographical Sketches of the Six Women of the Oregon Mission Who Made the Overland Journey in 1836 and 1838*. 3 vols. Glendale, Calif.: Arthur H. Clark Co., 1966.

Duniway, Abigail Scott. *Path Breaking: An Autobiographical History of the Equal Suffrage Movement in Pacific Coast States*. 2d ed., 1914. Reprint. New York: Source Book Press, 1970.

Dwight, Margaret Van Horn. *A Journey to Ohio in 1810*. Edited by Max Farrand. New Haven: Yale University Press, 1912.

Ellet, Elizabeth Fries. *The Pioneer Women of the West*. 1852. Facsimile reprint. Freeport, N.Y.: Books for Libraries Press, 1973.

Everett, Sarah. "Letters of John and Sarah Everett, 1854–1864: Miami County Pioneers." *Kansas Historical Quarterly* 3 (November 1939): 3–383.

Faragher, John Mack. "History from the Inside-Out: Writing the History of Women in Rural America." *American Quarterly* 33 (Winter 1981): 540–50.

——. *Women and Men on the Overland Trail*. New Haven: Yale University Press, 1979.

Farnham, Eliza W. *California, In-doors and Out; Or, How We Farm, Mine, and Live Generally in the Golden State*. New York: Dix, Edwards and Co., 1856.

————. *Life in Prairie Land*. New York: Harper and Brothers, 1846.

Filson, John. *The Discovery, Settlement And present State of Kentucke: And An Essay towards the Topography, and Natural History of that important Country: To which is added, An Appendix, Containing, The Adventures of Col. Daniel Boon, one of the first Settlers, comprehending every important Occurrence in the political History of that Province*. Wilmington, Del.: James Adams, 1784.

————. *Life and Adventures of Colonel Daniel Boon, The First White Settler of the State of Kentucky*. Reprinted and enlarged. Providence, R.I.: H. Trumbull, 1824.

Fiske, John. *The Notebook of the Reverend John Fiske, 1644–1675*. Edited by Robert G. Pope. Publications of the Colonial Society of Massachusetts, vol. 47. Boston: The Society, 1974.

Fithian, Philip Vickers. *Journal and Letters of Philip Vickers Fithian, 1773–1774: A Plantation Tutor of the Old Dominion*. Edited by Hunter Dickinson Farish. Williamsburg, Va.: Colonial Williamsburg and Princeton University Press, 1943.

Flint, Timothy. *Biographical Memoir of Daniel Boone, The First Settler of Kentucky: Interspersed with Incidents in the Early Annals of the Country*. Cincinnati: N. and G. Guilford, 1833.

————. *A Condensed History and Geography of the Western States, Or the Mississippi Valley*. 2 vols. 1828. Reprint. Gainesville, Fla.: Scholars' Facsimiles and Reprints, 1970.

Folsom, James K. *Timothy Flint*. New York: Twayne Publishers, 1965.

Force, Peter, comp. *Tracts and Other Papers, Relating Principally to the Origin, Settlement, And Progress of the Colonies in North America, From The Discovery Of The Country To The Year 1776*. 3 vols. Washington, D.C.: Peter Force, 1836–38.

Franklin, Wayne. *Discoverers, Explorers, Settlers: The Diligent Writers of Early America*. Chicago: University of Chicago Press, 1979.

Frost, John. *Heroic Women of the West: Comprising Thrilling Examples of Courage, Fortitude, Devotedness, and Self-Sacrifice, Among the Pioneer Mothers of the Western Country*. Philadelphia: A. Hart, 1854.

Fryer, Judith. *The Faces of Eve: Women in the Nineteenth-Century American Novel*. New York: Oxford University Press, 1976.

[Fuller, Margaret.] "The Great Lawsuit. Man *versus* Men. Woman *versus* Women." *Dial* 4 (July 1843): 1–47.

Fuller, S. M. [Margaret Fuller]. *Summer on the Lakes, in 1843*. Boston: Charles C. Little and James Brown; New York: Charles S. Francis and Co., 1844.

———— [Ossoli]. *Summer on the Lakes*. 2d ed. Edited by Arthur B. Fuller, 1856. Reprint. New York: Haskell House Publishers, 1970.

———— [Ossoli]. *Woman in the Nineteenth Century and Kindred Papers Relating to the Sphere, Condition and Duties, of Women*. Edited by Arthur B. Fuller. 1855. Reprint. New York: W. W. Norton, 1971.

Gates, Paul W. *Landlords and Tenants on the Prairie Frontier: Studies in American Land Policy*. Ithaca: Cornell University Press, 1973.

Gherman, Dawn Lander. "From Parlour to Tepee: The White Squaw on the American Frontier." Ph.D. dissertation, University of Massachusetts, 1975.

Gilman, Caroline Howard. *Recollections of a Southern Matron*. New York: Harper and Brothers, 1838.

Griffin, Susan. *Woman and Nature: The Roaring Inside Her*. New York: Harper and Row, 1978.

Hale, Sarah Josepha. "Editor's Table." *Godey's Lady's Book* 40 (January 1850): 76–77.

Hall, Clayton Colman, ed. *Narratives of Early Maryland, 1633–1684*. New York: Charles Scribner's Sons, 1910.

Hall, James. *Legends of the West*. Philadelphia: Key and Biddle, 1833.

Hart, James D. *The Popular Book: A History of America's Literary Taste*. 1950. Reprint. Berkeley: University of California Press, 1963.

Hawthorne, Nathaniel. Preface to *The Marble Faun, or The Romance of Monte Beni* (1860), in *The Complete Novels and Selected Tales of Nathaniel Hawthorne*, edited by Norman Holmes Pearson, pp. 589–91. New York: Random House, 1937.

———. *The Scarlet Letter and Other Tales of the Puritans*. Edited by Harry Levin. Boston: Houghton Mifflin, 1961.

Henry, Alexander. *Travels and Adventures in Canada and The Indian Territories, Between The Years 1760 and 1776*. New York: I. Riley, 1809.

Henson, Clyde E. *Joseph Kirkland*. New York: Twayne Publishers, 1962.

Hentz, Caroline Lee. *Lovell's Folly. A Novel*. Cincinnati: Hubbard and Edmonds, 1833.

Higginson, Thomas Wentworth. *Margaret Fuller Ossoli*. 1890. Reprint. New York: Greenwood Press, 1968.

Hoffman, Charles Fenno. *A Winter in the West*. 2 vols. New York: Harper and Brothers, 1835.

Holbrook, Stewart H. *The Yankee Exodus: An Account of Migration from New England*. 1950. Reprint. Seattle: University of Washington Press, 1978.

Holley, Mary Austin. *The Texas Diary, 1835–1838*. Edited by James P. Bryan. Austin: University of Texas Press, 1965.

———. *Texas. Observations, Historical, Geographical and Descriptive, In a Series of Letters, Written during a Visit to Austin's Colony, with a view to a permanent settlement in that country, in the Autumn of 1831*. Baltimore: Armstrong and Plaskitt, 1833.

Holmes, Julia Archibald. *A Bloomer Girl on Pike's Peak, 1858*. Edited by Agnes Wright Spring. Denver: Denver Public Library, 1949.

Hunt, John Dixon. *The Figure in the Landscape: Poetry, Painting, and Gardening during the Eighteenth Century*. Baltimore: Johns Hopkins University Press, 1976.

Irvin, Helen Deiss. *Women in Kentucky*. Lexington: University Press of Kentucky, 1979.

Irving, Washington. *A Tour on the Prairies*. Edited by James Playsted Wood. 1835. Reprint. New York: Pantheon Books, 1967.

Jeffrey, Julie Roy. *Frontier Women: The Trans-Mississippi West, 1840–1880*. New York: Hill and Wang, 1979.

Jones, Howard Mumford. *O Strange New World, American Culture: The Formative Years*. 1952. Reprint. London: Chatto and Windus, 1965.

Kelley, Mary. *Private Woman, Public Stage: Literary Domesticity in Nineteenth-Century America*. New York: Oxford University Press, 1984.

———. "The Sentimentalists: Promise and Betrayal in the Home." *Signs* 4 (Spring 1979): 434–46.

———. "A Woman Alone: Catharine Maria Sedgwick's Spinsterhood in Nineteenth-Century America." *New England Quarterly* 51 (June 1978): 209–25.

Kirkland, Caroline M. *Autumn Hours, and Fireside Reading*. New York: Charles Scribner, 1854.

Kirkland, Caroline M. "Bush-Life." *Sartain's Union Magazine of Literature and Art* 6 (January 1850): 69–72.

[Kirkland, Caroline M.] *Forest Life. By the Author of "A New Home."* 2 vols. New York: Charles S. Francis and Co.; Boston: J. H. Francis, 1842.

Kirkland, Caroline M. "The Hard Winter." *Union Magazine of Literature and Art* 2 (January 1848): 42–44.

Kirkland, Caroline M. "The Log-House." *Union Magazine of Literature and Art* 2 (June 1848): 274–75.

[Kirkland, Caroline M.] *A New Home—Who'll Follow? Or, Glimpses of Western Life. By Mrs. Mary Clavers. An Actual Settler*. 1839. Reprint. New York: Garrett Press, 1969.

Kirkland, Caroline M. *A New Home—Who'll Follow? Glimpses of Western Life*. Edited by William S. Osborne. New Haven: College and University Press Publishers, 1965.

Kirkland, Caroline M. *Western Clearings*. 1845. Reprint. New York: Garrett Press, 1969.

Kirkland, Joseph. *Zury: The Meanest Man in Spring County*. 1887. Reprint. Urbana: University of Illinois Press, 1956.

Kolodny, Annette. *The Lay of the Land: Metaphor as Experience and History in American Life and Letters*. Chapel Hill: University of North Carolina Press, 1975.

Langworthy, Margaret Wyman. "Alice Cary." In *Notable American Women, 1670–1950: A Biographical Dictionary*. 3 vols. 1971. Reprint. Cambridge, Mass.: Harvard University Press, Belknap Press, 1975. Vol. 1, p. 296.

Lee, Rebecca Smith. *Mary Austin Holley: A Biography*. Austin: University of Texas Press, 1962.

Lewis, R. W. B. *The American Adam: Innocence, Tragedy, and Tradition in the Nineteenth Century*. 1955. Reprint. Chicago: University of Chicago Press, 1965.

Marx. Leo. *The Machine in the Garden: Technology and the Pastoral Ideal in America*. New York: Oxford University Press, 1964.

Mather, Cotton. *Decennium Luctuosum. An History of Remarkable Occurences, In the Long War, Which New-England hath had with the Indian Salvages, From the*

Year, 1688. To the Year, 1698. Faithfully Composed and Improved. Boston: B. Green and J. Allen, 1699.

———. *Humiliations follow'd with Deliverances. A Brief Discourse On the Matter and Method, Of that Humiliation which would be an Hopeful Symptom of our Deliverance from Calamity. Accompanied and Accommodated with A Narrative, Of a Notable Deliverance lately Received by some English Captives, From the Hands of Cruel Indians. Whereto is added A Narrative of Hannah Swarton, containing a great many wonderful passages, relating to her Captivity and Deliverance*. Boston: B. Green and J. Allen, 1697.

Merk, Frederick. *History of the Westward Movement*. New York: Alfred A. Knopf, 1978.

Mitchell, Lee Clark. *Witnesses to a Vanishing America: The Nineteenth-Century Response*. Princeton: Princeton University Press, 1981.

Morgan, Dale, ed. *Overland in 1846: Diaries and Letters of the California-Oregon Trail*. 2 vols. Georgetown, Calif.: Talisman Press, 1963.

"The Mothers of the West." *Western Literary Journal and Monthly Review* (July 1836): 106.

Mott, Frank Luther. *Golden Multitudes: The Story of Best Sellers in the United States*. New York: Macmillan Co., 1947.

———. *A History of American Magazines*. Vol. 3, *1865–1885*. Cambridge, Mass.: Harvard University Press, 1938.

Noyes, Mrs. Charles P., ed. *A Family History in Letters and Documents, 1667–1837*. 2 vols. St. Paul, Minn.: Privately Printed, 1919.

Nye, Russel Blaine. *Society and Culture in America, 1830–1860*. New York: Harper and Row, 1974.

Osborne, William S. *Caroline M. Kirkland*. New York: Twayne Publishers, 1972.

Parkman, Francis. *The Oregon Trail*. 1849. New York: New American Library, Signet Books, 1950.

Pattee, Fred Lewis. *The Feminine Fifties*. New York: D. Appleton-Century Co., 1940.

Pearce, Roy Harvey. "The Significance of the Captivity Narrative." *American Literature* 19 (March 1947): 1–20.

Peck, John M. *Life of Daniel Boone*. Boston: Charles C. Little and James Brown, 1847.

[Pike, Mary Hayden Green.] *Ida May: A Story of Things Actual and Possible. By Mary Langdon* [pseud.]. Boston: Phillips, Sampson and Co., 1854.

Pinckney, Eliza Lucas. *The Letterbook of Eliza Lucas Pinckney, 1739–1762*. Edited by Elise Pinckney. Chapel Hill: University of North Carolina Press, 1972.

"The Pioneer Mothers." *Western Literary Journal and Monthly Review* (July 1836): 100–103.

Pomeroy, Earl. *The Pacific Slope: A History of California, Oregon, Washington, Idaho, Utah, and Nevada*. 1965. Reprint. Seattle: University of Washington Press, 1973.

A Remarkable Narrative of the Captivity and Escape of Mrs. Frances Scott, An Inhabitant of Washington County, Virginia. Printed for Chapman Whitcomb,

1800. Reprint. The Garland Library of Narratives of North American Indian Captivities. 111 vols. Compiled by Wilcomb E. Washburn. New York: Garland Publishing, 1978. Vol. 16.

Review of "*A New Home; Who'll Follow? or, Glimpses of Western Life* by Mrs. Mary Clavers—An Actual Settler." *North American Review* 50 (January 1840): 206–23.

Rowlandson, Mary White. *A True History of the Captivity and Restoration of Mrs. Mary Rowlandson, A Minister's Wife in New-England.* London: Joseph Poole, 1682.

Rowson, Susanna. *Miscellaneous Poems.* Boston: Gilbert and Dean, 1804.

Rusk, Ralph Leslie. *The Literature of the Middle Western Frontier.* 2 vols. New York: Columbia University Press, 1926.

Russell, E., comp. *Narative of Mrs. Scott and Capt. Stewart's Captivity. A True and Wonderful Narrative Of the surprising Captivity and remarkable Deliverance of Mrs. Frances Scott.* Boston: E. Russell, 1786.

Sanford, Mollie Dorsey. *Mollie: The Journal of Mollie Dorsey Sanford in Nebraska and Colorado Territories, 1857–1866.* Edited by Donald F. Danker. Lincoln: University of Nebraska Press, 1959.

Schlissel, Lillian. *Women's Diaries of the Westward Journey.* New York: Schocken Books, 1982.

Seaver, James Everett. *Life of Mary Jemison: Deh-He-Wä-Mis.* New York and Auburn: Miller, Orton, and Mulligan; Rochester, N.Y.: D. M. Dewey, 1856.

———. *A Narrative of the Life of Mrs. Mary Jemison, Who was taken by the Indians, in the year 1755, when only about twelve years of age, and has continued to reside amongst them to the present time.* Canandaigua, N.Y.: J. D. Bemis and Co., 1824.

[Sedgwick, Catharine Maria.] *Hope Leslie: Or, Early Times in the Massachusetts.* 2 vols. New York: White, Gallaher, and White, 1827.

[———.] *Live and Let Live; Or, Domestic Service Illustrated.* New York: Harper and Brothers, 1837.

Seelye, John. *Prophetic Waters: The River in Early American Life and Literature.* New York: Oxford University Press, 1977.

Shaw, Anna Howard. *The Story of a Pioneer.* New York: Harper and Brothers, 1915.

Shteir, Anne B. "Linnaeus's Daughters: Women and British Botany." In *Women and the Structure of Society: Selected Research from the Fifth Berkshire Conference on the History of Women,* edited by Barbara J. Harris and Jo Ann McNamara. Durham, N.C.: Duke University Press, 1984.

Sigourney, Lydia H. *The Western Home, and Other Poems.* Philadelphia: Parry and McMillan, 1854.

Sklar, Kathryn Kish. *Catharine Beecher: A Study in American Domesticity.* New Haven: Yale University Press, 1973.

Slotkin, Richard. *Regeneration through Violence: The Mythology of the American Frontier, 1600–1860.* Middletown, Conn.: Wesleyan University Press, 1973.

Smith, Henry Nash. *Virgin Land: The American West as Symbol and Myth.* 1950. Reprint. New York: Random House, Vintage Books, 1961.

Smith, Page. *Daughters of the Promised Land: Women in American History.* Boston: Little, Brown, 1979.

Solomon, Margaret. "A Study of Feminism as a Motif in 'A Journey to Pike's Peak and New Mexico' by Julia Archibald Holmes." In *Women and Western American Literature,* edited by Helen Winter Stauffer and Susan J. Rosowski, pp. 28–39. Troy, N.Y.: Whitston Publishing Co., 1982.

Soule, Caroline A. *The Pet of the Settlement. A Story of Prairie-Land.* Boston: A. Tompkins, 1860.

Southworth, Emma D. E. N. *India: The Pearl of Pearl River.* 1853. Philadelphia: T. B. Peterson and Brothers, 1856.

Stephens, Ann Sophia. *Fashion and Famine.* New York: Bunce and Brother, 1854.

———. *Mary Derwent.* Philadelphia: T. B. Peterson and Brothers, 1858.

———. *The Old Homestead.* New York: Bunce and Brother, 1855.

Stout, Janis P. *Sodoms in Eden: The City in American Fiction before 1860.* Westport, Conn.: Greenwood Press, 1976.

"A Surprising account of the Discovery of a Lady who was taken by the Indians in the year 1777, and after making her escape, She retired to a lonely Cave, where She lived nine years." In *Bickerstaff's almanack, for the year of our Lord, 1788.* Norwich, Conn.: J. Trumbull, 1787. Reprint. The Garland Library of Narratives of North American Indian Captivities. 111 vols. Compiled by Wilcomb E. Washburn. New York: Garland Publishing, 1978. Vol. 17.

Taylor, Bayard. *At Home and Abroad: A Sketch-Book of Life, Scenery, and Men.* New York: G. P. Putnam, 1862.

Tichi, Cecilia. "The American Revolution and the New Earth." *Early American Literature* 11 (Fall 1976): 204–12.

Tillson, Christiana Holmes. *A Woman's Story of Pioneer Illinois.* Edited by Milo Milton Quaife. Chicago: Lakeside Press, R. R. Donnelly and Sons, 1919.

Todd, John. *The Lost Sister of Wyoming. An Authentic Narrative.* Northampton, Mass.: J. H. Butler, 1842.

Trist, Elizabeth House. "The Travel Diary of Elizabeth House Trist: Philadelphia to Natchez, 1783–84," edited and with an introduction by Annette Kolodny. In *Journeys in New Worlds: Early American Women's Narratives,* edited by William L. Andrews, Sargent Bush, Jr., Annette Kolodny, Amy Shrager Lang, and Daniel B. Shea, pp. 181–232. Madison: University of Wisconsin Press, 1990.

Trumbull, John, comp. *The Adventures of Colonel Daniel Boon, One of the first Settlers at Kentucke: Containing The Wars with the Indians on the Ohio, from 1769 to 1783, and the first Establishment and Progress of the Settlement on that River. Written by the Colonel himself. To Which Are Added, A Narrative of the Captivity, and Extraordinary Escape of Mrs. Francis Scott An Inhabitant of Washington-County Virginia; who after the Murder of her Husband and children, by the Indians, was taken Prisoner by them; on the 19th of June, 1785.* Norwich, Conn.: John Trumbull, 1786.

Turner, Frederick. *Beyond Geography: The Western Spirit against the Wilderness.* New York: Viking Press, 1980.

Turner, Frederick Jackson. *The Frontier in American History.* New York: Henry Holt and Co., 1920.

Tuthill, Louisa C. *My Wife.* Boston: William Crosby and H. P. Nichols, 1846.

Unruh, John D., Jr. *The Plains Across: The Overland Emigrants and the Trans-Mississippi West, 1840–1860.* Urbana: University of Illinois Press, 1979.

Urbanski, Marie Mitchell Olesen. *Margaret Fuller's Woman in the Nineteenth Century: A Literary Study of Form and Content, of Sources and Influences.* Westport, Conn.: Greenwood Press, 1980.

Venable, William H. *Beginnings of Literary Culture in the Ohio Valley: Historical and Biographical Sketches.* 1891. Reprint. New York: Peter Smith, 1949.

Weil, Dorothy. *In Defense of Women: Susanna Rowson, 1762–1824.* University Park: Pennsylvania State University Press, 1976.

Wiggin, Eliza Johnston. *Impressions of Early Kansas.* Wichita: Grit Printery, 1915.

Williams, John. *The Redeemed Captive Returning to Zion: Or, A Faithful History of Remarkable Occurrences in the Captivity and Deliverance of Mr. John Williams, Minister of the Gospel in Deerfield.* 1707. Reprint. The Garland Library of Narratives of North American Indian Captivities. 111 vols. Compiled by Wilcomb E. Washburn. New York: Garland Publishing, 1978. Vol. 5.

Wilson, David Scofield. *In the Presence of Nature.* Amherst: University of Massachusetts Press, 1978.

Winthrop, John. *Winthrop Papers.* 5 vols. Boston: Massachusetts Historical Society, 1927–32.

Index